AMERICA'S LOST PLAYS

I

FORBIDDEN FRUIT
and Other Plays

II

FALSE SHAME
and
THIRTY YEARS

A series in twenty volumes of hitherto unpublished
plays collected with the aid of the Rockefeller
Foundation, under the auspices of the Dramatists'
Guild of the Authors' League of America, edited
with historical and bibliographical notes.

BARRETT H. CLARK
GENERAL EDITOR

Advisory Board

Forbidden Fruit

& *Other Plays*

BY DION BOUCICAULT

EDITED BY ALLARDYCE NICOLL
AND F. THEODORE CLOAK

INDIANA UNIVERSITY PRESS

BLOOMINGTON

Second printing April 1964

GENERAL PREFACE

THESE twenty volumes of *America's Lost Plays* are the result of the first sustained and coordinated effort to rescue a large and representative group of manuscript plays from the public collections of this country, and from the hands of private individuals. A constantly growing interest not only in the history of the American theater but in its plays—stimulated in recent times largely by the pioneer work of Dr. Arthur Hobson Quinn and the late Montrose J. Moses—had proved to many of us that the study of our native theater revealed much more than exclusively theatrical data: it necessitated and fostered further investigations into our social and political history as a nation.

We who have collected these hundred plays and are now seeing them published for the first time have sought to bring together an exhibition not only, and perhaps not primarily, of samples of the playwright's craft, but of curious and illuminating criteria of public taste over a period extending from the Revolution down almost to the present day. Far from claiming that the plays in these volumes complete the quota of our "lost" plays, we have established as one of our aims the intention of stimulating the further search among the vast stores of texts that remain to be rescued and made available to students. It is our wish not only to urge more research, but to encourage the searcher by assuring him that his quest will prove successful. For every play we are now publishing, there are five known to us that should be published: with the necessary time and means, it is our firm conviction that a great many more "lost" plays could be found than the five hundred we have unearthed. In one private collection alone there are fifty as yet unpublished plays of Dion Boucicault; in certain public libraries are complete sets of the plays of Charles Hoyt; there are over a hundred of Harrigan's works which it is hoped will some day be placed within the reach of students; and there is, finally, a collection of over two thousand manuscripts, most of which were never printed, that includes most of the characteristic plays seen on the stages of this country between 1880 and 1900.

For the sake of those who would trace the history of native playwriting, or investigate the broader aspects of the cultural development of the American people, the most characteristic examples of our dramatic output are of unquestioned value and interest. That plays of native authorship, until fairly recent times, are not artistic masterpieces (I speak of course only for myself, and not for my fellow editors) is entirely beside the point. If every aspect of the activity of man and its effect on his fellow men deserves our respect and our attention, then indeed the American theater is, I believe, quite as important to us as any other characteristic function and activity.

Our choice of "lost" plays was determined largely by the importance of the writer himself (hence the occasional presence in these volumes of certain relatively unimportant plays by important writers), and the popularity of the individual play, regardless of the author's distinction. It has been our intention in general to bring to light as many manuscripts as we could find that served to show us of today what plays of the past hundred and fifty years, as yet unpublished, were popular in their day, and to extend our knowledge of the work of such writers as were already known to a certain extent.

As for the term "American," it is used in the broad sense of plays, regardless of authorship, using American themes; plays, regardless of theme, written by residents of the United States or enjoying wide popularity in America; as well as plays of various sorts written by native-born writers whether actually produced in this country or not.

It was not to be expected that a venture of this sort, involving five years of research and considerable expense on the part of many persons, could ever pay for itself. This undertaking was in the first place largely subsidized by a grant from the Rockefeller Foundation. To Dr. David H. Stevens, Director of the Division of the Humanities, I am indebted not only for the actual financial grant, but for his enthusiastic cooperation, which was cheerfully offered and gratefully accepted. It is perhaps unlikely that, even with financial help, the project would have succeeded without his personal help and advice. To the Dramatists Guild of the Authors' League of America, official sponsors of the series, I should like to express gratitude for material encouragement; to Mr. Ligon Johnson particular thanks are rendered for a great deal of advice on complicated problems of copyright; to Mr. Joseph A. Brandt, Director of Princeton University Press, my special thanks for his unfailing and invaluable support and advice; to every member of my Advisory Board, and to the editors of each of the volumes, my thanks for assistance of almost every imaginable kind. To the many libraries, playwrights, editors, and others who have helped bring our long labors to a successful conclusion I can only express my gratitude in general terms: particular instances of help are so far as possible mentioned by each editor in the preface of the volume for which he is responsible.

BARRETT H. CLARK

DION BOUCICAULT

No EXCUSE need be offered for presenting Dion Boucicault as one of the authors of *America's Lost Plays*. It is true that, of the six plays chosen for this volume, two only, *Dot* and *Forbidden Fruit*, first saw the limelight of production in the United States, while three, *Louis XI*, *Flying Scud* and *Mercy Dodd*, originally appeared in England, and one, *Robert Emmet*, had practically simultaneous openings in Greenwich and Chicago. On the English stage of the late nineteenth century Boucicault is an important figure, no doubt, but no less important is he as a dramatist of the rapidly developing American theater of the 'seventies. Although born in Ireland and at one time "house dramatist" for Charles Kean, his contributions to the American theater were so vital and significant, his later activities so closely identified with the stage of this country, that no hesitation need be felt in including his plays in this series.

If one were asked to indicate Boucicault's chief talent, there could be little doubt concerning a correct answer: what marked him out from his contemporaries was inventiveness and ingenuity.

Others, such as Byron, Taylor and Brough, were as prolific as he; his grace in language is not particularly remarkable; depth and vision are lacking in his characters—but above all his companions he stood in the creation of theatrical novelties. Just what this means may need a word or two of explanation. Novelties in general are not difficult to introduce to the stage, but less easy is it to bring forward just those particular novelties for which an age has been unconsciously dreaming. Always Boucicault's inventiveness took the shape of an almost uncanny sense of what the inarticulate public wanted next.

At the age of nineteen, he showed this power in *London Assurance* (1841); and when, an old man of sixty-eight, he died in 1890, his grip on the pulse of his time was as firm and sure as it had been when he first started his career. When the mood for historical romances is approaching, he produces *Louis XI*; more domestic themes are likely to prove popular and *Dot* arrives; Ireland is to swim into the consciousness of the audience, hence *Arrah na Pogue*, *The Shaughraun* and *Robert Emmet*; American spectators would like to see native material dramatized and so comes *The Octoroon*; *Flying Scud* catches at the interest in horse-racing, *Mercy Dodd* at the appeal of the detective, while *Forbidden Fruit* anticipates Pinero's exploitation of the extended farce form of the 'eighties. With an extraordinary adaptability Boucicault, throughout the whole of his career, continued to divine aright the theatrical needs of audiences alike in London and in New York.

If his work does not show the result of that infinite patience out of which genius is born, at least it does not lack vigor, and he possesses to a high degree the essential dramatic power of conceiving his episodes in terms of the physical stage. His exploitation of new material is important; not less important are the scenic devices he introduces into his dramas. The wagon stage in *Dot*, the divided stage in *Mercy Dodd* and *Forbidden Fruit*, the rapid change from interior to exterior in *Robert Emmet*, the appeal to sensationalism in the horse-racing spectacle of *Flying Scud*—these are representative of the devices which made him a master craftsman in the art of stage management.

April 27, 1938   ALLARDYCE NICOLL

CONTENTS

FORBIDDEN FRUIT

FORBIDDEN FRUIT

Boucicault's dramatic activity continued almost unabated even in his latest years. Writing to his eldest son in 1874 about the opening night of *The Shaughraun*, he indicates his sense of pride in this: "My dear Willie—Another great success—perhaps the greatest of all—It seems to be so at present—and as 2000 people left the Theatre last night the universal opinion expressed was that 'Boucicault has beaten himself. The Colleen Bawn will be forgotten—it overwhelms Arrah-na-Pogue—'

"So you can say with Lady Macbeth 'Who'd have thought the old man had so much blood in him?' "

It is not surprising, even when he was rapidly approaching his sixties, to find still another successful and novel work from his pen. *Forbidden Fruit* is an early example of the three-act farce, with theme and situations similar to those later developed more fully by Pinero. There seems to have been some divergence of opinion concerning the moral implications of the piece; although the *New York Times* review made no complaint, William Winter twice referred to it as a tainted drama which "trailed the banner of the noble Wallack tradition in the gutter," and "caused Lester Wallack to disgrace Wallack's Theatre."

That *Forbidden Fruit* is a realistic picture of London life in 1880, the year of its first production in England, is carefully denied by G. A. Sala in the *Illustrated London News* for July 10. To him "the most amusing feature in this undeniably successful piece was its utter unreality as a picture of contemporary English manners." He mentions the "cabinet particulier" as a direct importation from Paris; the fact that English sergeants-at-law do not share the same chambers; that English female cartridges "are not ambitious to be put into the witness-box," and are the most retiring of quasi-dramatic womankind. And he adds that he liked *Forbidden Fruit* "all the better for these anomalies. Were it a realistic piece, the fundamental frivolity of the piece would make it not funny, but objectionable."

Two items of interest are connected with the staging of the play: the introduction of a real horse drawing a four-wheeled cab at the end of Act II, and the partitioning off of the stage into two compartments in Act I, and into two rooms with the intervening corridor in Act III. All of these effects were intended to accelerate the action of the play.

The original New York production took place at Wallack's Theatre, October 3, 1876, and had a cast including Beckett as Sergeant Buster, H. J. Montague as Cato Dove, Arnott as Captain Derringer, Miss German as Zulu, Miss Dyas as Mrs. Dove, and Mme. Ponisi as Mrs. Buster. The London première was at the Adelphi on July 3, 1880; the cast included J. G. Taylor as Sergeant Buster, Pateman as Cato Dove, Brooke as Captain Derringer, Miss Marie Williams as Zulu, Miss Bella Pateman as Mrs. Dove, Miss Helen Barry as Mrs. Buster, and Miss Clara Jecks as the barmaid.

A few copies of *Forbidden Fruit* were privately printed in New York in 1876; one of these has been used in the preparation of this edition.

F. T. C.

CAST OF CHARACTERS

MR. SERGEANT BUSTER, *Senior Counsel*

MR. CATO DOVE, *Junior Counsel*

CAPTAIN DERRINGER

PODD, *Clerk in the office of Buster and Cato*

SWALLBACH, *German Head Waiter at the Cremorne Hotel*

VICTOR, *A French Waiter*

JOSEPH, *Another Waiter*

RAILWAY PORTER

CONDUCTOR

CABMAN

MRS. CATO DOVE (JOSEPHINE)

MRS. ARABELLA BUSTER

ZULU, *The "Female Cartridge"*

MISS JULIA PERKINS, *Barmaid*

SYNOPSIS OF SCENES

ACT I. DOVE'S CHAMBERS IN THE TEMPLE.

ACT II. A RAILWAY STATION. THE REFRESHMENT ROOM.

ACT III. THE CREMORNE HOTEL. TWO ROOMS, WITH THE INTERMEDIATE CORRIDOR.

ACT I.

SCENE: *Cato Dove's chambers in the Temple. Clerk's office. R.H. Door in partition, R.C. Fireplace. Door. Podd discovered arranging papers, L.H. Bell rings. Podd goes into office, R.H. Opens door. Enter Zulu.*

ZULU. Mr. Cato Dove?

PODD. [*R.C.*] Will you please to walk in, Ma'am. [*Leads her into chamber L.H.*] This is his room. [*C. behind table*] Is it anything I can attend to? I am Mr. Dove's clerk.

ZULU. [*R.*] No; I wish to see him personally.

PODD. He is in the court at present—we have a motion on the list this morning!

ZULU. Is it anything interesting on the Brighton Scandal Case?

PODD. [*Handing chair L.*] No, ma'am. That case stands over till Monday next. May I ask, are you concerned in that matter?

ZULU. [*Crossing to C.*] Oh, very much!

PODD. A witness, I suppose, ma'am.

ZULU. Yes, sir; that is what I want to be.

PODD. For the defense, I presume.

ZULU. Well, sir, so long as I am a witness, it don't matter to me. [*Sits in chair L.*]

PODD. Yes, ma'am; but you see it matters very much to the case. Are you an important witness?

ZULU. The more important the better—that is what I want to see Mr. Cato about! I want to be well displayed!

PODD. Well displayed, ma'am! I don't quite understand! [*Bell rings, R. up stage in office*] Oh, here is Mr. Cato. [*Crossing to office*] I know his pull at the bell [*Enters office*]—a sort of snatch, as much as to say—It's me and I'm in a hurry! [*Opens door. Podd passes into outer office, opens door. Enter Mr. Cato Dove*]

CATO. Any letters? [*Down R. to desk, takes off his hat, gloves, and gives them and his umbrella to Podd, who hangs them up at back in office*]

PODD. Yes, sir; three, sir, and a lady.

CATO. [*Standing at desk*] Oh! [*Opening letters in outer office and reading*] Um! um! um! What sort of a lady?

Podd. [*R.C.*] Very peculiar lady, sir. Some new evidence [*Zulu walks round room, peeps into papers on table*] in the Brighton Scandal Case, strange lady, sir—says she wants to be well displayed.

Cato. [*Reading and unfolding a playbill enclosed in second letter*] What's this? Another playbill. Who is this individual who sends me every day her woodcut [*reads playbill*]—Mdlle. Zulu on the flying trapeze! Geni of the Ring? [*Zulu, who has been examining room, and looking into drawers in table, now mounts on a chair L.H. up stage—to look at a portrait hanging against the wall*]

Zulu. I wonder who that is! She has an ill-tempered mouth whoever she is.

Cato. [*Opening another letter, reads*] I forgot to enclose my photograph. Zulu! [*Takes photograph, cabinet size, out of letter*]

Podd. Oh, sir—

Cato. What!

Podd. She's in there! [*Points to Room L.H.*]

Cato. Who?

Podd. The photograph, sir! the lady! her as wants to be displayed!

Cato. The original of this likeness—is in my room, waiting for me. Are you sure?

Podd. Well, sir, the original in there has got so much dress and so little visible, and this likeness has so little dress and so much visible, that it is hard for me to swear!

Cato. [*After crossing to L. of Podd*] What can a flying trapeze want with me? [*After a moment's hesitation, he looks at the photograph and enters the room, finds her perched in the chair*] What is she about? I beg your pardon!

Zulu. [*Turning on chair*] No apology. I was admiring the pluck of that old fellow, to sit for his portrait at his time of life and in such a wig. What's his line of business?

Cato. [*Going to back of the table*] That is the Lord Chief Justice!

Zulu. [*Leaping down*] Thank ye. You don't mind my looking about, I hope?

Cato. [*Motioning her to the chair in front. He sits at table*] I am sorry to have kept you waiting!

Zulu. [*Advancing to L.C.*] No offense. I suppose you know me, so I need no introduction.

Cato. I believe I have the pleasure of receiving Mademoiselle [*looking at playbill*] Fooloo?

Zulu. Zulu, sir, not Fooloo. Zulu!

CATO. I beg your pardon. Foreign names are rather confusing.

ZULU. The flying Fairy of the Trapeze—the Geni of the Ring. I see you have received my card.

CATO. I have received your card—yes, that is—I received a—

ZULU. Card de visite.

CATO. Oh, yes—the photograph!

ZULU. You have not seen me at Cremorne?

CATO. I am ashamed to say—that is a pleasure to come.

ZULU. I am the original projectile, sir, the first person that ever submitted to serve as a Cartridge in a Cannon.

CATO. [*Rising*] Bless me, my dear lady.

ZULU. Yes, sir, I see the idea takes your breath away. You should see the faces of the public when the cannon is charged, and after leaping lightly on the tip of the muzzle and waving a graceful adieu to a crowd I slide down into the monster's iron throat! Hurried music in the orchestra—a pause to pile up the agony—Fire! Bang! I am shot in the air to alight like a bird on the rail of a trapeze! The sensation is thrilling, I assure you!

CATO. I feel that effect from your description only. I shall take an early opportunity of being thrilled. [*Drawing chair close to her C.*]

ZULU. Much obliged, but to the business that brings me here. Mr. Cato, I have followed the great Brighton Scandal Case in which you are engaged, with the greatest interest. I never miss a day in court!

CATO. All London is full of it. It is a painful exposure of the inner life of our upper classes.

ZULU. Painful! Sir, not at all. I am infatuated about it. I cannot get it out of my head. I dream of it. I breakfast and dine upon it. I know every one of your speeches by heart.

CATO. [*Aside*] He! he! the girl is gone on me, this is a decided case. Ha! ha! I am glad my wife is not here!

ZULU. For three years I've worked hard to get well displayed before the public, and never obtained more than three lines in the daily press, but here, sir, everybody is talking about the business and witnesses in this case, perfectly unknown people until you called them in the witness-box, once there they get columns of notice—I want to be a witness!

CATO. Dear me, madam, what do you mean?

ZULU. I want to be in the box, and have you talk to me, and make me tell all my life. I've made out a lovely biography, and I want to tell it! Draw me out as you did that lady you examined yesterday!

CATO. But what has your biography to do with the Brighton Scandal?

ZULU. No more than the biography of that lady; you made her confess a lot of things that had nothing to do with the case, but were so interesting.

CATO. But how can you be connected with it?

ZULU. Nothing easier, I've thought of that! You can ask me. (Ah, how well I know the tones of your voice.) "Miss Zulu, you are, I believe, an Equestrian Artiste?" Yes, sir. "One of the most distinguished and attractive in your profession?" Yes, sir. "You remember last Christmas a gentleman sending you some very costly presents of jewelry?" Really, sir, I receive so many tributes of that description, I cannot, amongst the number, distinguish the particular gentleman to whom you allude! "Come, come, Miss Zulu, you must know, I mean the defendant in this case; we are instructed that the defendant fell passionately in love with you last winter, lavished a little fortune on you in diamonds, besieged you with flowers?" I shall be covered with charming confusion, and you will make the most of it for the amusement of the jury. It will be delightful—you can keep me at it as long as you please!

CATO. [*Getting nearer to her*] It would be more delightful to enjoy your charming confusion here, as long as I pleased.

ZULU. Oh, Mr. Cato—how good you are and how I can scarcely believe my senses that I am really talking to you like this, and there you are! It is not possible! It can't be! I'm afraid it is a dream!

CATO. [*His arm over the back of her chair*] No, it is not a dream—or if it is—don't awake me.

ZULU. Oh, that voice! how it takes me back into court. What is the emotion that makes my heart throb and takes my breath away, when I am in court? Is it the depths of interest, or the want of ventilation? [*Cato takes her hand*] Oh, Mr. Cato, don't misjudge me, I am not an ordinary woman.

CATO. Oh, no! [*Leaning toward her*]

ZULU. I am a bundle of nerves, an electro-flying machine!

CATO. I am sensible of the fluid!

PODD. Their voices are got very low. I hope Mr. Cato is not getting out of one scandal case into another!

ZULU. Mr. Dove, will you allow me to call you Alfred? Will you pardon the liberty if I do? I'll tell you why. I had a friend, a very dear friend. Don't ask me what became of him, but whoever occupies the pedestal of my admiration at which he was the first idol—I call all my idols Alfred!

CATO. I should like to be Alfred the Great! [*Bell rings. Cato rises*]

ZULU. How provoking!

CATO. [*Aside*] I hope it is not my wife! [*Podd rises and goes to the door*]

ZULU. You can see me any evening at Cremorne, or I could come any day here you might be disengaged. How good of you to waste your time on me! [*Cato listens at door C. Podd opens the door. Enter Buster*]

BUSTER. [*C.*] Dove in?

PODD. [*R.*] Yes, sir, he is engaged with a client! [*They speak apart*]

CATO. It is Mr. Sergeant Buster. [*Returns to C.*]

ZULU. We see him nearly every night at Cremorne!

CATO. You shall hear from me.

ZULU. You won't forget me? [*Zulu goes to fireplace L. and settles her hat in the glass, as they speak*]

CATO. Impossible!

ZULU. Alfred! [*Points to a portrait on the wall L.*] Who is that person?

CATO. [*Aside*] My wife. [*Aloud*] That, oh, that is, a—Mrs. Buster. You see Buster occupies these chambers jointly with me!

ZULU. Oh, that's Mrs. Buster; I'm sorry for Buster, she is a cat. [*Enter Buster into L.H. room. Zulu pulls down her veil*] Good day. I hope I have not intruded on too much of your time. [*Going out. Buster retires up C.*]

CATO. Not at all! [*Following her to the door*] Good day!

ZULU. Good day. [*She bows to Buster, then says as she goes out, aside*] I am sorry for Buster. [*Crosses office. Podd opens door for her; Zulu exits. Buster crosses to fireplace. Cato after seeing her out returns to L.H. room and shuts the door. Buster stands with back to fire, turning faces Cato*]

BUSTER. [*Looks at Cato significantly*] If you have another client or two of that kind, I'll exchange with you a good—er—a railway case against one of them.

CATO. [*Crossing to table C. sits as he speaks*] My dear Buster, you are a dissipated luminary of the law. Your head is always running on petticoats. [*Sits at table and begins fussing amongst his papers*] I assure you that was a —a perfect lady, but I know your disrespect for the sex leads you to form ideas!

BUSTER. Cato, thou reasonest well! What are you looking for? [*Advances to L. of table*]

CATO. The Vice-Chancellor's opinion *in re* Tollemache.

BUSTER. [*Picks up Zulu's photo*] Is this it? [*Hands him it*]

CATO. Zulu!

BUSTER. Oh, it was Zulu? I thought I recognized her chin, and that equestrian swing in her walk—she cannot get—er—a—the trapeze out of it. My dear Cato, I congratulate you!

CATO. Now, Buster, really I don't like this kind of joke; it is in your way, I know—you go in for this sort of thing, but please to recollect I am a married man!

BUSTER. So am I, very much married. I—er—a don't know a man more married than I am! [*Crosses to R.*]

CATO. I love my wife!

BUSTER. So do I; that is, when I say your wife, I mean my wife!

CATO. [*Rising and going to fireplace*] Yes, sir, everybody's wife—anybody's wife that will give you the slightest encouragement.

BUSTER. Cato, don't be a fraud; pull down your flag! How would you like this specimen of a client to be submitted to the scrutiny of Mrs. Cato Dove?

CATO. Josephine?

BUSTER. Yes, Josephine; the unhappy Josephine; you designing Napoleon!

CATO. My dear Buster. [*Meets him C.*]

BUSTER. [*R.*] Confess, then, or I shall produce this evidence in court! [*Cato tries to snatch the photo from him*] Pull down your flag!

CATO. [*L.*] I—I—; yes, but I assure you this interview was not my seeking! [*Goes up stage to table, followed by Buster*] I never saw her before in my life; never heard of her. I—I found her here, and—[*Down R.*]

BUSTER. [*Following him*] Don't be mean, Cato; don't be a coward as well as a fraud. I have seen her sitting in court every day.

CATO. You have eyes everywhere.

BUSTER. Yes, wherever there is a pretty woman! I marked her down; thought—er—a—I had scored one, my wish was father to that thought; 'twas you who were the object of her attention, not the deponent. Well? [*During this scene Podd is seated at desk looking over playbill*]

CATO. She wants to be a witness in the Brighton Scandal Case! [*Poking fire*]

BUSTER. [*Looking at photo*] I'll go down to Cremorne tonight and serve a subpena upon her myself!

CATO. Don't be a fool!

BUSTER. It is the only character in which to approach a woman, effectually—it—er—a—reconciles her to the superiority of our sex.

CATO. There is no resisting you!

BUSTER. I wish you could make the women think so, my dear fellow! But in the mean time it gives me the greatest pleasure to welcome you as a fellow sinner. Your fidelity to Mrs. D. radiated a kind of cold atmosphere of propriety around you that chilled my good fellowship!

CATO. Mephistopheles!

BUSTER. So, to inaugurate the occasion, let us make a night of it; be a bachelor for twenty-four hours! You have had too much connubulating lately; a little change of air will do you good!

CATO. But my wife?

BUSTER. It will do her good; you are running down, dear boy; you want tone. Your mind is getting contracted within the limits—er—a—of your hearthrug, where you are becoming a mere—er—a—domestic machine, of which your wife is the motive power!

PODD. [*In the office*] If that woman comes slinging her trapeze here, Mrs. Cato will give her an engagement.

CATO. [*Bringing Buster down*] That is perfectly true! Buster, do you know she is growing terribly jealous?

BUSTER. Do you know why?

CATO. No.

BUSTER. You have never given her any cause!

CATO. I can't follow your reasoning.

BUSTER. There is no reason in a woman's caprices. She is jealous because —er—a—she has nothing else to do!

CATO. It is very ungrateful of her to suspect me, for I have not deserved it.

BUSTER. [*R.*] That's wrong. Deserve it—justify her suspicion and spare her your reproaches by taking her sin on your shoulders. The fact is, she finds you so perfect that she is impatient to discover a fault in you; be generous— gratify her!

PODD. [*Still looking over the playbill*] She wants to be well displayed. Well, if Mrs. Cato, his wife, catches her, she'll get all the display she wants.

CATO. [*L.*] I dare not look at a woman in the streets, but my wife asks me what I see in her to stare at. If I draw a deeper breath than usual, she wants to know what I am sighing about. If I put on a decent cravat when I go out, she inquires who I am dressing myself up to captivate. I am afraid to have eyes, lungs, clothes. [*Crosses to R.*]

BUSTER. All your fault! Look at my Arabella. Distrust is—er—a—firmly established in her mind, and she is thus relieved from all anxiety. Put your- self under my treatment. I am an old practitioner. I shall send Arabella a note not to expect me home to dinner, as I have a consultation at—er—a—let me see—at Nottingham, this evening, which may detain me until tomorrow morning. So I shall tell her not to wait up for me in case I am detained!

CATO. Does she stand that?

BUSTER. Broke her in early. You must give the same excuse to your wife.

CATO. I could not tell Josephine a lie if I tried. I should stammer, color up to the roots of my hair. I know I should.

BUSTER. Then write her a note. Notes don't stammer. Ink don't blush.

CATO. I am half inclined, only to give Josephine a lesson.

BUSTER. [*Sitting down R. of table and writing*] There is a charming lady engaged in the same troupe with Zulu, Madame Closerie Dalilah. I am writing to her to join our party. You write to Zulu. We can secure a private supper room overlooking the gardens—supper for four—it will be delightful!

CATO. Egad! I've a good mind.

BUSTER. Then don't change it. [*Finishes letter*] That's done. She'll come.

CATO. [*Sits to L. of table. About to write*] What shall I say?

BUSTER. [*Dictating*] Tonight, after the performance, happy to see you at supper, in reference to your desire to appear as a witness.

CATO. [*Writing*] At supper!

BUSTER. Don't sign your name; I never do. You ought to have an alias to sign it.

CATO. I have one [*signing*]—Alfred.

BUSTER. [*Goes to door, calls*] Podd!

PODD. Sir? [*Rises and crosses to door*]

BUSTER. Post these letters immediately. [*Hands letters to him*]

PODD. Very good, sir.

BUSTER. No, wait a moment; there are two other letters you may take at the same time.

PODD. Shall I copy these into the letter-book, sir? [*Going back to desk R.*]

BUSTER. No! [*Shuts the door*] What an old fool. [*Returns to table*] Now then sit down there and write to your wife, and I will write to mine.

CATO. Oh, Lord! what shall I say?

BUSTER. Follow my style. Affectionate, but offhand. Are you ready?

CATO. All right. My hand trembles so.

PODD. [*Reading addresses*] Madame Closerie Dalilah, Mademoiselle Zulu, Robinson's Circus, Cremorne Gardens. [*Holding letter in one hand and in the other the playbill*] I'm not surprised at Buster. He always was a music hall Don Juan. He married his housekeeper, a decent woman, who made his home so respectable he can't bear to live in it. But to think Mr. Cato should leave a pretty, lady-like, devoted wife for such an article as this. [*Cato sits R. of table*]

BUSTER. You must write to the same effect that I do. [*Writing*] My angel—

CATO. [*Writing*] My darling—

BUSTER. This infernal Brighton Scandal Case—

CATO. This eternal Brighton Scandal Case—

BUSTER. Obliges me to run down this evening to Nottingham—

CATO. Calls me away to Nottingham this afternoon—

BUSTER. To attend a consultation.

CATO. To see a witness.

BUSTER. So do not wait up for me tonight after twelve.

CATO. I may be detained very late—so you need not sit up.

BUSTER. It is an infernal nuisance, old Girl.

CATO. This is an awful bore, Ducky.

BUSTER. Go to bed early.

CATO. I shan't go to bed at all.

BUSTER. Your own Charley—

CATO. Your devoted Catydid. [*They fold, enclose and direct the letters*]

BUSTER. There! Podd can take this letter to a commissionaire, who will deliver them about the hour we are supposed to be getting on board the train —[*calls*] Podd—[*Rings a gong bell on the table*]

PODD. [*Rises*] Yes, sir. [*Enters room. Cato goes to fireplace—leans on mantel*]

BUSTER. Take these letters to a messenger and tell him to deliver them; there's the money! [*Hands him a piece of silver*]

PODD. Very good, sir! [*Returns to inner room*]

BUSTER. Well, Cato, how do you feel?

CATO. I don't know whether I feel frightened or happy; it is quite a novel sensation—it is like being in the Dock!

PODD. [*Reading addresses*] Mrs. Cato Dove—Mrs. Charles Buster! [*Cato walks about, Buster follows him*]

CATO. A day of freedom—a whole holiday!

BUSTER. Rule Britannia! Britons never shall be slaves. Where shall we dine?

CATO. I don't think I could eat a morsel just now! My heart is up here, in my throat. [*Returns to mantelpiece, L.*] I must digest that before I could swallow anything—Buster!

BUSTER. [*R.*] What?

CATO. I am beginning to funk fearfully—what shall I say, how shall I look, when I return home? Josephine will want me to give her chapter and verse for everything—I know her; she will expect a full account of all the consultation!

BUSTER. Give her a page out of—a—a—Chitty on Contracts; she will never stand it to the end—a—a—I never could!

CATO. Buster! [*Faintly*] Where do you keep your brandy?

BUSTER. [*Goes up to the back C.*] Here it is; what's the matter? Fright?

CATO. Yes, I think it is going for my stomach! [*Buster brings from a tin box, marked "Private Accounts," two case flasks*]

PODD. [*In the office, having taken his hat and umbrella*] Now to find the messenger! [*As he opens the door, Mrs. Cato Dove and Mrs. Buster appear at it, coming in*] Mrs. Cato!

JOS. [*Entering the clerk's office*] Yes, I met Mrs. Buster in Regent Street, and we thought we might drop in and give our husbands a surprise! [*Enter Mrs. Buster*]

ARAB. [*C.*] I suppose they are still in court?

JOS. [*R.C.*] No, Cato told me he would be home early today!

PODD. [*R.*] These letters are for you, ladies. I was just taking them to a messenger. [*Hands letters to the ladies. Josephine takes letter and crosses to L.*]

JOS. A letter for me? [*Opening it*]

ARAB. [*Takes letter down R.*] Some excuse, I suppose, to dine out, as usual! [*Opening hers*]

JOS. [*Reading*] Oh, dear! what is this? Going out of town?

ARAB. Nottingham! that means out all night!

PODD. [*C.*] The gentlemen have not started yet—they are in there, at work.

BUSTER. [*To Cato*] Take it straight—

JOS. Are they very busy? [*The two men drink out of the flask*]

PODD. They have a case in hand, I believe!

BUSTER. D'ye feel better?

CATO. I think I've got it under! [*Buster goes behind table C.*]

ARAB. Shall we interrupt them?

JOS. Dear old Catydid—he works too hard! I'll ask him to take me down to Nottingham with him! [*They enter the R.H. room*]

CATO. Josey!

BUSTER. My wife! [*They hide the flasks in their coat pockets*]

JOS. How pale he is! [*Crosses to L.*] My dear, really you are overdoing it. Isn't he overdoing it, Mr. Buster?

BUSTER. That is—er—a—just what I have been talking to him about—he should give himself a holiday!

JOS. What is this dreadful news? You are obliged to go to Nottingham? [*Arabella goes up, Buster down R.*]

BUSTER. [*R.*] You see how it affects him! Ever since I told him that he must go—he has been like that!

PODD. Now to post this letter to Mrs. Dalilah! [*Puts on his hat, takes his umbrella and goes out*]

ARAB. [*C., back of table*] I smell brandy, strongly—

BUSTER. Brandy? Impossible! [*Aside*] I forgot to cork it, and it is overflowing in my pocket! [*Aloud*] Oh, true, I forgot; Dove felt queer and took a nip!

Jos. Darling! I cannot let him go alone!

CATO. Josey, I must do my duty—but duty must be done without flinching! [*Crosses to L.C.*]

BUSTER. England expects that every man this day shall do his duty!

Jos. Can't I go and do it with you, dear?

CATO. No, we start immediately. Buster, when do we start?

BUSTER. By the five o'clock express—we may be detained all night!

Jos. and ARAB. All night? [*Arabella down C.*]

BUSTER. [*R.C.*] There is no knowing what circumstances may arise. We are going to attend the bedside of an invalid witness in our great case.

Jos. That horrid scandal!

BUSTER. Her evidence is vital!

Jos. Her! Is it a she? [*Crosses to C.*]

BUSTER. An aged lady of ninety-two.

Jos. Oh! [*Relieved*] Ninety-two!

BUSTER. Last birthday!

ARAB. [*Aside*] Buster is lying! There is an assumption of stupidity about his mouth, that he always prepares, when it frames a lie.

Jos. But can't I go with you, dear? Do let me, you won't find me in the way a bit!

CATO. [*L. aside*] Oh, Lord, wouldn't I? [*Aloud*] My precious, do be reasonable, bear up, don't add to my difficulties—how could you leave time without a—a—a—

BUSTER. A toothbrush—er—a—frisette, or—a—a razor?

Jos. I can drive home and pack my travelling bag!

BUSTER. We have not more than forty minutes to catch the express.

Jos. [*Stamping with childish grief*] Oh! oh! what shall I do all this evening alone?

CATO. My angel! [*They speak aside at fireplace*]

ARAB. [*Who has been watching Buster*] Charley, dear—

BUSTER. What does my Bonanza want?

ARAB. [*Taking him aside*] One lawyer is quite enough to get the evidence of this old party at Nottingham. Cato Dove will go down alone—he is your junior counsel; it is *his* business to get up the case.

BUSTER. My beauty, I—er—shall be wanted!

ARAB. Yes, *I* want you at home tonight, and home you must be, that is if you wish me to sign these papers. [*Produces deed*]

BUSTER. What's that?

ARAB. The conveyance of the land you are selling at Paddington.

BUSTER. Oh, true, has—er—a—the attorney sent the deed?

ARAB. Yes, here it is, he came with it to me this morning to obtain my signature.

BUSTER. Oh! a mere matter of form.

ARAB. Precisely—but without that mere form, you can't sell the land and get the money, can you?

BUSTER. Er—a—well—a—

ARAB. You can't. I know it—now if you dine at home like a good boy, and take me to the opera afterwards, I will sign the paper before I go to bed tonight!

BUSTER. What insect have you got down your back, my darling?

ARAB. No matter about the insect, you know my terms. [*Goes up R., crosses over to L. behind table*]

BUSTER. [*Aside with conviction*] She is a very superior woman.

Jos. Will you promise to send me a telegram from Nottingham the moment you arrive there?

CATO. But, my angel, I shall be back so soon.

Jos. No matter—I want to be sure you are thinking of me, and not of anyone else.

CATO. Oh! oh! as if I could—you will get the message by—let me see— Buster, when can Josey get my message from Nottingham?

BUSTER. From Nottingham? Arrive Nottingham eight o'clock, and give two hours—say two hours—for transmission and delivery—well, about ten.

Jos. I shall put it under my pillow and cry myself asleep over it! [*She embraces him and cries. Buster goes up R.*]

CATO. [*Speaking over her shoulder*] Oh! [*Aside*] 'Pon my life, it is too bad, I can't stand this much longer!

BUSTER. [*R.*] There, Mrs. B., look at that picture of connubial confidence! Why don't we assume occasionally that attitude.

ARAB. [*C.*] Because we should laugh over each other's shoulders, Mr. B.

BUSTER. [*Aside, coming down R.*] She is a very superior woman. [*Cato goes up to table*]

Jos. Since you must let me see the last of you, I can go with you to the station, can't I? Do let me?

CATO. [*Making up papers in a roll*] Certainly, my dear; of course, it will be very much out of your way—we must take a hansom cab, and I—I don't like you to be seen in hansom cabs—it looks so fast. Don't it look fast, Buster?

BUSTER. Very bad form, indeed. [*Crosses to fireplace*]

CATO. [*R. of table*] Even coupes are going out, ain't they, Buster?

BUSTER. [*At fireplace*] They are called loose boxes!

JOS. [*L. of table*] They may call them what they like. I am going to the station with you in your hansom cab, in defiance of all the proprieties! When you took me to Mabille in Paris on our wedding trip, I was timid—but you overruled my objection by saying: "If a married woman can't defy proprieties under the protection of her husband, what's the advantage of the bonds of wedlock; she obtains her freedom from prejudices by giving up her liberty." I got your very words by heart!

CATO. My love, of course I shall be delighted—[*Aside*] What the devil shall I do now? [*Aloud*] How are you going, Buster?

ARAB. [*R.*] Mr. Buster is going with me!

BUSTER. [*Aside*] Taken in charge.

ARAB. Mr. Podd.

PODD. [*At door*] Yes, ma'am!

ARAB. Please call up two hansom cabs! [*Goes up*]

BUSTER. [*Crosses to door*] Two cabs, Podd—pick out clean ones. [*Leaning out of door*] Hist, Podd!

PODD. Sir!

BUSTER. [*Whispers*] Don't post that letter to Cremorne!

PODD. It is gone, sir!

BUSTER. Oh, Lord!

PODD. [*Going out*] I see, Mrs. Buster has served a writ of *ne exeat* on the sergeant! [*The two ladies look into mirror over mantelpiece. Cato joins Buster R.*]

CATO. [*R.C. aside to Buster*] Buster—here's a go!

BUSTER. [*R.*] Yes, it is a go to Nottingham!

CATO. What on earth shall we do there?

BUSTER. Arabella has cornered me—I can't accompany you.

CATO. What? Oh, I say—I'm not going to be expressed to Nottingham! What's to be done? You got me into this scrape.

BUSTER. I like that—didn't I find you in it? Over head and ears in it— with Zulu?

CATO. I can't go wandering about the Midland Counties all night. What's to be done? I feel like a drowning man! [*Re-enter Podd into office*]

BUSTER. Then don't struggle—lie on your back and think—stop! Could not you get rid of her at the station, and slip out, leaving the train to start without you?

CATO. Splendid—I'll do it!

PODD. [*Looking in*] The cabs are at the door, sir! [*He retires*]

JOS. Now, darling, I am ready.

ARAB. Now, Charley, give me your arm!

JOS. Poor Caty, he *does* look sorry to go! Well, that is some comfort. I never saw him look so vexed. Don't, dear. There, I won't leave you till I see the train off!

CATO. [*Aside*] Oh, Lord! [*He looks despairingly at Buster*]

JOS. You shall see the very last glimpse of me!

CATO. [*Aside*] I am in for it. There is no escape! What a night I shall pass!

ARAB. Now, Sergeant, I am yours until tomorrow!

BUSTER. [*Aside*] Oh, Lord! What a night we both shall pass!

THE ACT DROP FALLS

AS THEY GO OUT

ACT II.

SCENE: *The refreshment saloon of a railway station. Large glass doors at back L.H. looking out on the street. "Ladies' Waiting Room" R.H. Refreshment counter R.H. at back. Door L.H.2E. Entrance to railway platform. Girl discovered behind counter R. Enter Capt. Derringer and a railway Porter carrying his valise L.H.D.*

DER. [*R.C.*] Leave my valise there, and call me a cab.

POR. [*Places valise up L.*] A hansom, sir, or a four-wheeler?

DER. [*Crosses to R.*] How delightful is that familiar sound! A hansom cab! It is four years since I rode in one. [*Back to C.*] No, my friend—get me a four-wheeler, as I have my luggage here—it will be more convenient.

POR. All right, sir. [*Exit D. in F. and off R.*]

DER. [*Crosses to L.*] Home again, after four years in India. How green the fields looked as we swept along—how cheerful every face appeared! [*Railway Porter outside heard to whistle and cry*]

POR. Four-wheeler!

DER. Nothing changed since I left this very railway station in '72. I think I can recollect that very girl behind the counter; they have not changed her. Dear old England! with all my faults, I love thee still! [*Takes out a cigar*]

Yes, nothing changed. [*Up C. to counter*] I recognize those cakes under a glass case—they are the very same! [*To the Girl*] My dear, can you give me a glass of ale?

GIRL. Yes, sir, if you please.

DER. Can you oblige me with a match to light my cigar?

GIRL. No matches, sir. Smoking is not allowed in this room—it is against the company's rules.

DER. Of course; dear old prejudices—fine old crusted conservative habits. [*Feels in his pocket*] If I had a piece of paper I might get a light at this lamp. [*Takes out a letter, rolls it up*] I never knew an English rule could not be covered with half a crown. [*Lights the paper at a lamp R.*]

GIRL [*R.C., serving him*] Glass of hale, sir—three pence—Hallsopp!

DER. Glass of hale—Hallsopp's hale; there's ten shillings—pray keep the change—and the H's.

GIRL. Hoh, sir!

DER. Her sweet cockney voice is worth the money! [*He throws down the letter half consumed, and treads upon it—taking up glass*] My dear, here's a good husband to you! [*Drinks*]

GIRL. I've got an 'usband, sir.

DER. Then, here's a second one with an H, for a change. [*Drinks*] By Jove! [*Crosses to L.*] What a surprise my arrival will be to my sister, Josephine. I hope I shall not find her changed after so long an absence, but marriage does make such a difference in women; it makes none in men; that's natural, of course. I wonder what sort of a fellow her husband is—[*crosses up to C. to finish ale*] Dove—what a name for a chap—and for a lawyer, too. I think she says in her letter he is a lawyer or a doctor—I forget which. [*Drinks*] Well, I never thought Josey would have thrown herself away on a lawyer [*down R.*]—when she might have had her pick of the army list; now if she had married a sawbones, he might have joined a regiment! [*Re-enter railway Porter, D. in F.*]

POR. [*Up L.*] Here is your four-wheeler, sir. [*Picks up the valise*] Where shall I tell the driver to take you, sir?

DER. [*R.*] Oh, true, my sister's address; I forget the number—it is in her letter [*feels in his pocket*]—at the top of her letter—the only one I have received from her these twelve months. Where have I put it? [*crosses to L.C.*] —it was certainly in this pocket. Oh, the deuce! [*Turns up*] I can't have lighted my baccy with it, surely? [*Picks up the half-consumed letter*] I have though, here it is! [*Reads*] "Your affectionate sister, Josey"—but the address is burned off! What's to be done now? Oh, stay! [*Turns to the Girl*] Will you oblige me with a look at your directory?

GIRL. [*C.*] We don't keep one, sir.

POR. [*L.*] You will find one at the newspaper shop, there's one in the next street—I'll show the driver where it is.

DER. [*R.*] That's a good fellow. Dove! There cannot be many doves in London! I shall look down the list of Doves in the directory, and easily pick out my brother. I hope the human Dove does not take after the prolific bird [*going up*], or I shall be hunting Doves all day long.

POR. [*Going up*] This way, sir. [*As they go up, enter Zulu, D. in F. from R.*]

ZULU. [*Down R.*] How provoking! I've just missed the 4:40 train.

DER. [*L.C.*] By Jove—what a splendid girl!

ZULU. [*To* DER.] Can you tell me, sir, if the five o'clock down train stops at Barnet? I want to go to Barnet.

DER. Would you accept a share of my cab?

ZULU. Sir! what do you take me for? But perhaps 'tis I who am mistaken. Are you not a railway official?

DER. [*L.*] Unfortunately, no. I wish I was. I am only a lieutenant of artillery.

ZULU. [*R.*] Oh, sir, a thousand pardons—you have a sort of uniform look that deceived me!

DER. Don't mention it. Can I be of service?

ZULU. I have a letter for a lady who resides at Barnet—Madame Closerie Dalilah—it is an invitation to supper tonight, at Cremorne, and it must be delivered to her in time.

DER. Cremorne, Dalilah—surely her name is familiar to me.

ZULU. Mine is not unknown to fame, sir—I am the great Zulu! [*The Porter drops the valise*] The Geni of the Ring. I may say, sir, that I'm in the artillery, also—for we have a real gunner in his full uniform to fire me off every night.

DER. [*Bowing*] I wish I was the target.

ZULU. I trust to rank you amongst my supporters; but how shall I get this letter to Closerie?

POR. Why don't you telegraph?

ZULU. I never thought of that!

POR. There's an office inside on the platform—it's only a shilling message.

ZULU. [*Crosses to R.H.*] I could have done that at Chelsea. How thought-less I was to come all this way when I might have spared myself the trouble and the cab fare.

DER. [*R.*] Allow me to bless your thoughtlessness, as it bestows on me the pleasure of your acquaintance.

ZULU. Oh, sir. [*Aside*] What a nice man!

DER. [*Bowing*] Hoping we shall meet again, allow me to offer you my card.

ZULU. Here is mine. Always at home, in the ring, from nine to ten P.M.

DER. True, I forgot! [*Hands her a card*]

ZULU. Reserved seats, half a crown! [*Hands him a playbill. Curtsies and exits L. Derringer opens bill and goes out reading, C. Porter goes with him leaving the valise*]

GIRL. Well, the impertinence of that woman! to go and make the acquaintance of such a splendid young man off-hand like that! What he could see in her. [*Railway Porter returns*] Did you see that, Jim?

POR. What—See her fired off at Cremorne Circus? Yes, and there's no fraud about it neither—real powder—the public feels of it afore it goes into the big gun—a real soldier to touch it off. She's a regular good plucked 'un, I tell you!

GIRL. Good plucked! I should think she was! See her fire herself off at the gentleman? [*Enter Mr. and Mrs. Cato Dove, and Mr. and Mrs. Buster*]

JOS. [*R.*] Ten minutes to five. I wish we had been too late!

BUSTER. [*C.*] Now, ladies, you had better sit down in the waiting-room, while Cato and I get the tickets!

JOS. I'll go with him.

BUSTER. By no means. I'll go. He can stay with you!

JOS. My dear Sergeant, how good you are.

CATO. [*R.C.*] What is the fare? No matter; there's a five-pound note!

BUSTER. [*Aside to Cato*] It is all right. I have thought of a rescue—leave it to me. [*Exit L.H. door*]

ARAB. [*L., looking after him*] My mind is not that easy it ought to be; Buster does not inspire me with confidence.

CATO. [*Aside, crossing to R.*] A rescue! What does he mean? [*Aloud*] This way, my dear! [*Going to waiting-room*]

GIRL. Beg pardon, sir, no gentlemen are admitted there! That's the rules of the company.

JOS. [*R.C.*] What a shame!

GIRL. There's a gentlemen's waiting-room, second door on the right.

JOS. That will do! [*Going L. with Cato and Arabella*]

GIRL. Beg pardon, ma'am, no ladies are admitted there!

ARAB. The sexes are committed to solitary confinement.

CATO. That's the rule of the company. [*Enter conductor of the train, who goes to refreshment bar and drinks*] My dear, you can't stop here in a drinking saloon; wait inside a moment until Buster returns. [*Josephine and Arabella enter room R.H. Re-enter Buster*]

BUSTER. [*L.*] Here's the tickets. [*Gives him a railway ticket*]

CATO. [*R.*] What's this? Why this is a ticket to Hornsey.

BUSTER. Hush! Don't you see, your wife will see you off by the Nottingham express. I find the train will stop at Hornsey; two miles off you jump out; return here and meet me at Cremorne.

CATO. But she will expect to receive a telegram from me tonight from Nottingham.

BUSTER. I've fixed that all right. [*Calls*] Conductor!

CON. [*C.*] Yes sir. [*Touches his cap and advancing*]

BUSTER. You go with the five o'clock express to Nottingham?

CON. Yes, sir.

BUSTER. Could you send a telegram for this gentleman when you arrive there, and accept this sovereign for the trouble? [*Gives him money*]

CON. Certainly, sir, there is a telegraph office at the Nottingham station. Where is the message?

BUSTER. [*Crosses to C. To Cato*] Go and write it—quick, you have not a minute to lose. Don't stand there like an idiot.

CATO. [*Crosses to C.*] I feel like one; all this is so complicated.

CON. [*L.*] This way, sir.

CATO. [*Going L.*] I'm so confused. I don't know what to say.

BUSTER. [*Following him to L.*] Make it hot and strong, with a squeeze of despair! [*Exit Cato, L.H.D. with Conductor*]

BUSTER. [*Returning to C.*] I would write it for him, but my style is too high flavored. Now, Cato, will come back and we can have a glorious carouse. I have extricated him splendidly! That move is Napoleonic, and he does not appreciate it! Yet nothing is more simple. After a painful parting, I tear the two ladies away and carry them home, and in ten minutes Cato will return here, while the telegram is speeding to Nottingham, from whence it will be dispatched tonight, affording legal evidence of his presence a hundred miles from London, while he will be enjoying a rosy time! Oh, stolen hours are sweet! [*Re-enter Josephine R.H. door*]

JOS. [*R.*] Where's my husband?

BUSTER. [*C.*] Gone to buy the evening paper [*Re-enter Arabella R.H. door*]—and a work of fiction! [*Re-enter Zulu L.H. door*]

ZULU. That is done. I hope Closerie will come; I am sure she will!

BUSTER. [*Aside*] Zulu, by all the artillery.

ARAB. [*R., measuring Zulu*] What a very loud person! Josephine, my dear, Cato was right—this is not a proper place for us! [*Crosses to R.C.*] Sergeant, give me your arm! [*Up L.*]

Jos. [*R., aside*] How the creature stares at me! I hope she is not going by the same train as Cato.

ZULU. Why, surely, 'tis Mr. Buster! [*Re-enter Cato L.H. door*]

CATO. [*Crosses to R.C.*] I have secured a corner seat.

Jos. I hope you are going in the smoking carriage.

CATO. My dear, I don't smoke.

Jos. [*R.C.*] No matter! I insist on your going in the smoking carriage! [*Aside*] There are no ladies admitted there!—rules of the company.

CATO. [*C., aside*] Zulu! The devil!

ZULU. [*Aside*] Alfred! [*Porter appearing at L.H. door*]

POR. Now, sir; if you are going to Nottingham you have no time to lose. [*Business*]

ZULU. [*Aside, crosses to R.*] Going to Nottingham! but how about our supper tonight?

CATO. Come, Josey, don't you hear? Oh, Lord! [*Bell heard outside*]

POR. [*Shouting at door L.H.*] Passengers for Bedford, Nottingham, Leeds and the North. [*Disappears. Exit Josephine and Cato L.H. door*]

ARAB. Sergeant, that person knows you and Cato! Who is she?

BUSTER. My dear, she is—er—a—simply—a—a witness in our scandal case!

ARAB. Yes, sir; I should say she has been witness of a good many. [*Looks at her with her glasses*]

ZULU. [*To the girl at the bar*] One of the penalties public people have to endure, is being stared at by the crowd.

ARAB. [*Aside*] Impudent baggage! [*Aloud*] Come, Sergeant! [*Exit L.H. door*]

BUSTER. [*Hastily*] Have you received the letter?

ZULU. Of course, I have; and have invited my friend to supper!

BUSTER. All right; we shall be there! [*Re-enter Arabella L.H. door*]

ARAB. Sergeant!

BUSTER. My dear! [*Exit with her L.H. door*]

ZULU. She has got the whip hand of him. Well, to see that man in court —brow-beating the judges, bullying the witnesses, and laying down the law to the jury, and then see him here cowed by a petticoat—one would never think it was the same person. [*Mimicking*] Sergeant, my dear! [*Exit L.H. door. Re-enter Derringer C. with a paper in his hand*]

DER. [*R.C.*] I found half a column of Doves in the directory—here they are—twenty-seven of them, beginning with Aaron and ending with William

Dove. I forget my Dove's name. I thought it was a Caesar or Brutus. Where the deuce shall I begin? [*Re-enter Josephine L.H. door*]

Jos. [*L.*] He has gone, dear old boy—he recovered his spirits just at the last!

Der. [*R.*] I must take a cab by the hour and call on every Mrs. Dove on the list!

Jos. Dove, who's this? Why, oh, it cannot be!

Der. I'll knock one over after the other! Let me see!

Jos. It is—it is!

Der. I will begin with Mrs. Dove, 24 Bedford Square.

Jos. No, begin with Mrs. Dove, 62 Boston Road.

Der. Sure, it isn't!

Jos. Yes, it is!

Der. Josey!

Jos. My dear Jack! [*They embrace*]

Der. Lord, what luck! why, do you know, I burned your letter by mistake, and forgetting your address, I was preparing to look up every Dove in London.

Jos. But why did you not write to tell us you were coming? We have not heard from you since my marriage.

Der. The truth is, I was laid up with a touch of sunstroke, invalided for six months. I did not like to spoil your honeymoon with bad news. As soon as I regained my feet, they gave me six months' leave, and I thought to take you by surprise.

Jos. Dear old Jack! I am glad to see you—how fat you have grown!

Der. Yes—the sunstroke seems to have agreed with me.

Jos. Mad as ever!

Der. But you must present me to your husband. Where is Dove?

Jos. You arrive just in time to miss seeing him. He was here ten minutes ago. He has just started for Nottingham.

Der. I am not sorry to have you all to myself for a few days.

Jos. Oh, but you won't—he returns tomorrow.

Der. Then let us make the most of today—you belong to yourself today—you are your own mistress!

Jos. [*Laughing*] And when my husband is here—I'm the master!

Der. What a happy fellow! What's his name? Scipio?

Jos. Cato.

Der. True—I forgot. I knew it was something with an *O*. Well, we must spend the day together.

Jos. We'll make a night of it!

DER. So we will.

Jos. Oh, what fun! [*Kisses him*]

GIRL. Oh! [*Re-enter Zulu L.H. door*]

ZULU. I heard a familiar sound. Who's kissing so loud here?—it is against the rules of the company. [*Josephine crosses to R.*] Oh, it is my gunner!

DER. [*C.*] My lovely bombshell!

ZULU. He is making the acquaintance of every girl he meets. Well, he did not get on as fast with me—she can't be much!

Jos. [*R. aside to Derringer*] Do you know this woman?

ZULU. Woman! No more a woman than you are, ma'am—and much more of a lady. Good day, sir. [*Aside*] Just like these common soldiers! [*Exit C.*]

Jos. Oh, let us get away from this place as soon as possible.

DER. Never mind her. Let us not mind anybody but our two happy selves. Recollect I have been four years away. Let us get a cab, and enjoy the rest of the day like two schoolboys. First, we'll dine at Richmond.

Jos. I must go home, then, and change my dress.

DER. I allow you fifteen minutes for the toilette.

Jos. I'll make as much haste as if you were my lover.

DER. Of course, you wouldn't hurry for a husband. After Richmond, we'll go to the Alhambra.

Jos. Oh, Jack, is that proper?

DER. Proper! It is the swell thing to do. There's a ballet, and I can smoke in the back of the box.

Jos. I shall lose my reputation.

DER. Leave it there—plenty of people in that place want one. Then, after the Alhambra, we'll go to Cremorne.

Jos. Out of the frying pan into the fire. Jack, I dare not do it.

DER. We can engage a private room overlooking the gardens—have a quiet little supper, and enjoy the fun.

Jos. Enjoy the fun! What a heartless creature I should be to enjoy any fun while poor Cato is shaking and jolting along all night in that horrid railway carriage, on his road to Nottingham!

DER. Do you think *he* would hesitate to embrace such an occasion as this because *you* could not share it?

Jos. My dear Jack, you don't know him. I am his only occasion. He would embrace nothing whatever but me!

DER. What a monotonous kind of a person he must be! Well, Josey, I'll be responsible for all the fun you will enjoy and I stick to my program. Here is the ladies' waiting-room; you must stay in here while I call up a cab.

Jos. Don't be long. [*Exit into R.H. room. Re-enter Buster, C.L.; he is nearly knocked down by Derringer*]

Der. Can't you see where you are blundering to?

Buster. Sir! I was just about to address the same question to you!

Der. [*Under his breath*] Stupid old tailor! [*Exit*]

Buster. [*Calling after him*] Why tailor! I don't perceive anything either ridiculous or degrading in the imputation—you may see it in that light—I don't. [*Comes down L.*] If he had waited I could have called him a volunteer, or a marine! These good ideas always occur to a fellow after he has lost the opportunity of expressing them. I have slipped through the matrimonial noose. When I got Mrs. Buster into the cab outside the station, I had a happy thought. "Arabella," I said, "we are close to the Agricultural Hall, where the Horse Show is in full force—the Royal Family will be there." (I baited the trap with that succulent lie.) "Shall we go?" She was delighted, and we drove to the exhibition. Two reserved seats in the gallery cost me half a sovereign. I had four pounds remaining of Cato's capital, so I did not mind the expense. When Arabella was safely squeezed in, after wading past forty people—eighty knees—I jammed her in a remote stall, and waited beside her for an opportunity of giving her the slip—it soon came. She admired a pair of ponies—miserable rats, but they had long tails, and that captivated her. "Bella," I said, "you have taken a fancy to this pair of ponies? They shall be yours!" "Buster," she cried, "you don't mean it!" "Mean it," said I, "you shall see," and I waded out. [*Looks at his watch*] Let me see, it will take me to examine these ponies and get a medical certificate that they are both unsound in every limb—will take me three-quarters of an hour! [*Re-enter Cato. He is dressed in a long linen duster, and has a soft broad-brimmed hat*]

Cato. I have returned.

Buster. Cato, where did you pick up that envelope?

Cato. At the station at Hornsey. They sell them at the bookstall! Where's my wife?

Buster. Safely at home!

Cato. What a relief. I can breathe freely! now I am getting accustomed to the excitement, the sense of danger being past, I rather like the feeling!

Buster. Don't you feel like a bird?

Cato. Yes, but while my wife was in sight, the bird felt he was within shot, and the sensation is very unpleasant!

Buster. Now you have an entire evening to enjoy yourself in our old bachelor fashion!

Cato. Yes. What shall we do to begin with?

Buster. Well, I must return to Arabella. [*Looks at his watch*] Time's up. (Those ponies won't carry me any longer.) I left her at the Horse Show!

Cato. You are not going to desert me?

Buster. My dear fellow, I can't leave my wife in the middle of a horse show, I must take her home!

Cato. Of course; but after you have left her at home, where shall we meet—when—how?

Buster. She insists on my dining at home, and then taking her to the opera!

Cato. But what am I to do all that time?

Buster. Go to the club!

Cato. I can't; half the fellows know my wife, and I couldn't take them—the whole club—into our confidence!

Buster. Go to Cremorne, dine there, and wait till I come.

Cato. Cremorne by daylight, before the lamps are lighted, with nobody but waiters and the checktakers on the premises! Can't you think of something that will occupy my time till nine o'clock?

Buster. What do you say to a game of billiards?

Cato. Splendid. I'll give you ten points in fifty, and play you for a sovereign!

Buster. Don't I tell you I can't leave my wife?

Cato. I'll give you fifteen points and make it a five-pound note.

Buster. Impossible!

Cato. But, my dear fellow, consider my melancholy situation. I dare not show myself anywhere in town!

Buster. Then take a cab and go for a drive in the country. My dear Cato, I proposed a night a Cremorne, but I did not undertake to find you employment for all the hours of the day. Stop! I know a quiet little public house, the Swan, at Chiswick, quite retired—not a soul there. They know me—take my card. [*Hands him a card*] There you are! Have a tea-dinner and a game of skittles with the landlord; he is a splendid fellow—will do anything for us. I defended him at the Old Bailey, case of burglary—got him off. He will treat you well—bye-bye! Supper is ordered at eleven; don't wait for me. I'll come, if I can! [*Exit C.D.*]

Cato. This is not what I expected when I entertained the proposal to make a night of it! When I entertained a vague idea of reckless dissipation, the picture of a tea-dinner in a retired public house did not present itself to my fevered imagination; a burglar, however splendid, was not the lovely companion, and skittles was not the occupation I dreamed of. Oh, dear, I begin already to repent. I feel depressed in spirit. I would not dare to confess it to Buster, but I want to go home to Josey! Can't I make some excuse? I can say I was taken suddenly ill on the train! Yes, that would do! No—I forget! It won't do; for after we had retired to rest that infernal telegram will arrive from Nottingham. I can't explain being in a telegraph office at Nottingham and being in bed in London at the same time. That alibi would convict me. [*Re-enter Buster hastily C. door*]

BUSTER. [*L.*]. Arabella is coming up the street; she has not seen me. I must slip around this way by the station and regain the horse show before she returns to the hall. [*Exit into railway station L.*]

CATO. [*Runs up and looks off R.*] Mrs. Buster coming! What shall I do? [*Enter Podd C. door. He looks up L.*]

PODD. I just escaped the rain.

CATO. Podd, my clerk, he must not recognize me! [*Turns to R.H. and pulls up his collar as he advances to R.C. Podd going across to L.H. door*]

POR. The train for Kentish Town, Hempstead, Highgate!

PODD. All right! I am going to Kentish Town. I'm just in time.

CATO. [*At R.H. door*] Where can I hide for one moment? [*He opens R.H. door—looks in suddenly—closes it*] Oh, Lord, my wife! She's in there! [*Podd at L.H. door, searches for his ticket to show the porter. A four-wheel cab drives up to door in F. Enter Derringer—gets out of it*]

DER. [*Down L.*] I thought I should never find a cab; this fellow is the only one on the stand. How it rains! [*He crosses to R.H. door and Cato runs up to C. door*]

CATO. Oh, dear! here comes Mrs. Buster. Podd blocks that door, and my wife is in there. I am surrounded on all sides. Oh! [*He opens the door of the cab and jumps in; closing it after him, he pulls down the blind. Enter Josey R. Exit Podd L.*]

JOS. What a time you have been! Have you found a cab?

DER. All right—here it is! [*Enter Mrs. Buster C. door*]

JOS. Arabella, why where is the sergeant?

ARAB. The monster, he left me in the horse show an hour ago; it is all over. They turned me out. I am looking for him.

DER. Now, jump in. [*Tries to open the door*] It sticks very fast. [*He opens the door of the cab; it is pulled to from the inside*] Hallo! what's that? There is somebody inside.

CATO. [*Inside*] This cab is engaged.

DER. That's cool; he says the cab is engaged; of course it is. I engaged it, sir; this cab is mine.

CATO. Drive on, coachman!

DER. Stop—not until I have your name.

CABMAN. Now, then, ain't you done?

CATO. [*Putting out his arm offers a card*] There, sir, is my card; take it.

DER. [*Taking the card and advances*] I will hold you answerable wherever you are.

CATO. [*Putting his head out at front window*] Cabby, Putney Common; a sovereign if you gallop all the way.

CABMAN. All right, sir. Hay! [*He whips his horse. The cab disappears*]

DER. [*Reading card*] Mr. Sergeant Buster, Pump Court.

ARAB. My husband! [*Derringer rushes up and shakes his fist after the cab*] [*Bell rings*]

POR. [*At door L.H.*] Passengers for Bedford, Leicester, Derby, Manchester.

ACT III.

SCENE: *Two rooms in a hotel, with the intermediate corridor. Doors in the partitions. Staircase and door at back. Supper tables laid. Swallbach, a German head-waiter, seated in R.H. room. Joseph, a waiter, is holding a back of a fire shovel to his eye.*

SWALL. Ah! ce—ahee—Gott in himmel! I zall be plind my life.

JOSEPH. How did you do it?

SWALL. Ach! you vool! It vas not me. It vas der gork der von champain bodel. [*Victor hurries in by corridor to R.H. room. He carries a bandage and a tomato*] I vas open it. I gut der string, ven bom—it dos dam gork—he zhot me in de eye!

VIC. Here is the best thing in the world for a black eye.

SWALL. Vas ist das? Ein domato!

VIC. Tomato! the finest plaster!

JOSEPH. It ain't to compare with a bit of raw beefsteak! That's the reg'lar cure!

VIC. Beefsteak! You English imagine to yourselves the beefsteak is cure for everything.

SWALL. Sacrement, vile you vight your beefsteak and domatoes, mine eye is glozing up. [*They bind the bandage over his eye, placing the tomato under it*] Ach! das vos goot, zo it is. [*Bell rings*]

VIC. There's the office bell!

SWALL. Quick, it is bardy for supper. Make ready. [*He rises. Exit Victor. Cato enters the corridor. His hat is smashed. His coat is covered with dirt and he wears a false nose*]

CATO. This is what Buster calls making a night of it! Buster drew out the program. Buster composed the entertainment, I consented to play a part in the piece; but if the incidents in store for the next three hours resemble what I have gone through already, I shall not live to see the morning. Waiter! [*Enter Joseph. Swallbach and Victor light the lamps in R.H. rooms and exeunt*]

JOSEPH. Sir, what can I get for you?

CATO. A clothes brush. [*Bell. Enter Victor*]

JOSEPH. Coming, sir. Victor, the gentleman wants a brush.

CATO. Stop—there's a cab at the door. Ask the fellow what's his fare.

JOSEPH. How shall I know which cab it is, sir?

CATO. You can't mistake it. Look at me; the vehicle is in a similar condition; so is the horse. You will find the cabman inside, very drunk!

JOSEPH. All right, sir. [*Exit*]

CATO. Now, I can release myself. [*Takes off his nose*] Oh, what a relief that is! After achieving that hairbreadth escape from detection by my wife, we drove at a most illegal speed to Turnham Green; pulled up once in Knightsbridge to buy this nose. When I got to Chiswick I found I had forgotten the address of Buster's friend, the cheerful burglar. It was only half-past six o'clock and raining in torrents. The cabman said his horse was done up, and as he had to go home to change his animal, I pulled out my purse—you cannot picture my despair when I found I had given all my money—five pounds—to Buster! I was obliged to stick to that cab. I have passed the evening in that cab. The fellow drove me home—to a stable-yard in the Old Kent Road. There he took out the horse and left me in the cab for two hours, at half a crown an hour. It was raining in torrents for two hours. He came back—drunk! Oh, so drunk that even the horse seemed to look on in doubt as to the propriety of trusting him with the reins. I had no alternative. I put him inside, mounted the box and drove the vehicle myself. It was raining in torrents. All went fairly—I may say swimmingly—till I tried to pass a dust cart in Millbank; caught the hind-wheel, and over we went. I landed amongst the ash-barrels. A friendly policeman soon put us right again. The cabman inside did the swearing, and I drove here! [*Re-enter Joseph*]

JOSEPH. The man says it is two sovereigns, sir, you promised to give him.

CATO. One! The rogue sees double.

JOSEPH. Well, sir, he says if you won't pay it he wants your number.

CATO. My number?

JOSEPH. You had best take his, sir, and give him your card.

CATO. [*Aside*] Oh, the deuce! that would never do! [*Aloud*] Pay the fellow what he asks, and put it on the bill.

JOSEPH. What name, sir? Who shall we charge to?

CATO. My name; oh, charge it to Buster. I am going to sup here with Sergeant Buster's party. [*Cato takes off his duster and hat—gives them to Joseph*]

JOSEPH. The sergeant is well known to us here, sir. Quite right, sir! [*Exit. Enter Victor with a brush*]

VIC. Here is a brush, sir—is that all for the present? [*Victor brushing him*]

CATO. You don't think a man who has eaten nothing since half-past eight this morning can stay his stomach with a clothes brush? I want a room—the best, warmest, cosiest you have, and supper for four.

VIC. Here is the very thing, sir. We kept this for Mr. Buster's party. [*Showing Cato into L.H.R.*]

CATO. [*Looking around*] Very snug—uncommonly snug—but what door is that?

VIC. [*Opening door in flat*] It slides back, sir; so as to throw the two rooms into one when we have a large party.

CATO. Ah! very convenient, but on this occasion if you have another party in there, they can overhear all that passes in this room. Have you not something more private?

VIC. Step this way, sir; here is the very room you require [*enters R.H. room*]—quite retired; tiled in, sir, with a window overlooking the gardens.

CATO. Excellent! Your name?

VIC. Victor!

CATO. Here's a crown for you! [*Feels in his pocket*]

VIC. Thank you, sir!

CATO. Put it in the bill—charge it to Buster! Now for the supper. I am as empty as a drum! [*Enter Swallbach*]

VIC. The head-waiter will take your orders, sir!

CATO. I feel as if I could eat an elephant roast and drink the Rhine. Has the supper been ordered?

SWALL. Not a yed, sir; de zergent he lefe it do me.

CATO. [*Aside*] Who is this foreign Cyclops?

SWALL. Ed a vayter, sir, to zerve you!

CATO. From Servia? So I should think from your appearance—got a Bashi Bazook in the eye?

SWALL. Nein, a gork in de eye, sir, in champayne.

CATO. Ah! reminiscence of the French war. Well, now for supper. Supper for four. Let me see—oysters, anchovy toast, cold salmon, a spatchcock, a

lobster salad—take care the insect is fresh; half a dozen woodcocks, broiled
—nicely underdone—on toast; dessert and Roman punch!

SWALL. [*Repeats to himself the list as he writes it down*] Hysters, toset
anchut; Solomon gold, mit a despatcher cock; zalad, mit lobster, afterwards
a would-be cock, broil on toset, unterdone, mit punch Romaine in de desert!
Now vor de wein!

CATO. Champagne—two bottles dry.

SWALL. Doo bodels! in der middle of four beeples—it is eight bodels!

CATO. Go it—eight bottles—they have got to last all night.

SWALL. Und dis is vor your aggount—to your name?

CATO. No; Buster. Charge it to Sergeant Buster, only serve it as soon as
you can, and, Victor—

VIC. Monsieur.

CATO. If anyone calls for Mr. Alfred—I expect a lady—two ladies—you
will show them in here; don't admit anyone else!

VIC. All right, sir. [*Exit*]

CATO. [*Aside*] I think I am pretty safe at last—snugly tiled in, no one will
recognize me here. [*Aloud*] You understand that I am Herr Alvred!

SWALL. Yaw, zir; anything you vish—you can rely on us, Mr. Dove.
[*Going*]

CATO. What did he say? What remark did that Polyphemus make!

SWALL. If I had mein eye—mitout dis—dot it is you shall not vorget
Swallbach, of de Café de la Mad'laine, Paris, vere you come so often to dine
mit dot putiful lady!

CATO. [*Aside*] My wife! [*Aloud*] You mistake me for another person.
I'm often confounded with him—he's a—a Scotchman from—a—Derbyshire.
I'm an American just arrived from—a—the Centennial—why, certainly—
don't you hear, I'm an American, I am!

SWALL. Zertainly—yaw—I gompre-end, I didn't see before. I make mistake.

CATO. Of course, how can you remember me with only one eye!

SWALL. Dass a fax.

CATO. My name is Tyler—Dewitt Q. Tyler, of Tippecanoe, New Jersey—
you will recollect?

SWALL. Yaw, Mr. Dove. I vill not forget.

CATO. Tyler!

SWALL. I understand, Mr. Dove; don't be avraid I vorget. [*Exit*]

CATO. That could not happen to anyone but me! now I must buy the
discretion of that one-eyed monster at any price. I must charge him to Buster.
[*Looks at his watch*] Five minutes to eleven, and not a soul arrived to relieve

my solitary misery. Six hours since I parted from my wife—it seems like six months—and this is making a night of it. May I never make another! Oh, Josephine! if you knew how I am being served out! You can't hear me swear, but I do, never again to go and *try the taste of forbidden fruit!* [*Enter Buster, C.*]

BUSTER. Waiter, which is Mr. Alfred's room?

JOSEPH. [*Meeting him*] This way, sir.

CATO. Buster—at last!

BUSTER. If you knew what I have gone through to get here—

CATO. Take it, put it under a microscope, magnify it 40,000 times, and you will see the horrible secrets of my life during the last six hours! but the clouds have cleared away. "The night has passed, and joy cometh with the morrow." Now we will enjoy ourselves, eh?

BUSTER. I wish I could, but it is impossible.

CATO. What?

BUSTER. I can't stop. I have left my wife at the opera; took a hansom cab, and came down here to tell you how unfortunate it has turned out.

CATO. Unfortunate!

BUSTER. I am in a worse fix than you are. I'm obliged to give up this party.

CATO. What—give me up?

BUSTER. I must run back to my wife, whom [*looking at his watch*] I left at the opera. I had the greatest difficulty in persuading her she was in fault this afternoon, when I left her at the horse show. I can't play the same card twice in one hand.

CATO. And you are going to leave me with these two ladies that you have invited?

BUSTER. Don't be alarmed. I have telegraphed Closerie not to come—I have put her off.

CATO. Put her off?

BUSTER. Certainly, and I have no doubt she has told Zulu—so neither of them will come.

CATO. But what am I to do?

BUSTER. Go home!

CATO. Go home!—I can't. You forget I am at Nottingham! how can I explain my return?

BUSTER. Say the locomotive broke down on the road.

CATO. How can I? At ten o'clock, according to your calculation, she received my telegram to say I had arrived there safely.

BUSTER. What the devil did you telegraph for? If you will spoil your wife by acceding to her caprices, you must accept the consequences.

CATO. I hope you are not going to leave me in for it!

BUSTER. In for it! I like that. I found you closeted with a lovely girl this afternoon—you agreed with me to have a jovial night of it. Here you are. I wish you joy, old man. I must be off. [*Exit*] I have barely time to reach the opera. [*Disappears off at C.*]

CATO. But stop. Where am I to sleep? I can't go home; I can't prolong supper until nine in the morning—that is the earliest hour I can decently present myself in Bolton Row. I shall be turned out of this place at two in the morning, then I must ramble about in the rain. It is raining in torrents still. I shall go and walk in front of my own house, look up at the windows [*re-enter Joseph with glasses*] not daring to enter; regarded with suspicion by the policeman. Oh, waiter! I ordered supper for four.

JOSEPH. It is ready, sir!

CATO. Be good enough to say I only want it for one.

JOSEPH. Impossible, sir. It is too late now. It is cooked and coming up. [*Exit*]

CATO. But I can't eat all that; it will look absurd. [*Enter Victor and Swallbach with dishes*] It is ridiculous. I can't sit down before all that, alone. I'll take a look into the coffee room, and if I see a congenial fellow there, I'll invite him to share my supper. [*Re-enter Joseph, preceding Derringer*]

JOSEPH. This way, sir.

DER. I want a quiet room for a lady and myself. [*Joseph enters L.H. room as Derringer follows him. Cato enters corridor C.*]

CATO. I'll invite the first I—by Jove, here's the very thing! There's a military jovial cut about him I like.

DER. This will do. I will go down and bring the lady. [*Re-enters corridor*]

CATO. Sir, I beg your pardon.

DER. Did you speak to me?

CATO. Yes, sir. I did myself that honor. I am a stranger here, you seem to be another.

DER. I arrived in London this evening.

CATO. In the army?

DER. Yes, sir.

CATO. So am I—that is, I am in the 21st Middlesex, Lawyers Corps. Further ceremony is useless. Will you do me the pleasure of supping with me?

DER. You are very kind. Another time I should be very happy to improve your acquaintance, but I have a lady waiting for me in a cab at the door, so you must excuse me.

CATO. You are going to sup with a lady. Happy fellow, I envy you. I was in a similar condition—

DER. I hope you will allow me—

CATO. I understand—

DER. [*To Joseph*] Lay supper for two—

CATO. Sir, your lady does not happen to have a female friend with her? If so, it would just suit me, for I have supper ready for four, and we could—

DER. [*Stiffly*] No, sir, the lady is not the kind of person you mistake her for. Good evening! [*Exit*]

CATO. I have no luck. [*Exit Joseph*]

SWALL. Der table is zerved!

CATO. [*Entering his room*] For four! [*Swallbach goes up corridor*] My appetite is gone! [*Sits*] I shall not forget this party of pleasure in a hurry. Supper for four!

VIC. Do you want anything else?

CATO. [*Rising furiously*] Yes, I want to break your head! [*Victor runs out*] The sight of those three empty chairs is a hollow mockery. [*Takes off the covers*] Where on earth shall I put all that. Oh, I wish my wife was here! [*Enter Swallbach with four bottles of champagne followed by Joseph with four bottles*] What is that?

SWALL. The champagne, sir, eight bodels—

CATO. You don't imagine I am going to drink eight bottles of wine?

SWALL. Eight bodels vas order. Eight bodels vos put on the ice. And ven it is ice it must be trunk. It is already in der bill! [*Exit Joseph*]

CATO. All right, charge it to Buster!

SWALL. Vera goot, Mr. Dove—

CATO. Tyler!

SWALL. I sall not vorgot. I am tiscreet, Mr. Dove! [*Exit*]

CATO. The Dutch idiot! He made me swallow an oyster the wrong way! [*Enter Derringer and Josephine by corridor into L.H. room*]

DER. This way. [*They enter L.H. room*]

JOS. Oh, this is charming! What a delightful day we have spent! There was only one drawback to my complete satisfaction, and that was the absence of my poor Cato. I wonder what he is doing now?

DER. Sound asleep, I dare say; what a spooney little darling you are? You made me drive all the way round by your house in Bolton Row to find that telegram.

JOS. [*Reads*] 62 Bolton Row, London. Dear old Catydid—I do spoil him!

CATO. Oh, Lord! I wonder what my wife is doing now! Snug in bed, no doubt, dreaming of me. I wish she were here—or I was there! [*Enter Victor with the dishes to L.H. room*]

VIC. There are the oysters to begin with—what will you please order to follow?

DER. Josephine, you must select the supper.

Jos. Must I? Let me see. [*Josephine writes with pencil on paper which Victor hands to her*] I'll ruin you with a delicious bill of fare.

CATO. This bird is done to a cinder. I'll try the lobster—I used to be fond of lobster. [*Eats*] What's this—white India rubber, flavored with phosphorus? Oh, this won't do! [*Rings the bell*]

VIC. [*Shouting from other room*] Coming, sir.

Jos. There I think that will be exquisite!

DER. Let the champagne be dry and not too cold.

VIC. [*Taking the list*] Very good, sir.

CATO. Will they never answer the bell [*rings furiously*] or must I tear the bell out by the roots? [*Victor crossing into R.H. room*]

VIC. Coming, sir. [*As he crosses he cries to Swallbach*] Monopole dry for No. 9.

CATO. Oh, you are here at last!

VIC. Beg pardon, sir, I was serving the party in the next room.

CATO. Take that insect away—disinfect it, and—what do you call that bird?

VIC. Woodcock, sir.

CATO. Yes, it is the woodenest I ever sat down to—take it away!

VIC. What would you like instead, sir?

CATO. How do I know? I can't choose—I can't think! What has that party ordered in the next room?

VIC. Here is their bill of fare, sir.

CATO. Let me see what they are going to indulge in. [*Swallbach entering L.H.R. with wine*]

SWALL. Dry Monopole. [*Places bottle on table*] Any oder ting, sir?

DER. Yes—brandy and soda.

SWALL. Vera goot, sir. [*Exit*]

CATO. [*Reading*] Chicken salad—why it can't be! This is the writing of my wife!

VIC. What, sir?

CATO. Nothing—I am deceived. Truffled partridge, macaroni Italienne. Those I's are Josephine's—I'd swear to her I's a mile off! My wife here! in such a place as this—at this time of night, when I am at Nottingham! Oh, dear! Waiter!

VIC. Sir!

CATO. What sort of persons are in the adjoining room?

Vic. Oh, sir—I—really—you must not ask me.

Cato. Speak! I'll—here's a five-pound note.

Vic. Well, sir?

Cato. Put it on the bill—charge it to Buster. But, speak, who is there?

Vic. A lady, sir.

Cato. Good figure—brown hair—regular features?

Vic. Yes, sir, that's it.

Cato. Dressed in blue?

Vic. Blue and grey.

Cato. She is alone, or with another lady?

Vic. The other lady ain't arrived yet, sir; she is with an officer. I think the gentleman is—

Cato. An elderly man, ain't he?

Vic. About twenty-six. You don't look well, sir!

Cato. It is the lobster!

Vic. Is that all you require, sir?

Cato. All I require? Get out—go! [*Victor exits*] All I require. It is very much more than I require. I cannot believe it to be possible, my wife—my Josephine—here—there—with a soldier. I'll not believe it. [*Entering the corridor*] No one here. What terrible truth am I about to discover through this keyhole? [*Looks through the keyhole L.H. room*] There they are; she is looking down; he is stooping over her. It is the young fellow I met here just now; his arm is 'round her—now she looks up. Ah! 'tis, 'tis she—my wife—Josey. I am losing my senses!

Der. You little fool, what is that paper?

Cato. Hush! they speak, he called her "a little fool."

Jos. It is the billet doux I received from Cato!

Cato. She is never going to read him my love letters—to feed him with my spoon!

Jos. Listen [*she reads the telegram*]: "Your darling one arrived here very sad—"

Cato. It is my telegram from Nottingham.

.Jos. [*Reading*] "far from his Josey. What a wretched night he will pass—"

Cato. The spirit of prophecy was on me when I wrote that.

Jos. [*Reads*] "But tomorrow, your faithful Bogamps will embrace you, his beloved."

Der. Bogamps?

Jos. That's a foolish pet name I gave him.

Cato. How well I remember the moment!

Der. Well, old girl, I dare say he would not be sorry to be in my place.

CATO. In his place. They are turning me into ridicule; he calls her "old girl." What shall I do? [*Enter Swallbach with brandy and soda*] Who is that? Where are you going with that wine?

SWALL. To the bardy in No. 9.

CATO. Stop—yes—that's a splendid idea. I—I'll do it—let me look at you!

SWALL. Excoos me!

CATO. Stop, I tell you. Will you earn ten pounds, fifteen, twenty?

SWALL. Zwanzig?

CATO. Lend me your apron—your bandage, all right!

SWALL. Vat vor?

CATO. Twenty pounds; hold that. [*Pulls off his bandage and gives him to hold while he puts on the apron, then the bandage, and finally takes the nose from his pocket and puts it on*] Now give me your bottles of wine!

SWALL. But I do not gombreend.

CATO. Twenty pounds; put it in the bill; charge it to Buster—all right!

SWALL. Ah! it is a joke, I zee—a joke mit dose beeples.

DER. Are those fellows never going to bring the wine? [*He rings the bell violently*]

SWALL. Gomming!

CATO. Clear out. [*Threatens Swallbach, who runs out*]

DER. Oh, here it is at last! [*Enter Cato to L.H. room*]

CATO. Gomming—yaw, mynheer—der wein—vat it is! [*Victor and Joseph bring dishes into L.H. room, lay them on table and exeunt*]

DER. Supper at last. Now, Josey, sit down!

CATO. [*Flourishing the bottle behind Derringer's back*] I'll Josey him!

JOS. What a singular looking waiter!

DER. He has only one eye, but that's a blazer! [*Cato opens bottle of wine and pours out three tumblers; hands them on salver*]

CATO. [*Aside*] I would like to break his head with the bottle!

JOS. [*Taking a glass*] I was dying with thirst.

DER. [*Taking a glass*] The fellow has poured out a third glass of wine. Don't you see there are only two of us, idiot?

CATO. Yaw—ein—zwei—drei—I but it avay. [*Retires and drinks it*]

DER. What are you doing? Are you out of your senses, or drunk?

CATO. You object to it, so I put it away.

DER. Leave the room—we wish to be alone. [*Derringer speaks to Josephine*]

CATO. [*Aside*] They want to be alone. The shameless woman. [*Sits down*] She hears him avow his desire to be alone with her, and she does not—

DER. [*Turns and sees him sitting down*] Will you get out?

CATO [*Rises. Aside*] She laughs. [*Aloud*] I go. [*Gains the door*] Oh, if I wasn't at Nottingham. [*Turns*] If you sall vant any tings, you ring, and I am here.

DER. Go to the devil!

CATO. Ring alvays, as ofden as you blease. [*Derringer offers to throw the bottle at him. Cato shuts the door—he listens*]

Jos. I do believe the poor fellow is crazy—there is something the matter with his head.

CATO. That's where it is!

DER. My darling Josey, you don't drink.

CATO. His darling!

Jos. Yes, I do, Jack.

CATO. He darlings her, and she Jacks him! [*Looking through the key-hole*] I won't lose a word, nor a look—nor a gesture. Oh, dear! I can't see. Hush! they are not speaking—that's a bad sign. What can they have to whisper about? It is not allowed in a respectable house. Hush! dead silence!

DER. [*After drinking again*] Oh, that's lovely! [*Cato bursts in on them*]

CATO. Gomming! [*Josephine screams*]

DER. Are you mad?

CATO. Don't you vant zometing?

DER. What the mischief brings you here?

CATO. [*As he retires*] It was nothing—false alarm. [*Meets Victor, who enters with salad, he takes it*] Salade!

DER. Put it down there; take these things away.

Jos. [*Aside*] How the creature eyes me.

DER. [*Aside to her*] Don't be afraid. [*Cato puts the salad on table—removes the dishes*] This salad is not mixed—where's the oil and vinegar?

CATO. Gomming.

DER. Waiter—champagne!

CATO. Gomming. [*Brings the oil and champagne. Aside, looking at Josephine*] I wish it was prussic acid and strychnine. [*He pours the oil in her glass and the champagne in the salad*]

Jos. Oh, what is he doing—he's helping me to oil.

DER. And pouring champagne in the salad. Will you get out and send us another waiter?

CATO. [*Aside, going out*] He orders me out. [*Bitterly*] Ah! This is making a night of it! [*He listens*]

DER. I'll stop further impertinent intrusion. [*He locks the door*]

CATO. He has locked the door.

DER. There now, we are rid of that idiot. I hope you have enjoyed your evening.

Jos. It has been delightful.

CATO. They have spent all the evening together.

Jos. It reminds me of the days we spent together five years ago, when we used to steal out together unknown to my uncle, and you took me to see the fireworks at the Crystal Palace.

CATO. I am seeing fireworks now.

DER. What fun we used to have.

CATO. Oh, it has been going on for five years.

Jos. My dear Jack, you were the only being in the world I had to love; and if you knew how I cried my eyes out when you joined your regiment.

DER. Dear old girl! [*He kisses her hand*]

CATO. He kissed her—I heard it!

Jos. But now, I shall see you every day.

DER. Certainly.

Jos. I shall introduce you to my husband.

CATO. Of course!

Jos. You will dine with us every day?

CATO. I must take him in to board!

Jos. You and Cato will get on splendidly. Why can't you come and stop with us altogether? I'm sure Cato wouldn't mind it!

CATO. Oh! Oh! Not mind it!

Jos. There is some one at that door. I heard a noise!

CATO. What are they about? [*Looks through keyhole*]

DER. Surely, that Dutch scoundrel cannot be listening. If he is, I will teach him to attend to his own business. [*He opens the door suddenly. Cato tumbles in. Derringer seizes him*] What were you doing there?

Jos. Oh, Jack, don't, pray don't.

CATO. Let me go!

DER. Not until I throw you out of the window! [*In the struggle Cato's bandage and his nose fall off*]

CATO. Oh, my nose!

Jos. My husband—it can't be you! it is!

DER. Your husband?

Jos. Why, Cato, what brings you here?

CATO. No, madam, that is not the question. I prefer to ask what brings you here! Sir, I am the unfortunate husband of that lady, who has not been the dupe she has imagined. This afternoon I pretended to leave for Nottingham.

Jos. Pretended!

Cato. It was a trap, madam, to detect you as I have done. I have followed you in disguise all day. I have been a witness to your conduct with this gentleman, whom you call your darling Jack. Don't deny it; it is useless.

Jos. I don't deny it. This is my brother, Jack Derringer.

Cato. Your brother! No! no!

Jos. Who returned from India this evening.

Der. And who certainly did not anticipate the pleasure of meeting you in this manner.

Cato. Oh, my angel! Oh, forgive me—if you knew—I thought—your hand, Porringer; forgive me.

Der. Derringer!

Cato. I beg your pardon. I am so confused—I mean so relieved.

Jos. And you really suspected me capable of acting such a part? Oh! Oh!

Cato. No! no! I didn't—that is, I was a jealous fool!

Der. [Lighting a cigar] It is past now. Let us forget and forgive.

Cato. I do—I forgive.

Jos. Oh, Jack, don't smoke here, please; it always makes me ill.

Der. All right, Josey; I'll take a turn in the garden and leave you together.

Cato. Let him smoke. You shall smoke all over my house. I am so grateful to him for being your brother. He shall do whatever he likes!

Der. That's hearty. I'll take up my quarters with you. Sling me a berth in any corner—brother Jack is not particular. [Exit by corridor]

Cato. Josey, Josey, throw your arms around me—take me home! Oh, if you only knew how I have loved you all this blessed—I would say infernal evening. Oh, never let us part again!

Jos. You dearest of foolish fellows! Do you think I regret your jealousy? Why, I am delighted you were miserable, for it shows the depth of your love for me. What! you have been suspecting me? That's delicious! And spying after me? Oh, Cato, you darling, there are so few husbands nowadays that love their wives well enough to be jealous of them!

Cato. Love you? Josey, I adore you! I never look at any other woman! [Cato embraces Josephine. Enter Zulu and Joseph into corridor]

Zulu. Which is Mr. Alfred's room? I am late.

Joseph. Mr. Alfred? [Bell rings] Coming!—the room on your right. [Exit. Zulu as he speaks has her back to audience]

Zulu. On my right. Oh, this is it; No. 9. Here goes; of course Closerie has not come. [Zulu knocks at L.H. door]

Jos. Someone is knocking. Oh, perhaps it is Jack, who has finished his smoke. Why does he knock?

CATO. He means it as a delicate attention. Dear old Jack! [*He opens door, sees Zulu and shuts it*] [*Aside*] Oh, Lord, Zulu!

ZULU. [*Knocking*] Don't shut the door, it's me!

Jos. Who is it? [*Cato keeping door shut and locking it*]

CATO. Nobody! It is an old gentleman who—who—has mistaken the room!

ZULU. [*Knocking*] Are you going to open the door? Come, I say, Alfred, none of your larks.

Jos. There, he is knocking again!

CATO. No; it is next door, I assure you!

ZULU. Will you open the door? Oh, don't be a fool!

Jos. Do see what the man wants.

CATO. Never mind him—he will go away when he's tired. [*Aside*] Oh, dear, what shall I do?

Jos. I will send him about his business. [*Goes to door*]

CATO. I am lost! Where can I retire? Oh, if I could subside into my boots! [*Sees the door in F.*] Ah, the next room! [*Slides back door, disappears as Josephine opens door R. and admits Zulu*]

Jos. A lady!

ZULU. I beg your pardon. Where is Alfred?

Jos. I beg yours, madam; there is no Alfred here.

ZULU. So I see, but he *was* here. We met this morning, and he invited me to sup with him this evening.

Jos. *My* husband invited *you* to sup here! It is false, ma'am, I won't believe it!

ZULU. Your husband! In what acceptation of the word, madam?

Jos. Oh, I can't stand this! [*Cato appears in corridor*]

ZULU. Nor can I. Where is he? I'll teach him to play the fool with me. Oh, here's another room. [*Exit door in F. followed by Josephine, as Cato enters R.H. room and locks door*]

CATO. Just escaped that explosive female! but how shall I explain my disappearance to Josey? I am becoming enmeshed in a web of lies. Caught in my own pretenses. I wish I had Buster here to help me! [*Enter Buster in corridor*]

BUSTER. I left Arabella at home. I said I would go out in our square to smoke a cigar, and here I am!

CATO. I don't hear the raging of the wild animals!

BUSTER. [*Trying door R.H. room*] Locked on the inside! [*Knocks*] Sympathy teaches us discretion.

CATO. There she is!

BUSTER. [*Whispering*] Whist! 'Tis I!

CATO. Oh, yes. I'm going to let you in—in a hurry! [*Re-enter Josephine into L.H. room*]

JOS. Where can Cato be? He was not there. He must have gone out by this door! [*As she opens door she meets Buster*]

BUSTER. Mrs. Dove! here!

JOS. Oh, Sergeant, how glad I am to see you! [*Buster enters L.H. room*] Where's my husband?

BUSTER. He's at Nottingham!

JOS. No, he is here!

BUSTER. Here? It can't be; you are mistaken!

JOS. I tell you I saw him!

BUSTER. It must have been an optical—er—delusion.

CATO. [*Listening inside his door*] I'll take a peep, and if I find the road is clear, I will run for it!

JOS. [*Sitting down and holding her head in helpless confusion*] Am I going mad? [*Re-enter Derringer down corridor*]

DER. Surely that lady talking to the waiter must be my little bombshell friend in the artillery!

CATO. Porringer! I am saved! Come, come in here! [*Drags Derringer into R.H. room and closes door*]

DER. What's the matter?

JOS. I spoke to him, I tell you; he followed me.

BUSTER. Where to—have you been to Nottingham?

JOS. Oh, you are all in a plot to drive me out of my senses!

CATO. I am in a frightful mess. You can save me, if you will. Not for my sake, but for hers—for Josey's. Listen! [*Cato speaks apart to Derringer. Re-enter Zulu with Victor*]

VICTOR. You mistook the room, Miss, this is Mr. Alfred's room.

ZULU. [*Entering R.H. room*] Ah! there you are!

DER. [*To Zulu*] Keep quiet. It is all a mistake. [*To Cato*] I understand it all. Leave it to me. I'll pull you through!

ZULU. I declare, it is my friend in the artillery. [*Enter Arabella, in corridor with Joseph. Derringer, Zulu and Cato speak apart*]

ARAB. So, you say Sergeant Buster has a supper party here, tonight?

JOSEPH. Yes, ma'am; one of the ladies is here—the other—

ARAB. One is enough, sir! [*Exit Joseph*]

BUSTER. My dear soul—don't take on so!

ARAB. That's his voice! He's with her in here!

JOS. Don't leave me!

Buster. I must get back to my wife, or she will suspect something is wrong.

Arab. [*Bursting into L.H. room*] Villain! I have detected you at last! Josephine—Oh! it was Mrs. Dove! This is too much!

Jos. What! do you dare to insinuate, madam, that you entertain any doubts about me?

Arab. None whatever, ma'am! The place, the position in which I find you, leaves no room for any doubt whatever.

Jos. Oh, this is too much! [*Josephine rings the bell furiously*]

Der. Rejoin your wife at once; we will follow you.

Cato. Zulu—Porringer—I shall owe you my life! [*Cato crosses from R. H. room to L.H. room*]

Arab. While your infatuated idiot of a husband is at Nottingham, you replace your fool with my knave. Cato!

Cato. Go on, Mrs. Buster. Take it out of me. I am used to it this evening.

Jos. Cato, you will explain to that lady how I came here.

Cato. [*Dignified*] My wife, madam, came here with her husband—with me!

Jos. She charged me with impropriety.

Cato. If she entertains such charges against any one here, charge them to Buster! [*Enter Derringer with Zulu*]

Der. I am sorry to confess I am to blame for all this. Allow me to explain. On my arrival this afternoon I met this lady, an old friend of mine and I invited her to sup here tonight. Miss—a— [*Aside*] What's your name?

Zulu. Zulu!

Der. Miss Zulu accepted the invitation, and in the excitement of meeting my sister, I totally forgot all about it. Miss Lulu came—

Zulu. Zulu!

Der. Found her place occupied.

Jos. Ah, then you were the Alfred she wanted?

Der. Yes; she always called me Alfred as a—a—short for Jack. We are such old friends. I—

Arab. Stop, stop, this is all very clear so far; but when I arrived here, the waiter downstairs told me that supper had been ordered for two ladies by Sergeant Buster.

Cato. [*Aside*] Now he's in for it—go it—charge it to Buster.

Buster. By *me*—ordered by *me!* Where is the waiter? [*Enter Swallbach*]

Swall. Gomming, sir. Here is der bill!

Arab. [*Taking it*] Twenty-seven pounds six.

Jos. Oh, what can they have had to come to that?

BUSTER. No, no; I appeal. My lords and gentlemen of the—that is—I forget. This is absurd! [*Aside*] Oh! the luxury of being falsely accused! It is a new sensation!

DER. Allow me to explain further. When I ordered supper for this lady and her friend the waiter asked me for my name, and I handed them my card, as I thought. By mistake, I gave them a card I received from a scoundrel of the name of Buster, who stole my cab this afternoon!

BUSTER. Arabella, tell him that was not *me*; say it was some *other* scoundrel. Save your husband's honor!

ARAB. It could not have been you, for I found you waiting for me at the Horse Show. I will do you that justice!

BUSTER. Virtue is triumphant!!!

CATO. Who could it have been?

SWALL. Das ist vera good; but who is to pay the bill?

DER. I'll settle it! [*To Zulu*] I think the supper is ready in the other room. [*Exit Zulu into R.H. room*]

CATO. No, we can't allow you to pay! [*He takes the bill from Swallbach*] Can we, Charley? We demur. Waiter, this is our affair. Buster, we must settle this. [*Exit Swallbach into R.H. room. Buster and Cato follow Swallbach into corridor. Derringer takes the wine and pours out glasses full for the ladies*]

DER. Come, ladies, in the absence of your husbands, let us drink a toast!

CATO. [*Drawing Buster forward*] My dear fellow! one word with you. You tempted me to make what you called a night of it!

BUSTER. You did not know how to make one!

CATO. Possibly! but I'll never attempt to make another! I have tried the taste of forbidden fruit. I don't like it! A fast life looks charming to those who see it as spectators look at a play, but you have introduced me behind the scenes, and I prefer the illusion to the reality!

BUSTER. [*Mournfully*] There is no illusion about Arabella.

DER. Now, ladies, are you ready?

CATO. [*Listening*] Hush!

Jos. Here's to my darling Cato—the best, truest, most devoted of husbands.

BUSTER. Do you hear?

CATO. I do, and I blush!

ARAB. Here's to my dear old Charley, whom I confess I have wronged by my suspicions. [*The ladies drink*]

CATO. And you said there was no illusion about her! Oh, Charley, Charley! if you found your wife out in such infidelity as you indulge in daily. Ah! what would you say?

BUSTER. [*Wiping away a tear*] I'd say—charge it to Buster!! [*They embrace—as the ladies drink the toast*]

CURTAIN

LOUIS XI

LOUIS XI

THAT Louis XI has not previously been printed is a minor mystery
of theatrical publishing, for it has four production dates of importance:
January 13, 1855, the original production at the Princess's Theatre,
London, under the management of Charles Kean; September 7, 1858, the
first production in America at Laura Keene's Theatre, New York, under the
management of that lady herself; March 9, 1878, at the Lyceum Theatre,
London, during the series of Sir Henry Irving's revivals; and October 11,
1879, at Booth's Theatre, New York, when Dion Boucicault essayed the
character of Louis.

John W. Cole, in his biography of Charles Kean, states that this play
"silenced all pertinacious denials of Mr. Kean's hardly won preeminence as
the leading tragedian of the day. Even the most determined opponents at
length yielded up their prejudices to the public verdict. During his long practice of twenty-eight years, he now for the first time stood before his judges in
an original part of first-rate importance." That this is not a prejudiced statement of a Kean enthusiast is substantiated by the reviewer in *The Times*
(January 15, 1855), who reported that "even the most fanatical" of Kean's
detractors, who might "refuse to see any merit in his other performances,
will be compelled to make an exception in favor of Louis XI. We can scarcely
conceive anything more perfect." Of the other members of the cast of this
original production we have, unfortunately, little record; however, it is
known that Ellen Tree (Mrs. Charles Kean) played the part of the Dauphin.
When Kean produced the play on April 27, 1865, at the Broadway Theatre,
New York, he retained the character of Louis, and was supported by J. F.
Cathcart as Nemours, George Jamieson as Coitier, Miss Chapman as the
Dauphin, and Mrs. Kean as Marthe, "a very subordinate rôle, contributing
her name to the entertainment rather than her unrivalled powers."

The originality of Kean's interpretation has been questioned. William
Winter, in his account of Henry Irving as a manager, states that it was mod-
elled, to a considerable extent, on that of Ligier, who originated the part at
the Théatre Français; and John Coleman narrates in his loose but graphic
style a conversation in which he quotes Boucicault as saying, "I was in Paris
at the time of its first production." Charley and Ben Webster used to go night
after night and glare at each other. They were neither of them very pious,

but 'pon my sowl!—soul I mayne—I b'lieve aich prayed every night that the other might be dhrowned on the way home, that the survivor might have the first shy at Louis in London." Whether Kean's creation was totally original or not, the fact remains that the success of this play established a decisive period in his career as an actor.

The performance of *Louis XI* at Laura Keene's Theatre is significant merely for its being the first production in America, preceding Kean's tour of this country by seven years and Irving's performances in New York by twenty-five years. The occasion was the opening of the 1858-1859 season, and the cast included Culdock as Louis, Miss Laura Keene as the Dauphin, Sothern as Nemours, Burnett as Coitier, and Miss Sara Stevens as Marie.

What has been said of the importance of the rôle to Charles Kean is almost equally true of its value to Henry Irving. Clement Scott believed that "the Louis XI of Mr. Henry Irving will be recognized as his most complete and scholarly study," and William Winter remarked that "Mr. Irving's Louis XI is so excellent a work that it surpasses even the great performance of that part which was given by Charles Kean; and to say this is to offer an uncommon tribute." Perhaps there is some significance, too, in the fact that Irving chose to play Louis for his last regular London performance, on June 10, 1905. A complete description of Irving's production appears in Clement Scott's *From The Bells to King Arthur*. The cast of the original Lyceum production included, in addition to Irving, F. Tyars as Nemours (a part afterwards played by William Terriss), Andrews as the Dauphin, J. Fernandez as Coitier, W. Bentley as Tristan, and Miss Virginia Francis as Marie.

The last important production of this play is closely associated with Dion Boucicault himself, and permits us an intimate glimpse into his ambitions as an actor. It is manifest that Boucicault had wanted to play the part of Louis for years before he finally appeared in the part in New York in 1879. In the conversation previously quoted from George Coleman, Boucicault is said to have remarked, "Oh yes, Kayne—I mayne Kean—is right enough, but wait till you see *me*!" It was unfortunate that anyone was given the opportunity. The *New York Times* for Sunday, October 12, 1879, reports the occasion in part as follows: "Mr. Boucicault's acting was weak and incomplete. He portrayed the abjectness of the King's character with undoubted ability, with much of that peculiar talent which he has so often and so successfully employed in his impersonations of Irish vagrants, but its malignancy, its terrible bloodthirstiness, its thrilling contrasts of bantering cupidity and sudden fury —these were hardly suggested. In fact, his performance was all in one key, and that a minor key . . . and can only be regarded at best as a misapplied effort."

Townsend Walsh in *The Career of Dion Boucicault* relates an anecdote about this same performance, as told by George Clarke, a member of the company who was in the audience on that fatal night. He says: "It was weird without words. At first the audience sat in dumb amazement; then came titters and giggles, and finally roars. Never did monarch receive less grave and reverent treatment. Boucicault's brogue came out thick and strong. If he had been impersonating Brian Boru instead of Louis XI, he would have been funny enough, but a French king with a Dublin brogue was too excruciating an anachronism for the audience. To make matters worse, three of the principal parts were also played by Irishmen—John Brougham, Dominick Murray and W. B. ('Billy') Cahill. They all spoke Casimir Delavigne's blank verse 'wid that lovely accint' that one hears on the banks of the Liffey, but never by any chance in Plessis-les-Tours. As the tragedy—or, more properly speaking, the tragic farce—progressed, John Brougham, who loved a good joke better than anything else in the world, began to exaggerate the unctuousness of his own fine, natural brogue. Next John Clayton, an Englishman and the son-in-law of Boucicault, who was playing Nemours, felt in duty bound to fall in line with the others, and he too assumed a broad brogue. The rest of the company, either out of deviltry or catching the infection, became Gaelic instead of Gallic, and before the play was half over the French tragedy had degenerated into an orgy of Hibernian dialects." And so ends the story of Conn, the Shaughraun as Louis XI, King of France.

In addition to the cast mentioned, Dion Boucicault, Jr., made his professional début as the Dauphin, and Miss Coghlan appeared as Marie.

The source of the play is Casimir Delavigne's work of the same title; Boucicault's adaptation follows the original accurately, differing only in the concluding scene. But, as Clement Scott says, "He has turned its course occasionally toward the lighter paths of drama, has given it scientific opportunities and chances for theatrical effect."

The manuscripts which form the basis for this edition were secured from the Lord Chamberlain's Office in London, and from Mr. Julius Tolson of Harrisburg, Pa.

F. T. C.

CAST OF CHARACTERS

Louis XI, *King of France*

Duke de Nemours

The Dauphin

Tristan L'Ermite, *Grand Provost and Executioner*

Philip de Commine, *the Historian*

Jacques Coitier, *the King's Physician*

Oliver, *the Barber Minister*

François de Paule

Cardinal d'Alby

Monseigneur de Lude

Cranford, *Officer of the Scottish Guard*

Marcel
Richard ⎱ *Peasants*
Didier

Count de Dreux

Montjoie, *Herald of France*

Toison d'Or, *Herald of Burgundy*

Marie, *Daughter of Philip de Commine*

Marthe, *A Peasant*

French and Burgundian Lords, Guards, Priests, Pages, Courtiers, Citizens, Peasants, Etc.

SYNOPSIS OF SCENES

ACT I. EXTERIOR OF THE CASTLE, PLESSIS-LES-TOURS.

ACT II. THRONE ROOM IN THE CASTLE.

ACT III. AN OPEN SPOT IN THE WOOD NEAR THE CASTLE.

ACT IV. THE KING'S BEDCHAMBER.

ACT V. THRONE ROOM IN THE CASTLE.

ACT I.

Exterior of the castle, Plessis-les-Tours. Tristan enters with the prevotal guard. Richard enters from hut.

Trist. Thy name?

Rich. Richard, the swineherd.

Trist. Thy dwelling?

Rich. There.

Trist. The King forbids all egress at this hour.

Rich. Death is beneath my roof. I seek a priest
       To thrive a fleeting soul.

Trist.   Back to thy kennel!
        Or else thy carrion swings on yonder oak
        To mark the wakeful justice of the King.

Rich. My son—

Trist. Obey!

Rich. —is dying.

Trist. Darest thou prate to Tristan?

Rich. Tristan! Heaven preserve the King! [*Exit. Enter Cranford with Scottish Guard*]

Officer. Halt! Who goes there?

Trist. The Grand Provost.

Officer. The countersign!

Trist. Faithful!

Officer. France! [*Exeunt. Enter Philip de Commine*]

Com. The day shows faint and sickly in the east.
      Welcome, my only hour of calm repose,
      Robb'd from the body's rest to rest the mind.
      Hark, 'tis the watch-cry of the Scottish soldier
      Hired to defend yon Tours, and guard the life
      Of Louis, King of France. Château de Plessis—
      Tomb of a living King! Thy watch and ward,
      Thy lofty ramparts and thy deepest fosse
      Will never scare th' assassin who now seeks
      The life of Louis. Yet a few poor days
      He may dispute with death, and then—[*Enter Coitier and Richard*]

COIT.   Fear not;
        He sleeps. The danger now is past; he yet
        May live. [*Exit Richard*]

COM.   Coitier!

COIT.   Commine!

COM.   Dare you thus
        Neglect your duty to the King?

COIT.   The King—the King—
        Always the King!

COM.   His life from day to day hangs on your skill.

COIT.   My skill were well bestowed elsewhere.

COM.   Somewhat has angered you.

COIT.   Smother wanton crime. This swineherd's son
        Was wounded nigh to death last night. Forsooth
        He dared to linger near the castle walls
        Gaping in wonder at the gloomy pile.
        A Scottish archer from the battlement
        Transfixed him with an arrow.

COM.   Louis of this is innocent.

COIT.   The King who tolerates a crime commits it.

COM.   Thou art the only man who dares thus chafe him—
        But haste thee in—already he has waked
        And calls for Coitier.

COIT.   Let him call and bawl,
        And when he's tired he'll wait, 'tis well he should,
        Patience is a medicine he must gulp,
        'Twill soothe his choler. Thus I can repay
        The sufferings he heaps on me. He hates me,
        Taunts me with lack of skill, and mocks my art—
        That's when he's well—but when from fever'd sleep
        By some avenging spectre he is chased,
        To me he cries for help. Coitier must wake;
        To Coitier is exposed his ulcered soul,
        Creeping with terrors and alive with crime.
        'Tis then my turn to taunt, to jeer and mock!
        We change our parts; the tyrant I become,
        And he, the abject slave.

COM.   Thou art too hard
        Upon a dying man.

Coit.   'Tis true he dies.
      But like a snake with all the venom quick
      And ready in his tooth, to the last pulse
      There's a murder in him.
Com.   Why, then, toil
      With all thy art to keep such crime alive?
Coit.   My mission is to heal, and not to judge.
Com.   Does not his abject fear of death move you
      To pity?
Coit.   Dost thou ask me
      For pity for the murderer of Nemours?
Com.   Nemours was guilty—
Coit.   'Tis false! His only guilt
      Was his offensive goodness. Louis could bear
      No virtue save in a priest. Beneath his roof
      I passed my youth where I was born a serf.
      Nemours first lifted my intelligence,
      And bade me think. Sustained by him with hope
      I struggled on, and by his help became
      The wonder of the time. Nemours built up
      My fortune—yet when his own ebb'd fast,
      When he and his three children lay immured
      In the Bastille, Louis denied my prayer.
      Nemours, my master, benefactor, friend,
      Fell by the tyrant's axe. One child alone
      Was saved; aided by thee he was conveyed
      And hid away.
Com.   Coitier—
Coit.   I say by thee.
Com.   In Heaven's name speak lower!
Coit.   Then why say Nemours was guilty?
Com.   Be more just to me.
      I loved Nemours; and when he fell, did I
      Mourn idly? No! I sounded anxiously
      The King's intent, and found his thirst for blood
      Unslaked. The children of Nemours still lived;
      I roused them from their grief and bade them fly.
      The eldest only would be warned in time,
      And sought the shelter I had found
      For him with Charles of Burgundy.

COIT.   A welcome guest.
     If Charles the Bold should need an instrument
     Of cold, determined steel, there is the weapon,
     Steeped in the hideous poison of revenge,
     And hungry for the heart of Louis.

COM.   Such
     Was the Duke's design, but foiled ere ripe.
     My daughter Marie, then a child, was lodged
     Beneath the roof where I had placed Nemours;
     She was the sole companion of his exile.
     They grew to love; their union is agreed
     When Heaven shall bring back brighter days to France.

COIT.   You mean, when he is gone.

COM.   Who?

COIT.   He!

COM.   Beware!
     I hear footsteps.

COIT.   'Tis Marie

COM.   My child!
     No more, she might betray us.

COIT.   How! Dost fear her?

COM.   Not so—but hush, she comes.

COIT.   By Heaven, he has suspicions
     Of his own child. [*Enter Marie*]

MARIE.   Ah! my father—good morning, sir.
     How fares the King?

COIT.   He is in his hour
     Of excellence—his only gentle mood.
     He sleeps. But whence that glow upon your cheek?

MARIE.   The King last night bade me and Bertha rise
     Before the dawn and ride across the wood
     To watch the coming of the holy man,
     François de Paule, and quick to bring the news
     When from the distant spires the pealing chimes
     Rang out a joyful welcome—and each town,
     Village, castle and hut poured forth its life
     To greet the hermit.

COIT.   You have seen him, then,
     This anchorite, this miracle performer?
     Who by his intercession is to heal

The ills of mind and body, and restore
The King to youth and health?
MARIE. Dare you to doubt
His power? Have you not heard his wond'rous deeds?
COIT. Oh, yes,
I have heard.
MARIE. Yet what simplicity!
No sacerdotal pomp—no purple robe
To command the homage of the eye; no crook
Of gold he wields; no jewelled mitre gleams
Upon his head; but neatly clad, not rudely;
Modest, not vainly humble.
A simple staff supports his aged limbs,
And as he sheds his blessings on the crowd,
His silvered brow is luminous with love
And seems to radiate benevolence.
COM. Yesternoon the Dauphin left Plessis
To seek this hermit.
MARIE. They met François de Paule beyond Amboise;
The Dauphin straight dismounted, and his train
Walked by his side. The nobles laid apart
Their weapons, and, bareheaded, prayed his blessing.
Then high the people waved their fresh-hewn boughs
And chanted hymns of praise. The peasant girls
Strewed all the path with forest flowers; and thus
To Plessis comes François de Paule.
COM. Thou shalt awake the King with this good news.
MARIE. A word, my father.
COM. Go, Coitier, do thou
Announce these happy tidings to the King.
COIT. Good news from Coitier? He will ne'er believe it. [*Exit*]
COM. He is gone.
Now tell me, Child, what happy secret
O'erflows your eyes and flutters on your cheek.
MARIE. Can you not guess?
COM. News from Peronne!
MARIE. The village
Of Plessis is thronged with knights who bear
The badge of Burgundy.

Com. It is the envoy of the Duke. He comes
　　Full-mouth'd with war. Louis has given aid
　　And succor to the revolted Swiss. Even now
　　A deputation from the Cantons here within
　　Craves audience. On the Burgundian border, too,
　　Brancas and Chabannes have by surprise
　　Seized on the frontier citadels. For this
　　Charles will demand most ample satisfaction.
　　Didst learn this envoy's name?

Marie. The Count de Rethel.

Com. Rethel! I know there was an ancient house
　　Long since extinct who bore that name, Rethel.
　　Amongst the nobles of Peronne heard you
　　Of such a one?

Marie. Rethel? No!

Com. Strange!

Marie. I hoped
　　This envoy might be bearer of some news
　　From him.

Com. Nemours?

Marie. Nemours! Who knows; ere now
　　He may have quite forgot Marie.

Com. Nemours forget!

Marie. In childhood it was I who sought Nemours,
　　A cold, abstracted, silent youth, who fled
　　The commerce of the court, its plays, its jousts;
　　But did I speak
　　Of Louis, his hand would grip his dagger hard;
　　He gazed upon me, yet he knew me not.
　　I chased away the drops of agony
　　That beaded o'er his brow, but he felt not
　　The tears I left there.

Com. Hush! Another year
　　Will give another king to France.
　　Nemours may then return.

Marie. Oh, were the gentle Dauphin on the throne
　　He would not let me sue in vain. Nemours
　　Would be recalled.

Com. Marie, I have observed
　　The Dauphin courts thy company.

MARIE. He does,
     Poor youth.
COM. That youth one day will be a king.
MARIE. Must I for that avoid him when he comes
     To seek me; implores my aid to read
     The chronicles of France?
COM. Enough! Enough!
     He is too old to learn from lips like thine,
     And thou too young to teach a guileless task!
     He loves thee.
MARIE. Father!
COM. Avoid his company!
     Hark, they approach.
     Come, let's in. [*Exit. Enter Peasants, François de Paule, Dauphin,*
Duke de Nemours, Nobles, Toison d'Or]
FRAN. Forbear, sweet Prince, and leave me here awhile
     To rest from weary state.
DAUPHIN. Father, permit
       That I precede thee to the King, who craves
       Thy blessing. He will come forth, and to the dust
       Abase himself before thy saintly presence.
       My lords, attend me! [*Exit*]
FEMALE. Father, pity my child; he's sick to death,
     And 'tis my only one.
MARC. Reason has fled
     My mother's brain; restore it ere she die
     That she may bless me.
RICH. Enter my hut;
     Look on my dying son, and he will live.
FRAN. Arise, my children, from your knees. 'Tis thus
     Heaven only should be sought. Why look on me?
     I am a man most feeble and infirm,
     Bow'd down with age. Judge then, had I the powers
     You claim of me, should I be thus?
RICH. Had I been noble,
     He had healed my son.
MARC. But what are we?—Are we
     Deserving of a miracle?

NEM. We are alone, my son—
    Alone with Heaven—
    For Heaven is with thee, my father.
FRAN.   As with all
    Who put their trust therein.
NEM. Beseech its mercy
    For one whose hours are numbered.
FRAN.   Not for thine—
    No, thou art young; thy cup of life is full.
NEM. Ay, full of blood, held by my father's spectre
    To my lips, and as I quaff, 'tis filled and filled
    From my murdered brother's gaping wounds.
FRAN.   What would'st thou do?
NEM. What is thy mission here?
FRAN.   To comfort and console.
    What thine?
NEM. To bear the vials of Heaven's wrath. Hard on the priest
    Cometh the headsman.
FRAN.   These words are wild, my son.
    What ill design do they import? Reflect—
    Pause!
NEM. Bless me, my father.
FRAN.   Willingly, my son. Thou hast my blessing.
    But what shall it avail thee if thy heart
    Meditates evil? If thy thoughts are pure,
    Mercy will better plead for thee above
    Than my poor words. Yet I do bless thee.
    Fare thee well! May Heaven be thy guide. [*Exit*]

ACT II.

The Throne Room in the castle. Marie discovered. Enter the Dauphin.

DAUPHIN. Marie!
MARIE. Your highness! [*Rises*] Pardon; I saw you not.
DAUPHIN. And now you see me, does the sight repel
    And drive you from me?
MARIE. Ah, your highness,
    My service is commanded by the King.
DAUPHIN. Stay!

MARIE. 'Tis late. Indeed I must—

DAUPHIN. Remain,
Marie, I pray you. I—command.

MARIE. Your highness,
I obey.

DAUPHIN. No, no, forgive me, Marie,
You have my leave to go—yet do not go.
Do as thou wilt—ay, leave me.

MARIE. In disgrace?

DAUPHIN. There is a saying, "Happy as a king."
There might be one, "As wretched as a prince."

MARIE. You wretched!

DAUPHIN. Ay. My father hates me.

MARIE. Hush!

DAUPHIN. Far from his thought or care, my childhood passed
Within the gloomy walls of Amboise. There
I grew as the wild flowers grew—unheeded,
My only lesson was to fear the King,
And tremble at his name.

MARIE. All his love and care
Lie in his kingdom.

DAUPHIN. Oh, that my kingdom were
Some little, unregarded isle, and thou
My only subject.

MARIE. 'Tis time I should begone.

DAUPHIN. Stay! Goes the King forth today?

MARIE. He does.

DAUPHIN. To hunt? Well, I will ride beside thee.

MARIE. No.

DAUPHIN. What then?

MARIE. A pilgrimage.

DAUPHIN. A pilgrimage? What for?

MARIE. My lord—

DAUPHIN. I mean, to whom? Whither?

MARIE. The King
Today will seek the village shrine hard by,
The Chapel of St. Martin in the Woods, and there
Will pass the vesper hour in prayer.

DAUPHIN. I wish
    Thou wert a saint, then I would be devout.
    My father wears his saints about his cap,
    But I would wear thee in my heart.

MARIE. I must
    Begone.

DAUPHIN. Stay yet—come hither—see what I have here.

MARIE. A book!

DAUPHIN. And full of pictures. Look!
    Knights, combats, and great feats of arms!

MARIE. I tremble did the King suspect. How came
    You by it?

DAUPHIN. I stole it from my uncle, Orleans.
    Come, let us read it.

MARIE. No!

DAUPHIN. Why not?

MARIE. I fear.
    You know the King forbids that you shall read
    From any book but that which he himself
    Has writ for your instruction.

DAUPHIN. Yes, I know,
    But his book is so stupid.

MARIE. Hush! A king
    Is never stupid. What is your book about?

DAUPHIN. That you shall teach me. Come, sit here, and so
    Now if I mistake, correct me.
    [*Reads*] "The Chronicles of France, written in the year
    Of Grace—" There come figures. I will
    Skip the figures.

MARIE. For certain reasons.

DAUPHIN. "Wherein there is recited all the feats of
    Arms of those most noble knights, Dunois, Lahire,
    And—and—
    Lahire, and—and—Du—du—Du—guess—"

MARIE. Dugueschin!

DAUPHIN. Oh, what a hard word.

MARIE. Ay, but a great name.

DAUPHIN. "And how the Realm of France,
    Being oppressed, was saved by

The great prowess of a shepherd girl named
Joan of Arc."

MARIE. The Maid of Orleans!

DAUPHIN. I know of her,
And of another whom the late King loved,
Agnes Sorrel. I have often thought
That thou, Marie, shouldst resemble her.

MARIE. The mistress of a king.

DAUPHIN. She might have been
His Queen.

MARIE. I am too lowly born for that;
Too nobly, to be the toy of any man.

DAUPHIN. Then, when I am King
I can, alas, in nothing shew my love
For thee. Yet, take this ring.

MARIE. My lord—

DAUPHIN. Take it,
And come the day I may a service grant,
Claim it by token of this ring; and here
I pledge my knightly faith and royal word,
What title, lands, or grace soe'er.

MARIE. Even should I pray you to recall
An exile, and to grant him pardon?

DAUPHIN. Him!
Whom?

MARIE. One who pines, afar from home and kin.

DAUPHIN. Ha! You love him.

MARIE. Ay.

DAUPHIN. You love him. Marie!
Give me back the ring.

MARIE. 'Tis here, my lord.

DAUPHIN. No, retain it, it is thine. I did but jest.
You love this exile—it is well. You hold
His pardon, come what may. The Dauphin's word
Shall by the King be faithfully redeemed. [*Exit*]

MARIE. The pardon of Nemours. [*Enter Commine*]

COM. How now, Marie,
That name upon your lips.

MARIE. You bade me check
The Dauphin's suit.

Com.   What have you done?

Marie.   I have confessed my love and cast myself
   Upon a prince's generosity.

Com.   Imprudent girl! The rashness of your heart
   Will prove your lover's ruin.

Marie.   Father, list.
   Go sit beside the King, and deal out law
   To cure those ills that ail the commonweal,
   For thou'rt a very crafty councillor.
   But if thou wouldst preserve that high repute,
   Leave love alone! Or should the question start,
   Seek counsel of a fool and shut your eyes.

Com.   Away, and take thy folly with thee. Go! [*Exit Marie*]
   The Count of Rethel scarce arrived, demands
   An instant audience. I am bid to sound
   This proud Burgundian ere the council meet.
   He must be bought—but how? That rests with me
   What coin to offer—titles, gold, or laurels. [*Enter Officer*]

Officer.   The Count de Rethel. [*Enter Nemours*]

Com.   Nemours! Thou here, Nemours?

Nem.   Here then he lives; here in this naked tomb.

Com.   Hast thou forecast thy peril? Knowest
   Thou the very echoes here are spies; the stones
   Are traitors?

Nem.   Fitting palace for a king!
   As I approached the walls, I saw the track
   Of Tristan's gory footsteps. The very river
   Blushed for its human burthen; each tree bent,
   Shame bowed, with its unnatural quiet. The air
   Is clogged with death.

Com.   And yet you came.

Nem.   Confiding in your faith, your love.
   The secret of my name is known to you, Marie,
   And Coitier. Which of ye will betray me?

Com.   None, none!

Nem.   Think you the King will recognize in me
   The child, who only once stood in his presence,
   When I and my two brothers were thrust forth
   Beneath the scaffold where our father fell?

Com. Why seek him now whose hand
  Has crushed thy race?
  The Duke did ill to send thee here, Nemours;
  Another would have served his end as well.

Nem. Louis had bribed another; but in me,
  Charles in his wrongs, in hate, in person—all
  Is represented. Like me, alone survivor
  Of his house—like me too, by a murder left
  An orphan without home or kin.

Com. Nemours, who knows thy wrongs so well as I.
  But is there no soft word that can disarm
  Thy wrath? Marie—

Nem. Marie!

Com. Listen, my son,
  France is thy home, thy country; for her sake
  Forget thy wrongs. Louis and Charles are foes,
  But thou canst make them friends, and thus at once
  Canst salve the country's wounds, and heal thine own.
  Thy titles, lands and home will be restored;
  The King will pardon and forget.

Nem. Forget!
  He will forget! What do I hear? Forget
  That night of crime—the victim of the block—
  Three children made to kneel beneath the scaffold,
  Clothed all in white as if beneath a shrine,
  Assisting at a joyous ceremony. Sudden,
  The sound of footsteps came, and then a voice.
  'Twas his, my father's; he was murmuring
  A prayer he taught me. Then he spoke my name,
  And those of my two brothers. "My poor children!
  Heaven shield my helpless children." Then he prayed
  Again; and then, silence—no more. No more!
  Stretching my arms towards him in the gloom,
  As I would kiss him for his prayer, I felt
  What seemed to be his tears, that drop by drop
  Fell on my face. His tears! No, no! Those eyes
  Could shed no more. They were no tears that fell.

Com. Nemours!

Nem. 'Twas blood! 'Twas blood! My father's blood!
  Forget! He may, that king who watched the deed,

And saw the stream, which still flows here, let out
My father's life. He may forget; I never!

COM. Nemours, be calm; they come.

NEM. Oh, fear me not. In presence of my foe thou'lt see
Who best can play the master. [*Exit*]

COM. Perdition seize the Duke. Why hath he sent
This frenzied youth to raise the foul fiend here?
How finely has my mission been achieved!
When Louis asks me what report I bring,
What shall I say? [*Enter an Officer*]

OFFICER. His majesty the King! [*Enter Louis, Oliver, Coitier, Tristan,
Count de Dreux, Courtiers and Citizens*]

LOUIS. Look to't, Sir Count, look to't. Let me but hear
A murmur from people, and my hand
Is on ye. My doubts confirmed, I send you straight
To Heaven for mercy. Therefore make you up
Betimes, the budget of your soul, d'ye hear?
As for your body, that I'll see to.

COUNT. Sire, might I—

LOUIS. Ay, ay! My people you'll depress,
Exacting more from them than I, their King.
My people and myself are one; the least of them
Is part of me; touch 'em, and you raise your hand
Against my royal person. This you have done.

COUNT. Dread sire—

LOUIS. You have! I beg you beg from these,
My friends, good honest citizens of Tours,
Five hundred crowns for me—raised two thousand;
Robbing them and me—me most especially.
Why, look on me; upon this king you count at nought.
Am I dead? Ha! Or quick? Look, man, look up!
I'm not so near the grave as some may think.
You're paler, Count, than I. Why, by my faith,
You die first now. Have you an heir?

COUNT. [*To Coitier*] Save me—interpose—in mercy!

COIT. Ho, sire, come! Enough of this. You must not yield to anger;
'Tis hurtful.

LOUIS. True! But I am well today;
I may indulge. The sight of that good Saint
François de Paule has quite refreshed my life.

Coit. Dismiss me then, and trust to him. But still
       This useless rage and vengeful eye, methinks,
       As little do become the Christian sire
       As the invalid.
Louis. Coitier!
Coit. Oh, do not waste
       Big words on me. You're wrong.
Louis. Coitier!
Coit. Yes, wrong, and I am right.
       See now, why look
       The mischief's done; your
       Face is changed already.
Louis. Eh, what! Is't changed, indeed?
Coit. Ay, is't.
Louis. Well, then, I'll be more calm.
Coit. Oh, not on my account, go on. Suffer
       And die. 'Tis your affair.
Louis. There, there, now, Coitier.
Coit. You're the King.
Louis. Come, come.
Coit. Why, do then as you list,
       But afterwards, don't come to me complaining.
Louis. There, good Coitier, there, forgive me. So,
       Look now, Sir Count, hark ye! What you have ta'en
       From these good folk restore within three days,
       For that's the price I put upon your head.
       Which, if it suit you, well. If not, I'll take it;
       But without anger—to which I am forbade
       As being hurtful.
Count. Sire, I submit.
Louis. You hear?
       How say ye, am I my people's champion? Ha!
       Oliver, thou'lt see these fifteen hundred crowns
       Repaid. 'Twas he denounced yon traitor from the start.
       You'll freely give my faithful Oliver
       Five hundred crowns—that is, if he accept.
Oliver. Sire!
Louis. He refuses.
Oliver. No; I say your word is law.

Louis. A thousand crowns remain. But there's
    My faithful Coitier.

Coit. No! I'll none of it.

Louis. He will. Press him. So, that's settled.
    Now let's on to State affairs.
    Speak, Oliver.

Oliver. My liege, the deputation of the Swiss await.

Louis. Let 'em begone!

Oliver. Unheard?

Com. Your majesty
    Has recognized their rights, their liberties.

Louis. Their liberties! I hate the word, freedom. What next
    Will they demand, these chamois hunters? Ha!
    What is their country worth?

Com. The Duke of Burgundy
    Can tell. They make good head against his grace.

Louis. Let them begone. The Count de Rethel else
    Would charge us with their entertainment. No!
    You bear me witness, all, I bid them go
    Unheard. [*Aside to Oliver*] Treat with them.

Oliver. How?

Louis. You know—you know!
    Give the least they'll take, and promise all
    They ask.

Oliver. Enough!

Louis. [*Aloud*] Shall I take part with them
    Against my cousin, Burgundy? Foster rebellion?
    No! Let them have hospitality, no more,
    And their good speed.
    [*To Oliver*] Ply 'em with wine, d'ye hear?
    The Swiss drink hard;
    You'll catch them in their cups.

Oliver. Ne'er fear me, sire.

Louis. How now, my good Commine!
    Say, have you seen that envoy, ha?

Com. Ay, sire.

Louis. Well—well—eh?

Com. I find him incorruptible.

Louis. Bah!

Com. My liege—

Louis. I tell you, no.

Com. He's honest.

Louis. Then you confess
    That you have bid too little. I must see to't.
    Go—bring him here. We will receive him now.

Com. If I may venture to advise your majesty,
    Avoid this audience.

Louis. Tut, man, go do my bidding. [*Exit Commine. Enter Marie*]
    Come hither, truant, let me sun myself
    Beneath thy smiles.
    How fares our saintly guest?

Marie. I scarce have left him, sire.

Louis. The odor of his sanctity still clings to thee.
    Tell me, what miracle has he performed already?

Marie. Not one, sire.

Louis. No! He garners up his power
    To let the fullness of it fall on me.
    But hark! the Dauphin greets the envoy of the Duke.
    They come. Leave us, sweet gossip, leave us.

Marie. My liege, I would entreat your leave to stay.

Louis. Know you this Count de Rethel?

Marie. No.

Louis. Indeed! You must
    Have seen him at the court of Burgundy?
    Look where he comes.

Marie. Ah!

Louis. Ha! How now?

Marie. 'Tis he.
    I leave you, sire. [*Aside*] It is Nemours!

Louis. What's this?
    She's troubled. Ha! I'll fathom this. Begone! [*Exit Marie. King ascends the throne*]

Mont. The envoy of
    The most high and mighty Prince Charles, Duke of Burgundy and Flanders,
    Heralded by Toison d'Or, humbly entreats your majesty
    To grant him audience.

Louis. Admit the Count. Tristan, be on your guard.
    Close round me, gentlemen. [*Enter the Dauphin and Commine. Flourish*]

Louis. Largesse to Toison d'Or. How now, Sir Count,
　　　　Our presence troubles you; you tremble and look pale.
Nem. If so, it is with anger, sire. The wrongs
　　　　That bear me here are ocean wide, and though
　　　　I fain would curb them, still you see they burst
　　　　And foam upon my face.
Louis. Out with them, then.
　　　　Let us hear them.
Nem. Right speedily you shall.
　　　　Know then, that my most puissant lord, Duke Charles
　　　　Of Burgundy, first peer of France and sovereign prince—
Louis. Enough, I know the states and vassals of my crown.
　　　　Pass to the facts.
Nem. To you, then, King of France,
　　　　His brother and ally, he sends me in his name
　　　　To charge thee with foul breach of faith and treaty.
Louis. Ha!
Nem. You have consorted with his foes, the Swiss,
　　　　Sending them secret aid; and even now
　　　　You entertain their chiefs within these walls.
Louis. I have not seen 'em; bear me witness, all.
　　　　They are dismissed unheard. Now, sir, what more?
Nem. This much! Lords of Brancas and Chabannes
　　　　Have crossed our frontiers, and by treachery
　　　　Surprised and seized upon our citadels.
Louis. If this be so, these lords must bear the blame;
　　　　'Twas done against my will.
Nem. Give me a proof.
Louis. Agreed!
Nem. Ay, sire, but prompt, and on the spot.
Louis. Well—well?
Nem. Their punishment!
Louis. Sir Count, you ask too much.
　　　　Would this be fair? Should I condemn these lords
　　　　Unheard?
Nem. Oh, sire, your ever-ready axe
　　　　Ere now has fall'n for less than this
　　　　On nobler heads than theirs.
Louis. Ay? Whose head?

NEM. Heaven knows,
    And when your hour of judgment comes,
    He who condemns will shew it ye.
LOUIS. Your head is in my power.
NEM. Why, take it, then, but first
    Attend, for you shall hear my message out.
LOUIS. Ha! Charles the Bold is represented well.
    He never merited that name till now!
    How say ye, gentlemen?
    Pursue, Sir Count, pursue.
NEM. Hear me then, Louis of Valois, and you,
    Most noble knights and lords of high estate.
    Duke Charles, whose wrongs this paper doth set forth,
    Demands and will have justice; or by me declares
    The Lion Banner of great Burgundy, unloosed
    For every duchy, barony and fief
    He holds in vassalage from thee; he now
    Casts off his fealty—Avenger of the past!
    He doth invoke in aid that ghostly train
    Of murdered peers whose blood anoints his cause.
    Their champion, Charles the Bold of Burgundy,
    As knight thine equal, and as prince thy foe,
    In single combat will this quarrel try
    With thee or thine. In proof, there lies his gage.
    Lift it who dare.
DAUPHIN. That do I
    For Valois and for France.
ALL. I—I—sire!
LOUIS. Ha!
    Well done, brave sirs, and he my son, the first
    Amongst them all—so young—so brave. 'Tis well
    He is a child of France.
DAUPHIN. My father—
LOUIS. So—so—enough!
    Here, Toison d'Or, take back
    This glove. [*To Nemours*]
    And thou, to whom in mercy
    I restore it, thank my clemency
    Which doth exceed thy madness.
    But I esteem thy boldness as fidelity.

We will confer in council on this matter,
And, as Heaven guide us, we'll do right and justice.
Today, after our pious pilgrimage,
And in the presence of our saintly guest, François de Paule,
This treaty shall be canonized.
Till then I must resign my heart to prayer,
And in my own misdeeds ease thought off thine. [*Exit Nemours
with escort*]

Louis. Commine! Tristan!

Com. You would not be advised.

Louis. I like these angry folk, one sees them all
    At once. This treaty must be signed.

Com. How, sire!

Louis. That seems a grave mistake, eh, gossip, eh?

Com. Most grave, sire.

Louis. When with pen and ink you make
    An error, have I not seen you scratch it out?

Com. Ay, sire.

Louis. Ay, with a knife—go to, then, gossip—
    If I make a blot, I'll use the knife,
    But not till then. Marked you the Dauphin?

Com. Ay, I did, my liege.

Louis. His royal blood o'erflowed.

Com. What princely valor!

Louis. Ay, he might prove dangerous
    If he rebelled.

Com. Oh, sire!

Louis. Ay, ay, I know. I know
    How much a royal son can do against a king. I was
    A dauphin once.
    Tell me—ha! This Count de Rethel knows Marie?

Com. My daughter, sire?

Louis. Reply!

Com. I know not, sire.
    When she resided at the Court of Charles,
    Amongst the noble youths who sought her, she—

Louis. Distinguished him.
    Speak man!

Com. Sire, I did hear,
    To Marie's beauty—

Louis. Ay, ay, ay!

Com. He was not insensible.

Louis. He loves. You know it, and you said
        That he was incorruptible. Go, go, my good Commine,
        Go! I'll know the truth from her. [*Exit Commine*]
        Tristan!

Trist. Ay.

Louis. Come hither.

Trist. I am here.

Louis. Nearer.

Trist. So.

Louis. Nearer.

Trist. Speak low; I'll listen with my eyes.

Louis. Well, gossip, ha! You heard this haughty vassal?

Trist. Ay.

Louis. I pardoned him.

Trist. You said so—umph!

Louis. And I did right.

Trist. The King can do no wrong.

Louis. I sign this treaty, yet if Heaven decree
        Some dire reverse to Charles—perhaps defeat—

Trist. And Heaven send it soon, that same decree.

Louis. That's an unchristian wish—a wicked wish.

Trist. It is an honest one.

Louis. Still, if mishap
        Befall the Duke, were it so well, d'ye think
        This treaty should arrive in Burgundy?

Trist. The Count is in your power.

Louis. How! Violate
        His sacred office? No, let us respect
        The laws of nations.

Trist. Oh!

Louis. I can allow
        Nothing to happen—here.

Trist. How then regain
        The treaty if you let him go?

Louis. Can't I
        Provide him with a trusty escort?

Trist. Ay, you must.
        To do him honor, protect him to the frontier.

Louis. Ay, gossip, as you say,
    To do him honor.

Trist. Who will command the troop?

Louis. I thought of thee, eh?

Trist. Oh—of me! And how
    Shall I compose it?

Louis. As thou wilt.

Trist. I see. Fellows I can trust.

Louis. Ay! So!

Trist. And numerous.

Louis. Double his band—to do him honor.

Trist. Good! It shall be done.

Louis. And then, d'ye hear, who knows
    When in some lonely wood—
    Ha! What's that? The Angelus? [*Bell rings*]

Trist. Ay, sire.

Louis. Who knows, when in some lonely wood,
    A cause of quarrel may arise?

Trist. It shall.

Louis. Your people, by his guards insulted.

Trist. Ay. I'll see it done.

Louis. You will defend yourselves.

Trist. We will.

Louis. And so, you may regain the treaty.

Trist. Ay, but then, the Count—

Louis. The Count? How dull you are.

Trist. Heh! Must I—

Louis Ah! you smile, old friend.
    You understand me, then.

Trist. I comprehend.

ACT III.

An open spot in the wood near the castle, Plessis-les-Tours. A village fête.
Music. Marcel, Didier, Richard and Villagers, Male and Female. Dancing
groups about the stage.

Marthe. [*C.*] Who knows how the King fares today?

Marcel. [*L.*] No worse—no better.

Marthe. A King, it seems, is very long a-dying.

MARCEL. The place is such a good one.

MARTHE. Who can tell why Master Tristan bade us here? The chapel is
         Prepared; the altar decked with flowers, and we have orders
         To assemble here to sing and dance.

DIDIER. And be most joyful.

MARCEL. Ay, on pain of death.

RICH. Beware! I hear a footstep.

DIDIER. 'Tis Master Oliver.

MARCEL. The Barber Minister. Quick, to your places! Strike music! [*They
dance and sing. Enter Oliver*]

OLIVER. Good—this is well! Sing—dance—be happy!

MARCEL. You see, my lord, we can't be happier.
         When once the Grand Provost said, "Be joyful," we know there's
         No excuse.

OLIVER. Well done. Proceed! Perhaps the King
         May venture out amongst ye.

DIDIER. The King!

RICH. Here?

MARTHE. Amongst us?

OLIVER. Why not? Why do ye recoil?

MARCEL. 'Tis the—the—joy—I feel when I hear his name.
         I feel a—a—respect for him that makes my blood run cold.

OLIVER. When he comes, you will speak to him, but freely, gaily—

MARCEL. I speak—a—gaily? Noble sir, I am of a sad temper,
         But here is Richard who sings an excellent song, let him speak.

RICH. No, you, Didier.

DIDIER. Me?

MARTHE. I'll do it. What am I to say?

OLIVER. Open your hearts, and tell him all you think.

MARTHE. I have it! I will let him know we hate his Scottish guard.

ALL. Ay! Ay!

DIDIER. And how our crops are ravaged by his game.

ALL. Ay! Ay!

OLIVER. How now? What insolence is this?

MARTHE. Pardon, sir, you bade us tell him all we think.

MARCEL. That's true! Tell us, sir, what is our opinion?

OLIVER. You love your king.

MARTHE. We'll think so.

OLIVER. Like a father.

MARCEL. I never thought of that till now.

OLIVER. Tell him so—speak frankly—raise his spirits with
    Your rude and rustic merriment. Laugh loud, and if he jest—
MARCEL. Eh?
OLIVER. Reply in sort, and keep his humor up.
    Hush! Here he comes.
ALL. Where?
MARCEL. What? That old, decrepit man?
OLIVER. Decrepit! Fool, do you prize your head?
    He is in excellent good health.
MARCEL. Yes, sir, I see now. So he is.
OLIVER. Sing, dolt!
MARCEL. [*Sings rather trembling a line of the previous melody*]
OLIVER. Louder! Quick, be gay! Sing, all of ye, and dance.
    It is the King! [*They do so. Louis enters, leaning on Tristan, and
followed by Scottish archers who remain at back. Goes to back and sits.
Oliver creeps over to him. The peasants gaze in terror*]
LOUIS. The sun is fierce today; the air is heavy; it weighs upon
    Me, and yet the air of France used to be pure. Methinks the
    Climate must have changed since I was young.
OLIVER. It has been so remarked, sire.
LOUIS. Ah, Oliver.
OLIVER. Look, sire. These peasantry were happily
    Engaged here as you came; join in their gaiety.
    Speak to them. They do not
    Recognize you.
LOUIS. I will. I'll play the King incognito.
OLIVER. This noble lord would speak with you, come near.
LOUIS. Aha! Come hither, rosy face.
MARTHE. Please you, sir.
LOUIS. Bounty of nature! You deserve a prize for
    Health. How came you by it?
MARTHE. How? Hi—hi—hi!
LOUIS. Ah! How?
MARTHE. It comes by stealth, I know not how, no more
    Than why the grape grows. Perhaps it comes from heaven
    By night, fattening the heart with happy dreams.
LOUIS. But you have sorrows?
MARCEL. Why—ay. Life has its changing weathers, sir. All is
    Not sunshine. But sorrows come like rain; they freshen up
    A man. Sorrow's a good providence.

MARTHE.   And a light heart flows over it. The hardest lot
          Can always find some wretch to covet it.
MARCEL.   There's cousin Mallard owes five quarters' rent.
          That comforts me who only owe a half.
LOUIS.   [*To Oliver*] These wretches find a cause of happiness
          In everything. But when disease arrives, and strikes ye down?
MARCEL.   Ah, when our sheep have got the rot.
LOUIS.   Nay, your own mortal sickness. When you behold
          Your substance lavished upon doctors?
MARCEL.   We're no such fools. Doctors, forsooth!
          When I am sick, I draw a horn of wine,
          And laugh at 'em. Who pays a doctor robs his son
          And heir. When a man's due, death lays his hand
          On him, and never asks a doctor's leave.
LOUIS.   You speak of death as if you feared it not.
MARCEL.   I do believe death is not near so bad
          As folks would make it. 'Tis a bad life that makes
          Death so dreadful. When I behold a train
          Of weeping mourners, and think that he they follow is
          Preceded by a black account of crime, ill-gotten wealth,
          Murders—
LOUIS.   Oh!
MARCEL.   *Then* death alone has terrors. The bearers of the dead
          Seem fiends.
LOUIS.   Perdition!
MARCEL.   *Then* fear I death. Yet why, I know not, for
          I never wronged my neighbors, nor shed fellow creature's blood.
LOUIS.   Begone!
MARCEL.   What have I said?
OLIVER.   Idiot!
LOUIS.   Death—hell—eternal torture! Heaven pity, help me!
          Hence! No, come answer me. Who bid thee, wretch,
          To speak these words to me?
MARCEL.   Nobody. Nobody.
LOUIS.   Thou'rt paid to do it. Speak!
MARCEL.   No, as I live.
MARTHE.   Not he, sir, there's no harm in him. I'll warrant him—
          He's but a fool.
MARCEL.   A downright, well known fool, sir. Ask all the neighbors.
LOUIS.   I did but jest. He's your husband, then?

MARTHE. I would not ask a better.

LOUIS. Then you shall earn his pardon.

MARTHE. That will I. How?

LOUIS. He says he has no sorrow. I will provide him one.
        He, he! Hark! With such a buxom air, those ruby lips
        And sparkling eyes, you must have lovers in the village
        On the sly. Name them!

MARTHE. Lovers, sir? Not I!

LOUIS. Take care; his pardon hangs on it.

MARCEL. Name them all, Marthe; as you love me, out with
        Their names—I'm deaf!

MARTHE. Well, if I had a choice—

LOUIS. Ay, ay?

MARTHE. Amongst the men I've seen, I'd choose—

LOUIS. Who? Who?

MARTHE. You!

LOUIS. Me! He, he!

MARTHE. Be quiet.

LOUIS. Would you fear an old hunks like me?

MARTHE. Not so old neither; you've a sly look.

LOUIS. [Aside to Marthe] Good, good!

MARTHE. A sturdy form.

LOUIS. He, he!

MARTHE. A fool would be the maid would trust you.

LOUIS. You think so?

MARTHE. I only wish our good old king had such an air,
        And bore his years as well.

LOUIS. What, what?

MARTHE. Then for his precious life we'd have no fear,
        For you will live to see a hundred years.

LOUIS. A hundred years! You love your king?

MARTHE. Love him? Ay, do we all. France has but one voice,
        And you have heard it.

OLIVER. There, sir, you can't accuse them of flattery.

LOUIS. A hundred years, that I shall live to see. [Kisses her]
        The King thus thanks you for your prophecy.

MARTHE. The King!

ALL. Long live the King!

LOUIS. Good souls, good souls! For France and myself I thank ye.
        Ah, I shall see a hundred years. For every year of that good

Wish, here is a crown. Take these jewels; take 'em all.
Go sing, dance, drink, pledge me good health—long life. Drink
To my hundred years!

MARCEL. I shall tell everyone the money I have received.

MARTHE. Yes, and I shall tell how I have received
Two kisses from the King.

ALL. Long live the King! [*Shout and exit U.E.L.H.*]

LOUIS. 'Tis sweet to be thus loved.

OLIVER. And when the avowal comes from hearts that know
Not how to feign.

LOUIS. A hundred years! Did you mark, Oliver?

OLIVER. These common people predict with wondrous truth.

LOUIS. You jest, gossip.

OLIVER. Not I.

LOUIS. Her words agree with my nativity.
My horoscope portends I shall outlive my foes.
Oh, life, life! Let me but live
To see these sores of France, these sovereign vassals
Levelled to the herd. Their lands, their crowns,
Their very pride I would escheat to swell
The royal power, till there should be in France
But one estate—the people. Ay, all people—
Except me!

OLIVER. Blessed hour!

LOUIS. Let me secure my cousin, Charles the Bold of Burgundy,
And in a good stout coffin see him cribbed, and then, my
Well beloved subjects, ye great dukes of Burgundy shall never
Chaffer with the knight of France for right or privilege.
But hush, he lives. Tell me, this Count of Rethel, has he
Seen Marie?

OLIVER. Not yet, sire.

LOUIS. So. Bid him come hither. [*Shouts "Long live the Dauphin!"*]
What shouts are these?

OLIVER. It is the Dauphin, sire. The people greet the Prince.

LOUIS. Their love is too profuse; it worries me. He is not yet
Their king. He comes—begone! [*Exit Oliver into the chapel.*
Enter the Dauphin]
How now, what mean these transports?

DAUPHIN. Sire, the people crowded on my path, invoking blessings on me.
I was moved to tears.

Louis. Tomorrow you return to Amboise.

Dauphin. So soon?

Louis. So, you would taste of popularity,
    The people's breath!
    'Tis a foul poison, Prince.
    To win their voices, throw but a crown or two, and while they
    Fight for 'em, they'll cry ye deaf. You deemed their shouts
    Were hearty? Eh! 'Twas I who bade 'em do't. They had
    Been paid for't.

Dauphin. How! 'Twas ordered?

Louis. Ay; by me.

Dauphin. Oh, sire!

Louis. Now let this be a lesson, so—begone and meditate upon it.

Dauphin. What have I done?

Louis. Thou? Nothing! What dared? What could you do?

Dauphin. Alas, not even please you, sire. And yet—

Louis. What?

Dauphin. I dare not. Sire—my liege—my father—
    If you could grant me your love.

Louis. How! What it seems that I do not love you, heh?

Dauphin. Oh, pardon, sire.

Louis. I hate you? So! So! I am a savage, an inhuman father. This
    Has been prompted; 'tis not of your thought. Who told you
    This? Ha, 'twas your uncle, Orleans. Come, Charles, my son,
    Tell me in confidence, who was it?

Dauphin. My uncle once did say that France sooner or later must
    Own me for its master.

Louis. [*Aside*] Ah, the traitor! And said he not that old and sick
    I must ere long—I—Ha! 'tis false! And then he said the
    Crown was well-nigh in your grasp.

Dauphin. Oh, sire.

Louis. 'Tis false again! Does its weight make me bow? I tell ye,
    Boy, another diadem, and yet a third heaped on this wrinkled
    Front, would lighter sit than that same silken cap upon thy
    Baby brow.

Dauphin. My father, live—live long; it is my only prayer—my hope
    Beneath your sway, may France grow great, and if my days
    Could serve to lengthen yours, I'd pray that Heaven may take
    Me in my youth, and add my life to thine.

Louis.   My son, my son, this is weak. Begone! [*Dauphin exits*]
        That's a good son who still perhaps deceives his father. [*Enter*
Marie from chapel]
        Ah, 'tis she. Come here, child. What brave attire! Thou
        Never hast thy beauty thus enshrined for me.
Marie.   You bade us to a ceremony where I thought—
Louis.   To meet some cavalier.
Marie.   I do not understand you, sire.
Louis.   Your cheek does. Well, let's speak of something else. You
        Shall be secret, yet if there be a thing I love, 'tis to make
        Young lovers happy.
Marie.   You are a great king, sire.
Louis.   Ay, I know some newly married folk that say as much. I hoped
        I could have lent my aid to thee, but since you love not—
Marie.   I, sire?
Louis.   Let us speak of something else.
Marie.   But—what then did you think?
Louis.   Come, sit you here. I thought that at the Court of Charles
        Some brave and handsome cavalier—what more natural—had
        Touched your heart. I saw him, as I thought, at your feet—
        A noble youth—let's see, should he be noble?
Marie.   Oh, yes, sire, noble and most unhappy.
Louis.   True! A count! And then I dreamt this swain, so lost in love
        Was he, that in the guise of envoy came to see this fair.
Marie.   Oh, Heaven!
Louis.   Nay, had arrived today, and even had my royal word obtained
        To sign—
Marie.   A treaty!
Louis.   And a marriage bond.
Marie.   And you—you, sire?
Louis.   Methought that I consented—but 'tis false. 'Tis all dreams.
Marie.   You know then, sire?
Louis.   Let's speak of something else.
Marie.   'Tis true! Oh, pardon—
Louis.   Ah, you have secrets from me. I will be revenged.
Marie.   Pardon—I ask it on my knees. Who had betrayed him?
Louis.   Who? Commine.
Marie.   My father! He has told you all, and you forgive?
Louis.   I do.
Marie.   Nemours—

Louis. [*Aside*]   Ah, 'tis Nemours!

Marie. Ah, give me leave, my liege, to fly to him and join my
   Hopes to his;
   To bless your royal name, and mingle prayers for your prosperity.

Louis. Not for his life. Hark, he believes himself unknown. Ha, ha!
   Thy father and myself have planned a plot, see? I'm a traitor
   For I let it out. Well, we have planned the moment and the
   Place to lift the mask from this impostor's brow.

Marie. Oh, sire!

Louis. You know I love my jest. Come, then, and swear to me by all
   Thy hopes of heaven and love, never this matter to divulge.

Marie. I promise, sire.

Louis. Upon that silence rests thy lover's life, which I have sworn
   To spare. Redeem thine oath, and I'll remember mine. [*Aside*]
   Nemours! And in my grasp! A word, a look and he is dead.
   But what may then ensue? I'll think on't. Tristan! [*Tristan
enters*]
   Adieu, dear child, adieu! [*Exit*]

Marie. Must I not speak? Oh, treason to my love. Must I then have
   A joy which he has not? No, it will overflow, as now it does
   At these rebellious eyes. Yet he will come. A word I sent
   Him by my page will guide him hither. Ah, a footstep!
   To its tread my heart keeps time. 'Tis he! [*Enter Nemours*]
   Nemours! Once more we meet, and, as I oft foretold we should,
   Beneath our native sky.

Nem. Look on me; let me not see beyond thine eyes, nor roam beyond
   Thy heart. Speak to me, and let me hear thy voice.

Marie. I have one theme, and that is all my language. Hope, Nemours;
   I speak and bid thee hope. Thy fortune still is in the royal
   Hand that plucked it from thee. By another word, the voice
   That banished thee may bid thee back.

Nem. I see a meaning in your eyes, Marie, that overtakes thy tongue.

Marie. I dare not tell thee more. Already I have said too much.
   Hush! See! [*Procession advances from the chapel*]
   The chapel doors unclose; they come! Farewell! [*She separates
from him. Enter the Burgundians. Nemours joins them. As Marie advances
towards the chapel, Louis, François, Oliver, Tristan, the Cardinal, d'Alby,
Craven, Commine, Priests and Courtiers appear on the steps. Louis holds the
treaty in his hands*]

Louis.   There ends unholy strife. Bear witness, Heaven, I do approve
          And sign the bond of peace. The Count de Rethel hath his
          Mission done with haughty menace, which I had avenged did I
          Not hold my people's happiness above my pride.
Nem.   He who can read the human heart doth know how much of it
          Is on thy tongue. Not for myself I speak, but in
          The name of him I serve. Duke Charles now holds
          His wrongs atoned, and justice done.
Louis.   To Charles of Burgundy, my dear ally, before these holy symbols
          And in sight of Heaven, I swear most solemnly this bond
          To keep most unviol—[*Enter Dauphin hastily followed by Dunvis
and de Lude*]
Dauphin. Hold! Oh, hold, my father!
Louis.   How now?
Dauphin. News, news, my liege, of moment. Pardon! There has arrived a
          Despatch from Burgundy—a messenger who brings the tiding.
          Charles, thy foe—
Louis.   My foe! Charles, my brother—my ally!
Dauphin. Has been defeated.
Louis.   How? How say ye? Speak!
Dauphin. I say defeated—utterly undone—and lost!
Nem.   Charles—
Louis.   Art sure of this?
Dauphin. The lords of Loucy, Dunvis, and de Lude assure it true.
          One of his captains did betray his cause.
Louis.   Ah, the coward!
Nem.   This is a false report, which soon a glowing triumph will belie.
          Charles the Bold—
Dauphin. He's dead.
Louis.   Dead? Dead? The proofs!
Dauphin. They are here. [*Hands Louis despatches*]
Nem.   Duke Charles defeated—dead. 'Tis false, and Count de Rethel
          With my life maintains—
Louis.   'Tis true—Duke of Nemours.
Dauphin and All. Nemours!
Nem.   Betrayed!
Louis.   Ay! True it is—impossible. See you now, Heaven's vengeance
          Has overtaken him, as sure as mine shall now find thee.
          Secure him!
Nem.   [*Drawing sword*] Death—treachery! A rescue! Burgundy!

Louis. [*Retreating*] Upon them, France!

Fran. Hold, in Heaven's name, whose temple you profane.

Nem. Put up your weapons, gentlemen, and yield. This is my cause
Alone. Alone I'll fall. If Charles still lives, the terror
Of his name will better aid me than your bravery.
If he be dead, alone I'll follow him. [*Casts sword at King's feet*]
To meet thee, I had need like thee to feign. For my design,
I'll render an account above. Cast thou unto my father's
Murderers another prey, but there is one delight you cannot
Have—I have no son, no brother, no not even a friend whom
Thou canst force to kneel beneath my scaffold to receive the
Blood that thou wilt shed.

Louis. Tristan! Tonight, his judgment, and at daylight, the rest.

Fran. Have pity, sire; thou art a king.

Louis. Ay, as a King, my father, I might pardon, but I am
The Church's head; he hath insulted her, and to approach
Those sacred relics there with sacrilegious—Oh, I will
Avenge! Go, prepare his soul.

Fran. And thine, my son. Dost give no thought to that? [*Exit with his train*]

Louis. Montjoie, St. Denis—ha! Demois, gather six hundred spears—
Ride for Peronne, to Arras, Baudrecourt with all the force
You can. Let Artois ere one month be France. Down upon
Flanders, you. Burgundy is ours! I give it ye as spoil.
Seize what and where you can, and rend the soil amongst ye.
Counties and fiefs—for all who win shall wear 'em. But hold!
Hold ye awhile! The noble duke has met a hero's fate. He
Was my foe, but all my wrongs are hid and buried in his tomb.
He was my cousin. The court will wear full mourning for a
Week.

ACT IV.

The King's bedchamber. Enter Coitier followed by Nemours.

Coit. Come in, my son, thou art in safety here.

Nem. Good Coitier.

Coit. Look on me, Nemours, and let me trace
The features that I love upon thy face.
Methinks thy father smiles upon me now.

NEM. The likeness ends not there—the same dire fate
Awaits his son.

COIT. By Heaven, it shall not be. I'll guard thy life;
Ay, with my own. Fear not this toothless wolf.

NEM. Yet I am caged—these bars—this gloomy cell.
It is a prison still.

COIT. 'Tis the King's bedchamber.

NEM. This?

COIT. This. Behold yon relics! See how they are worn by his
Impassioned kisses—A poignard—he dares not touch,
Yet fain would always have beside him. There
His bed, where he would hide in vain his terrors.

NEM. Why have you brought me here?

COIT. The King desires to speak to you.

NEM. Alone?

COIT. He dares not. No, he'll come surrounded by his
Myrmidons.

NEM. What would he with me?

COIT. Thou art beloved by all the chiefs and citizens
Of Burgundy; the idol of the soldiers; thy
Friends command in all the citadels. I told
The King that on thy bidding, Artois would submit
And Flanders yield a bloodless victory.

NEM. Thou said'st so, Coitier?

COIT. The remedy's extreme, I own it, but thy peril—

NEM. How! Betray—despoil my benefactor, Charles?
For whom? the headsman of my race? No! Never! It
Were a murder of my father's memory, a burial
Of his wrongs alive.

COIT. Nemours, thou art resolved?

NEM. To die, if't must be so.

COIT. Behold this dungeon! 'Tis the sole retreat
Where I am master. When I bound myself
The tyrant's slave, not all his wealth could buy
My ministry, had he not yielded me my liberty
And right of free egress. See! See! This key opens
The postern gate. Take it. It was my freedom,
Now 'tis thine.

NEM. But then—his vengeance!

COIT. Tut—he suffers.

NEM. His rage when my escape is known!

COIT. He suffers.
    Fear not, I know him well. Away! Stay!
    Take this dagger—descend the spiral stair,
    A vaulted passage leads to the moat—
    Then a few steps—a door that key provides
    For—then the open fields, the wide free heaven
    And liberty, Nemours.

NEM. Give me the dagger.

COIT. There! Now, go! Begone! I hear a step! It is
    The King. Away! I fly to meet him. Speed!
    Speed, while I retard his coming. [*Exit*]

NEM. My liberty! No, Coitier, no! Thou hast bestowed a
    Treasure still more priceless. Revenge! [*Conceals himself. Enter
Louis, Commine, Marie, Tristan and Coitier*]

COIT. Believe me, sire, the air will do you good.

LOUIS. No, no, 'tis cold; see how I quake. [*Aside*] Where is Nemours?

COIT. You are in pain, sire.

LOUIS. Ay, in every limb it leaves me no repose; the
    Very air is like a serpent's tooth. Oh, endless,
    Endless death! Nemours—what said he?

COIT. There, sire, warm your starved limbs.

LOUIS. Ah, ah, a fire!

MARIE. Sit here. May it revive you, sire.

LOUIS. Why cannot thy young and glowing heart give
    Heat and life to mine? Come, smile.

COM. [*Aside to Marie*] Courage, Marie; obey.

MARIE. Alas, I am unable. [*Weeps*]

LOUIS. Tears! You sadden me. Go, or cease weeping. I can repair
    The past—cure everything.

MARIE. And will you, sire?

LOUIS. Ay, and I will. [*To Coitier*] Nemours—

COIT. Be bidden, sire, for once to bed.

LOUIS. Not yet. [*To Tristan*] Where is Nemours? Go bring him here.

TRIST. You know he is no longer in my keeping.

LOUIS. He is in thine. [*To Coitier*]

TRIST. He was my due—judged and condemned. I love to finish
    All that I begin.

MARIE. Ah, father!

COM. Hush!

LOUIS. True, true! Thou, Coitier, hast him. Why is he not here?

Coit. Because he would not come.

Louis. He would not?

Coit. No, he would have braved you.

Louis. Ay!

Coit. You would have killed him.

Louis. Well?

Coit. That crime, at least, I saved you. He is gone.

Louis. Gone!

Coit. Ay, escaped!

Louis. Aided by thee!

Coit. Your victim is beyond your rage. Pursuit were folly.

Louis. Wretch, thou darest say so, villain! [*To Tristan*] And
Thou, thy boasted vigilance and power he has evaded.
Oh, ye are traitors, all. Whither has he fled? Speak,
Dog! Away, away! Alive or dead, I'll have him.

Marie. Oh, mercy, sire. Mercy for me, by whom he
Was betrayed. Oh, at your latest breath may Heaven
Deny your prayer for mercy if you now are deaf to mine.

Louis. [*To Commine*] Take her away.

Marie. Give me to death; spare, spare Nemours.

Louis. Away with her! For you, traitor, death. Tristan—
Tomorrow—death.

Coit. Why say tomorrow? Strike at once—today.

Louis. Away with him!

Coit. Farewell, we soon shall meet.
I'll give you just ten days to live.

Louis. Ah, villain, be it so; then I will die, I will; but still
I'll—I'll—[*To his suite*] Go! Begone! [*To Coitier*]
Stay you. [*Exeunt all but Coitier*]
Think not thou wilt escape thy fate. No—No—for thou
Shalt die in torment. Ay, thou shalt.

Coit. So you have said already, sire. Now do it.

Louis. Ay, I will. Ha! you think I prize your skill.
Ha! Ha! I laugh at it, your art! What has it done for me?
Go, cheat the herd with quackery. I'll do without ye, and
I'll live by my own will alone. I feel I can.

Coit. Excellent! Will try?

Louis. Ay, thou traitor, ay! François de Paule can with a single
Word repair my life; his breath can give me youth.

Coit. He'd best make haste, then.

Louis. Ay, he can.

Coit. Of course—no doubt of it.

Louis. Oh, Coitier, ungrateful Coitier, have I deserved this of thee?

Coit. Why, look ye, sire, ungrateful I had been, had I not saved
My benefactor's child.

Louis. Your benefactor!

Coit. Ay! I owed his father all.

Louis. What then, have I been scant? I give, and count not what I
Give. What gave this benefactor, then, to be so much preferred?

Coit. His love! What right have you to gratitude? Thank Heaven,
I owe you none. We give and take, and owe each other nought.
Come, sire let's be honest. You give from fear; I take from
Interest. I give my life, consume it, to prolong
Your days. I sell, you purchase. 'Tis a bargain.
You kings imagine all is bought with gold; you
Pay a courtier, and you buy a slave, but not a friend.
Oh, sire, there's but one price for him—that's love.

Louis. Then Coitier, I will love thee tenderly. Nay, I do love thee.

Coit. Ay, for thyself.

Louis. No, as I live. I am in dreadful pain. See now, I do believe
This holy man may, if he will, restore me. Yet behold, I do
Forgive thee this that thou hast done. Ay, freely. [*Enter Oliver*]

Oliver. Sire, François de Paule attends you. [*Enter François*]

Louis. See, my father, he has braved his king, yet I have pardoned him.
Go, Coitier, go rest thee awhile within. Dear friend,
Adieu. [*Exit Coitier*]
Ah, traitor, come the day when I've no need of thee. We
Are alone.

Fran. What seek you with me?

Louis. Let me unveil my heart.

Fran. Arise, my son.

Louis. Let me abase myself, my forehead in the dust, and kiss the
Print thy saintly feet have made.

Fran. Reserve thy kneeling for Him to whom alone we owe that
homage.
Rise!

Louis. So great the blessing I would ask,
I know not how to stoop too low for it.

Fran. What can I do?

Louis. All. I know your wondrous power.
Endowed by Heaven with gifts miraculous.
Fran. My son?
Louis. Since at the peasant's prayer you pour the dews
Upon the parching earth, pour young red blood
Into my veins; refresh this arid heart.
Command this broken frame to knit its thews
And rise again invigorate with youth.
Stretch out your arms, and lift me up to health.
Touch these pale, livid features with your hand,
And smooth this wrinkled brow.
Fran. Blaspheme no more.
What am I?
Louis. Ten years!
Oh, say ten years, my father; grant me that,
And I will load thee with my gratitude.
Hear me. I have precious saintly relics
Beyond all price. They shall be thine, and more
If I obtain these twenty years I spoke of.
I have power at Rome, and thou shalt find
A place 'mongst the saints. Amongst what, say I,
Above all. I'll lay a tax
Upon my faithful subjects; dedicate
A temple to thee. But for such expense
A score of years is surely not enough.
No, let me live on—life—life—ah, grant me that.
Prolong my life!
Fran. Can I cry halt to time?
Change at my will the laws of nature? King,
That life thou seekest, thou must have indeed,
But not on earth.
Louis. I'm weary of that prate.
Won't do thine office? Exercise thy power,
Or I have means to make you. I am King!
Ah, no; pray pardon me; I know not what I say.
Fran. Thy mortal malady
Is but remorse. Repent.
Louis. I will. Then shall I heal and live?
Fran. It may be so.
Louis. Then I repent, and will confess.

FRAN.   Sinner, who call'st me to this holy office,
       Speak, speak, what hast thou done?
LOUIS. The King, my father, died; his ailment, it was said,
       Was terror of the Dauphin.
FRAN.   A son abridge the old age of his father?
LOUIS. That Dauphin was myself.
FRAN.   You!
LOUIS. The crown was tottering, and France was lost.
       State reasons supersede the ties of nature.
       I had no choice.
FRAN.   Thou wicked son, confess thy crimes, but
       Seek not to excuse. Proceed!
LOUIS. I had a brother.
FRAN.   Well?
LOUIS. He also died.
FRAN.   How?
LOUIS. By poison!
FRAN.   By thy command?
LOUIS. It was so suspected. Some did suspect so.
       Would they who said it had fallen in my clutch!
FRAN.   'Tis not so, then?
LOUIS. I said not that.
FRAN.   Oh, Heaven! 'Tis true!
LOUIS. But he deserved his fate.
FRAN.   Unutterable horror! Dost thou find
       Excuses fast as crimes? Down to the dust!
       Thou art no more a king. Down, on thy knees,
       Thou fratricide!
LOUIS. Pardon—
FRAN.   Pour out thy leprous soul.
       Repent, and cleanse thy heart.
LOUIS. I do—I do!
       See—on my knees—I do. I've yet a crime untold.
FRAN.   What! More?
LOUIS. Nemours. He did conspire;
       His guilt was proved, but still his death was crime.
       I forced his sons to witness it, while from the scaffold
       His life-blood fell on them.
FRAN.   Most barbarous!

Louis. I confess. Yes, I have judged
  With rigor.
Fran. Judged!
Louis. No—no!
  They are crimes—foul crimes!
  The silent wave has been my executioner;
  The earth, my jailer. Here beneath these walls
  My captives groan, forgotten and unknown.
Fran. This crime can be atoned, thank Heaven for that.
  Come!
Louis. Where?
Fran. To release these prisoners.
Louis. Stay—stay—you ask too much.
  The Church has pardons which a king can buy.
Fran. Not so; they must be merited.
Louis. Then they are mine by right of misery.
  Oh, could you look into my soul, my father,
  My body's anguish is but half my pain;
  The present is a terror, but the past—
  Oh Heaven, I dare not turn and look on that!
  My days are wretched, yet they bring relief,
  And come to scare away my nights of terror.
  The gloom takes forms to mock and gibe at me;
  The silence whispers names I loathe and dread;
  And when I sleep, a demon sits and broods
  Upon my heart. I thrust him off, and then
  A naked blade held in a viewless hand
  Pierces my throat. I try to rise; my couch
  Swims in a sea of blood, whose gory waves
  Rise up to drown me. Such my daily life!
  And quitting it, I thirst for more. To drain
  This poison'd cup is all my fear.
  To eke it out, my only hope.
Fran. One act of mercy will restore thy peace.
  Free these, thy captives.
Louis. Tomorrow—I will think it out.
Fran. Death may come ere then—tonight—this instant.
Louis. Death! From whence? No, I am too well defended.
Fran. Adieu, then. Merciless thyself, how canst thou hope for mercy?

Louis.   Ah, you condemn me.
Fran.   No, 'tis not my office.
       But, oh, my son, wouldst thou release thyself?
       Undo these prisoners' chains, and free thy soul.
       Their curses drown thy prayers! Make them be still,
       And thou'lt be heard in Heaven. Farewell! Farewell! [*Exit*]
Louis.   Father! He leaves me! Stay! I do consent!
       I—No! That were but weakness! He is gone!
       Oh, who will aid me now? [*Enter Nemours*]
       Sweet saint, I pray thee plead for me. Thou knowest
       My heart is pitiless. A king must use the power he holds
       From Heaven, or wrong his trust. In punishing
       The guilty I would
       Prove my right to thy protection. In return
       I'll build thee
       Churches; load thy shrines with gifts.
       But let me gratify
       My just revenge for thine especial honor,
       And mine too.
Nem.   Silence!
Louis.   Silence!
Nem.   Not a breath!
Louis.   Not one.
Nem.   Thou art well defended.
Louis.   Oh, Nemours!
Nem.   Who dares to risk his life is master, then, of thine.
Louis.   What would ye?
Nem.   Justice!
Louis.   Oh, be merciful.
Nem.   I am not thy judge.
Louis.   Who, then?
Nem.   My father!
Louis.   No! Thou—thou!
Nem.   My father!
Louis.   Thou, Nemours!
Nem.   My father!
Louis.   He would kill me.
Nem.   Thou hast said it.

Louis. Hear!
     Oh, hear me first!
Nem. As thou didst hear my father's dying prayer.
Louis. Nemours!
Nem. 'Tis here!
     Look on it now; he bore it on his breast,
     When by thy fell command he suffered.
     'Twas sent
     By him to thee to melt thy heart to pity.
     Thine answer wouldst thou see? 'Tis there—his blood!
     Come, read! Read!
Louis. Mercy!
Nem. Read, I say!
Louis. I cannot.
Nem. Beneath the fatal weapon he could write.
     Read, as he wrote.
Louis. No, no! I cannot!
     That horrid steel distracts me—blinds my sense.
     I cannot!
Nem. Listen, then.
Louis. Oh, spare me! Pity me, Nemours!
Nem. [*Reads*] "My most merciful and gracious sovereign,
     With all my humble heart I plead to your offended majesty
     For pity and for pardon—"
Louis. I will restore thy title—thine estates,
     Make expiation, full and humble.
     I do repent. See, see, my tears?
     Put me but to the proof.
Nem. Listen. [*Reads*] "I will atone my sins and serve you
     So well and faithfully that my repentance
     Shall o'ertop my crimes. Oh, let my tears
     Assuage your anger."
Louis. My son, think of my child! Nemours,
     Leave him not fatherless.
Nem. [*Reads*] "Yet not for me, but for my children's
     Sake! Oh, for Heaven's charity, my liege, con-
     Demn them not in me. For my transgression
     Will they in dishonor live to beg their bread.
     Oh, sire, have pity for my unoffending children."

Louis. I will deliver to thee Tristan;
      He it was who did the deed. Deal with him
      As thou wilt.
Nem. [*Reads*] "May Heaven preserve your majesty, and
      Imbue your heart with mercy for your
      Childhood's loved companion."
      See! Murdered! See! Read! Read thyself!
Louis. I cannot.
Nem. There!
Louis. [*Reads*] "Your childhood's loved companion, Jacques
      Of Armagnac."
      You weep, Nemours; let fall those tears on me.
      Wash out my sins.
Nem. Oh, thou shalt pay them dearly.
Louis. Nemours! Nemours!
Nem. What tortures can avenge me? where to find
      A forfeit equal to his crimes?
Louis. He'll kill me!
Nem. Ah, there is but one.
Louis. My death!
Nem. No, fiend, thy life!
      I know thy anguish; I have heard thy woe.
      Die on! Die slowly! Mass up crimes each hour.
      Linger till death with lagging steps arrive
      To seize thee still more guilty. Live in torment!
      Heaven in its justice listens to thy prayer,
      And grants thee life to double my revenge.
Louis. Help, Tristan! Help! the villain murders me!
      Tristan! that dagger! Hew him down, I say. [*Tristan and guards
rush on*]
      Tristan—the traitor's there—the door—pursue—
      O'ertake the assassin—there!—search!—look!—the curtains
      Behind the bed—that's where he hides! How, wretches,
      Can ye not find him? He'll slay me in the midst!
      Surround me!—close! No, traitors!—back away!
      I fear ye all!—Ah, there's a shadow—there!
      See, Tristan! Help, he's here again! He strikes!
      His dagger's red with blood! Help! Tristan! Kill! [*Falls in con-
vulsions*]

ACT V.

Throne Room in the Castle. The stage is filled with courtiers.

LUDE.   Is't true, my lord? They say that Coitier
        Was an accomplice.
LORD.   Ay!
LUDE.   Messire Tristan,
        Can this be so? Nemours and Coitier?
LORD.   Ay!
        They are judged—to death; and when the King revives,
        To sign their sentence, justice will be done.
LORD.   The Parliament convoked, the peers assembled—
        This looks like death. [*Enter Commine*]
COM.   A page, ho! Quick!
        This to the Duke of Orleans—away!
        This to the Lord of Beaujeu!
LUDE.   The Duke and Beaujeu! Then the King is *in extremis.*
COM.   There is no hope.
TRIST. See how they flock about the coming reign.
LUDE.   Be comforted, sweet Prince.
COM.   Think of Nemours.
        Let your first act be one of mercy, sire.
DAUPHIN. Have I the power?
COM.   Speak but one word to Tristan.
DAUPHIN. Be it so.
COM.   Tristan, you have heard. Nemours—
TRIST. His highness needs but look to be obeyed.
LUDE.   See, here is the Cardinal. [*Enter Cardinal d'Alby*]
DAUPHIN. The King, my lord, the King?
CARD.   Fast fleeting, Prince, inanimate.
        Yet still, my lord, be comforted in this
        That by his gifts and great beneficence,
        The Church assures his life to come. Let us
        All hope to make as Christian-like an end.
DAUPHIN. Then there is no longer hope?
CARD.   Accept the throne; it is your burthen, sire,
        Which we will help to bear.

DAUPHIN. And he will die
         Without a word—a look.

COM. My lord, 'tis hard.

LUDE. He is unnatural! He ever treated you
         With cruelty.

DAUPHIN. Silence! He was my father.
         That which he did seemed fit to him, and must
         Seem so to me. [*Enter Oliver*]

OLIVER. My lords, our prayers are heard.
         The King revives.

DAUPHIN. He lives!

CARD. Providence be praised.

OLIVER. There is no fear, his senses have returned.
         There is great hope. He has desired this couch
         To be prepared. Prince, he would be alone;
         All must retire but Commine and Tristan.

DAUPHIN. But this affects not me; I am his son.

OLIVER. Alas, my lord; trust to my offices,
         And he shall ask for you anon.

DAUPHIN. Accept my gratitude.

COM. And mine.

LUDE. A king
         Thus undecided if to die or not,
         Compromises everybody now.
         Who knows which way to turn? to whom to bow?

OLIVER. We are alone.

COM. Well?

TRIST. Will he live?

OLIVER. Of course, to them I said so, but 'tis doubtful
         Still.

COM. Speaks he of Nemours?

OLIVER. No, he forgets.

COM. Come death—ere he remember.

OLIVER. His brain is gone.
         Just now, why, nought would serve him but he must
         Preside at council. On his haggard brow
         I needs must place the crown, though with the weight
         His wizened chin sunk upon his breast;
         And o'er his ague-stricken form, he wears
         The royal mantle. Then he will walk, forsooth,

But scarce has made one pace, when, breathless, helpless,
He sinks back, crying that he never felt so well. Faith,
He never felt so well! See, he comes.

TRIST. Has such a phantom life? [*Enter Louis and an Officer*]

LOUIS. What men are those?

OLIVER. Commine. Tristan.

LOUIS. Think you I cannot see 'em?
One would suppose my eyes were failing me.
Good day, sirs.
Leave me, fellows; let go your hold.
Can I not stir without ye?

OLIVER. There, repose; rest you awhile, sire.

LOUIS. I am not weary.

OLIVER. No.

LOUIS. I am strong and capable.

OLIVER. Most capable.

LOUIS. Since you will have it so,
Why stands he there,
And gazes on me so? Does he find me changed?

TRIST. I, sire? I never saw you look so hale.

LOUIS. That's well. This room is spacious; there is air in't;
I can breathe. [*Dozes*]

OLIVER. He sleeps.

COM. Remember, gentlemen,
He bade us once when his last moment came
To warn him.

TRIST. Ay.

OLIVER. He might desire to make
Some last bequest to us.

TRIST. In that case, we'll
Let him be told.

LOUIS. Tristan, art thou there?

TRIST. Ay, sire.

LOUIS. Watch—guard me—guard!

TRIST. Fear nought.

COM. He sleeps again.

OLIVER. Who will assume this office?

TRIST. It must be done by one who can convey
The matter tenderly. [*To Oliver*]
You are the man.

Com. The very man, indeed.

Oliver. I would accept, but faith, I love him so
    I could not keep my feelings in command.
    Nay, it must be firmly done, and you,
    I think, would do it best of all.

Trist. He's right.

Com. I am willing; but why thus prolong
    His woe? 'Twere better and more merciful
    To speak outright and break the truth
    At once, as you would do. [*To Tristan*]

Oliver. Why, so it would.

Trist. Eh, gentlemen,
    Let us confess the thing is delicate.

Louis. Why do ye whisper there?

Oliver. We bless the day for your recovery.

Louis. Why is not Coitier here?
    Where does he lay? Go fetch him!

Trist. Sire, you know—

Louis. I know—I know he never is where I
    Would have him be.

Trist. But, sire, you bade—

Louis. Away! I bade you bring him here. No words! Obey! [*Exit Tristan*]
    I feel in cue for
    Hearty exercise. Go bid my grand equerry have the train
    In readiness.

Oliver. How, sire?

Louis. I'll hunt the wolf
    Today. Announce it loudly to my court.

Oliver. But, sire—

Louis. Begone!

Oliver. Were it not well to pause
    Till Coitier—

Louis. Again?

Oliver. He is himself again. [*Exit*]

Louis. Remove this idle pomp, Commine. My crown—
    Why have they thrust it on me? Place it there.
    Nearer! Nearer still; beneath my eyes; under my hand! [*Enter
Coitier and Tristan*]

Coit. From my lips he shall learn what you so fear
    To tell.

Louis. Ah, Coitier, art thou there? Whence came ye?

Coit. Whence! This is too much!

Louis. Why, speak!

Coit. Look on my wrist, still blushing with the rust
    Your manacles have left there. Whence come I!
    Job's patience! from the dungeon.

Louis. A dungeon! Thou? Who gave the order?

Coit. Who? You!

Louis. I!

Coit. 'Fore Heaven,
    He will deny it now. You in my presence
    Gave it.

Louis. Where? For what?

Coit. Accuse me of a deed
    So vile! Why, man, had I the stomach for it
    What hindered me? A drug—a remedy o'erdone—
    One drop too much, and I had done with ye.
    But, introduce a midnight murderer
    While ye were sleeping—

Louis. Hold! Hold! That vision
    In the night—behind those curtains, said ye?

Com. Coitier, what have you done?
    He had forgotten.

Louis. No, no, I do remember now. Thanks, thanks!
    'Twas he—Nemours! Nemours! A dagger raised
    Against my life. [*To Tristan*] Speak! He's dead?

Trist. I waited, sire.

Louis. How, traitor, he is not dead?

Trist. The Dauphin, sire, forbade the execution.

Louis. Ah, ah! My son! Doth he presume
    To reign so soon? 'Tis doubtful he may reign at all.

Coit. Oh, sire, think not on such designs.
    Have done with vengeance; look to your own affairs.
    Your hour is come.

Louis. Eh? How, say you?

Coit. The truth!
    Look well, I say, to what you do,

For by the light of Heaven, this day will be
Your last.

LOUIS. If so, it shall be also his.
Tristan, come here. Let it be now, at once; and hark,
No juggling with me, or your head shall answer it.
Begone!

COM. Tristan!

TRIST. My life or his, you hear.
I have no choice. [*Exit*]

LOUIS. My blood grows chill,
Deserts my limbs and gathers round my heart.
Nay, this weakness is but a spasm; 'twill pass,
'Twill pass, so wipe my brow. It is the sweat
Of agony, and not the dews of death.
Ah, mercy!—now it comes. Ay—go—the Dauphin—
Quick!

COM. I fly, sire.

LOUIS. No, come back!
If thus he saw me, he'd believe 'twas past
And over with me. Oh, look not so, sirs,
This is mere pain, not death. It cannot be.
Save me, Coitier! Oh, give me air—air!
Oh, all my treasure for one breath! Take, take,
But save me. Quick!
'Tis not death; 'tis not—[*Falls*]

COIT. Ah, but it is. Away, apprize the Dauphin.
Tell him he is King of France. [*Exit Commine*]
I am free at last.
These shrunken lips and sightless glazed eyes
Bear impress of the livid seal of death. He's gone—
And Nemours, Nemours is saved—
The heart beats still! He may survive the spasm,
And live awhile—that is, if I revive him.
Wherefore? To eke his anguish out one hour?
Just time enough to act another crime—
The murder of Nemours! No, 'tis enough. Nature,
Do as thou wilt. I yield him up to thee. [*Enter the Dauphin, Commine and Courtiers*]

DAUPHIN. My father, I am here; I come.
How now, his face is changed, Coitier. What means

This silence? Is it too late? He is no more. Leave me;
I would be alone.

Com. My liege—

Dauphin. Away!
I do command ye. [*All retire*]
Oh, my father;
Oh, my sovereign, let thy spirit hear me
And listen to thy son. Believe my heart,
Unknown, forbidden, and outcast by thee.
This poor cold hand of thine which now I take
To warm with tears. 'Tis not thy tenderness
But death that gives me leave to kiss it thus. [*Places his hand
on the crown*]
This fatal bauble stood between our hearts,
Symbol of earthly power. [*Marie rushes in, followed almost
immediately by the Court*]

Marie. My liege!

Dauphin. Marie!

Marie. He is condemned, sire. Tristan is engaged
Upon his fatal work. Stay—stay it, sire.
I claim your royal word; see, here is your pledge.
I ask the pardon of Nemours; his life.
His life or mine! They lead him out to death.

Dauphin. The King redeems the Dauphin's word. Nemours— [*During
this the King revives; the Dauphin quickly withdraws his hand from the
crown*]

Louis. No, keep it; it is thine. My hour is come.

Marie. Nemours—one word for him—

Fran. You hear—

Marie. My liege, my liege, as thou dost hope for pardon,
Extend it now. [*Bell*]
The bell! 'Tis for his death!
Oh, Heaven! See! Nemours, Nemours!

Dauphin. One word, my father; speak and give him life.

Fran. Sire, while thou yet hast time.

Louis. If I forgive,
Shall I, too, in my turn find mercy?

Fran. Would'st thou
Contract with Heaven, and die accursed
As thou hast lived?

Louis.   No—no—
          I pardon. Save him! Save him!
Marie.   Hold! Ah—My life for his. [*Rushes out*]
Louis.   Father! Speak—save—absolve!
          Is there no hope? Oh, mercy! Mercy!
          The mortal foe! See! See you not? It comes!
          I feel his icy grip. Pray! Pray for me!
          I do entreat ye all—pray! I command—[*Dies. Montjoie breaks his
staff*]
Mont.   The King is dead. The King is dead!
          Long live the King!

CURTAIN

DOT

A Fairy Tale of Home, from
The Cricket on the Hearth,
by Charles Dickens

DOT

Dramatizations of Dickens' *Cricket on the Hearth* were made immediately after the publication of that story in the winter of 1845, but according to statements made in the press and in other theatrical notices, none of these attained the success of the Boucicault version. *The Times* review of the London première says: "All the early versions of *The Cricket on the Hearth* were attempts to reduce the book to theatrical shape with as little alteration as possible. Scenery took the place of description, the dialogue was preserved intact, and the development of the story in the play was precisely similar to that in the narrative. . . . Mr. Boucicault . . . adopts a totally different principle." His chief innovations were the strengthening of the dramatic suspense by revealing immediately to the audience the real character of the deaf old man whom John Peerybingle brings home in his cart; and the introduction of the company of fairies, which furnishes opportunities for striking pictures in the prologue and at the final curtain.

The first production of *Dot* was seen in New York on September 14, 1859, when the Winter Garden was opened under the joint management of William Stuart and Dion Boucicault; three years later, on April 14, 1862, the play was produced at the New Adelphi in London, Mr. Benjamin Webster, sole proprietor and manager. The circumstances leading up to these two productions show an interesting similarity, for it was Boucicault who suggested the part of Caleb Plummer to the leading actor in each of the two companies. Joseph Jefferson in his *Autobiography* tells us: "Previous to the commencement of the season, Mr. Boucicault and I had some conversation in relation to the opening bill. I told him I was rather apprehensive of my hitting the part of Caleb Plummer, as I had never acted a character requiring pathos, and, with the exception of the love scene in *Our American Cousin*, as yet had not spoken a serious line upon the stage. He seemed to have more confidence in my powers than I had, and insisted that I could act the part with success. I agreed therefore to open in Caleb, with the understanding that I should finish the performance with a farce, so in the event of my failing in the first piece, I might save my reputation in the last. He assented to the arrangement, but warned me, however, that I would regret it; and he was right, for when the curtain fell upon *Dot*, I should have much preferred not to have acted in the farce."

We read of a parallel situation in J. L. Toole's *Reminiscences*: "A version of *The Cricket on the Hearth* had been done, but it was not a success, and Boucicault suggested to me a more dramatic and ambitious version of the story, in which I consented to play, fearing at the same time that I was making a new departure that I might perhaps not justify. I read Dickens, and tried at home and while about in the streets to put myself in the position of Caleb. I think I succeeded in getting inside the part. I know I felt for the sufferings of the poor old chap, and did my best to make my audience feel them." That Toole also was successful in shifting to more serious comedy is shown by the review of *The Times* of April 16, 1862, which said, "Mr. Toole's Caleb Plummer is finished to the highest degree, with a greater depth of humour and pathos than, perhaps, this clever actor ever yet displayed." It may be bold to suggest, but it is certainly consistent with the theatrical judgment and perspicacity of Boucicault, that, by influencing these two great comedians of the period, he was partially responsible for the more realistic and serious tone of later nineteenth century comedy.

Another point of significance, and one typical of Boucicault's attitude toward the drama, was the introduction of a "sensation scene" in the production of this domestic comedy. The scene calls for what seems to have been an early use of the wagon stage. For a description of it, I quote again from the *Times* review. "The situation by which this jealousy (John Peerybingle's of Ned Plummer) is aroused is also contrived in a manner entirely novel. To show the part of the action that takes place in Caleb Plummer's room, his cottage is regularly built upon the stage, a wall being left open to show the interior, while the rest of the picture is filled with the farmyard and stable, covered with snow. When Tackleton would call the attention of John Peerybingle to the conduct of Dot with the stranger, the cottage, with all the personages in it, gradually slides to the side of the stage, leaving the courtyard in the middle, with John in frantic despair at the scene he witnesses in the building on the opposite side."

The original casts of both these productions show strong companies, famous in theatrical annals of the nineteenth century. The Winter Garden company included Harry Pearson as John Peerybingle, Joseph Jefferson as Caleb Plummer, A. H. Davenport as Edward Plummer, T. B. Johnstone as Tackleton, Miss Agnes Robertson as Dot, Mrs. John Wood as Tilly Slowboy, Miss Sara Stevens as Bertha, Mrs. W. R. Blake as Mrs. Fielding, and Mrs. J. H. Allen as May Fielding. A playbill of the Adelphi gives the London cast: S. Emery as John, J. L. Toole as Caleb, Billington as Ned, C. H. Stephenson as Tackleton, Miss Louise Keeley as Dot, Miss Woolgar (Mrs. Alfred

Mellon) as Tilly, Miss H. Simms as Bertha, Mrs. Marston as Mrs. Fielding, and Miss Latimer as May.

For those who may be interested in a production of this play, the musical numbers, taken from the same playbill, may be suggestive:

Dot—Overture—La Part du Diable—Auber.

1. Entr' acte—Le Tour du Monde—Set of Valses—O. Metra.

2. Entr' acte—The Cuckoo and the Cricket Polka—Herzog.

The manuscript which forms the basis of this edition is a prompt copy which had belonged to J. L. Toole, dated 1871, secured through the courtesy of Mr. Cyril Hogg, of Samuel French, Ltd., London. The manuscript has been collated with two other originals, both used in this country. The first is deposited in the New York Public Library, and is the more interesting because it includes notes in what I believe to be Boucicault's hand. If this assumption is correct, Boucicault added these notes from a manuscript similar to or identical with the Toole copy, perhaps his own original prompt copy. The second collated manuscript, from the William Seymour Collection at Princeton University, is one of a production at the Boston Museum; the date is unknown. Both of the American manuscripts show a rearrangement of scenes in the first act, and I have accepted that rearrangement for this edition. Although transposed, the scenes retain all of the original lines, with the addition of but two speeches to effect the transposition. My primary purpose has been to evolve from these three scripts the best reading and acting version of the play.

F. T. C.

CAST OF CHARACTERS

Characters in the Fairy Episode:

OBERON

TITANIA

ARIEL

PUCK

HOME

KETTLE

CRADLE

CRICKET

Characters in the Drama:

JOHN PEERYBINGLE
"Oh, Mother Nature! give thy children the true poetry of heart that hid itself in this poor carrier's breast."

CALEB PLUMMER
"A little, meagre, thoughtful, dingy-faced man; he seems to have made himself a great coat from a sack-cloth covering of some old box, for when he turned he disclosed upon his back the words, 'glass with care' in bold characters."

MR. TACKLETON
"The toy maker, he was a domestic ogre, who had been living on children all his life, and was their implacable enemy."

EDWARD PLUMMER

DOT
"Fair she was and young, though something of the dumpling shape. The Cricket, good gracious how it chirped."

TILLY SLOWBOY
"She was of a spare and straight shape, her garments drooping off her pegs of shoulders, and always in a state of gaping admiration at everything."

BERTHA
"Happy blind girl, how merry she was in her exultation."

MAY FIELDING

MRS. FIELDING

SYNOPSIS OF SCENES

ACT I. SCENE I. (PROLOGUE: THE FAIRY VISION) A WOOD.
      SCENE 2. DOT'S COTTAGE.

ACT II. SCENE I. THE OUTSKIRTS OF A VILLAGE.
      SCENE 2. CALEB PLUMMER'S ABODE. A POOR CHAMBER. THE FARMYARD AND
          STABLE.

ACT III. DOT'S COTTAGE.

ACT I.

TITANIA. The wind is cold, it bites me through and through,
   My rosy wings are frozen till they're blue.
   Oberon! why, Oberon! He comes, the lazy thing. [*Music. Enter Oberon R.U.E. carrying faggots*]
OBERON. [*R.C.*] Here's a condition for a fairy King.
   Reduced to gather faggots in the wood. [*Throws faggots off*]
   Where just two hundred years ago I stood
   The center of a fairy Court. My Duck,
   Where's Ariel? [*Music. Enter Ariel R.*]
ARIEL. [*R.*] Here, Master.
OBERON. [*C.*] And where's Puck? [*Music. Enter Puck L.*]
PUCK. [*L.*] Here!
OBERON. [*R.C.*] My faithful ones, sad remnant of the past,
   Of all the ancient fairies we're the last;
   For what these mortals call civilization,
   Has quite exterminated all our nation.
ARIEL. [*R.*] I always said that modern education
   Would be of fairy land the ruination.
PUCK. [*L.*] We've no more woods where we by night can roam;
   They have improved us out of house and home.
   We're not believed in.
ARIEL. To ride the tempest once I had the power;
   But tempests scare the mariner no more,
   He steams by preference against the gale,
   And says, a head wind blows his fires up well.
PUCK. In olden time I put a girdle round
   Earth in forty minutes; now they've found
   The time I took to fly was o'er plenty,
   By telegraph they do the job in twenty.
OBERON. The axe has felled the forest glades and now
   The woodland lies beneath the ruthless plow.

ARIEL. And worse than all, the meadows where we held
    Our fairy circles are with turnips filled.
PUCK. Our day has passed!
ARIEL. I fear our race is run.
OBERON. Is then the fairies' occupation gone? [*Music. Enter Home L.
knitting*]
HOME. [*C.*] Not quite, King Oberon, you're but dethroned.
    Your Kingdom by another monarch's owned.
OBERON. [*R.C.*] Pray, who are you?
HOME. [*C.*]   Queen of new fairyland.
    O'er all the household elves I hold command,
    My throne the chimney corner, my sceptre this.
    A knitting needle—emblem of cheerfulness.
    My name is Home. What ho! my merry elves!
    Come from your cozy nooks and shew yourselves!
    Kettle! [*Music. Kettle appears L.*]
    Cradle! [*Music. Cradle appears R.*]
    And now my little Cricket quick come forth;
    Leave for awhile your corner on the hearth. [*Music. The spirit of
the Cricket appears from tree*]
HOME. [*L.C.*] My Prince!
CRICKET. [*C.*] My Queen!
HOME. Behold the elfin band
    That rules the realms of modern fairyland.
OBERON. Oh, wretched hour!
    Has such a homely elf usurped my power?
PUCK. Oh, Shakespeare!
TITANIA. And, oh, Spencer!
OBERON. Can it be!
    Farewell, Romance; adieu, sweet Poetry!
HOME. Fairies no longer trip upon the green,
    But round the peasant's homestead we are seen.
    We dwell hard by within a peasant's cot,
    The guardian fairy of his wife, named Dot;
    The dearest, kindest, little thing that breathes.
    Wouldst see her home? [*Waves wand*]
    Come forest by your leaves. [*Music. The wood opens and discov-
ers Dot's cottage. Lower float*]

FIRST VISION

OBERON.   Lives Poetry beneath that humble shealing?
CRICKET.   'Tis not so low but that the most noble feeling
      Can stand upright in it.
HOME.   Within these walls, a nobleman of Nature's making dwells.
CRICKET.   He'd wear a coronet, if crowns were made
      To fit the heart of man, and not the head.
TITANIA.   Who can, to such a miserable thatch
      A feeling of romance or love attach?
HOME.   A little child around that cot once played;
      'Twas many years ago. Since then he strayed;
      Far over distant climes to roam. [*Music. Waves wand. The wood opens and discovers Edward Plummer asleep on the mast of a ship. Lower float*]

SECOND VISION

HOME.   Behold him now; the ship boy dreams of home.
OBERON.   A lovely scene that home must surely be
      That thus enchains his sleeping spirit. [*Music*]
HOME.   See! [*Waves wand. The wood opens and discovers the interior of John Peerybingle's cottage. John, Dot, and Tilly taking tea*]

THIRD VISION

HOME.   For all the palaces of Greece and Rome
      He would not change that humble, happy home.
      See Dot! and John! and Tilly at their tea
      Talk of poor Ned that ran away to sea.
      Those thoughts and messages we fairies take,
      And so to distant hearts communicate.
      Visions away! [*Music. Wood closes*]
OBERON.   Romance and poetry
      Belong to noble hearts, not to peasantry.
HOME.   That is one of your old, exploded follies
      That Grace's heart was finer made than Molly's.
      Listen! John Peerybingle, though advanced in life,
      Has got a young and very pretty wife,
      Called Dot.
TITANIA. [*L.*]   Othello o'er again.

HOME.   [*Crossing to L.*]   The same.
    We'll play the very tragedy you name
    Upon this vulgar hind.
TITANIA.   [*Crossing to R.*]   And then we'll see
    Who shows the nobler heart, the Moor or he.
OBERON.   Agreed! Come on, as Shakespeare used to say,
    "My soul's in arms, and eager for the fray."
HOME.   [*Up C.*]   Then follow me; over the wood we go,
    And light upon Dot's cottage in the snow.
    Then down the chimney from whence issuing forth
    We'll form our fairy circle on the hearth. [*Music*]

CHORUS

Over the forest, over the lea,
    Through the air we glide,
Over the moonlit silver sea,
    Floating along the tide.

Fairies come, no longer stay,
    Moonlight is our fairy day;
Over the forest, over the lea,
    Through the air we glide.

[*All the Fairies exit L.1. and 2.E. singing the chorus till it dies away gradually. Change scene. Lights full up*]

SCENE 2: *Dot's cottage. Music. Enter Dot R.2.E. with a kettle, and her kirtle
thrown over her head.*

DOT.   [*C.*]   There I lost my pattens in the mud, and splashed my stockings,
too.—But where's Tilly and the baby? Why they haven't both got into the
cradle, have they? No. [*Calls*] Tilly! Tilly! [*Music. Enter Tilly carrying
baby. R. door*]

TILLY.   Yes, mums, here I be's. [*Crosses to L.*]

DOT.   [*At table*]   Here, help to set the table. John will be home 'ere his
supper's ready. Put the kettle on the fire, while I lay the tea. Handy now,
handy!

TILLY.   Ees, mums! [*Goes to fire for kettle, shifts the baby from one arm
to the other awkwardly. Takes kettle*]

DOT.   Then toast the bacon, Tilly. Come, quick, lass.

TILLY.   Ees, mums! [*Runs to flitch of bacon L. gets bewildered between
bacon, kettle, and baby*]

Dot. Why put the child to bed, you goose, and the kettle on the fire.

Tilly. Oh, ees, mums. [*Runs down. Puts kettle in cradle L. and is going with child to fire*]

Dot. Oh! My gracious, Tilly! [*Snatches child*] You horrid thing! She was going to boil the child.

Tilly. No, mums. [*Goes to cradle L. and rocks it*]

Dot. And now she be a-rocking the kettle. The lass be crazy sure. [*Takes kettle out*]

Tilly. Ow! ow! ow! [*Cries*] Oh, mums, please don't scold. I couldn't help it. Ow! ow!

Dot. Oh, don't cry, dear Tilly. There, take the baby. It ain't your fault if you've got no brains in your head.

Tilly. No, mums.

Dot. Well then, don't stir now; let me work.

Tilly. [*L. to child*] Was its Tilly going to boil a precious dear? [*Music. Enter May Fielding L. door*]

May. [*L.*] Dot.

Dot. [*R.*] May Fielding, come in—wha-what's the matter coom t'ye?— Ye are as pale as a potato cake.

May. Are we alone, Dot? Oh, I have dreadful news. I hope you won't despise me for what I've done.

Dot. What's the matter?

May. How many years ago was it since poor Ned went to sea?

Dot. [*R.*] It's just four years this Christmas, when old Caleb, his father, was took for debt. My John lent the money to get him out of prison; and he stood on yonder hearth, and swore he'd never rest till he'd paid my John back, and us could not persuade him agin it. So he went aboard ship in search of fortin in the Golden South Americas. Poor Ned! He was a wild fellow, worn't he? And when the news came home that his vessel and all aboard was lost—

Tilly. Oh!

May. He is dead, Dot. [*Crosses to R.*] And I wish I were dead beside him.

Dot. What's the matter?

May. My mother has incurred a debt much larger than we can pay. The man to whom this debt is due is rich, and—and—

Dot. And wants a wife?

May. Y—yes.

Dot. Well, tell him you're not for sale.

MAY. Dot, were I sure that Ned was drowned and lost to me for ever, I had rather marry a man that I could not love.

DOT. [*Going to table*] If I were you, I'd rather be the widow of Ned's memory than Queen of England, and I'd give no man the right to take his last kiss off my lips, his lock of hair out of my breast, his image from my heart, and his own beautiful, dear, dear letters from under my pillow. Them's my sentiments. [*At table*]

MAY. Oh, Dot, Dot, you break my heart. [*Weeps*]

TILLY. [*L.*] Ow! ow! mums, ow! don't breaks her hearts. I couldn't abear to see it. Ow! ow!

DOT. Hold your tongue, you big fool. [*Music*]

TILLY. [*Gulping down her tears*] Ees, mums. [*Distant harness bells heard and barking of dog*]

DOT. [*Crosses to door L.C.*] Hark! There's Boxer's yelp. I hear the cart wheel. John is coming. Dry your eyes, May, and let us tell him all.

MAY. No, no, I couldn't meet his face. I will run out the back way.

JOHN. [*Outside*] Whoa! Down, Boxer!

MAY [*R.*] Good-bye, Dot, good-bye. [*Music forte. Exit May R. Enter John L.*]

JOHN [*Speaking off*] Wo, woho! quiet! Ha, where's my fairy wife? [*Music stops*] Where's my Dot? Where's my little corner of heaven broke off and fallen down on this earth to shew what up there's made of?

DOT. [*R.*] Ha' done, John. [*She takes his coat, hat and whip*]

JOHN. [*L.*] I won't; I can't; how can I help going on? Why, as my old cart rolls along the road, and Boxer racin' ahead afore me, the old dog runs into every cottage door, and out he flies again followed by all the population, cryin', "How are ye, John? How's Dot? God bless her, how's our little Dot?" And the children climb into the cart and ask for you; and the minister stops by the wayside and greets me with, "A fine day, John. How's the little wife, God bless her?" It's like a music played afore and around me.

TILLY. [*L. Taking child from cradle*] Did its fathers comes homes, and never notice his precious? No!

JOHN. [*L.C.*] What, Tilly and the little pip? Let's look at him.

DOT. Hush, he's asleep. Ain't he nice? Don't he look as you could eat him up every bit?

JOHN. [*Takes child*] He ain't more'n a mouthfull, is he? He, he! Hollo!

DOT. What?

JOHN. He's opened his eyes, and he's turning 'em up awful. That ain't right, is it? And now he's gasping like a gold and silver fish. [*Lets go child*] I ain't hurt him, have I?

DOT. [*Taking child*] You don't deserve to be a father. [*Gives child to Tilly and crosses to R.*]

JOHN. Well, when I look at that mite of a thing, I feel like an elephant that's found himself the father of a canary. [*Crosses to C.*]

DOT. [*Crosses to L.*] Here, Tilly, take the baby, and don't let him fall under the grate whatever you do.

TILLY. I'll try, mums.

DOT. [*Up to table and down R.*] Now, John, sit down to your supper, all's ready. There's the tea, [*pours it out*] and the fresh loaf, and the eggs and ham, and [*Cricket chirps*]—Listen! There's the cricket, too. D'ye hear?

JOHN. Our little cricket is merrier than usual tonight, ain't he? [*Eating*]

DOT. He and I sing together many a time, and I do think it knows my voice a little. What parcels have we? What's this, John? Why, it's a wedding cake.

JOHN. [*Seated*] Leave a woman alone to find out that. I do believe if you was to pack a wedding cake in a pickled oyster barrel or a turn-up bedstead, a woman would smell it out.

DOT. [*R.C.*] A wedding here? Whose is it?

TILLY. [*L.*] Oh, don't I wish it was mine.

JOHN. Your wedding!

TILLY. [*Grinning*] Noa, my cake.

DOT. Stay, here's a direction. What! Tackleton! Old Caleb's master! Tackleton at the toy shop!

JOHN. [*At table R.*] Ees. I got it at the pastry cook's, and I've been thinking all the way home who it is he be agoin' to marry. I've scratched a hole in my head a-thinking. There's no single girl here about; it can't be Mrs. Bixer, she's bedrid; nor Bertha, Caleb's blind girl; nor old widow Fielding, May's mother.

DOT. [*R.*] Ah! [*Utters a cry of horror and drops the cake*]

TILLY. [*L.*] Ow! [*Utters a cry of fright and drops the baby*]

JOHN. [*Down C.*] Dot! Tilly! What's the matter?

DOT. Nothing, John, nothing. I dropped the cake. [*Laughs*] It ain't hurt though, not a bit.

TILLY. [*Having picked up baby*] Not a bits; it's a massy it fell on its head.

DOT. [*Aside*] It's old Tackleton that May Fielding's going to marry.

TILLY. [*To baby*] Was it old Tackletons, the toy makers, den, and did it call at pastry cook's for wedding cakes, and farders brought 'em homes?

JOHN. [*Going to fire*] Why, hello! I've clean forgotten the old gentleman.

DOT. [*R.*] The old gentleman?

JOHN. In the cart.

TILLY. [*L.*] Oh, don't let him come in, please. Oh, mums! It ain't the old gentleman with the tail and horns, mum, is it?

JOHN. [*Opens L. door and calls*] Hoy, sir! He's as deaf as a codfish. Hoy! This way, sir. [*Music. Enter Edward L.D. disguised*]

JOHN. [*R.C.*] He can't hear a word. I found him seated by the wayside; he hailed me; I took him up, and there he be.

EDWARD. [*L.C.*] Put me with the other goods to be left till called for.

DOT. [*C.*] Poor old man!

EDWARD. [*Aside*] 'Tis she, my own little Dot. This disguise succeeds; she does not recognize me. [*Aloud*] Your daughter, my good friend?

JOHN. No, wife.

EDWARD. Oh, your niece.

JOHN. [*Taking his arm*] No, my wife.

EDWARD. Oh, indeed, sure—rather young. Um, baby yours? [*John nods*] Girl?

DOT. [*C.*] No, boy!

EDWARD. [*L.*] Ah, I thought so. Very fine little girl.

DOT. [*C.*] B-o-o-y! The idea of taking our baby for a girl.

JOHN. Why, Dot, here be old Caleb Plummer out in the snow.

EDWARD. [*At fire—aside*] My father!

JOHN. Come in, man, come in. [*Music. Enter Caleb*]

CALEB. [*L.C.*] Good evening, mum. Good evening, unbeknown. Good evening, baby, how d'ye do? Boxer's pretty well, I hope?

JOHN. [*R.C.*] All thriving, Caleb. Sit down beside the fire and warm yourself; it's a bitter night.

EDWARD. [*Aside. L. of table*] My poor, old father! Oh, how changed!

CALEB. [*L.C.*] Thank ye, John, no; I'd rather not go near the fire, it makes me want it, yer know, and I can't afford to have a fire at home every day.

EDWARD. [*Aside*] What do I hear?

TILLY. [*Hearing Edward groan*] I think the old gentleman is got wrong insides, mum.

CALEB. Have you got anything for me in the parcel line?

JOHN. A small box. Here you are.

CALEB. [*Reading*] For Caleb Plummer with—with cash. Eh, with cash, John? I don't think it's for me.

JOHN. [*R. pointing*] With care. Where do you make out cash? [*Puts his spectacles right*]

CALEB. [*C.*] Eh? So it is—with care. Yes, my eyes ain't as good as they used to be. Ah, if my dear boy that went away to the Golden South Americas had lived, it might have been with cash, too.

EDWARD. [*L. aside*] His son! He speaks of me.

CALEB. [*L.C.*] My poor Ned. My merry, noble-hearted boy. You loved him like a son, didn't you? You needn't say you did. I know when he left us, I was doing a thriving little business in the toy shop line, but since his—his death, my business fell off; perhaps I fell off just; but down, down, down, I went, like my poor son sinking in the sea, and here I am at the bottom, like my dear boy.

EDWARD. [*Aside*] I can't contain myself much longer.

TILLY. [*Watching him*] He's broke something inside. [*Takes baby*]

CALEB. [*Reads*] Caleb Plummer, with care. Yes, it's a box of doll's eyes; this is for my poor, blind, daughter's work.

EDWARD. [*Aside*] My sister blind!

CALEB. I wish it was her own sight in a box that you had brought me, John.

JOHN. [*R.C.*] I wish it was.

CALEB. [*C.*] Thank ye, you speak very hearty. To think that she can never see the dolls, and them staring at her all day—the lifeless bits of wood that look at her so steady, and she with her blinded eyes before 'em; that's when it cuts, Dot, don't it? Well, what's to pay, John? What's the damage?

JOHN. [*R.C.*] I'll damage you if you enquire. Stop, Caleb, here's a little flower I bought for Bertha.

CALEB. You're very kind. Bertha's very fond of flowers. Anything else, John?

JOHN. Here's something for your employer, old Tackleton.

CALEB. [*C.*] He isn't a pleasant man, is he, John? Although he does sell toys, 'pon my word I think he always likes to sell those that make children uncomfortable—ogres, with jaws, and devils all over hair, and jack-in-the-boxes. Oh, he loves 'em! He revels in what's ugly! [*Edward goes back to fire*]

JOHN. Don't forget, Caleb, that tomorrow is Christmas Eve, and Dot and I and Tilly and the baby is coming over to spend the evening with you and Bertha. It's my wedding day! And we'll bring a few eatables, so you needn't get nought ready. And the next day being Christmas, you'll dine with us, won't ye? That's right! [*Goes to fire*]

CALEB. Thank ye, John.

DOT. [*R.C. at table*] Are you busy just now, Caleb?

CALEB. Pretty well, mum; it's a good time of the year for the toy business. There's rather a run on Noah's Arks just at present. I wish I could improve Noah's family, but I don't see how it's to be done at the price. It goes agin my conscience to make sheeps and elephants and flies all of one size. Well, I must be going. [*Returns*] Bye the bye, you couldn't have the goodness to let me pinch Boxer's tail, mum, for half a moment, could you?

DOT. [*R.*] Why, Caleb, what for?

CALEB. Oh, never mind, mum, p'raps he mightn't like it. But there's a small order for barking dogs just come in, and I'd like to go as near nature as I could for sixpence, that's all. But never mind, mum; good night, thank ye. [*Music. Going out is met by Tackleton. Enter Tackleton down C.*]

TACK. Oh, here you are, are you?

JOHN. Mr. Tackleton.

TACK. [*C.*] Don't say you're glad to see me now, because you're not, you know.

JOHN. Well, I won't.

TACK. [*L.C.*] I suppose you've heard the news, eh? You smelt a rat in the wedding cake, eh?

DOT. I think a rat would have more business in one than you.

TACK. He! he! very good! Your little wife is honest, ain't she? Speaks her mind straight out. I like it, I do. Well, next Thursday is your wedding day.

JOHN. One year ago I married Dot.

TACK. On that day I shall marry May Fielding.

EDWARD. [*Rising L.*] How!

DOT. [*R. up stage*] I knew it!

TILLY. [*L. corner*] He's broke out!

CALEB. [*L.C.*] May, our May Fielding, your wife!

TACK. [*C.*] D'ye think the girl is going to snivel over your son all her life?

CALEB. [*L.*] Poor May; my Ned loved her so well.

TACK. Why, one would think the girl was going to the county jail instead of the church. She has forgotten your son.

DOT. She'll begin to remember him from this time out. [*Exit D.R.H.*]

TACK. I want you to spend the day with us. You and your wife have a comfortable sort of look that makes marriage seem agreeable—of course, you have your little, homely rows when nobody's by.

JOHN. What are you talking about? [*Re-enter Dot R.3.E.*]

TACK. I want your wife to praise up married life and all that sort of thing; tell May that next Thursday is to be the happiest day of her life; you know, that'll make her believe it.

DOT. [*R.C.*] You mean to say she don't believe it, then?

TACK. Oh, that's all nonsense, you know; love is only the gilt and paint on marriage, it all comes off with a little handling; it's only a toy.

DOT. [*Crosses to child. Crosses to L.*] That ain't no toy; handling won't rub that out. Well, that's like love after marriage. If it's love of the right sort, it grows and grows, until in old age it becomes the prop and stay of life. [*Crosses to John*]

TILLY. [*L.*] It won't be rubbed out, a precious, no it shan't. It shall be a prop, it shall, and a pair of stays, too. Ketcher, ketcher, ketcher!

JOHN. [*R. corner*] Don't mistake, Mr. Tackleton, it isn't every man that has a house who can bring his wife to a home.

TACK. Bah! What's a home? [*The Cricket chirps*] Four walls and a ceiling. [*Cricket chirps*] Why don't you kill that cricket; I would. I always do. I hate their noise. [*L. corner*]

JOHN. Oh, you kill your crickets, do you?

TACK. I scrunch 'em, scrunch 'em. Pooh! Romance and feeling and sentimental stuff; it's all well enough in story books, but look at your own case. You're young, you know, quite a child, and John is nearly old enough to be your father.

JOHN. Quite old enough. She's eighteen, and I'm more than double that.

TACK. Well, you liked him well enough at first, and now you honor and obey, and all that sort of thing, but you don't pretend there's anything more in it.

DOT. [*Crossing Tackleton*] I think my John would chuck any man out of the window who said there wasn't.

CALEB. Don't you think we'd better go, sir?

TACK. [*Helps cake on Caleb's shoulder*] Exactly—of course—come, Caleb.

JOHN. Stay, sir. Here's an old gentleman that would like to be set down at the village inn, I suppose. Would yer mind giving him a lift? [*Music*]

EDWARD. [*Aside*] No, I must remain here—I must take Dot into my secret. [*To Dot*] Dot, dear.

DOT. [*Starting*] Ah!

EDWARD. Hush! Don't you know me? 'Tis I, Ned Plummer. [*Raises his wig and discovers his face. Dot screams and totters forward. Tilly howls and falls R.H.*]

JOHN. [*Catching Dot in his arms*] Eh! what coom! Dot, my darling, speak, what is it? Are you ill? [*Edward replaces wig and sits by fire*]

DOT. No! no, it can't be, but it is. He! he! he! I'm dreaming, surely. No, 'tis he. Ha! ha! ha! [*Claps her hands and laughs*]

JOHN. What's this?

TACK. She's mad! Is she often took like this?

DOT. I'm better, John, it was nothing—it was a shock that old gentleman —something—I don't know what it was, but it's gone, quite gone.

TACK. Oh, is it? I'm glad it's gone. I wonder where it's gone to? Caleb, who's that with the gray hair?

CALEB. [*L.C.*] I don't know, sir, but I've been studying him this last half-hour. What a beautiful figure for a nut-cracker, quite a new model; or a great mogul with a screw jaw opening down into his waistcoat. He'd be lovely.

TACK. Not ugly enough for a great mogul.

CALEB. Or a fire-box! You might unscrew his head to put the matches in, and turn him heels up'ards for a light. He'd be lovely for a gent's mantelpiece what smokes cigars.

TACK. Not half ugly enough—nothing in him at all. Come, we must be moving. [*To Dot*] All right now, I hope.

DOT. Yes—yes—good night.

JOHN. Stay, I must rouse up this old fellow.

DOT. John, don't turn the poor old man out on such a night. I'll make up a bed for him.

JOHN. Very well. Put him down beside the fire to toast his old toes, while I go out to unharness Dobbin, and give him a feed.

TACK. She is very anxious about the old idiot. If he was a young man, eh, we might understand.

JOHN. Understand what?

CALEB. We'd better go, sir.

TACK. Oh, nothing. Come, Caleb, take care how you carry that box—let it fall, and I'll murder you. [*Music*] Good night! Eh, call this a good night? —black as pitch, and weather worse than ever. [*Exit L.D.*]

CALEB. Good night, John, we shall expect you to spend the day with us tomorrow, recollect.

TACK. [*Outside*] Here, are you coming or not? [*Exit Caleb and John L.D. Dot watches them off*]

DOT. Come, Tilly, bustle now, go and draw a jug of ale. I'll mind the baby.

TILLY. Ees, mums. [*Exit R. Edward jumps up, runs to window, looks after John*]

EDWARD. [*Throws off his coat*] Don't you know me, Dot? [*Pulls off his long wig and appears in his sailor's dress*] Don't you know me now?

DOT. It is! no, it isn't! It can't be! Yes, it is! Ned!

EDWARD. [*R.*] Yes, Dot, your own dear Ned. Your own Ned come back.

DOT. [*Embracing*] Ah! so it is; so it is. Oh, Ned! Ned, how could you keep away so long and let us think you dead and gone?

EDWARD. I was wrecked and cast away upon a shore seldom visited by our ships. There I lived among savages. After a long time, I accomplished my sole purpose, for I escaped. I made my way to the Spanish Main.

DOT. [*L.*] And you never forgot May Fielding?

EDWARD. Never, Dot, never. As I lay rocking on the maintop crosstrees, or swinging in the hammock of my Indian hut, the form of May Fielding followed me. At length I got back to English soil, and was hastening home, when what did I hear at the market town below? why that the banns for May Fielding's wedding was on the church door. Then I bought this disguise so that I might see with my own eyes what my heart refused to believe. [*Crosses to R.*]

DOT. And thy heart is right, Ned. May loves your memory better than all the living men in the world.

EDWARD. And the story of her going to be married is not true?

DOT. Well, not exactly, but I must tell you—

EDWARD. [*R.*] To whom? To whom?

DOT. [*L.*] I don't know, and all I do know is she was here not half an hour ago, crying her eyes out, and saying she'd rather be dead beside you than the wife of a king.

EDWARD. She did? Oh, Dot, is it so? Oh, let me be sure of that; let me see it, hear it, know it.

DOT. You shall. But let me call in John. He will be so happy to see you. [*Going to door L.*]

EDWARD. [*Stops her*] No, Dot, John is too honest, too clumsy to keep my secret as it must be kept. And you will promise me that you will not betray it to May Fielding until I prove that her heart is the same as I left it? If you refuse me, I'm off to sea again.

DOT. Don't ask me to have a secret from John.

EDWARD. Only for one day, Dot, and for my heart's sake. [*Dog barks without*]

JOHN. [*Without*] Down, Boxer; down, sir!

DOT. Here comes John. Quick, then, put on that horrid wig and coat.

EDWARD. Lord bless me, I feel fit to jump out of my skin.

DOT. Here comes John; quick, put on your wig. [*Runs to door*]

EDWARD. Fol de rol! [*Puts on wig*] She is my own May after all, and we shall all be happy again. We shall all be—fol de rol de rol! [*Dances. Enter Tilly who stops astonished. Comes slowly forward and looks at him. Edward stops suddenly*]

TILLY. He broke out in a fresh place.

EDWARD. [*To Tilly*] Boo!

TILLY. [*Starting*]   St. Vitus in his legs. [*Enter John L.D.*]

DOT.   Come, I'll show this old man to his room. Tilly, you stop here and mind the baby. [*Takes a light*] Come! [*Exit Dot and Edward R. Lights down*]

JOHN. [*Looking after her*]   Bless her, how kind-hearted she is. And to think that young thing loves me; me, old enough to be her father. I don't know how it is, but the words of that old Tackleton do somehow worry at my throat. I wonder if she wishes me a little younger sometimes.

TILLY.   Did its moders and the old gentlemans dance, then? And was its hair brown and curly under its old, gray wig?

JOHN.   What are you talking about? [*Re-enter Dot*]

DOT.   There—ah! I'm so glad he's sleeping under our roof. [*Aloud*] Oh, John, I feel so happy tonight, so happy.

JOHN.   Are you? Then, so am I. And d'ye never think that I'm so much older than you?

DOT.   Yes; and that makes me feel I'm such a useless, little thing; and when I look into the fire, and think so, the cricket says to me, "I'm little, Dot; your baby is little; and so are you, Dot. Cheer up, cheer up." Oh! this is a happy tune for me, and I love the cricket for its sake. [*Cricket chirps*]

JOHN.   D'ye hear him? Come, Dot, fill my pipe, and sit there beside me. And you, there, Tilly, and baby.

DOT. [*Sitting at his feet and filling his pipe*]   When you brought me home a year ago, the first voice I heard was that of the cricket on the hearth.

JOHN.   It was glad to see you.

DOT.   I love it for the many times I've heard it. [*Cricket chirps*] And the good things its harmless music has put into my heart. Sometimes in the winter twilight, when you were away with the cart, and I was alone, for baby wasn't here then, John, I felt so sad. But then the cricket would cry, "Cheer up, cheer up, Dot, he's coming; John's coming. Cheer up, little one, here he comes." And you did come. [*Cricket*] Hark! It hears me. Oh, John, it's a good thing to have a cricket on the hearth. [*They sleep. The stage grows gradually dark. The room is lighted by the glow of the fire. Music. The back of the chimney opens, and discovers fairies, etc.*]

CRICKET.   "I love it for the many times I've heard it; and the sweet music it has put into my heart."

Sleep on, sweet Dot. Sleep, gentle, little wife.

The cricket watches over you through life. [*Scene opens. Lime light on chorus. Ring. Fairies repeat chorus. Curtain*]

ACT II.

Scene 1: *The outskirts of a village. Music for rise of curtain. Lights one-half down. Enter Tackleton followed by Mrs. Fielding R.U.E.*

TACK. [*L.*] Your observations ma'am, are like yourself, admirable.

MRS. F. [*R.*] Mr. Tackleton, you are about to enter into a family, which, though I say it that perhaps oughtn't, still I will say, sir, can look back; and have always looked back.

TACK. Hear! hear!

MRS. F. To the time, perhaps, when we had liveries of our own—

TACK. [*Aside*] Wore 'em, perhaps.

MRS. F. And when we rode in a carriage. I might refer to those matters, but I won't; and I might say that a certain calamity, not unconnected with the indigo trade—

TACK. [*Aside*] If she gets into the indigo trade, she never gets out again.

MRS. F. But no, these are subjects too painful to contemplate.

TACK. Yes, ma'am, much; don't let us talk of 'em.

MRS. F. I cannot give you a fortune with my daughter, May.

TACK. Quite the contrary, ma'am. I hold a little note of yours, which, when I receive your daughter's hand, I propose to hand you over the counter —I mean the altar.

MRS. F. Here comes my sweet child.

TACK. She does not look as if tomorrow was going to be the happiest day of her life. I hope that sort of thing ain't going to last.

MRS. F. Mr. Tackleton, you understand toys, wooden things, but the delicate organization of woman's sensibilities, and women, who, like my daughter, can look back—

TACK. That's what I object to, ma'am. For when your daughter looks back, she sees an infernal sailor chap who interferes with the view of what I want her to see. [*Music. Enter May dejected R.*]

MRS. F. My dear child, why are you so sad?

MAY. [*R.*] I am on a sad errand, mother. I am going to see Caleb and Bertha to tell them I have given up all hope of Ned's return, and to bid them farewell.

TACK. What pleasure can you find in the society of that old fool and his blind daughter?

MAY. Oh, could you hear the gratitude, the enthusiasm, with which Bertha speaks of you. She attributes to you the comforts of their home.

TACK. Comforts! It's a worthless shed I rented to Caleb to save him from the almshouse.

MAY. She does not know how poor they are. When she lost her sight, Caleb was well off, and surrounded with comforts. She remains ignorant of his ruin, and he makes her believe that their miserable abode is a neat cottage, and their life is what it was.

MRS. F. [C.] How very improper! The man's existence is a panorama of lies.

TACK. [L.] That's what I say. He could save a decent living if he only had himself to support. Why don't he put the girl in the asylum? [Dog barks]

JOHN. [Outside] Woho! hie, Boxer, ho!

TACK. 'Tis John Peerybingle and his family. They are going to Caleb's. I must get there first. Mrs. Fielding, if you will condescend to join our little party at Caleb's, we shall all feel it an honor. There will be a small supper to which we each bring a mite. Say yes. Very well, we expect you. [Kisses May's passive hand. Aside] Not a look; obstinant as the devil. Wait till we're married. [Exit L.]

MAY. Oh, mother, mother! Must I indeed be that man's wife? Is there no help, no alternative?

MRS. F. My dear, don't forget yourself; think of your family. Look back!

MAY. [R.] No, no! To look back breaks my heart, and to look forward fills me with horror.

MRS. F. [L.] Horror, my dear! Control yourself. [Music. Enter John and Dot R.]

JOHN. What, May! And old Mrs. Indigo, as I'm a sinner.

DOT. [Looking off R.] Oh, look at Tilly; she can't get down out of the cart.

JOHN. [Speaks off R.] Hello, Tilly, why don't you get down?

TILLY. [Outside R.] I can't, please, the cart is too high, and my legs is too short. [Exit John laughing R.]

DOT. [R.] Why, go and help her, do. [To May aside] Let John and the old lady go on first, I want ye. D'ye see yon old man?

MAY. [L.] Just alighted from your cart?

DOT. [Aside to her] He has just come from furrin parts. He knew Ned.

MAY. Ned!

DOT. Hush! [Tilly screams then enters with baby]

TILLY. Ow, if you please, mums, that old gentleman is after this precious baby.

DOT. Nonsense!

TILLY. Well, mums, it's either me or the baby, for he's been a-pinchin' both of us all the ways along. Ow! 'Ere he comes! [*Edges off to L. Enter John and Edward disguised*]

JOHN. [*Laughing*] Why the gal be afeared that the deaf old man be the devil coom to take her away.

TILLY. [*L. Aside and feeling*] He's got several pieces of me already.

JOHN. [*R.*] Coom, let's jog on, Mrs. Indi— I would say, Mrs. Fielding; take my arm. We're not far off a pair, are we? He, he! [*Crosses to Mrs. F.*]

MRS. F. Ah! You are just the height of my poor husband who died shortly after that calamity, to which I won't refer, but may observe that it wasn't unconnected with the crisis in the indigo—

JOHN. Exactly, ma'am, I was there at the time. [*Exit John and Mrs. F. L.*]

MAY. How strangely he regards me.

TILLY. [*L.*] Don't let him coom within pinchin' distance, don't.

DOT. [*C.*] May, what do you think yon old man's brought you? Heart alive, lass, don't faint.

MAY. Speak, what is it?

DOT. [*R.*] A letter.

MAY. [*C.*] From him? From Edward?

EDWARD. [*Aside*] She trembles like the ague. Oh, she loves me!

DOT. Bear up, May. Yes, from him, writ many years ago. The last he writ before his death, if indeed he be dead.

MAY. Give it me, give it quick. [*Dot hands letter to May and makes signs to Edward*] Yes, 'tis his, his own. [*Kisses the letter passionately and crosses to R. Edward, delighted, cuts a caper. Dot tries to repress him. Tilly stares in wonder*]

MAY. [*Reads. Letter written*] "My own sweet May. I write these lines to let you know I'm well, and that my love for you is as deep as the deep sea beneath me." Dear, dear, Ned. [*Edward is going to embrace her and is stopped by Dot*]

TILLY. [*Aside*] He's got a fresh pinchin' fit on.

MAY. [*R. corner reads*] "Whatever betide, never despair. But if death overhaul me, why then, May, when you come to love another, and why should you not, then give to Dot my letters and the lock of hair I gave you at parting; they might only cause you regret to look on, and I would not cross the path of your happiness with a single cloud. God bless you. Your lover, Ned."

Dot. [*Crosses to May*] May, dear, is your mind made up? Shall I ax ye for that letter and the lock of poor Ned's hair?

May. This letter and this. [*Draws locket from bosom*] My Ned, my own! [*Kisses locket. Crosses to R. Ready to change lights down*]

Edward. [*C.*] Will she fail me?

Dot. [*R.C.*] Coom, lass, give it back to me. What does Tackleton's wife want with a lock of Ned Plummer's hair on her breast? Give it me.

May. [*R.*] Dot, I—I can't—I can't.

Dot. Oh, May, dear! [*Embraces her*]

Edward. She can't! Ha! ha! It's all right! Huzza! [*Edward embraces Tilly*]

Tilly. [*Struggles from him*] Ow! If you please, don't! Ow! [*Tilly's bonnet gets turned sideways on her head*]

Dot. Coom, lass; coom, May, let's get on to Caleb's and cheer up. [*Crosses to L.*]

May. Oh, Dot, what can I do? Have I any alternative?

Dot. Ees, you can do what's right and what's wrong. Take your choice, and I'll help you. [*Music. They go out L. Edward follows them to the side, expresses his delight and love. Tilly, afraid, but desirous to pass him, hovers round behind him. He turns and makes a move toward her. Very frightened, she avoids him, and at last makes her escape followed by Edward. Scene changes. Wait for characters to get round to back. Lights down at change*]

SCENE 2: *Caleb Plummer's abode. A poor chamber. Music. Lights down to blue in front. When Caleb lights second candle run up two front wing ladders and turn up front very slowly. Snow falls as scene opens. Two candles. Lime light.*

Caleb. [*R. Singing as he holds up a baby horse*] There we are, as near the real thing as I can get it. I must hurry, or John and Dot will arrive before my work is done. [*Music. Enter Bertha L.D.*]

Bertha. Father, I have dressed myself in my best to welcome John and Dot. How do I look?

Caleb. You look like an angel in brown merino.

Bertha. [*L.*] Is our room as tidy as usual? [*Crosses to chair*]

Caleb. Oh, beautiful! homely, you know, Bertha, but snug.

Bertha. The walls are hung with blue, ain't they?

Caleb. Yes, you can scarce see 'em for the pictures.

Bertha. I remember the portrait of my dear brother, Ned, is over the mantelpiece.

CALEB. Y—yes. There is a general cheerfulness and neatness in the building that makes it very pretty.

BERTHA. [*C.*] I hope the rain last night did not hurt your new blue coat.

CALEB. [*R.*] Not a bit. No, but I'm half ashamed to wear it; 'pon my word I'm such a swell.

BERTHA. I can see you, father, as plain as if I had the eyes you gave me— a blue coat, is it not?

CALEB. Yes, bright blue.

BERTHA. The color I can just remember in the blessed sky.

CALEB. And brass buttons.

BERTHA. Oh, I remember your round, merry face and laughing eyes, and dark brown, curly hair. Your figure rather stout, you know.

CALEB. Middling, my dear. [*Rises and places her a stool*]

BERTHA. But so active, light, and handsome.

CALEB. Hollo! Hollo! I shall be vain directly.

BERTHA. Oh, you must not think that I forget you. But I am idling, I must get to my work. [*Sits at R. of table and works. Business of needle and thread*]

CALEB. [*Aside*] Poor child, she lives in a world that I have made for her. She little dreams of the wretchedness around her. Thank heaven that suffering has been all for me. She has her own affliction to bear; that's enough— too much—too much.

BERTHA. [*Seated R.*] You are speaking softly, father. Are you tired?

CALEB. Tired! What could tire me, hearty and strong as I am? [*Sings*]

TACK. [*Outside, speaking through the singing*] Hollo! You, Caleb!

BERTHA [*L.*] Hark! 'tis Mr. Tackleton's voice, our dear, kind master.

CALEB. [*R.*] Yes, so kind, yet with so rough a manner; you know, a rough diamond, eh, Bertha?

BERTHA. [*Seated R.*] Yes, I know. But why does he conceal his generous and kind nature under so rude a manner?

CALEB. It's his joke. While he speaks so harsh, he is winking at me all the time; he's such a man to joke, but so kind at heart. [*Aside*] And if she only knew the brute he is. [*Sings. Enter Tackleton C.D.*]

TACK. [*C. Bertha gets R. during this speech*] What? you are singing, are you? Go it! I can't sing. I wouldn't if I had the voice. [*Crosses to L. corner*]

CALEB. [*Aside to Bertha R.*] If you could only see him, how he's winking at me. Such a man to joke. You'd think, if you didn't know him, that he behaved like a brute to me, wouldn't you?

BERTHA. [*C. Laughing*] Yes, but I know him.

CALEB. [*At back of table R.*]   Yes, eh? [*Aside*] Heaven forgive me.

BERTHA.   Always merry and light-hearted with us, Mr. Tackleton.

TACK. [*L. corner*]   Oh, you're there, are you? Poor idiot! Well, being there, how are you?

BERTHA. [*C.*]   Quite well, and as happy as your kind heart could wish me. [*Rises*]

TACK.   She's a lunatic, a confirmed lunatic.

BERTHA. [*C.*]   You sent me a little rose tree yesterday.

TACK. [*L.*]   The devil I did!

CALEB. [*R. Aside*]   Oh, dear, I shall be found out.

BERTHA.   I placed it in my window that it might see the sun, and this morning when I woke, I heard its voice, for its odor is its voice to me. Its song filled all the room.

TACK.   Bedlam broke loose. She'll want a straight waistcoat before long.

CALEB. [*Aside to Bertha*]   The extent to which he's winking at this moment! Oh, my gracious!

BERTHA. [*Crosses to Tack. L.*]   Ah! [*Takes Tackleton's hand, raises it to her lips*]

TACK.   Hollo! What's the matter now?

BERTHA.   May all the blessings you bestow on others be repaid you hereafter.

CALEB. [*Aside*]   Amen! A clear slate.

TACK.   Not a gleam of reason left—mad as a March hare! Come here, you, what's your name? Bertha. This is the evening little what-d'ye-call-her—spoiled child—John's wife, and her fool of a husband spend the evening here, don't they?

BERTHA.   Yes.

TACK. [*L.*]   Well, I want to join your party.

BERTHA. [*C.*]   Do you hear that, father?

CALEB. [*R.*]   Oh, yes. [*Aside*] I wish I didn't.

TACK.   You see, next Thursday I'm going to be married.

BERTHA.   Married! [*Staggering back to C.*]

TACK.   I do believe she's such a confounded idiot, she don't know what marriage means.

BERTHA.   Married!

TACK.   Yes! Church, parson, clerk, bells, breakfast, bridecake, marrowbones, cleavers, and all the rest of the tomfoolery! A wedding, d'ye understand? A wedding!

BERTHA.   Yes, I—I understand.

TACK. Oh, you do, do you? It's more than I expected; you've got a lucid interval, I suppose. Well, I shall come and bring my bride.

BERTHA. Your bride?

TACK. Yes, d'ye think a man can get married without a bride? She's off again! My bride, May Fielding. Now I want you to puff me. You know, make her think I'm everything that's beautiful. Just go it in your mad kind of way. It all helps to make her mind up. I shall be back again as soon as I can, so you'll expect me.

BERTHA. [*Turning away towards L. corner*] Yes.

TACK. [*Crosses behind to C.*] I don't think you will. She seems to have forgotten about it already. Caleb!

CALEB. Sir?

TACK. [*At door*] Take care she don't forget what I've been saying to her.

CALEB. She never forgets, it's one of the few things she ain't clever in.

TACK. Yah—every man thinks his own geese, swans. Well, good-bye. Look at her mooning still—poor devil. Oh, now what should I do with such a daughter? [*Exit C.D.*]

CALEB. [*Comes from table L.*] You'd kill her in a week. [*Aside*] I'm always nervous when he's here, I'm afraid she'll find me out.

BERTHA. [*R.*] Father.

CALEB. [*L.*] My child.

BERTHA. I am lonely in the dark. I want my eyes, my patient, willing eyes.

CALEB. Here they are, always ready. What shall your eyes do for you, my dear?

BERTHA. Look at May, and tell me, is she very beautiful?

CALEB. Very, very beautiful.

BERTHA. [*Sighs*] Her hair is very dark? darker than mine?

CALEB. Golden brown, and her voice is musical.

BERTHA. I know it.

CALEB. And her shape; well, there's not a doll here that can compare with it—a sweet, kind mouth, and such a pair of eyes, such eyes.

BERTHA. Such eyes?

CALEB. No, no, I don't mean that, Bertha, I—I—[*embraces her and sings*]

BERTHA. Go on, dear father, tell me more. Is Mr. Tackleton older or younger than she is?

CALEB. [*L.*] Eh! Oh, well, a little older, not to signify—[*Aside*] I don't think he was ever young. He's like a man made by human hands, come out of a hardware shop—all spikes. [*Footstep*]

BERTHA. [*R.*] I hear a footstep. Hush, 'tis here. 'Tis May, and another is with her.

CALEB. [*At table*] Who is it? [*Going to fire*]

BERTHA. Can't you hear it, clear, light, and happy? It is Dot. [*Music. Enter May and Dot C.D.*]

DOT. [*C.*] Here we be. I've brought Tilly and our baby, and Boxer; and I would have brought our cricket, too, if he'd a coom.

BERTHA. [*Kissing Dot*] Ah, Dot! no house wants a cricket where you are.

MAY. [*L.*] Bertha. [*Bertha starts*] You tremble. Will you not kiss me? [*Crossing to her R.C.*]

BERTHA. [*R. corner*] Yes, May, I wish you all the happiness that—that— [*Pauses, turns away*] Father! [*Seeks him*]

DOT. [*Aside to May*] D'ye see? She turns from you; she minds that ye were her brother's sweetheart. [*Enter Edward at door*]

BERTHA. [*L.*] Who is that?

DOT. [*R.*] It is an old man, dear.

BERTHA. No.

EDWARD. [*Aside*] My sister, my poor, blind sister!

CALEB. Yes, indeed, Bertha, a stranger.

BERTHA. No, it is not the step of an old man, and a stranger would pause at the door.

EDWARD. [*L. Aside*] Her heart sees plainer than the old man's eyes.

CALEB. You are wrong this time, Bertha.

DOT. He is our guest at home, and begs for him a corner at your fire. He's as deaf as a door-post. [*To Edward*] Sit thee down, man. [*Sits by fire. Enter Tilly with the baby*] Why, Tilly, where have you been?

TILLY. [*L.C.*] I've been a-running, please mums. I thought the old gentlemans was after me. [*Enter John and Mrs. F.*]

JOHN. [*C.*] Caleb man, how be ye? Hearty, eh? And Bertha, too, eh? Coom, Dot, Tilly lass, let's help Caleb to set table. Here's a chicken I brought to add to our sociability. [*Produces a large turkey*]

CALEB. [*L.C.*] Oh, John, what a bird. It ain't a fowl, it's a phoenix. [*Goes to Tilly*]

MRS. F. Now here's a bottle of wine. There was a time we had a cellar, and if a certain crisis in the indi—[*Goes up stage*]

DOT. Yes, ma'am. And here be a pinch of tea; I thought it might be useful; and Tilly, where be the sugar and the cake? [*Goes to her*]

TILLY. Ees, mums, I've got it somewhere, please. [*Rolls over the baby and searches*] Oh, it's here, mums, I ain't a-dropped 'em, only I just can't tell which is the baby, and which the cake. [*Produces long parcel not unlike the form of the infant*]

JOHN. Coom, let's all help. Lead the way, Caleb. [*Music*]

CALEB. Coom along. [*Throwing turkey over shoulder. Exit Caleb, Dot, John, and Tilly C.*]

MAY. [*R.C.*] Mother, do not ask me to marry Mr. Tackleton.

MRS. F. [*L.C.*] Good gracious, not marry him! What a sentiment!

BERTHA. [*R. seated*] Ah! What do I hear?

MAY. I still love poor Edward; I love him with all my heart, and I had rather join him in the grave than meet this man at the altar.

EDWARD. [*L. At fire*] I should like to wring that old woman's neck.

MRS. F. May, I am astonished at you. And if I had my heartshorn here, I don't know what my feelings might not be. Have you not given your word?

MAY. Given it, yes! As the traveller gives his purse to the highwayman who holds his weapon to his throat. Given my word, mother! Yes; he said, "Your love, or your life!"

MRS. F. And think of your being reduced to work for our living, like Caleb here. This is the home your sailor lover would have brought you to had he lived. I don't speak for myself, for I have learned to suffer, but I have known better times, before that unfortunate crisis in the indigo trade, which your unlucky father—but never mind—I can descend one step further—there will be enough left out of the wreck of our means to buy me a respectable coffin.

MAY. Mother!

MRS. F. And a silver plate, perhaps, or a white metal one, recording simply that I did know better days.

MAY. Dear mother!

MRS. F. I need not refer to that unhappy crisis?

MAY. No, you have suffered enough. It is now my turn.

MRS. F. Bless you, dear, for that noble thought. It is one of the principles I instilled into you at an early age, and now I am reaping the benefit of it.

BERTHA. [*Aside*] She does not love him—Oh, why does my heart rejoice? [*Creeps to May, embraces her, both sit. Music. Re-enter John, Tilly, Caleb, and Dot bearing supper*]

CALEB [*C.*] Here we are. Now then for supper. It isn't often we do indulge in dissipation, is it?

JOHN. Dissipation? One bottle among six! [*Enter Tackleton L.D.*]

TACK. Eh! Here we are. Bravo! Let's make a night of it, eh? There's my contribution—I've brought a tart. [*Produces a small one*]

DOT. [*R. Looking at it*] Tilly, put that where the flies won't get at it.

TILLY. [*L.*] Ees, mums. [*Sits L. and eats tart—swallows it at one mouthful*]

CALEB. Now, all's ready. Now, Mrs. F., mum. [*Offers his arm and escorts Mrs. F. to table in a formal manner. All sit*]

TACK. May, my dear.

JOHN. [*Going to Edward L.*] The old gentleman hugs the fire; so be it. No ceremony, so here goes. [*Sits*]

TACK. Now this is sociable, ain't it? [*Mr. Toole's business with Tilly and Baby (plate)*]

DOT. I didn't know you liked being sociable.

TACK. [*To John*] Your little wife will have her joke at my expense.

DOT. It's the only thing I can have at your expense.

JOHN. Ah! She had ye there, man.

OMNES. [*Laugh*]

CALEB. How comfortable we do look. Ah, if my poor boy could be amongst us. [*Helps Tilly*]

DOT. How many things have changed since he has gone; there's May, quite a woman grown.

CALEB. And you, Dot, married.

JOHN. Yes, and got a baby.

DOT. Hold your tongue.

JOHN. Eh! Did I say anything to—

DOT. Take some pie, [*helps him*] and don't talk with your mouth full.

CALEB. Ladies and gentlemen all, I rise to give a toast. Here's to the bride and bridegroom, which tomorrow's wedding will join.

TACK. Hear! Hear! [*Tilly puts plate on Caleb's chair*]

CALEB. And particularly to the bride; and I wish her many happy returns of the day.

DOT. Hear! Hear!

CALEB. And the old lady, too. Your good health, mum; my respects. [*They all drink*]

MRS. F. [*Rising and bowing*] Ahem! My friends, Heaven has given me a good and dutiful child. I don't take the credit of it myself, you observe, although she owes me more than I choose to say. Although the husband I have chosen—

CALEB. [*Aside*] She alludes to the late Mr. Indigo.

MRS. F. [*Looking fiercely at Caleb*] Although the husband I have chosen for my child, I refer to a person present, has been rejected many times by my daughter—

DOT. Hear! Hear!

MRS. F. I refrain from mentioning that fact. He enters a family, which, but for circumstances not wholly unconnected with a crisis in the indigo trade, might have been wealthy; but that is a subject I disdain to enter upon. I beg to conclude by stating that tomorrow is the only day I desire to behold. After that, I earnestly desire to retire to an early, but respectable grave in any genteel place of burial. [*Sits*]

JOHN.   Brayvo! Now, Dot, it is your turn. Can't you give us a sentiment, or a song on the occasion?

DOT.   What occasion? May's marriage?

CALEB.   Surely.

DOT.   Ees, I know a song that'll fit it to a T. It tells of a young lass that loved a sailor boy, who went off to sea. She was over-persuaded by her friends to marry an old fellow, and when she was in for it, back comes her young lover.

JOHN.   Oh, lord!

TACK.   There the story don't apply.

CALEB.   Sing it, Dot, if it will bring back my boy. [*Dot sings "Auld Robin Gray"*]

CALEB.   My boy, my poor Ned.

TACK.   [*Aside R.*]   She has made May weep, confound her chirping. Oh, I'll be even with this infernal cricket. I'll scrunch her.

JOHN.   Horraw! I'm getting sociable. Dot, give me my pipe, and it's your turn to call for a song. Coom, May, Bertha. [*Dot searches for John's pipe in his coat*] What, not a note, eh? [*Edward crosses behind the table and makes signs to Dot. Passes out at R.D. quickly*] Caleb, won't you tip us a stave, man? [*Song, Caleb, "Drown It in a Bowl"—three times*]

TACK.   [*Aside*]   Hollo! the old gentleman is telegraphing to Dot. [*Goes to fire to warm himself, but watches. Dot gives John a light for his pipe*]

DOT. [*Aside*]   He beckons me. [*Caleb and John sing. Dot, after a hurried glance, exits R.D. Tack. crosses from L. to R. behind the table and looks out at window—draws the rag of a curtain which hangs over it. After the first verse of Caleb's song he creeps out stealthily*]

JOHN.   Caleb, Caleb, you've sung that verse before.

CALEB.   I know twenty or thirty more verses, but they're all the same as that.

JOHN.   Come, Tilly, you give us a song.

TILLY.   Oh, I can't.

JOHN.   Yes, Tilly, you give us a song, and I'll give you a Christmas box. [*Tilly sings, "My Lover Was a Sailor Boy"*]

JOHN.   Stop! Stop!

TILLY.   I won't sing any more, there!

CALEB. Tilly's got a very good voice for a parish clerk; or in the milk line she'd do very well. [*Re-enter Tackleton at door*]

TACK. [*L.*] Oho! He! I've caught 'em; I've caught 'em!

CALEB. [*L.C.*] What shall we do? play a round game, or tell fortunes on the cards.

TILLY. [*L.*] Ow, do tell fortins, it frightens a body so nice. [*Caleb gets cards from mantel-shelf L.*]

JOHN. [*R.C. Seated*] My fortune don't need no wizard to tell it. The best wife alive.

TACK. [*L. Upstage*] Ho! ho! [*Jerks his thumb toward door*]

JOHN. A happy home over my head, a blessed baby, and a cricket on my hearth. What are you squirming at there, like a bob worm on a fish hook? [*To Tackleton*]

TACK. Look round ye. Where's Dot, eh? Where's the old deaf gent, eh? They're gone, ain't they, eh?

JOHN. Gone where?

TACK. I'll show you where. Come! Hush! [*Music. Snow here*]

JOHN. What d'ye mean? [*Tack. draws him off at door*]

CALEB. Now cut three times. [*Mrs. F. cuts*]

TILLY. Oh, I feel it a-coming all over me.

CALEB. What's here? There's the king of diamonds—that's John—and there's a black knave.

TILLY. That's Tackleton.

CALEB. He stands between John and the queen of hearts.

BERTHA. [*L.*] Dot is the queen of hearts.

CALEB. There she is along with a light man, who comes across the water. I wish it could be my boy. What's this? A bundle?

TILLY. A bundle—that's baby.

CALEB. I can't make it out. [*Studying the cards. Takes second pack. Re-enter Tackleton and John at back*]

TACK. Come here.

CALEB. There's that infernal knave again. What's he about?

JOHN. Why have you brought me here?

TACK. John, be cool, don't fly out. The old man, your guest, that your wife was so urgent should stop under your roof, is no old man at all, but a strapping, young fellow in disguise.

JOHN. [*Seizing him*] Ye lie, varmin, ye lie. [*Snow begins to fall*]

CALEB. I don't like that knave.

TILLY. He do stick out bad, don't he?

TACK. I tell you they are together in yonder barn. I saw 'em through the keyhole. Look! Look!

JOHN. My wife! Shew it me, and then I'll trample soul out of ye, d'ye hear?—Stop!—Stay! I'm faint—sick—my head is full of blood—I—I—go on —on, I tell ye—

TACK. Hush, look here. [*Creeps to door R. opens it and discovers Dot and Edward. Tableau in barn lighted up by calcium. Dot and Edward standing smiling at each other. She replaces Edward's wig.*]

JOHN. My wife! Dot in his arms—aah, let me tear him—let me tear—oh! —when—Dot! [*Staggers and falls in the snow C.*]

CALEB. Look there, the little queen seems in more trouble still.

TILLY. She don't stand out well, do she? [*When John falls—Ring. No picture. Curtain slow*]

ACT III.

Dot's cottage—same as Act I. Chandelier one-third down. Lights up one-half full and then gradually up. John discovered seated by the fire R.C. Music for curtain.

DOT. John, dear, what has come to you? You have sat here all night through. The fire has gone out on the hearth; you are cold.

JOHN. Go, Dot, I would be alone. [*Turns away*]

DOT. John, I have been crying all night. I could not sleep because I have a secret from you that I promised to keep. I know I have done wrong, but I have promised, and I hope you'll forgive me when you know all.

JOHN. Very well, Dot, so be it; but leave me now.

DOT. [*Going*] I will, dear. [*Returns*] Won't you kiss me, John? [*Music. John does not move. Dot turns away slowly and exits weeping R.*]

JOHN. The fire has gone out on the hearth; you are cold. Ay, Dot, here is the hearth where the fire has gone out, and never can be lighted again— never. [*Music. Enter Tackleton L.D.*]

TACK. [*Touching him on shoulder*] John, my good fellow, how goes it this morning, eh? You look a little streaky, eh, don't ye?

JOHN. I have had a poor night, Master Tackleton, but it's over now, and so I want to say a word to ye.

TACK. [*L.*] Go on, John, I'm all sympathy and attention.

JOHN. [*R.*] Last night you showed me my wife alone with that man.

TACK. In his arms, John. I saw it; so did you.

JOHN. I did, and the livelong night through I've seen nothing else. And I've thought on it, until now I've thought it out. [*Crosses to L.*]

TACK. [*R. Enter Dot behind from R.D.*] You will act as an outraged husband should?

JOHN. I'll act as a man ought, a rough and plain one, perhaps. Listen! I married my little wife because I had seen her grow up from a child in her father's house, and I knew how good she was. I stood beside her life as she grew and grew, until, like a creeping plant, year by year she twined herself round my heart, and stood under the shelter of my o'erspreading love. Love, selfish love, blinded me. I did not consider what I was doing. I did not consider what she was.

TACK. Young, giddy, frivolous! Ah, I understand.

JOHN. No, you don't; and you'd best not interrupt me till you do. If yesterday I'd a struck down the man who dares to breathe a word against her, today I'd set my foot on his face, if he were my own brother.

TACK. I didn't mean, John—I—go on.

JOHN. Did I consider that I took her, a child, at an age when she had not sense enough to know how beautiful, how good, she was? Noa! I cheated her, and I married her because I loved her, not because she loved me.

TACK. But she has deceived you, hasn't she?

JOHN. She has.

TACK. Ah!

JOHN. For when she found she could not love me as she thought she might, why, she kept that knowledge from me. And now I begin to feel how hard she has tried to be a good and dutiful wife.

TACK. Hollo! What d'ye mean?

JOHN. I mean I sat upon that hearth last night, all night, where she has often sat beside me; that hearth which she has blessed and brightened; that hearth, which but for her were only a few stones and bricks and rusty bars, but which she made the altar of my home; beside which we knelt together in nightly prayer, blessing Him that gave us to each other; so that the smoke from yon poor chimney has gone up a better fragrance than the incense of the richest temple in the world. It was on that spot I knelt and prayed last night, and it has given me strength of heart to know what to do. I'll make her all the reparation in my power.

TACK. Make her reparation? I don't hear you right.

JOHN. Don't ye? [*Seizing him*] Then listen to me, and take care you do hear me right. Listen to me! Do I speak plain?

TACK. Very.

JOHN. As if I meant it?

TACK. Uncommonly as if you meant it.

JOHN. I acquit her of all blame—all. This day one year ago, she became my wife, and this day I will take her back to her father's house, and if any man wants to say a word agin her, he's got to strip and stand up afore John Peerybingle. Now do you hear?

TACK. Distinctly. I'm uncommonly sorry for this affair, but you'll excuse me, I'm going to be married today, in half an hour. [*Going*] I thought I'd come in and gratify myself with a view of things in general. May Fielding makes no shew of her affection for me, that's why I have no suspicion of her sincerity. Ha! ha! This is really altogether the happiest day of my life! [*Music. Exit door L.*]

JOHN. Farewell, Dot. Farewell, my little wife. If I can't make you love me, ye shan't despise me anyway. No, it's a tough fight, but I'll act like a man, like a—[*Breaks down and covers his face with his hands as he goes out R. door*]

DOT. [*Coming down sobbing*] I don't know what I've done, but I feel it's something I oughtn't to a done. [*Enter Tilly with the baby R.D. Looks back after John*]

TILLY. [*Howling*] Ow! ow! if you please, don't; it's enough to dead and bury the babies, so it is, if you please.

DOT. [*L. Crying*] Oh! Oh!

TILLY. [*R. Seeing Dot*] Ow! ow! Don't, mums, oh, don't, ow! What has everybody been and gone and done with everybody, making everybody else so wretched? Ow! ow! ow! [*Enter Caleb L. door*]

DOT. [*R.*] Caleb!

CALEB. [*L.*] How d'ye do, mum? Thank ye, I'm in trouble, a peck of trouble.

DOT. [*Drying her eyes*] What is it?

CALEB. All last night Bertha walked about her room, stoppin' now and agin, mum, and giving out such a sigh—

DOT. [*Aside*] Like John.

CALEB. At daylight she crept out; I followed her; she went to the church, and felt her way until she came to her mother's biding-place. There she lay clasping the ridge of grass; and fur off I stood, and I dusn't ask her why she left me to seek her dead mother. I've done something bad, mum.

DOT. So have I.

CALEB. [*L. corner*] I dusn't speak to her for fear she'd say to her father, "You have deceived me." Oh, Dot, perhaps she has found me out.

TILLY. [*Looking out of window*] Oh, mums, here's the blind girl, feeling her ways along the road.

CALEB. [*L.*] Bertha!

DOT. [*R.*] Let her come. Don't ye move. Don't say a word. [*Music. Enter Bertha. Dot runs to her. Bertha goes toward Dot*]

BERTHA. Dot, dear, I have come to you.

DOT. [*R.*] What ails ye, dear?

BERTHA. [*C.*] Dot, we have had a good genius in our house, one who has been so kind and good to us. So rough in manner, but so gentle in deed.

CALEB. [*Aside*] She means Tackleton.

BERTHA. [*C.*] The portrait my father drew of him made me love him.

DOT. [*R.*] You love him? Him!

BERTHA. Could I help it? And when this morning the village bells pealed for his union with another, to one who does not love him because she does not know him as I do—

CALEB. [*Aside*] Gracious power, have I deceived her from her cradle to break her heart at last? [*Business of Caleb's*]

BERTHA. Who's that? [*Starts. Feels her way toward him. Stops and whispers*] My father!

CALEB. Bertha, I have heard your confession, and now you must hear mine. Hear me kindly, darling, won't ye? Hear me, and forgive me.

BERTHA. [*C.*] Forgive you, so kind, so good.

CALEB. [*L.*] I meant to be. Your road in life was rough; I meant to smooth it for you; so as I wandered from the truth, I have altered objects around you, changed the characters of people.

BERTHA. Changed their characters?

CALEB. I must tear the veil from your eyes that I put there. I have deceived you. Mr. Tackleton is a stern, sordid, grinding, man; a hard master to me for many a year; ugly in looks, cold and callous in nature.

BERTHA. He! He!

CALEB. He is a demon that I have made your idol. [*Turns away*]

BERTHA. Oh, father, father, what have you done? [*Weeps*]

CALEB. Don't cry, Bertha dear. Oh, don't let me see the tears coming from those blind eyes. Oh, what shall I do? Shall I go away, and never see you any more? Where's John to beat me? [*Tilly runs for John*] Oh, dear! Oh, dear! [*Sits. Exit Tilly*]

BERTHA. Dot, you will not deceive me. [*Goes to her*] Tell me, what is my home?

DOT. It is a poor place, Bertha; the house will scarce keep out the wind and rain.

CALEB. [*L.*] Oh, dear! Oh, dear! [*Half rising and seating himself again in a supplicating manner*]

Dot. The roof is in rags, and the walls are all patched like the sackcloth of Caleb's only coat.

Caleb. [*In agony, half rising*] Oh, no, no, do leave me my blue coat.

Bertha. Look across the room where my father is, and tell me what you see.

Dot. I see an old man, lean and haggard.

Caleb. [*Groaning*] Oh, lord, oh, dear, she'll hate me now.

Dot. Wore to the bone with care and work.

Bertha. I see! I see!

Dot. Hunger and misery have been round you, but he only knew it, so his love has turned your blindness into a blessing.

Bertha. Oh, to think I might have died and never known I had such a father. [*Crosses to him*]

Caleb. What have I done now?

Bertha. [*Embracing him*] Father, at last I know you.

Caleb. And you don't miss the blue coat?

Bertha. No, no.

Caleb. And the brass buttons, dear?

Bertha. No! Peace has returned to my breast, and I have now an idol for my love that no one can take from me. I could not feel happier. [*Bells and music*]

Dot. [*Runs to door L.*] Yes, you could; you could, and you will, too. Hark! those bells! What d'ye hear, Bertha? Listen!

Bertha. [*C.*] I hear shouts and the sound of wheels. They come nearer; they stop at this door. [*Re-enter Tilly L.*]

Tilly. They're a-comin', mums, everybody's coming. They're got married, and everybody's married, and coach and fours, marrowbones and cleavers. Here he be!

Dot. [*Putting her hands over Caleb's face*] No, you shan't look at him. [*Enter Edward L. in sailor's dress*]

Edward. It's over, Dot; she's mine. Hurrah! Fast as the parson can make her.

Dot. D'ye hear that voice, Caleb? Speak; d'ye know it?

Caleb. [*L.C.*] Oh, dear; oh, mum! No, it can't be.

Edward. [*C.*] Ain't it?

Caleb. If my Ned, my boy from the Golden South Americas were alive—

Dot. He is. [*Taking her hands away*] He is! And there he is! [*Pushes him to Ned*]

Caleb. [*Staggers back*] M—my son! [*Goes toward Ned*]

EDWARD. [*Runs and catches him*]   Father!

CALEB. [*C.*]   It is, it is; oh, mum! oh, lord! Here, look here! Ned! Ho! ho! ho! My boy! My son! [*Embracing*]

BERTHA. [*R.C. Up a little*]   My brother! My little brother!

CALEB.   Her little brother! Ho! ho!

DOT. [*Smiling; coming between Edward and Caleb, pushing Caleb*]   Get away, you've had enough. Hush! [*Leads Bertha to Edward. She seeks for him as if for a child. Dot slowly raises her hands to his shoulders*]

BERTHA. [*With a cry of surprise and joy*]   Ah, I had forgotten. [*Embraces him*]

CALEB. [*L.*]   There he is, and there's the real blue coat and brass buttons, at last. Hooraw! I feel as if I was a jumping-jack, and somebody was a-pulling at me and making me dance all ways at once.

DOT. [*R.*]   Ain't he splendid?

CALEB. [*L.*]   He looks like a ship in full sail.

EDWARD. [*R.C.*]   Dot, dear Dot. [*Embraces her*] How much don't I owe you. [*Enter John R. Door*]

JOHN. [*C.*]   Dot!

DOT. [*R.C.*]   Here I am. Come here, John, d'ye see who this is?

CALEB.   Take a long look at him, he'll stand it, my boy.

JOHN.   Ned! Ned Plummer!

CALEB.   From the Golden South Americas—that you fitted out and sent to sea.

JOHN. [*Gazing on him R.C.*]   Ned! No, no! It is! [*Clasps his hand*]

CALEB.   Ecod, for a minute I thought he was going to say it wasn't.

DOT. [*L.*]   Now tell him all, Edward, and don't spare me a bit.

EDWARD. [*R.C.*]   I was the deaf old man, John. Forgive me for deceiving you for a while, but when I left here many years ago, I loved May Fielding. Dot alone knew that love; to her alone I confided the secret of my presence, that she might prove to me that May was still honest and true.

DOT. [*C.*]   And when I asked him to let his old friend, John Peerybingle, into the secret, he said that John was much too open-hearted, for he'd be sure to go and haw-haw it out in his dear, old, clumsy way; and I promised to keep his secret if he wouldn't run off to sea again, as he would a done, until I showed him May faithful and constant as ever. And I did it, John; and they were married, John, an hour ago; and here [*runs to door and brings in May*]—here's the bride. And old Tackleton may hang himself, or die a bachelor. [*Coming down L.C.*]

JOHN. [*R.C.*]   My own, my darling!

Dot. [*C.*] No, John, no! Hear all before you love me again. It was wrong to have a secret from you, and I am very sorry. I didn't think it any harm.

John. Dot, my wife, my little wife. [*Struggles with Edward*]

Edward. [*R.*] No, no.

Dot. You doubted me, John; I overheard it, and you thought to send me away. Oh, how could you do it?

Caleb. [*L.*] How could you do it?

John. [*R.C.*] Because I was a darned fool. [*Struggles*]

Dot. Not yet.

Caleb. [*Squares up between them*] Not yet! Keep off!

Dot. If I could have loved you better than I do, the noble words you spoke this morning to old Tackleton, and the shaking you gave him, would have made me; but I can't. So now, my dear husband, take me to your heart; that's my home, and never, oh, never, think of sending me away to any other. [*They embrace. Music. Enter Tack. and Mrs. F.*]

Tack. [*L.C.*] Hollo! I say, what's this? There's some mistake here.

Tilly. [*R.*] Ees there be, and you made it. [*All laugh*]

Caleb. [*L.*] Well said, Tilly.

Mrs. F. My daughter in the arms of a blue stranger.

Caleb. [*L.*] In the arms of my son, mum. Look at him. [*To Tack.*] Take a long look; there's no extra charge.

Tack. [*To Edward*] I beg your pardon, sir, I haven't the pleasure of knowing you, but if you'll do me the favor to spare that young lady—she has made rather a particular engagement with me this morning.

Edward. [*R.*] I'm very sorry, sir, but this young lady has made rather a particular engagement with me this morning.

Tack. What! My parson ready, my beadle ready, my boys ready to shout —three pence a head—all at the church—nothing wanting but the bride.

Edward. The bride has been to church once this morning, and I found everything as you stated. Much obliged for your attention.

Mrs. F. Married! Oh, that I should ever live to see the day. Carry me to my grave. [*Leans on Tackleton*]

Tack. [*L.C.*] Don't be an old fool. [*Pushes her off*]

Mrs. F. Oh, dear! Good gracious! Who would be a mother?

Tilly. I would.

Tack. Allow me to understand all this. This is Mr. Plummer, then, I infer?

Dot. [*R.*] That's the name.

TACK. Oh! Certainly! To be sure! It's all right, quite correct. Miss Slowboy, will you have the kindness to throw that wedding ring in the fire. [*Gives ring in piece of paper*] Thank ye.

TILLY. [*Crosses to Tack. L.*] Perhaps I might want it for myself. [*Puts it in her bosom. Goes up*]

TACK. Good morning! I haven't anything to observe, nothing whatever; it's quite correct—ladies and gentlemen, all around—perfectly satisfactory—good morning! [*Exit. Ready to lower lights in front*]

TILLY. If it ain't, I'll marry him. [*Music. Follows him off. Shouts outside*]

JOHN. [*Looking at door*] Huzza! Here come all the neighbors. They come to wish Caleb joy of Ned's return. Huzza! Come in, lads; come in, lasses. [*Enter peasantry*]

ALL. Bless you, Caleb. What, Ned! [*Shake hands*]

JOHN. [*C.*] There he is, and there's my little wife, and there's the bride. And, oh! this is a happy day. Hurrah, boys, a cheer for us altogether! [*All shout. Enter Tilly with a cake*]

TILLY. [*C.*] Please, mums, here's Mr. Tackleton coom back with his compliments [*Comelbents*][1] and says, if you please, as he hasn't got no use for this cake himself, perhaps you'll all eat it.

CALEB. Law!

TILLY. And his extra comelbents, please, and he's got a few toys for babies, mums, and they ain't ugly noways.

DOT. [*R. Upstage*] What do he mean? Come in, man. [*Enter Tackleton with toys*]

TACK. [*L.C.*] May I? Thank ye. It means that the village is empty, and all the folks are flocking here; and, friends one and all, my house is very lonely today. I have not so much as a cricket on my hearth; I've scared 'em all away. Don't be hard upon me, neighbors, as I have been on you, but let me join your happy party.

DOT. Join us! Aye, shall you; for if we can make you happy, you become good and kind. [*Crosses to him*]

CALEB. Coom, clear the room for a dance. Is there never a fiddle here? Hollo, Bertha, I'm young and fresh and fat again. I'm twenty-one years old; I'm dressed in blue and pink, and brass buttons breaking out all over me. Hooraw! Places, boys and girls!

JOHN. [*R.*] Tap the ale in the cellar, Tilly. Bless us all! everyone! Caleb—bless his old coat and bald head! Bless you, Ned and May! And old mother

---

[1] "Comelbents" inserted into New York Public Library manuscript in what I believe to be Boucicault's hand, as an explanation of Tilly's pronunciation.

Indigo—bless her old wig! And bless Tilly, too! And bless my darling, little wife, my Dot!

TILLY. [*Coming down R.*] And the babies! [*Cricket chirps*]

DOT. And don't forget the cricket on the hearth!

ALL. Hurrah! [*Music. They all take partners and places for a cushion dance. Toward the end of dance—stage darkened*]

Group of Fairies descend in chimney. The chimney is the large hood in C., and the front of hood is drawn up like a window blind and discovers group. Red fire. Tableau. Curtain.

Dance: John and Dot, Caleb and Tilly, May and Edward, Tack. and Mrs. F., Peasants and Peasants.

Special business of each: Bertha is led to a seat and enjoys the music; Dot and John—hearty and jubilant; Caleb and Tilly—he childishly joyous and comic in his senility, she awkward and comic from ignorance of the figures; they correct her and get her through them; May and Edward—truly loving and ingenuous; Tack. and Mrs. F.—he frowning and aspersive in his comic looks at having to dance with her, she, thoroughly self-satisfied, and when her turn comes to run and be caught, she at once goes to cushion and kneels, and complacently prepares for the kiss. He runs away from her—she chases him all over, in and out, and enters with him in triumph—he, vanquished, yields.

Dance: Forward in couples—turn partners—opposite corners advance to C. and back—opposite corners advance and dos a dos—first couple go up C., cast off, and down outside, chase, take lady to cushion, kneel and kiss—all cast off—first couple join hands and the rest pass under—repeat figures for each couple—alternate couples back to R. and L.—whole and half turn at sides—form two small rings at sides—hands round and back—keep up dance till curtain.

CURTAIN

FLYING SCUD;
Or, A FOUR-LEGGED FORTUNE

FLYING SCUD;
Or, A FOUR-LEGGED FORTUNE

THE production of *Flying Scud* cannot be said to have added anything to the reputation of Dion Boucicault as a literary dramatist, but it certainly swelled his popularity with both English and American audiences; it ran for two hundred nights in London and forty-one performances in New York. The opening night of the Holborn Theatre (October 6, 1866) was the occasion for the first presentation of the piece, and a wild and boisterous night it must have been. *The Times* of October 8 gives a vivid picture of the enthusiastic reception. "The last scene of the act represents the course on Derby-day, enlivened with all those minute realities that are combined in Mr. Frith's celebrated picture. . . . To describe the excitement of the audience during this scene would be impossible. Carried on by the course of events, they had so completely identified their own feelings with those of Nat Gosling that they watched the progress of the mimic race with an anxiety that could scarcely have been surpassed if every one of them had actually put his money on Flying Scud. The shout from pit, boxes, and gallery that greeted the old jockey when he came forward as the victor expressed not only violent approbation, but a strong sense of relief. Thank goodness! the 'legs' are defeated and the Derby winner is Flying Scud."

The drama is built in a series of sensational and novel episodes. As Professor Odell says, it was "one of the first plays to center in a horse race," and Townsend Walsh calls it "one of the first of that interminable series of plays called 'racing dramas,' full of direct claptrap appeals which the gallery never fails to answer." According to *The Times*, the actual race was shown to the audience by means of "small profile horses in the background and at the end Nat appears in front, seated on a real, live Flying Scud." The duel scene on Calais sands gave opportunity for another elaborate and beautiful setting as well as a new thrill; and the introduction of a *divertissement* executed by a chorus of jockeys, all played by women, presented a "Terpsichorean intrusion . . . highly relished by the spectators."

The first American production at Wallack's Theatre on April 24, 1867, was equally exciting. The advertisement which appeared in the *New York Daily Tribune* on the day of the opening announced the drama as "showing the ups and downs, crosses, double crosses, events and vicissitudes of life on the turf."

The casts of these performances included the following: in the London production, George Belmore as Nat Gosling, G. Blake as Tom Meredith, G. Neville as Captain Goodge, E. Garden as Colonel Mulligan, Vollaire as Mo Davis, Miss Fanny Josephs as Lord Woodbie, Miss Charlotte Saunders as Bob Buckskin, Miss Bessie Foote as Katey Rideout, and Miss J. Fiddes (Mrs. Dominick Murray) as Julia Latimer; and in the New York production, A. W. Young as Nat Gosling, Frederick Robinson as Tom Meredith, B. T. Ringgold as Captain Goodge, W. H. Norton as Colonel Mulligan, Charles Fisher as Mo Davis, Miss Mary Barrett as Lord Woodbie, Mr. J. C. Williamson as Bob Buckskin, Miss Maud Elliott as Katey Rideout, and Mrs. Clara Jennings as Julia Latimer.

The arrangement of scenes in the manuscript used in preparing this edition seems to vary somewhat from the descriptions in contemporary papers. *The Times* indicates that the play "may be said to consist of two parts, almost distinct from each other, in each of which two acts are comprised." From the running description of the scenes in the New York paper, too, it is obvious that the original Act II is the Act III of our manuscript, and that Boucicault in reworking the play has made changes of lines and incidents to knit the two stories more closely, thereby increasing the suspense of the horse-race scene, and heightening the excitement of the whole play.

The typescript used in editing this play was secured through the courtesy of Samuel French, Ltd., London.

F. T. C.

CAST OF CHARACTERS

Tom Meredith

Nat Gosling

Lord Cecil Woodbie

Captain Grindley Goodge

Colonel Mulligan

Mo Davis

Chousir

Bob Buckskin

Ned Compo

Jerry

Mr. Quail

Jackson

A Servant

Katey Rideout

Julia Latimer

Lady Woodbie

Stable Boys, Bailiffs, Tenants, Policemen, A Waiter, Thimble Riggers, Negro Minstrels, Venders, Supers.

SYNOPSIS OF SCENES

ACT II. SCENE 1. THE CLUB CARD ROOM

       SCENE 2. CHAMBER (IN ONE)—MULLIGAN'S LODGINGS

       SCENE 3. HYDE PARK (IN TWO)

       SCENE 4. CALAIS SANDS

ACT III. SCENE 1. NEAT CHAMBER IN NAT GOSLING'S LONDON LODGINGS

       SCENE 2. MULLIGAN'S LODGINGS

       SCENE 3. FRONT SCENE ON ROAD TO STABLE

       SCENE 4. STABLE YARD AT NIGHT. ILLUMINATED VILLAGE IN THE DISTANCE

       SCENE 5. EPSOM DOWNS

ACT IV. SCENE 1. MULLIGAN'S LODGINGS

       SCENE 2. STREET SCENE (IN ONE)

       SCENE 3. THE GARRET

ACT I.

SCENE 1: *Love Lane, near Doncaster. Nat's cottage embowered in shrubbery R. A pump L.C. Cottage R. Railings, etc. Enter Jerry and Lord Woodbie L.U.E.*

JERRY. Well, my lord, we shall be very sorry to lose you, I'm sure, nobody will be sorrier than the boys in our stable.

WOOD. I've been here now much longer than I intended; I should have gone before, but I thought I might as well wait till after the reading of the will—not that it's got anything to do with me—but the Squire was always a decent sort, and I am rather curious to know how he has left his money.

JERRY. The reading of the will has been fixed for three o'clock; notices have been sent to several of the principal tenants on the estate to attend. Poor Squire, I'm sorry he's dead; he might have lived till after the Derby. I know he had great hopes of one day pulling off the big race, but now he's dead and gone. Bless him, he was a right down good sort.

WOOD. Yes, I've always heard him spoken of as a steadfast friend, and where once he took a liking he was never known to change his mind. Have you seen Miss Latimer this morning?

JERRY. No, my lord, I don't think she's come out of the grounds yet. I saw her last night with her uncle, Colonel Mulligan.

WOOD. Oh, all right. I dare say I shall see them presently.

JERRY. I'm just going to look after the stable lads; they've got the horses out for an airing. If I should see Miss Latimer shall I tell her that you were asking after her?

WOOD. Yes—no—I mean, don't trouble; I dare say I shall see her myself.

JERRY. No trouble, if I happen to see her I'll mention it. Good morning, my lord.

WOOD. Good morning. [*Exit Jerry L.U.E.*]

WOOD. Oh, Julia, Julia, you've much to answer for. Here's another night I've passed without a wink of sleep. I never knew what it was to be in love before; it's a most awful complaint and I've got it very badly. I don't know what mama will say when she knows all about it. I'm afraid she's got higher notions for me, but I know she'll give her consent when she knows how much I love her. [*Laugh outside*] Good gracious, what's that? [*Enter Bob Buckskin L.U.E. smothered in blankets and speaking off*]

BOB. Yes, you may laugh, ye unfeeling monsters, you may laugh. You're a set as would laugh if you saw an omnibus run over your mother-in-law; necessity knows no law and I'm bound to do it. Here goes for another lap. [*Starts running around stage*]

WOOD. Good gracious! My good fellow, what are you doing?

BOB. Beg pardon, I didn't see you, my lord. I've just got off another three ounces. I'm bound to do it, there's no help for it. I'm making too much fat and this is the only way I can keep it down. While the stable boys have got their horses out for their exercise, I'm taking mine; I've done twelve miles this morning, had two doses of salts and senna, and three pints of boiling water. Oh, it's a splendid thing. I'll soon be as thin as the living skeleton who was being shown for a penny at the shop in High Street.

WOOD. You will kill yourself if you go on like this.

BOB. Not a bit of it. I'm bound to do it to keep myself in condition.

WOOD. You must have a good constitution to stand it.

BOB. Yes, my lord, my constitution has been a curse to me; everything I take turns to fat, everything I eat or drink agrees with me. It's all my constitution. If I lived on fat bacon for a fortnight, I shouldn't be able to get my clothes on or off. Milk I ain't allowed to touch; taters, I daren't look 'em in the face; every bit of bread I eat has to be toasted to a cinder; and as for beer, oh lor, beer. [*Grimaces*]

WOOD. Well, don't let me stop you; go on with your exercise.

BOB. Just what I was thinking. I'm getting cool here and the perspiration must be kept up. My lord, you might time me thirty times round the haystack over yonder. I'll back myself to do it in fourteen minutes.

WOOD. Come on then, we'll see.

BOB. This is my form. Watch. [*Runs twice round stage and exits R.U.E. Lord Woodbie follows laughing. If horses are used, all enter L.U.E. with Jerry and stable lads and all exit R.U.E. followed by Katey in riding habit. She looks round as if followed, then exits behind cottage. Music. Enter Goodge hastily L. He looks round*]

GOODGE. Where is she? Surely I have not mistaken the road? No, she disappeared round that corner and dived into this lane. Ha! A cottage hiding under the rose bushes. [*Looks over the paling*] The very nest for such a bird; I must waylay one of the servants and find out who and what she is. [*Enter Nat R. with a bucket and smoking a pipe*] Here is one.

NAT. [*Sings*] In '44 I won the Hoaks
        And then they put me up
        To ride Sir Tatton's little mare
        As took the Chester Cup. [*Pumps water into bucket*]

GOODGE. The very fellow for my purpose.

NAT. [*Sings*] But, oh my, oh cry, it was just then d'ye see,
    The pootyest gal in Doncaster, she fell in love with me.

GOODGE. I say, my man.

NAT. Sir to you, sir. [*Sings*]
    She said she would be mine, ven I was growed a little bigger.
    She didn't know I dussn't put no meat upon my figger.
    Oh my, oh cry, vot is a chap to do
    Ven he's in love and got to ride,
    Vell under six stun two.
    [*Spoken*] Saddle and bridle included, mind you.

GOODGE. Do you live in that cottage?

NAT. Ess. [*Is going in with bucket*]

GOODGE. [*Holding up a sovereign*] D'ye see that?

NAT. [*R.*] Ess, how much do you want for it?

GOODGE. A very lovely girl rode down this lane a few minutes ago, on a bay horse with black points.

NAT. [*Sings*] Oh, yes, she's as beautiful as a butterfly.

GOODGE. Confound the fellow, he's as bad as a barrel organ! Does she live in that cottage, and can you tell me all about her?

NAT. Ess, her name is Katey Rideout, and she do live yonder.

GOODGE. Alone?

NAT. Nay, but wi' her auld grandfather.

GOODGE. What's his name?

NAT. He be called Nathaniel Gosling, but more often old Nat, hereabouts.

GOODGE. Then he is grandfather to an angel.

NAT. Yes, a thoroughbred 'un, and sich a temper, she's as sweet as milk, as fine as silk, and as soft as a dooey morning.

GOODGE. Poetical. [*Hands him money*]

NAT. And all included in the sovrin. [*Pockets it*]

GOODGE. Does old squeezebags keep a sharp eye on the girl?

NAT. Lord love ye, I can get over him.

GOODGE. Egad! then I have hit on the right man to do my business for me.

NAT. You may bet your last shirt button on it.

GOODGE. I'll pay you handsomely if I win the girl.

NAT. I allus takes my tip for sporting information. [*Takes up the bucket*]

GOODGE. Then tell her that I am Captain Goodge, Grindley Goodge, of Nobbley Hall. [*Going R.*] Stay, what is your name, my man?

NAT. Well, I be called Nathaniel Gosling, but more often old Nat hereabouts.

GOODGE. The grandfather himself! I have been done.

NAT. [*Enthusiastic*] Yes, you have been done brown. I've got the sovereign, no money returned. [*Exit R.*]

GOODGE. And here I stood, I, Grindley Goodge, to be reckoned up and turned into cash by a yokel like that. Can this old cub be the grandfather of such a lovely being as that girl? [*Enter Tom Meredith L.*]

TOM. I beg your pardon, sir, for addressing you, but I saw you in the lane and I hoped you would pardon my intrusion.

GOODGE. Speak out, my man. Who are you, one of my tenants, eh?

TOM. Yes, sir, my name is Meredith, Thomas Meredith. I farm the low meadows.

GOODGE. I know nothing about the estate except that I shall come into possession of it some day. What do you want?

TOM. I have received notice this morning, sir, to quit my place. I have no lease. Your uncle, before he died, said I would never be dispossessed.

GOODGE. Then why did he not give you a lease?

TOM. He said I should never want one while he lived nor afterwards.

GOODGE. Nor afterwards?

TOM. These were his very words.

GOODGE. What a pity those words were not in black and white.

TOM. There never was a scratch of a pen between us. You see, sir, my father, Colonel Meredith, owned this estate. He was a great racing man. Your uncle was his groom. But when my father was ruined and sold up, your uncle stepped into Nobbley Hall and became the squire. Perhaps when he found me his poor tenant, he remembered how good and generous my father had been to him, for though close-fisted to all the world, he was ever open-handed to me.

GOODGE. It's more than he ever was to me, the old screw. I'm sorry I can't oblige you, but I must have all my meadow land for my racing stock.

TOM. I'll take in all your stud, sir. I trained for your uncle. There's a two-year old in the stable now, that never had any hand but mine over him.

GOODGE. Thanks, but I have my own trainer. [*Going, crosses R.*]

TOM. See, Captain Goodge, I—I can't take no for your answer; it will just be ruin to me to quit the low meadows. I—I am in hopes of being married, sir. Now if you deny me I shall have no home to offer my young wife, for every penny I have is dug into your land or spent on the house I hoped that she would one day share with me. Don't turn me out like a dog, sir. Come, sir, let her add her persuasions to mine. She lives yonder.

GOODGE. In that cottage? Are you then the accepted lover of that beautiful girl?

Tom. I can't say that she has out and out said yes, but I know that she likes me better than anyone else.

Goodge. How are you sure of that?

Tom. I've often told her that if I caught any fellow fooling round her, I'd break his neck, and she didn't object.

Goodge. I can't stop to see the lady; I am rather in a hurry. [*Crosses L.*]

Tom. But you will renew my lease, sir?

Goodge. No, I want the land. You've had your answer, go. [*Aside*] And I want the girl, so I must clear this fellow out of the estate. [*Exit L.1E.*]

Tom. There he goes, the thoroughbred heartless sporting character. He's all there with his napless drab hat, his drab face where all the wrinkles he is up to keep watch round his eyes; he looks clean shaved all over, and covered in air, tight from the choker to his boots; as much as to say, I don't think there is anything about me you can catch hold of, and there is so little any-body would care to take. [*Enter Katey Rideout R.*]

Katey. Well, Tom, what's the matter?

Tom. I am ruined, that's all. All I have worked for is to be swept away into the pocket of yonder eelskin, and I am left homeless.

Katey. A man who loves and is loved again, however poor he may be, is never homeless. Home is not built with bricks and mortar, Tom, but with flesh and blood.

Tom. But is there such a thing as home for me? am I loved again? Nobody can answer that but you. [*Nat appears and looks over paling*]

Katey. When you were in luck and I could have had you any day, I did not know my own mind, but now you are ruined, I feel jealous and exas-perated.

Tom. What does that mean?

Katey. It means, Tom, that when you are turned out by the world I shall say, "Come home." [*They embrace*]

Tom. Ah, what a comfort that is to a fellow in his misfortune. [*Nat's business with rose plant*]

Nat. [*C. At back*] They ort to have their picters took jest so. What a hinterest even for their children.

Katey. [*R.*] Do you feel ruined now, Tom?

Tom. [*L.*] I feel reconciled to it, dear.

Katey. Well, I don't. We are as poor as mice. If you lose the farm, what are we to live on? We are not going to sponge on my old grandfather.

Tom. No, I'd never be a burden to the old man. Never! Never! Never!

Nat. Hear! Hear! Hear! [*Retires behind cottage*]

KATEY. Then you must have that lease. [*Crosses R.*] Leave the captain to me; I can move his heart.

TOM. How?

KATEY. Never mind how, that is my business. [*R.*] The lease you shall have. Never ask me how I obtained it. Good-bye, Tom. [*At the door*] Have you not forgotten something?

TOM. Ah! [*Runs to kiss her, she shuts the door in his face*] Bless her, what a treasure she is. [*Crosses. Enter Nat*]

NAT. Don't rely on her to make your fortune. A man as reckons on a woman to make his way in the world ain't no better than a child.

TOM. I tell you, Nat, I have not a hundred pounds in the world.

NAT. And I tell you, lad, I have ten thousand. Hist!

TOM. Ten thousand pounds?

NAT. Every blessed copper on 'em.

TOM. Where?

NAT. In the stables at Nobbley Hall. That 'ere capital is stowed away in the loose box No. 14, in the form of the two-year colt.

TOM. Flying Scud?

NAT. Hist! I tell you, d'ye want to ruin me? Speak low. Yes, Flying Scud. For two years the Squire has been keeping that colt dark, and as month after month he grew under your training, we sor the bit of stuff coming an' comin' out as sure and clear as the ye'rly mornin' and then we kept it darker. Last June he was entered for the Criterion Stakes and then we slipped him in for the blue ribbin at Epsom. Nobody took no notice, while I got him on at 100 to 1. I swore I'd never back anything as wore hoofs, except to lose, but I've backed him to win and he will, he will. I've been a jockey, man and boy, for fifty-nine year, and never saw his match. Slip your money on him, Tom. Pitch it. Melt down your best breeches and put your last teaspoon in the pot, for as sure as we stand here, you and me has bred and trained a Derby winner. [*Crosses to L.*]

TOM. You take my breath away!

NAT. That's what I reckon Flying Scud will do to bigger men than you and me, when ahead of his horses he shows the field his plates. [*Whispering*] Ooraw! Ooraw! Ooraw!

TOM. I'll back him, Nat, I'll back him.

NAT. 'Old 'ard, lad, the colt belongs to Goodge. That is, he will belong to him, for this afternoon the lawyer comes from London with the old Squire's will, which he will read at the 'all. Then Flying Scud with all his engagements will become the property of Captain Grindley Goodge.

TOM. Well?

NAT. Well, when our beauty wins the Criterion Stakes, he'll be at evens for the Derby before Christmas.

TOM. I won't edge a penny, Nat, I'll stand or fall by him. [*Crosses L.*]

NAT. Then you'll fall, lad, for then Goodge will lay against him for the Derby, and he'll be run to lose. That's always the game them sort play.

TOM. What can we do?

NAT. Keep dark, lad, and let me work the oracle. There's three men, pals of hisn, now on a visit at the 'all. Mo Davis, Colonel Mulligan, and Chousir. Them three and Goodge are known as the quadruped.

TOM. The quadruped?

NAT. Ay, the four legs. And the heap of money they've run away with! Afore they've found out what's in Flying Scud's skin, you get your money on with all of 'em. Let 'em smell your money, they'll make it easy for you; then we'll let the light in upon them, and when Goodge finds he has got a flyer in his stable, a Derby crack, he'll give you the lease or whatever you ask him, for fear you should blow the secret and spoil the odds.

TOM. But I would not betray my employer.

NAT. I know it, lad, but he don't believe in honesty except what's paid for ad valorum, and that's where three sharp 'uns get licked. Leave it to me, boy. Off with you to the stable, I'll follow you.

TOM. Success, Nat, I feel success. Oh, my bright and bonny colt, when you've rubbed your nose against my cheek and looked so kind at me out of your dark eyes, did you know that you were going to win for me, not the Derby, but a greater prize than ever was contended for on the English turf, Katey Rideout, the girl I love better than my life, the prettiest girl in Yorkshire? [*Exit L.1E.*]

NAT. There goes a square, honest, good bit of stuff. His character is as sweet as new mown hay; free from dirt, of a fine nose, and jest such as any woman or friend may thrive on. [*Exit R.*]

SCENE 2: *The garden at Nobbley Hall. Front Cloth. Enter Goodge followed by servant.*

GOODGE. Has Joe gone down to the station to meet Mr. Quail with the dog-cart?

SERV. Yes, sir.

GOODGE. Let lunch be ready in the library at three o'clock. Have the principal tenants been notified to attend?

SERV. Yes, sir.

GOODGE. Very good. [*Exit servant L.1E.*] I wish to enter into possession in style. Today will make me master of Nobbley Hall, and it comes not a day too soon, for my creditors began to look cloudy. Here comes two of them. They stick to me like leeches. Ah, my very dear friends, when can I afford to kick you out! Won't I pick my heaviest pair of boots for the festive occasion—in the meanwhile— [*Enter Mo Davis and Mulligan L.1E.*] Ah, Mulligan, how are you enjoying yourself? Eh, Davis?

Mo. Ve have been taking stock of the place. Beautiful, ain't it, Mulligan?

GOODGE. It's good for the thousand I owe you, Mo, and for the seven hundred I am in your debt, eh? What do you think, my rollickers?

Mo. A thousand was it? Vell I never think of it, Grindley, s'elp me, it never crossed my mind.

MULL. Don't mention it, old fellow.

GOODGE. Well, I won't. Have you any news from Lord Woodbie's trainer? How are the horses we sold him?

Mo. Vulcan has broken down, and Tripod has been and justified his name, and goes on three legs. He says the stable looks like a coffin lid, it's full of screws. You couldn't paint von of them to look like a horse.

GOODGE. Where's the young lord now?

MULL. Playing billiards.

Mo. His Lordship is a comfortable annooity to me, and Mulligan makes a settled income out of him at billiards.

GOODGE. While you and I manage his stable and advise him how to lay his money out.

Mo. Ah, he's a young mine of wealth, as ve've discovered, and ve've all shares in him.

GOODGE. And a pretty sharp lookout we've kept upon each other to see that we shared alike.

Mo. Oh, honor, ve couldn't get on nohow unless we had some principle; I say, Mulligan, go and keep an eye on young Lord Woodbie.

MULL. All right, I'll see to him. [*Exit. Enter servant L.1E.*]

SERV. Miss Rideout, sir, wishes to see you. She has just rode into the strawyard.

GOODGE. Miss Rideout, are you sure?

SERV. Yes, sir. [*Speaks apart to Goodge*]

Mo. Vy, here comes Mr. Quail, the lawyer.

GOODGE. I must leave you, Mo, to receive him, for the prettiest girl in Yorkshire is waiting for me yonder. [*Exit with servant L.1E. Enter Quail R.1E.*]

Mo. Ah, Quail, welcome to Nobbley Hall. You bring de vill, eh?

QUAIL. I see that Captain Goodge has taken possession already.

Mo. Vy not, ain't he a right to it; ain't he the heir?

QUAIL. You are an old and valued client, Mr. Davis. Ahem! Goodge owes you a thousand pounds.

Mo. Vell, vell, he will pay me when he fingers the old Squire's spondoolicks.

QUAIL. Don't make too sure that he will ever touch a penny of them.

Mo. Vot, vot, I thay, no jokin'! You don't mean to tell me the Squire has cut him off?

QUAIL. I have no right to say so much, but as you are an old client—

Mo. Oo, Oo, jumpin' Moses! I'm in a hole! Oo, Oo, it's ruin. A thousand pound! What's to be done?

QUAIL. Six months ago you instructed us to sue Goodge for this debt.

Mo. No, no, you was sent on by a third party. I didn't vant to quarrel vid him.

QUAIL. We obtained judgment. I issued execution yesterday. The officer is waiting at the village inn. Now the rest is your business, but take my advice. Put the screw on while Goodge is in feather. Let him borrow the money or get security now, for by tonight there may not be a feather left upon him. [*Exit L.1E.*]

Mo. Jumpin' Moses! Here's a pretty kettle of fish. There's no trustin' nobody. Even ven a fellow's dead and buried, he's down on you in his will. Poor Goodge, I pities him, s'elp me, he's out of luck. Vat's to be done? If I put the screw on, dere's young Lord Woodbie vill never let him be arrested; he'll pay it or go security. I'll offer to jine in a bill. I'll give the bums an 'int; I've not got an hour to act in. Poor Goodge! Vell, vell! I wouldn't 'urt 'im, but it's for his own good, 'cause ven he's down in the vorld agin I can lend him a fiver; I'll put the screw on. I wouldn't do it, but it's for his own good. [*Exit L.1E. Enter Julia Latimer L.1E.*]

JULIA. Did he see my signal? I waved my handkerchief to him through the billiard room window. Yes, he's coming. [*Enter Lord Woodbie L.1E.*]

WOOD. You wished me to join your ramble?

JULIA. I am afraid I interrupted your game.

WOOD. Oh, it is all right. I was playing with your uncle, Colonel Mulligan, but when I saw you beckon to me, I threw up the game and paid my stakes.

JULIA. I do not wish you to play billiards with my uncle.

WOOD. Why not? I can beat him, I can give him ten points in fifty.

JULIA. [*Aside*] Poor fellow. [*Aloud*] I know you can, but my uncle cannot afford to lose his money.

WOOD. Then I am so glad he has won somehow of me a few hundreds by flukes. I never saw such a fellow to fluke.

JULIA. He is almost as lucky as Mr. Chousir.

WOOD. By Jove! Chousir is the worst hand at ecarté I ever did see. The blunders he makes!

JULIA. But I thought he rose up a winner last night?

WOOD. So he did, to his great amusement and surprise. But the beginners always have such extraordinary luck.

JULIA. [*Aside*] Poor boy. [*Aloud*] Can you find no occupation more pleasing than cards or billiards?

WOOD. Well, yes, I prefer to walk with you. I say, Miss Latimer.

JULIA. Well, my lord?

WOOD. I wish you would call me Cecil. I—I wish you'd tell me what to do to please you, because, I—I want to awfully. Do tell me something.

JULIA. Don't bet, you lose your money; don't drink, you can't stand it; don't smoke, you don't like it.

WOOD. Oh! By Jove! I can't get up in the morning till I've had a cigar, and positively I could not get over the afternoon without a pick-me-up at two and a stiff tod before dinner.

JULIA. Well, I don't like it, and if you wish to please me—

WOOD. Wish to please you. Oh, by Jove, if you only knew, 'pon my soul—

JULIA. Don't swear.

WOOD. Oh, I say, you're awfully hard on a fellow.

JULIA. You are an only child, Lord Woodbie.

WOOD. Yes.

JULIA. The only child of a widowed mother?

WOOD. Solitary chicken of the old bird.

JULIA. Don't speak so of your mother; you don't feel it. When you are at Naseby Castle do you smoke in bed of a morning?

WOOD. Well, the old lady will come and wake me, just as she did when I was a kid; it's an awful bore.

JULIA. Do you take pick-me-ups and your tods there?

WOOD. No, because she's always kissing me, and the infernal things smell so.

JULIA. Do you swear in her presence?

WOOD. [*After a pause*] No!

JULIA. Lord Woodbie, do not affect vices for which you have no taste, nor mimic manners of which you are really ashamed. Smoking makes you sick, I have seen you grow pale at your second cigar.

WOOD. Me?

JULIA. You abhor brandy, yet you drink it neat, just to show off. Tobacco and spirits offend your mouth, and you wince when you swear.

WOOD. I will do anything you tell me, you know I will, because—because—you won't be offended?

JULIA. Because?

WOOD. I love you. Oh, I do indeed, Julia. I never said so before, but you must know it. Don't you, don't you?

JULIA. Hush! Yes!

WOOD. Oh, Julia, if you knew how I go on about you when I am alone; I've laid for hours outside your door, and kissed the boots you had left there; I've been the most infernal idiot to go on so, but I can't help it.

JULIA. No, no, you must not love me.

WOOD. I shall have seventeen thousand a year when I become of age, and when my granduncle dies I'll be a duke. I'll marry you at once.

JULIA. I am not fit to hold the rank of your wife.

WOOD. You are fit to be a queen.

JULIA. What I am is best known to myself, but I will not impose on your heart.

WOOD. I see what it is. You look on me as a child, to be pitied and to chide, not to be loved.

JULIA. Think what you please, but believe me, what you ask is impossible.

WOOD. It is all over then? You turn away from me; very well, you love someone else; I hope he loves you, 'cause then you—you won't feel as I do now. Oh, what shall I do! What shall I do!

JULIA. Cecil, forgive me. [*She takes his hand*] Won't you speak to me?

WOOD. No! [*Throws her hand away and runs off L.1E. Enter Mulligan with billiard cue in his hand*]

MULL. [*R.*] What is the matter?

JULIA. [*L.*] Lord Woodbie has proposed to me.

MULL. That's elegant.

JULIA. I have refused him.

MULL. Refused, refused an earrul! Refused seventeen thousand a year?

JULIA. The boy does not know I am an adventuress.

MULL. A what? You, my sister's child, wid the blood of the Mulligan in you, an adventuress? Show me the man who will say it to my face.

JULIA. No, but I will show you fifty that will say it every day behind your back. They say that I have been employed by you and your companions to dazzle and blind such victims as that young lord, while you pick their pockets.

MULL. Are you mad or dhraming?

JULIA. No, I am wide awake; I wish I had been so three years ago when I left school to partake of your home and to become what I am, your accomplice.

MULL. Is this the gratitude for the education I've wasted on you?

JULIA. Marry me to a rich man; take your price, pay yourself; I am ready to be sold, but let it be to one I am not expected to love.

MULL. Do my sinses decave me? Do you mean to tell me that you love this slip of a boy?

JULIA. Yes, I do, and that is why I have refused him; [*goes R.*] I cannot cheat him in love as you do in play; I will not enter his family like a thief. [*Exit R.1E.*]

MULL. Once in, who cares how you get there? Refuse seventeen thousand pounds a year! There's no counting on a woman. When you've won the game for her, she'll revoke and play the divil wid your finest combination. [*Exit L.1E.*]

SCENE 3: *The Stable. Door R. in F. Door L. in F. with No. 14 painted on it. Hayloft R. with ladder up to it. Stable boys take two horses out through D.F. for airing. Jerry and stable helps discovered.*

JERRY. Bob not yet in? He's been out for some exercise, he wants a lot of flesh taken off him; in fact he wants regularly pulling through a sieve.

BOB. [*Outside*] Hallo, Jerry!

JERRY. Ah, here he is. [*Enter Bob, dressed up in wraps and looking very fat*]

BOB. Give us a peel, lads.

JERRY. Take 'em off very cautiously; don't let the wind come on him too suddenly. [*Business*] My eyes, ain't he drawed fine?

BOB. I've had an eight-mile bust, I was twenty-nine ounces over weight this morning, let's see if I've left them on the road. [*Jumps into scale*]

JERRY. [*Counting in weights*] Nine fourteen and a half and three pounds. Nine stun ten.

BOB. That vos my mornin's averdoopise. Take out a pound. Ooraw! I'm flying still; take out another. Ah, I'm comin' to that. Eight stun eight and a pinch of snuff. [*Jumps out*] There's a waste. Now I'll take a feed; wot's the bill of fare?

JERRY. Here you are. [*Points to a paper on the wall*]

BOB. [*Reads*] Cold tea, sop biscuit, stale toast and a mug of water. Oh, Lord! [*Enter Nat D.F.R.*]

NAT. Ah, my little pips, here we are, eh?

ALL. It's Nat! it's Nat!

JERRY. Blow'd if it ain't "Old Boots" hisself.

ALL. Ooray!

NAT. How are ye, boys? It does my witals good to see you.

JERRY. Sit down. Why, what form he is in, boys; he is jockey all over still, ain't he? Now, Bob, go and get him a drop of beer.

BOB. All right, give us the jug.

JERRY. You will find one on the table. [*Exit Bob D.F.*] Ah, Nat, when I look at you I always thinks of the glorious old times when it was reckoned the greatest honor a man could have, to hold the blue ribbon of the turf.

NAT. Ah, them was days and no mistake.

JERRY. You was well thought of, and your friends ought to have been proud of you.

NAT. I believe they was. I was laid down right as a boy, lads; I'd a father as wouldn't stand no fat, and he skinned me close before I could walk. He brought me up in the weight I should go and when I was old I didn't depart from it.

JERRY. Have you saved much?

NAT. Well, I might have saved more if I hadn't spent so much, but I suppose I mustn't grumble. You see I does pretty well even now; I gets all the information from the boys in the stables, I advertises in the "Pink un," and I sells tips, straight tips too, not like some on 'em. I can truly say that I've never done anything yet that I'm ashamed of, and I can look back on the past with the knowledge that I have never wronged man, woman, or child.

JERRY. If all had been like you, Nat, the turf would stand much better than it does.

NAT. Cf course there are black legs in every calling, and the turf is no more free from them than anything else.

JERRY. I was talking to a jockey the other day, Nat, who said he could always ride better after having a glass of champagne. What's your opinion of that? [*Re-enter Bob with a pewter pot of beer*]

NAT. Rot, utter rot! No man ever did anything better through being under the influence of drink; and my advice to every jockey would be, never touch a drop of liquor till after the race. You've heard of the time when I rode Skyrocket for the Great Metropolitan Stakes.

JERRY. Yes, when Scaramouth won by two lengths.

NAT. Not a bit of it, Scaramouth won by two glasses of champagne.

JERRY. Two glasses of champagne? Why, how was that, Nat?

NAT. Well, I'll tell you. It wants a clear head to ride a race; there's no excitement in the world equal to it. I hadn't had much to eat on the morning of the race, and although it's bad to eat too much, still it's bad to ride on an empty stomach. I was feeling rather faint, and just when I was on my horse, my backer says, "Have a glass of champagne, Nat; it will do you good"; so I took it. It was beautiful and cool, had been standing in ice, and tasted to my parched throat like nectar. I looked longingly at the bottle and he generously offered me another glass. I took it and sure enough I did feel the better for it. "I'll win," says I, and off I started. I headed them all the first hundred strides. I dug my spurs into my horse, and he answered to it and I felt it was a sure thing. The champagne seemed to bubble all over me, and I felt as light as a feather. We sprung up the rise like a whirlwind. The roar of the people, the swarming of the carriages, the bright colors on the grandstand all flashed across my eyes like a dream. It was just then I felt the horse flag in his pace; my head began to swim and I seemed to lose my presence of mind as I heard the second horse close behind me. I lost my grip and control, and my blood seemed to turn to liquid fire; my brain seemed to be a blaze and my head felt like bursting. I could feel the second horse behind me, but my sight seemed to get blurred; my own horse seemed to slip out of my grasp, and I couldn't regain my hold. It was my fault. I had given him too much to do at first, and he couldn't keep it up. The second horse came abreast of me; I could see the jockey; we glared into each other's eyes as we went along neck and neck, stride for stride, until we came within a hundred yards of the winning post. Then the other jockey lifted his horse, yes, fairly lifted it, past me and won by two lengths. But he didn't, he won by two glasses of champagne. I had the best horse, but my horse hadn't got the best rider. Then I took a sacred oath never to touch a drop of intoxicating liquor on the day of a race, and I've never broken my word; and I advise you chaps to always do the same.

BOB. Well, that puts me in mind of what happened to me when I rode Blue Bell in the Ladies Plate; only I lost mine through the mare, Vixen, and not through having anything to drink.

NAT. Oh, that's an old story, and has got about, and been told over and over again.

BOB. Well, never mind who's been telling it, it really happened to me.

JERRY. What was it, Bob?

NAT. You've heard it before, Jerry, scores of times.

JERRY. Never mind, a good thing is never the worse for telling over again.

BOB. Well, I had a spell of very bad luck; hadn't won a race for the whole season, when I got a chance with Blue Bell for the Ladies Plate.

There was only two in it as far as the race was concerned, Blue Bell and Vixen—you know, the squinny-eyed mare. I rode Blue Bell, and Tommy Comfit rode Vixen. Tommy was always a bit nasty with me, and never lost a chance of queering me; and as for Vixen, we were never friendly. The betting was five to four on Blue Bell; the mare was in grand form, and I felt something inside me which seemed to say I had a sure win. When Vixen came out of the stables she seemed to look out of the side of her squinny eye in a vicious, nasty, spiteful way—something like this. [*Business*]

NAT. Don't go on like that, Bob, or you will be struck with a squint.

JERRY. Well, if ever I saw a mare look like that, I should think there was sommat up.

BOB. And so there was sommat up. Vixen had made up her mind that Blue Bell shouldn't win.

JERRY. 'Ow did she prevent it?

BOB. That's what I'm coming to. The starting bell was rang, and off we went.

NAT. Where was you, Bob?

BOB. Mounted on Blue Bell, to be sure.

NAT. Oh! I thought you said you fell off.

BOB. Now that just shows what attention you were paying to my story.

NAT. But I've heard it before.

BOB. Well, you've got to hear it again. Off we went. Blue Bell took the lead and kept it till the end of the race. Vixen kept coming slowly but surely on, till she got alongside Blue Bell, and there she stuck. Tommy Comfit was so close to me that I could smell his breath; I remember it distinctly, for he had been eating onions at the time.

NAT. P'raps he wasn't so close to you as you thought; the flavor of onions may be carried a long way.

BOB. I dug my spurs in Blue Bell's flanks, and tried to lift her forward; Tommy did the same thing with Vixen. I lashed Blue Bell; Tommy quilted Vixen, and there we kept side by side—nothing to choose between us. The other horses all fell behind, but on we went till the winning post came in sight. Then came the last grand struggle. I lashed at Blue Bell, and Tommy laid on to Vixen. The shouts on the course roared like thunder in our ears. On we went, foot to foot, muscle to muscle, head to head, neck to neck, nose to nose; and then Vixen gave such a look as never came out of a horse's eyes before, and put out her tongue and won. Won by a tongue. [*Enter boy with jug of beer*]

NAT. Bob, my son, what's all this here? You told me as you wos on a regiment! Oh, this won't do! This must all come off! D'ye drink beer?

Bob. A drop or so.

Nat. You look it. And you eat butter; I see it in yer. And cheese! What d'ye expect to come to with a constitootion and a career like wot you have?

Bob. I don't know what to do with myself.

Nat. Tomorrow, lad, you'll breakfast on a pint and a half of warm water, and you'll put that in it. [*Gives him packet*] Hepsom salts! So called 'cause they prepares the body for training. Then you'll put yourself on dry toast, stale bread, and arf a pint o' tea a day, no milk in it, mind ye. Ye mustn't look at sugar, and if you dream of beer at night, take another dose of salts in the morning.

Bob. Very good, sir.

Nat. Fifty years ago, they knew how to breed jockeys, but, love ye, I'd split a pen, and make more of a jockey than half the boys that gets the crack mounts now. And Nat Goslin', though I say it, was the pink of the Pig Skin in those days. You heard how I took the Chester Cup in 'fifty-nine? Ah! I'll tell you about that adwenter.

Song. [*With chorus of boys*]

"THE OLD JOCKEY'S LAMENT"

In 'forty-four I von the Hoaks, and then they put me up
To ride Sir Tatten's little mare as took the Chester Cup.
But, oh, my! oh, cry! it vos just then d'ye see,
The pootyest gal in Doncaster, she fell in love with me.

[*Spoken*] She vos a prize gal, sech a chest, deep and full forard, and well let down.

She said she would be mine ven I was growed a little bigger,
She didn't know I mustn't put no meat upon my figger.
Oh, my! oh, cry! vat is a chap to do,
Ven he's in love and got to ride vell under eight stun two.

[*Chorus of "Oh, my!, etc."*]

I vos in form to go to scale, but, Lord, so small a mite
I never shall forget the day when I was coortin' she.
She undertook vith all her veight to sit upon my knee.

[*Spoken*] Fourteen stun six, I thought the roof had fell in.

I've heard that girls in general, vos made of hoop and bustle.
This gal of mine, her crinoline vos made of bone and muscle.
Oh, my! oh, cry!, etc.

[*Chorus of "Oh, my!, etc."*]

My little dear, ses she to me, I'd be afraid to take ye,
For if I'd give ye half a squeeze, it's two to one I'd break ye.
Next week as I was walking my five-miler on the downs,
I met her walking with a six-foot sergeant of Dragoons.

[*Spoken*] He'd got his arm 'round her vaist. "My lad," ses he,
"Take my advice. Next time you want to marry,
Jest handicap the gals, and see what weight you're fit to carry."
Oh, my! oh, cry!, etc.
[*Chorus of "Oh, my!, etc." After which the boys start into a jockey hornpipe,
general dance, solos: Nat, Bob, and Ned*]

I RIDE TO WIN

(Gentleman's Version)

The Queen of my heart is Rosie my own,
A trainer's fair daughter is she,
Her dad had to win a certain great race
Or ruined for life he would be.
He gave me the mount; that evening I met
My dear little Rosie, who cried,
"If you win the race, your wife I will be."
I kissed her and boldly replied,

[*Chorus*] Rosie, Rosie, to win I ride,
Rosie, Rosie, then you're my bride;
The mare's all right, and I'll make her spin,
For love and life, for wealth and fame, I ride to win.

The race day arrived, and there on the course,
A bookie crept up to my side,
And whispered, "A thousand if you will lose."
"No, never, you villain," I cried.
I saw the old man, his face full of care,

With Rosie close by all the while,
And then at the post, all eager to start,
I shouted to her with a smile. [*Chorus*]

The flag quickly fell; the lot got away,
But I kept the bonnie mare back;
Till swift as a dart, she worked through the crowd,
Got foremost of all on the track.
I touched her but once with whip and with spur,
Bent forward and gave her her head;
We shot past the judge—hurrah! we had won.
My cap proudly waving, I said. [*Chorus. After song and dance, Nat exclaims*]

NAT.   Ah, here comes Master Tom Meredith with Flying Scud from exercise. [*Enter Tom leading horse*]

TOM.   Soho! my beauty. There, that'll do! He is a shaving too heavy in the shoulder, Bob. Tomorrow morning at eight, you will give him a gentle pipe opener in his breast cloth.

BOB.   Yes, sir.

TOM.   Put him in his box. [*Business putting horse off*]

NAT.   Well, Tom, I don't know what you think, but I consider the horse in first-rate form.

TOM.   He's a picture. He looks as if he knew his own secret and revelled in it. Bob, I hope you never quit him.

BOB.   Quit him? I sleeps in his manger; me and the cat.

NAT.   Has any of the gentlemen down from the Hall been to look at him?

BOB.   They all come, and chucked an eye over him. One said he vos too slack; t'other said he'd got 'ocks like a cow, and axed me what I wallied him at, so much a pound.

NAT.   I'm agoin' to make your fortin, lad, for you're gettin' overweight for your business, and should lay by a trifle, for nobody knows the day when fat will come on him, and put him into private life.

BOB.   Please, sir, I've two pun ten saved up agin such an ewent.

NAT.   Then I'll put every shilling of it on the Scud for you, Bob. Now be off and take a constitutional four-miler, and get down some of that hextra.

BOB. [*Downcast*].   I'm afraid it's bred in me, sir.

NAT.   No, Bob, 'tain't bread, it's beer. [*Exit Bob*] Now, Tom, you're going to meet these turfited, and don't be afeared.

TOM.   But how shall I begin?

NAT. Leave that to me. I'll cut out the running for you. It ain't the wally of the money only, but, oh, to see them four legs on the gridiron, and to see 'em getting it hot. Well, it will be a sight improvin' to youth, and gratifyin' to declining years. [*Enter Woodbie L.D. in F.*]

WOOD. Here I shall be alone. I cannot see those fellows with red and swollen eyes. [*Sees Nat and Tom*] Deuce take it. [*Turns away*]

TOM. That's one of them. [*Rain and thunder*]

NAT. [*Aside*] No, no.

WOOD. It's beginning to rain. [*Looks out*]

NAT. He's a gentleman all over; his money wouldn't have no flavor in it. Foller me; I'll point the covey. Pardon, sir. [*Exit passing Woodbie and followed by Tom L.D.*]

WOOD. What a fool I am. I will go back to Naseby and try to get over this feeling. [*Opens and reads letter*] "My darling boy: Let me entreat you to return to me, if only for a week. I hear you are wasting your youth and health sadly; and worse than all, you have formed an attachment for a worthless and designing woman, by whose arts you are retained amidst a bad set of men. I do not regret the money you have lost to these scheming persons, but I do regret that your affection should be shared between a heartless adventuress, and your attached mother, Cecilia Woodbie." This "designing adventuress" refused me; refused to be a countess because she could not love me. Hark, someone is coming here. [*Looks out*] 'Tis Goodge, and a lady. They are seeking shelter from the rain. I am not fit to be seen. [*Wipes his eyes*] I'll wait in the loft above until they are gone. [*Goes up ladder R. into loft. Enter Goodge D.F.*]

GOODGE. [*L.*] It is only a shower; this place will afford you shelter. [*Enter Katey D.F.*]

KATEY. [*R.*] I do not mind a ducking.

GOODGE. Nor I; provided I can choose my duck.

KATEY. I beg you to leave trifling, and consider my question. If you turn young Meredith out of the farm, there is not a tongue in the county that will not cry shame on you.

GOODGE. I care more for one word from your lips, than for what all the tongues in the kingdom can say.

KATEY. Then you will grant me a favor?

GOODGE. Will you grant me that word?

KATEY. You are jesting.

GOODGE. No, for I love you, and I am ready to make any sacrifice for your sake.

KATEY. I cannot listen to you. Let me go. [*Crosses R.*]

GOODGE. You must; you shall. You knew that I loved you, and you came here to avail yourself of that passion to obtain a favor from me, to bestow it on my rival, young Meredith.

KATEY. I came to plead to your good nature.

GOODGE. You cannot ask me to mend his fortune. [*Locks door L.*] Let me rather offer you a share in mine.

KATEY. Stand from before that door, if you please.

GOODGE. I cannot part with you. I love you. Well, there, I offer you my hand.

KATEY. Your case must indeed be desperate. [*Tom knocks at door D.F.*]

GOODGE. Nay, you shall not go. [*The door R. is tried*]

KATEY. Thank heaven, there is someone!

GOODGE. From the first hour I saw you, I marked you as mine, and mine you shall be.

KATEY. If you are a gentleman, sir, you will cease this importunity. [*Knocking at door*] Why do they not come in?

GOODGE. Because I have bolted the door.

KATEY. Bolted the door?

GOODGE. Hush! You must wait now till they have gone away.

KATEY. Oh, why did I come here?

TOM. [*Outside*] Hallo, Jack! Stephen! Who has locked the door?

KATEY. It is Tom's voice. Oh, sir, what can I say? How can I explain such a position?

GOODGE. You cannot, but you can pass out this way. Quick! [*Opens the R.H. door. She enters the stable of the Flying Scud. He locks her in, and then opens the R.F. door. Enter Tom, Chousir, Mulligan and Mo Davis R.*] Well, gentlemen, what do you want?

TOM. [*C.*] I beg your pardon, I did not know you were here.

MO. [*R.*] Ve have been accommodating this young gentleman vith the hods on the hanimal hinside there.

MULL. The odds to fifty pounds, Mr. Meredith.

TOM. I'll take them again.

MO. Done.

TOM. And again to you, sir.

GOODGE. [*R.*] I am sorry you should have backed Flying Scud, for it is my intention to withdraw him.

TOM. Withdraw him? Scratch Flying Scud?

GOODGE. I don't intend to run the horse, and therefore have no further need of your services. I'll trouble you for the key of these stables.

TOM. But, sir, the horse was engaged by your late uncle.

GOODGE. So were you. I discharge you both. Fetch me the keys. I'll show you who is master here.

MO. So, if you have dem monnies runnin' about doin' nothing, you may fetch dem as vell, and square up at once.

TOM. [*Aside*] If the Scud is scratched, I am ruined, and so is Nat. [*Exit L.*]

GOODGE. I must get rid of these fellows and release the girl. What a state she must be in! [*Enter two bailiffs L.1E.*]

1ST B. Captain Goodge?

GOODGE. Yes.

1ST B. We want you, if you please, sir, at the suit of Joel Lawrence.

MO. Vot is it? Why these vagobonds is hofficers.

MULL. The devil they are! [*Exit door L.*]

GOODGE. I am arrested.

MO. Vell! Dis is truly ridiculous. Vere is Lord Woodbie? He will go security. [*Enter Jerry door L.*]

JERRY. Mr. Quail, sir, sent me to say that he is waiting in the library to read the late Squire's will. [*Exit*]

MO. Vere is Woodbie? Dis vill never do; ve must take you out between us.

GOODGE. No, I'll attend the reading in custody. In half an hour I shall have my uncle's banking account at my mercy.

MO. No, Goodge, old fellow, let me and Woodbie pay this, just to show you ain't without friends as is friends. He von't let me put the young lord in. Ain't it selfish? [*Exit D.F. A pause. Katey knocks at door*]

KATEY. [*Inside*] Sir! Sir, are you there? For Heaven's sake, unlock the door. [*Enter Tom with keys R.D.*]

TOM. Here are the keys. Ho! nobody here? I suppose they are gone back to the house. [*Katey knocks*] What's that? [*She knocks again*] There is someone in there. [*He tries the door*] 'Tis locked. Hush! I hear sobs. It is a young woman. Ho! I understand why all the doors were locked; the captain had a girl with him, and we surprised their billing and cooing.

KATEY. [*Inside*] Sir, sir, Captain Goodge, do unlock the door.

TOM. That voice! It is—it is hers.

KATEY. They are all gone now, and I can get away unperceived.

TOM. 'Tis she! 'Tis Katey! She was concealed here. [*He buries his face in his hands*] She said she had an influence over him. I see what sort it was; and I was fool enough to think she loved me. [*Enter Nat D.E.R.*]

NAT. Tom, my lad, they are waiting for us in the library.

TOM. [*Aside*] If he knew!

NAT.   You are as white as if you were all in a lather. What's up?

TOM.   Come away, Nat, come away. We have no business here.

NAT.   Why, what's the matter?

TOM.   Don't speak to me; my heart is breaking. [*Hurries him away*]

CLOSE IN

SCENE 4: *Front exterior on the road to the Hall. Enter Bob L.1E.*

BOB.   Well, they're agoing to read the old Squire's will up at the Hall, and I don't suppose there's much chance of him leaving me anything. People do say as how everything is a going to this Mister Grindley Goodge. He's a cove as I never did like; a sort of a domineering, overreaching, bullying, regular bad un. He's a regular hot un. His mother must have weaned him on pepper and mustard. Well, if he's going to be boss, it'll be the chuck out of all of us. If so, I think as how I shall get married and settle down. The awkward part of it is in making a selection of the proper party. My father used to say there was no depending on a woman. Oh, woman, woman, woman, woman! But there, I was allus susceptible of female loveliness.

"If to their share some trifling errors fall
Look in their faces, and you'll forget 'em all."

—*Shakespeare*

There's one girl as would jump at me, the parlor maid at the Cat and Saucepan. True, she's got a glass eye, and a bit of a limp—something like this—but that's rather an advantage, for if I wanted to get out of her way, she couldn't very well run after me. And as for her glass eye, if ever I did anything wrong, and didn't want her to see me, I could get on the blind side of her. [*Exit. Enter Lady Woodbie with letter*]

LADY W.   This letter which I have received puts it beyond all doubt that Cecil has formed an unfortunate attachment for a reckless adventuress, who is connected with a notorious gang of unprincipled scoundrels. Whatever happens, and at whatever cost, the affair must be broken off at once. [*Enter Mulligan and Mo Davis*]

MO.   I tell ye, it's true. He's arrested and taken down to Nobbley Hall to hear the will read. Oh! Jumping Moses! If it's true what the lawyer hinted at, we shan't get enough to buy a return ticket to London.

MULL.   Well, don't look at the worst side of things; let's get down to Nobbley Hall at once.

LADY W.   I beg your pardon, gentlemen, did you say Nobbley Hall?

Mo. Yes, mum, ve vos just a-going there to hear the vill of the old Squire read.

Lady W. I am a stranger here, and have missed the road on which I was directed; can you point out the way to Nobbley Hall to me?

Mo. Allow me! Just over there, and turn to the right; then you'll come to a cross on the road, go over by the left, and take the second turning on the right, and there you are.

Lady W. Thanks. [*Exit L.*]

Mo. Who is the old party? Quite an aristocratic old geezer.

Mull. Why, don't you remember her?

Mo. Vell, I seem to have a kind of a glimmering kind of an indistinct notion as I've seen her somewhere afore, and yet I can't be quite certain where.

Mull. Well, I've seen her somewhere, I'm certain.

Mo. Oh, sender me! I remember now! Don't you remember Lord Woodbie a showin' us some portraits the other night, and among them was one of his mother?

Mull. His mother?

Mo. Yes, his mother! Now what's she down here about?

Mull. Why, can't you see? It's plain enough to me; she's got scent of what we're up to, and is going to queer our pitch with the young Lord Woodbie.

Mo. Oh, s'help me! It's like taking the bread out of honest people's mouths! We're in a hole! we're in a hole! What a blooming schermozzle. [*Enter Jerry R.*]

Jerry. Beg pardon, sir, but if you want to hear the will read, you had better come at once, as the lawyer said he's going to start sharp to time.

Mull. Well, come along, we might as well know the best or the·worst.

Mo. Jumping Moses! There'll be no best about it, but all the worst.

Mull. Perhaps the old man may have revoked before he died; but in any case, whether we've lost in pot over Grindley Goodge or not, we must keep a tight hand over Lord Woodbie.

Mo. Tight hand; tight hand! These frisky young fools have got a nasty way of kicking over the traces and deserting their old friends. It's an old saying, but a true one, "Bring up a child in the way he should go, and when he's old, he'll do what he likes." [*Exeunt R.1E. Enter Lady Woodbie and Cecil L.1E.*]

Lady W. How strange that I should meet you, Cecil.

Wood. Yes, dear mother, I was on my way to Nobbley Hall, as I had been invited to attend the reading of the will, but changed my mind as I could have no interest in it, and preferred to take a meditative walk in the fields.

Lady W. Now, Cecil, look me straight in the face.

Wood. [*Aside*] Oh, Lord! What's coming?

Lady W. I believe you to be still the dear, loving-hearted boy that I have doted on from childhood, and incapable of a deceitful action. Believe me, that anything I have to say is for your own good. Now answer, is there any truth in that letter?

Wood. [*Hurriedly reading it*] Who could have written it? Yes, yes, dear mother, it is true. I do love her, love her devotedly.

Lady W. I was afraid you would say so. 'Tis a mad infatuation! You must learn to forget her.

Wood. Impossible! I can never forget, or cease to think of her. Believe me, mother, she's an angel.

Lady W. Yes, they're all angels before marriage, and I've often heard it said that's the reason husbands often wish their wives in Heaven soon afterwards.

Wood. If you only knew her, you wouldn't speak like that.

Lady W. Come now, Cecil, you are getting quite a man, but you don't know your own mind. You must give her up. Remember, it's only a couple of years since you thought you were in love with Sir Francis Reynold's niece.

Wood. But that was only a boyish fancy; I was not old enough to know my mind.

Lady W. And you are not old enough now to decide so serious a question. You must give up all thought of such a union. I am a woman of the world enough to tell you that more than half of the misery and unhappiness in this world is caused through ill-assorted marriages.

Wood. Mother, you are mistaken in your estimate of Julia. She is different from other women, different from any other woman I have ever met. But as I loved you in my childhood's happy days, so I love you now, and I promise you, my darling mother, that I will do nothing without your consent to my marriage with Julia. I will give her up, even if it should break my heart to do so.

Lady W. Spoken like my own true-hearted boy, Cecil. Cecil, you are still more than all the world to me, and, believe me, you shall never regret listening to the warning words prompted by a mother's love. [*Exeunt L.1E.*]

SCENE 5: *The library. Full stage. Door L. Window R. Quail at table R.C. arranging papers. Mulligan, Goodge, Mo Davis, and tenants discovered. Two policemen near door L. Enter Tom and Nat.*

QUAIL. [*C.*] Take a seat, Mr. Meredith.

GOODGE. [*L.*] Stop, sir; allow me to do the honors of my own house, if you please. [*To Tom*] You can stand there, my man. [*Gives chair to one of the tenants*]

NAT. [*L.C.*] No offense, sir. I say, Tom, we are the only upright men in the crowd.

QUAIL. [*Opens the will*] The will, gentlemen, I see is short and holograph.

MO. Vat's that?

NAT. It's short for sweet, I hope.

MO. But what does "holograph" mean?

QUAIL. Why everyone knows it means written entirely by one's own hand.

MO. Ah! Some of my friends get writing other people's.

QUAIL. [*Reads*] "To Katherine Rideout, granddaughter of Nathaniel Gosling, I leave two hundred pounds in affectionate remembrance of the bunches of flowers she used to leave me."

NAT. Bless his heart, he didn't forget my dear Katey. Two hundred pounds in affectionate remembrance, Lord love him.

QUAIL. "To Dr. Dryden, who nearly caused my death by giving me enough physic to kill a whole stable of horses, I leave the—"

NAT. How much? The doctor is not here; I wonder what he'll think of his luck? Shall I go and fetch him?

QUAIL. Wait a minute. "I leave the empty pill-boxes and physic bottles, hoping they may never be refilled."

NAT. I shan't go and tell him; one of the others can go and let him know of his good luck.

QUAIL. "To Jeremiah Cobbler—"

NAT. Hallo, Jerry, it's your turn now.

QUAIL. "The sum of twenty-five pounds in consideration of his general good behavior."

JERRY. Twenty-five pounds? Then I'm going to have a holiday. Twenty-five pounds! I didn't expect twenty-five pence.

QUAIL. "To the proposed school for children of old jockeys who have never had a black mark against them, I leave the sum of five hundred pounds."

NAT. He couldn't have left it for a better purpose.

QUAIL. "To the hospital at Doncaster, I leave the sum of three hundred pounds."

NAT. Hear! Hear! Good again!

GOODGE. [*Aside*] Confound his generosity! All that will come out of what should be mine.

MULL. Cheer up, Goodge, those small legacies are merely flea-bites; merely flea-bites.

NAT. Order, gents, please! Order!

MULL. Yes; let's have a scotch and soda.

QUAIL. [*Sternly*] Eh?

MO. Jumping Moses! I forgot where I was.

QUAIL. "To the members of the Jockey Club, I leave fifty pounds to be spent in a good dinner to be eaten within twelve months from the time I go up aloft."

GOODGE. Or below; a mere matter of opinion.

MO. Above or below, I don't suppose it matters much. He's got friends in both places.

QUAIL. Silence, gentlemen!

MO. Yes, let's have a bit of silence, gentlemen, I am surprised at yer.

QUAIL. "To Robert Buckskin I leave the sum of twenty-five pounds, with a strong recommendation to spend it in Anti-Fat, as I believe he is naturally stout, and inclined to make flesh, and no amount of training will keep him a reasonable size."

NAT. Well, Bob, you and Jerry share and share alike.

BOB. I'm sure I didn't expect it any more than Jerry did. Twenty-five pounds! What'll I do with it?

MO. I'll bet you 250 to 25 that Kiddle-a-wink doesn't win the Esher Plate.

BOB. Right you are; book it a bet.

NAT. I'll stand in half with you.

BOB. Right you are.

QUAIL. Really, gentlemen, this is most unseemly. Silence! "To my legal advisers, Messrs. Quail and Fitter, I leave the sum of one hundred pounds each, and hereby appoint them trustees of this my last will and testament."

NAT. That's his will sure enough, but I don't see any testament.

BOB. P'raps it's one of them books on the table?

GOODGE. Proceed, sir, get on with the reading of the will.

NAT. I haven't heard your name yet, Tom. For your father's sake I should have thought he would have left you a few hundreds.

Tom. I respect his memory just the same, whether he has left me a thousand farthings or a thousand pounds.

Goodge. A thousand farthings is more like the figure than anything else.

Nat. Well, I'm not so sure about that.

Quail. No more am I. Listen to this, gentlemen: "Subject to the payment of all the before-mentioned legacies, I give and bequeath everything of which I die possessed to Thomas Meredith, the son of my old master. I wish to restore the property I made out of his father, and therefore I give and bequeath to him my estate at Nobbley Hall, together with all my property of every kind therein and thereon, on the following conditions: that whereas my bay colt, Flying Scud, by Hurricane, out of Sunshine, is entered at Newmarket and Epsom, the same Thomas Meredith shall run the horse on his fair merits for these races, and shall fulfil all the engagements previously made for the said Flying Scud."

Goodge. Then what is left to me?

Quail. Nothing. [*Stop music*] Your name is not mentioned in the document.

Mull. He hasn't even cut you off with a shilling.

Quail. Mr. Meredith, I congratulate you, sir.

Mo. Vell, you might knock me down with a fedder.

Nat. Ooraw! Ooraw! Three cheers, lads, for Thomas Meredith, the Colonel's son, the heir to Nobbley Hall.

All. Hurra! Hurra! Hurra!

Nat. What's the matter, Tom? The lad's stunned; he's knocked silly with his good fortune. Oh, lud! Where's my Katey? That's who he wants; my Katey, gents, that will be the lady of the manor, after all.

Tom. No, Nat. Katey and I can never be anything to each other now.

Nat. What d'ye mean? Oh, I see; you are rich. It's all off between ye; the girl is scratched; she won't suit your book no more.

Tom. [*Sternly*] Captain Goodge, I must beg you to hand me over the key of Flying Scud's stable.

Goodge. So that's where it bites him, is it? [*Goodge gives him the key after a pause*]

Tom. [*Handing it to Nat*] There, Nat, unlock Flying Scud's stable, and you will learn why your grand daughter can never be anything to me again. [*Nat is bewildered. Tom is surrounded by Mulligan, Chousir, Mo Davis and Quail, who congratulate him*]

Quail. I congratulate you, Mr. Meredith, you're a rich man now.

Tom. [*Losing self control*] Rich! I'd give every penny of my fortune if I could only think her the good and pure girl that won my heart's first love.

GOODGE. [*Aside L.*] Jealous, eh! Then there may be a chance for me yet. [*Aloud to Tom*] Cheer up, Mr. Meredith, don't think so badly of her, perhaps she's no worse than many another girl.

TOM. Don't you dare to speak of her. Quit the house at once!

GOODGE. [*Furiously*] Quit the house?

TOM. Yes, quit the house and never darken the threshold of it's doors again. Remember, *I* am now the master here.

TABLEAU

ACT II.

SCENE 1: *The club card room. Mulligan and Mo Davis discovered.*

MULL. Here, Mo, aisy wid that champagne; pass a taist of it this way. [*Business. Enter Goodge C. from L.*] Here's Goodge! Well, Captain, wot's the state of the funds?

GOODGE. [*L.C., drinks*] Well, gentlemen, we have got tied up in an infernal tangle. Money has become tight with us for some time. The bills we have forged and paid into the bank in Lord Cecil Woodbie's name, become due in two days after the Derby. I think our horse, Voltigeur, is sure to pull off, and if so, we are safe.

MO. Vell, I never feel safe till we're out of danger.

GOODGE. If you could only get Julia to extract a promise of marriage from Woodbie, we should be all right in any case, because his lordship would scarcely dare to prosecute us then for forging his name.

MULL. I don't like the whole business, and I'm afraid Julia may kick over the traces.

MO. Quite right. You can never rely on a woman, they're as bad as horses.

GOODGE. Tom Meredith is coming here tonight, and has promised me my revenge for the large sum I lost to him the night before last. I don't propose to begin playing cards with him till he gets half drunk, and then I fancy I shall be able to turn him inside out.

MO. Jumping Moses! he always seems to be inclined to turn us inside out.

GOODGE. Curse him, I'll be even with him yet. He's never forgiven me that affair with his sweetheart, Katey Rideout.

MO. And he's not likely to, either.

GOODGE. Well, it's a sharp game between us, and we shall see who will win. He's flush of money lately, and if I only knew how to get a thousand or two cash tonight, I believe I could skin him out.

MULL. All the money we've got is out on the race, and I don't know which way to turn for more. If Voltigeur wins the Derby, we're all made men.

Mo. And if he loses, we shall have to make off somewhere else. All my bets are to be paid the day after the race, and if it goes against us, the day will be very useful to give me time to start off somewhere else, and set up business on the continent.

GOODGE. I must get a couple of thousand ready to meet Tom Meredith at cards tonight. You, Moses, can look over his hand, give me the tip what cards he holds, and losing is an impossibility.

Mo. That's all very well, but where are we to get the ready? I'm stoney broke.

MULL. Then what's to be done?

GOODGE. Something must be done; I cannot sit with Meredith tonight until this money is forthcoming. Have we no resource? Come, Mo, can't you make a raise?

Mo. Two thousand pounds! You might as well ask me for the crown of England.

GOODGE. That I shall win ten times this amount is sure.

MULL. It's a moral certainty. If any respectable married man could see you slip them cards, he'd advance the amount at once. Have you no plan yourself? [*To Goodge*]

GOODGE. I see only one hope now, Mulligan. You must invent some tale about Julia and tell it to Lord Woodbie, who has returned to London. [*They all start up*]

Mo. The bank is going to resume payment.

GOODGE. I met him in Rotten Row. He has just arrived from Vienna. The name of Julia brings the blood to his cheek; he is more in love with her than ever.

MULL. I know it. Ever since he has been abroad, he has written to her every week. She would not answer his letters, but she would sit up at night crying over them, and console herself by scrawling replies. Then she tore them up after relieving her feelings.

Mo. Just like me ven I was stone broke. I used to draw checks on the Bank of Elegance, and tear 'em up.

MULL. One day last week I found one of those letters on her desk, and, be jabers, sir, I posted it.

GOODGE. He has told me that he was coming to this club tonight. That letter has recalled him, Mulligan, you have saved us. [*Crosses to L.*]

Mo. He deserves the Victoria Cross.

MULL. Hush, here is Julia. [*Mo crosses behind table to C. Enter Julia C. from L.*]

JULIA. Uncle, I must say one word to you. Your pardon, gentlemen. [*Bows to Goodge*]

GOODGE. [*L.C.*] We were just going into the smoke room. [*Bows*] Good evening, Mull. Come, Mo. [*Crosses up C.*]

Mo. [*Aside*] I say, Goodge, she looks hagitated, don't she; out of sorts; her eyes is all staring, her features looks all ruffled up the wrong way.

GOODGE. Hush! Good evening, Miss Latimer. [*Exit C. and L.*]

MULL. Wait for me, Mo.

Mo. I'll smoke a cigar with you, just to show there's no narstymosity. [*Exit C.*]

JULIA. Lord Woodbie is in London, I have just seen him. He is following me; he did not know I saw him. I dare not trust myself to speak to him again. He must learn to forget me.

MULL. [*R.C.*] What has brought him back, I wonder?

JULIA. Uncle, I implore, do not ask me to receive him. Tell him I cannot, will not speak to him again. Say that my affections are engaged elsewhere. Hark! I hear his footsteps. [*Crossing R.*]

MULL. How do you know that?

JULIA. He followed me here from the park. [*Exit R. door. Enter Mo Davis from L.*]

Mo. He's come! [*Crossing down R.*] Lord Woodbie is here!

MULL. She won't see him. [*Enter Woodbie C. from L. Mulligan R.C.*] Ah, my lord, you are right welcome. [*Shakes hands. Aside to Mo*] Stick to me, I see a chance to get a rise for Goodge. [*Aloud*] Welcome, my lad, you've just got home in time for the Derby.

WOOD. [*L.C.*] You look rosier than ever, Mull. How do, Davis. I hope Miss Latimer is well?

MULL. Poor Julia! She is sadly changed, eh, Davis?

Mo. [*R.C.*] Ah, you might pass her off for somebody else.

MULL. I mane in spirit. [*Business. Kicks Mo*]

Mo. Vy did you not say so then? [*Kicks Mulligan*]

MULL. She lives a retired life, sees no one, especially since that unfortunate affair.

Mo. Ah, that was when she vos took worse. [*Aside*] Vot work is he hengergeneering now?

Wood. I trust that Julia—Miss Latimer has met with no—

Mull. It was a cousin, but he bore the name of Mulligan. That was enough!

Mo. She couldn't stand that. [*Aside*] Vere is he going to?

Mull. He was the manager of the Universal Bank; he was behind hand with the accounts. Poor devil, it might happen to the best of us, but he was unlucky enough to get found out. He was in the hands of the police.

Mo. I didn't care so much for him, as I did for his young vife and family. [*Aside*] Vere the devil is he going to?

Mull. That's what touched Julia. The poor girl was distracted about it. She never told me a worrud, sir, of what she was going to do.

Mo. Not a syllable. [*Aside*] It's a hole; he's hexcavating a hole.

Mull. But she packed up every ornament she had; she took the rings off her fingers, the earrings out of her ears, even the ould diamond of the Mulligans that come down by female line from Mohelly Egan, the Prince of Gath-na-cush.

Mo. Every blessed Irish diamond in the family. [*Aside*] It's a hole.

Mull. And in the night she disappeared; pawned them, my lord, raised two thousand pounds; paid the dirty bank its claim; rescued the name of Mulligan from detection.

Mo. Two thousand pounds!

Wood. Noble girl! It was just like her.

Mo. Don't you see the blood of the Prince of Got-no-cash coming out strong in her?

Mull. She did not care for the loss of the jewels, not a bit; she never wore them.

Wood. Just what I was going to remark.

Mull. She enjoyed them in secret; she doted on the ould family associations.

Mo. And besides, they wasn't set fashionable.

Wood. My dear Mulligan, I hope you will not be offended, but will you—will she allow me to restore these jewels? [*Takes out check book and goes up*]

Mull. Restore! What do you mean, my lord?

Wood. [*Writes at back*] Let me send at once to the place where they are deposited and release them. Nay, I will take no refusal.

Mull. She will never allow it.

Wood. Then do not mention my name in the matter. Here is a check for the money. [*Gives it*]

Mo. Beautiful! [*Crossing C. takes check*] I'll undertake the hopperation. [*Goes up C.*]

MULL. Give me your hand, Lord Woodbie; you have the heart of a lion.

Mo. [*Aside*] And the head of a goose. [*Exits C. and L.*]

WOOD. Shall I not have the pleasure of seeing her this evening?

MULL. She's in the club. She came here with a message for me. I'll tell her that you are here; she will be astonished to hear it. [*Aside*] I'll have them together, and leave Master Cupid to do the rest. He's fairly caught. [*Exit C. and R.*]

WOOD. Here is the dear little letter that brought me back. [*Reads*] "Dear, dear, dearest Cecil, I have been reading your dear letters, but they are sadly blotted with my tears. Ah, why are you not beside me to kiss them away? I have learned them all by heart. I sleep with them clasped to my heart; thus only can I rest. How I love you, Cecil, how I love you! Write no more to me, but come; I am weary of this resistance; come to your own Julia." When I read those burning whispers, I thought I had lost my senses, that I was dreaming. [*Enter Julia R.D. crosses to R.C.*] Ah, dearest Julia—

JULIA. Pardon me, my lord, I beg you not to address me in that manner.

WOOD. Why are you so cold to me?

JULIA. Has not my uncle informed you that I am about to be married?

WOOD. To be married?

JULIA. And as my feelings, my affections, are engaged elsewhere, I—I cannot listen to your expressions of attachment.

WOOD. Am I dreaming? You are in love, and not, not with me?

JULIA. Ah, Lord Woodbie, why have you returned to inflict this needless pain on me and on yourself?

WOOD. You ask me why I have come back? You who have learned my letters by heart?

JULIA. What do you mean?

WOOD. Have you been trifling with me, or do you really sleep with them clasped to your breast? Is this the cry of your heart: "How I love you, Cecil, how I love you!", or is this a wicked forgery? [*Shows letter*]

JULIA. That letter! How came you by it?

WOOD. It reached me in Vienna by post.

JULIA. [*Sinks in chair, head on table*] Betrayed, betrayed!

WOOD. No, no, not betrayed, but confessed. Oh, Julia, how could you love me so, and rob me of so much happiness? Do not hide your eyes from me; you said you were weary of this existence.

JULIA. So I am! Be it for good or evil—I know—I know not how I have been betrayed. I have struggled honestly with my heart, but there are limits to suffering, and I have reached them. [*Rises*] I love you, Cecil, I love you. When I sent you from me—ah, may I never repent your return.

WOOD. You never shall, Julia. We are both young maybe, but when a fellow is old enough to love as I do, he is as much a man as he ever will be. [*Embrace. He leads off L.1E. Enter Bob and Nat*]

NAT. Bob, I want to see Mr. Meredith. [*Bob stamps L. and dances*] Hullo, Bob! What's a-swelling you out?

BOB. Please, sir, they've been at me, they have. Mr. Davis come an' hoffered me a tanner if I'd shut him in with Flying Scud in his box for ten minutes.

NAT. Kalkelation on Joovenile depravity! Well, Bob, you behaved like a honest boy, I hope.

BOB. Yes, sir, I took his tanner.

NAT. Eh!

BOB. And shut him in with the animal for ten minutes.

NAT. Wot!

BOB. Yes, sir, but I didn't mention that a policeman was there on dooty. Oh, sir, if you'd a seen Mo Davis' face arter he comed out.

NAT. He axed you to let him, and so you did. Good boy! Ah, them's the hactions that when you come to my age o' life, you'll look upon with satisfaction to your innards. Go along and tell the lads at Leatherhead I shall be amongst them tonight at the Pigskin Club. And, Bob, how's your weight now?

BOB. Eight pounds over still, sir.

NAT. Put yourself in a double rug, and take a five-miler.

BOB. Oh, dear, I don't know where it comes from. Ain't it haggerawaitin'? I can't pass a brewery, but the very smell, I b'leeve, puts a hounce on me for hevery sniff. [*Exit up C.*]

NAT. That's a virtuous character in spite of his weight; but perfection can't be expected in this world. [*Loud laughter heard R.U.E.*]

TOM. [*Outside R.*] Wants to see me, eh? Well, here I am. [*Enter Tom, wildly laughing*]

NAT. Good evening, Master Tom.

TOM. Ah, good evening, Nat, how are you?

NAT. Pretty well, tank ye, sir, not so bad for an ould 'un. Sorry to say you're not looking so well. London air doesn't agree with you like the country. You don't look half so well as when you were in the training stable at Doncaster.

TOM. And I don't feel half so well. I daresay many envy me, but they little know what I think of myself. I was never intended for the so-called "fast life" in London. I'm getting pretty sick of it. Late hours and heavy drinking are enough to break the strongest constitution, and although I am regarded as the fortunate Tom Meredith, my money has no value for me. The smiles of lovely women make my heart ache. [*Down R.C.*] But what did you want to see me about, Nat, eh?

NAT. [*L.C.*] Well, sir, I've just come from Tattersall's. Our horse, Flying Scud, is steady at 5 to 4 on him. [*A little up L.C.*]

TOM. And you feel sure that he will win the Derby?

NAT. There ain't a hanimal in the list that the Scud couldn't give seven pounds to, and a licking—Voltigeur included. What did I tell you a year ago? Ain't he answered hevery particular?

TOM. You have doubled my fortune, Nat, and if I carry the Derby prize, I shall be a rich-man. But I'd exchange place with my own stable boy if I could believe the story Katey told me.

NAT. I don't blame you for doubting it, and she don't blame you neither. It did look bad, and my poor girl don't see how she could get out of it.

TOM. Sometimes the conviction of her innocence comes over me, and then a hateful suspicion crawls back to my mind and drives me mad. [*Crossing L.*]

NAT. If Flying Scud could speak, he'd tell you what passed between her and Goodge, for he was the only human being present in the stable except theirselves. But speech is the only thing that can't be expected of him, bless his heart. Ah, if only horses could only speak, they'd have some strange stories to tell.

TOM. I don't mind confessing to you, Nat, that I love her still, most passionately.

NAT. D'ye think I don't know it? What takes you out to the Tottenham Club every night till arter daylight, gamblin'? What's druv you to drink, Tom? Why, your love for my gal. And I ses to her, "It's a heatin' into his constitution, and the only cure for him is just what he can't take, and your blessed self, my dear."

TOM. What is the use of a fortune that I can't share with her? Wine makes me forget her for a while, and when I gamble, it is with Goodge, for I'll ruin him, or he shall ruin me. [*Exit L.1E.*]

NAT. Goodge ruin you! Not while I'm on the green side of the turf he shan't. [*Exit L.1E. Enter Mo Davis with notes L.D., and Mulligan C. from R.*]

MO. I've got the check cashed; here's the spondoolicks. [*Enter Goodge C.*]

GOODGE. Quick, Mo, have you got the flimsies? Here's Meredith coming half drunk, mad for play, and ripe for plucking.

Mo. Here's the hoof. [*Business, Gag, one short, business*] Ain't he selfish? [*Enter Tom, half tipsy, C., followed by Bob, waiter with brandy and water, Woodbie re-enter L.*]

TOM. Now, Goodge, I've come to give you your revenge. Bob, s'more brandy. [*Waiter fills, Tom drinks, sits L. of table*] Five hundred on this game. [*Cuts cards*]

GOODGE. [*Deals*] Five hundred, you say. [*Three cards each*]

TOM. [*Playing*] Thousand, if you like. [*Goodge wins*]

Mo. [*Makes a sign to Goodge behind Tom's back*] Oh, I'm backing Meredith, and Goodge winning all my money. [*Goodge cuts, Tom deals, plays again*]

WOOD. [*L.C.*] Is Goodge in luck? Then I'll back him for a hundred. [*Puts notes on table*]

TOM. I cover it. [*Does so*] Goodge wins again! [*Mo, business*]

GOODGE. [*Dealing again*] Does the same bet stand? Five hundred again?

TOM. [*Playing*] As I said just now, a thousand, if you like.

WOOD. No, no, Meredith, you don't know what you're doing. It is not fair, Goodge, to let him go on.

TOM. [*Rising*] What do you mean, my lord; do you 'sinuate that I can't play?

ALL. No, no, Meredith, sit down.

GOODGE. A thousand it is.

TOM. If you can't afford the stake, who asked you to bet?

WOOD. I never lay a stake on, sir, that I am not prepared to pay.

TOM. Then where is your stake? I don't see it. Where is it? [*Playing*]

WOOD. There! [*Throws down notes. Goodge wins again*]

TOM. That is five hundred I owe you, my lord, there it is. [*Giving notes*]

WOOD. Thanks, I—I—don't wish to take it. I am at liberty, I presume to consider the bet off?

TOM. No, sir, I allow no man to take such a liberty with me.

WOOD. Then I decline the money because I have not won it.

Mo. Not won it!

WOOD. No! I saw Mo Davis making signs behind Tom's back.

Mo. Me? Oh, jumping Moses, what a haccusation.

MULL. I hope you don't mean to insinuate, my lord, that there has been unfair play?

WOOD. Yes, I do!

ALL. What!

GOODGE. Are you mad, Woodbie?

WOOD. I watched you, Captain Goodge, and I saw you signal the cards.

GOODGE. You lie! [*Dashes cards in Woodbie's face, business; guests enter C. Glass crash, Mo business with Bob*]

TOM. Stick close to me, Lord Woodbie, I'll see you through. [*Tom, Bob, and Woodbie fight their way out C.*]

CLOSE IN

SCENE 2: *Chamber in 1. Mulligan's lodgings. Enter Julia to begin, L.1E.*

JULIA. My uncle and his companions have not yet returned from the club. What can detain them? Lord Woodbie begs me to go with him and see his mother at once, to add my entreaties to his to gain her consent to his marrying me. How can I ever expect to make her ladyship think that I should ever be worthy of him? Oh, Cecil, Cecil, why weren't you born without a name, and without a penny? Then I could show you how much I loved you. Ah, footsteps! My uncle returned, and Captain Goodge with him. The more I see of that man, the more I dislike him. They both look upset. What can have happened? I'll listen. [*Retires R. Enter Goodge and Mulligan L.1E.*]

GOODGE. Now, Mulligan, what's to be done?

MULL. I am at my wit's end.

GOODGE. Who could have forseen such a result? We are ruined irretrievably. [*Knock L.*]

MULL. There's Mo Davis wid news of what happened after we left the club. Perhaps Woodbie will apologize. [*Enter Mo L.1E.*]

GOODGE. Well?

MO. Lord Woodbie repeats his haccusation. It was no use of me giving my word of honor; do all I could, nobody believed me.

MULL. [R.] Is the word of a boy like that to be taken against the protestations of three honorable gentlemen like us?

GOODGE. Yes, when there is no doubt that he is a gentleman.

MULL. Do you mean to say that we are not?

GOODGE. You're a fool!

MULL. Captain Goodge, I don't permit you to call me a fool! As the poet says, "The man that calls me a fool—"

GOODGE. Tush, man! Tomorrow morning, the magistrate at Bow Street may call you a felon. Do you suppose that Meredith is going to pay one shilling of his losses?

MO. Oh! Oh! Then how is all the paper I've given to be perwided for?

GOODGE. When this affair gets wind, all the creditors will come down on us like vultures.

Mo. They are sure to. I shall be the first victim. Oh, vy didn't I stick to the cigar and cabbage leaf line? The swindle was small, but it was sure.

GOODGE. Where's Chousir?

Mo. He's gone to enquire vot country there's no extradition treaty wid.

MULL. Do you mean to tell me, Captain Goodge, that you have placed me in the disgraceful position of being found out?

Mo. Look at me; I shall be found out for passing those bills, but I'll swear I'm innocent party. Let us all be innocent, and leave Chousir in the hole.

MULL. That's an idea, and Chousir's only the son of a butcher, so he has no character to lose. Besides Julia can beg him off with Woodbie. We'll call the forgeries a slip of the pen. [*Knock*]

Mo. There he is! I'll let him in. [*Exit L.1E.*]

GOODGE. I have no doubt you will, and let us all in if you could.

MULL. We must stand by one another, Goodge. This is a desperate business entirely. Is there no escape for us?

GOODGE. None that I can see. To obtain the money now is impossible; and Woodbie, after my insult to him, will be pitiless. [*Crosses and looks off R. Enter Meredith L.1E.*]

TOM. I beg your pardon, but as I entered, Mr. Davis left the house. He informed me that I should find Captain Goodge here. [*Goodge turns and bows R.*] I am commissioned by Lord Woodbie to deliver a message.

GOODGE. To what effect?

TOM. Are you prepared to avow the foul play practised by you and your confederates, and to tender him a full apology?

GOODGE. What if I decline?

TOM. In that case, I am directed to arrange a hostile meeting.

GOODGE. [*Crossing*] Ah! Will he fight? Will he fight?

TOM. You must feel that you cannot meet one who is little more than a boy.

GOODGE. Then why do you bring this message?

TOM. To ask you the favor he refused me; let me take his place. We have a long account to settle, Captain Goodge, and I am anxious to wipe off the score.

GOODGE. Oh, Katey Rideout's affair! You have taken a long time thinking it over; I thought you had forgotten all about that. Why didn't you settle up about her before?

TOM. Because I believed her guilty, but with my knowledge of your unscrupulous character has grown the conviction of her innocence. I did not believe that a man could behave as she accused you of doing, but you have taught me of what men such as you are capable. There is nothing too mean for you to attempt; you're a liar and a thief! a disgrace to manhood! And you ought to be expelled from every club in London, and warned off the turf.

MULL. You cannot stand that, Goodge.

GOODGE. [*To Mulligan*] One thing at a time, sir. [*To Tom*] When I have disposed of this young lord, I'll teach you what I'm capable of in another line, but I must give him a lesson before I attend to you. Here is my friend. [*Crosses R.*]

MULL. [*R.C.*] I think you might give Mr. Meredith the preference. Fight him first, and then settle with young Woodbie.

TOM. If he faces me first, the meeting with young Woodbie will never take place.

GOODGE. I know my own business best. Tonight, then, on the sands behind Calais Pier, at ten o'clock, after I have settled matters with you and your friend.

MULL. [*To Meredith*] Is that convaynient?

TOM. Perfectly.

MULL. [*To Goodge*] Pistols, I suppose? [*Goodge bows*]

TOM. Agreed! We shall be there.

MULL. At ten o'clock.

TOM. At ten o'clock. [*Bows and exits L.1E.*]

MULL. Good Heavens, Goodge, you don't mean to fight the boy. It will be infanticide.

GOODGE. I'll kill him, Mulligan. When he proposed this duel, I saw it at once, our only chance of escape. I am a dead shot, and Woodbie shall never return to dishonor the bills we have drawn in his name, and so expose us.

MULL. I never thought of that.

GOODGE. The frauds can never be traced to us without his evidence. As for Chousir, he will not betray us when he knows that he himself is out of danger. [*Crosses L.*]

MULL. I believe you are right.

GOODGE. I must practise for an hour or so, and get my hand in. I shall start for Dover by the early train. [*Exit L.1E.*]

MULL. [*Crossing L.*] I will meet you at the station. [*Enter Julia R.E.*]

JULIA. No you won't, uncle.

MULL. Julia!

JULIA. Goodge will kill him; he is a dead shot; and Woodbie will never return to prove your villainy and expose you.

MULL. Did you hear that? Then you know what hangs over me?

JULIA. I don't care what hangs over you; let the guilty suffer, not the innocent. I will go to Lord Woodbie and tell him all I have heard.

MULL. What, that Goodge is a dead shot, and that he may escape fighting this duel by accusing his adversary of felony? Do you know what such a spirit as his would do? He would pay the money, tear up the forged bill, and meet his man.

JULIA. And as you reckoned on his folly to bring him to ruin, you reckon on his honor to lead him to death; and I, I have brought him step by step to this.

MULL. What have you to do with this?

JULIA. [Crossing L.] You shall see.

MULL. [Taking her wrists] You are not going to betray me?

JULIA. I will not betray anyone, but, come what may, I will protect that poor boy from the consequences of his infatuation for me. [Throws Mulligan off] Go your way, I will go mine, and Heaven forgive you for what will be the result when we meet again. [Exit L.1E.]

MULL. What the devil is she going to do? [Exit L.1E.]

SCENE 3: Hyde Park. In two. Enter Bob with black eye and letter.

BOB. The Guvnor has given me this letter to be delivered to Lord Woodbie at once. Vot's in it, I wonder? Something seems to whisper to me there's summat up. I wos to be sure to give it into His Lordship's own hands, and wos to bring back an answer. [Going R.] After I've done it, I'm going to square up with Goodge's lad; I'm not going to have this black eye for nothing. [Enter Julia L.1E.]

JULIA. Stop, Boy! Lord Woodbie is going to fight a duel with Captain Goodge; your master is to be Lord Woodbie's second.

BOB. I ain't so sure about that.

JULIA. That letter is from your master to Lord Woodbie.

BOB. Well, yes, I was to be sure to give it to the young lord, and bring back an answer.

JULIA. I am going to Lord Woodbie's. Give me the letter. [Bob hesitates] Be assured that your master, Mr. Meredith, runs no risk from Captain Goodge. I know the gentleman's designs, and I am about to defeat them. [Takes letter]

BOB. She's on a lay! When she let Goodge's name out of her mouth, her eyes snapped like lucifers.

JULIA. [*Reads*] "Dear Lord Woodbie, I have seen Captain Goodge and his friend Colonel Mulligan. Our rendezvous is Calais Sands, behind the pier, at ten o'clock. T.M."

BOB. She has opened master's letter, and read it. Beg pardon, Missee, but this here won't do, you know.

JULIA. Hush! Be silent, and you will learn that I am your master's friend. [*Aside*] If this letter reached Cecil, no power on earth would prevent him keeping his appointment. It must not be delivered until it is too late for him to reach Calais this evening.

BOB. Hexcuse me, Miss, I'm very sorry for the young Lord Woodbie, but if he don't turn up when they've pitched the ropes, *my* master will have to go and pull his coat off. Now if this 'ere is a plant, and there's going to be any murder cropping out of the transaction, I'd as lief my master wasn't first come, first served.

JULIA. Your master shall be in no danger, I promise you, and Goodge shall find an antagonist who will inflict on him indelible disgrace. Go back and tell your master that Lord Woodbie will be there at Calais Pier tonight at ten o'clock.

BOB. Well, I believe, Miss, that you mean square, and I've no objection to serve his lordship, but I'm a-going with master this over the water business, and when I'm there, if I sees any sign of a cross, or my master getting in a hole, I'll split.

JULIA. Yes, you may do that. Farewell. [*Exit Bob*] Ah, Cecil, Cecil, how many times have I sworn to devote my life to you! Now he shall know how Julia keeps her word. [*Exit L.1E.; enter Katey and Nat R.*]

KATEY. Oh, Grandfather, Tom is in some great trouble; in the park there, he clenched his hand and bit his lip. I was watching him; I was watching him. [*Looking off*]

NAT. Of course you was; it's a lucky as heyes ain't got tooth, or you'd eat him.

KATEY. [*Looking R.*] I can see him still.

NAT. You are wuss than a cannibal; you live on that 'ere human bein'. Come, you'd best give him up.

KATEY. I can't! I can't! I love him more than ever.

NAT. Of course you do, now you can't get him.

KATEY. Oh, Grandfather, Grandfather! [*Hides her face on Nat's breast*]

NAT. Nay, I didn't mean to hurt ye. Don't cry. There. Why, to see thee married to that lad, I'd lay down in my own grave, and pull the turf over me. [*Katey sobs*] I would! There, deary, put up your tears; save 'em. Hush! yonder is Goodge.

KATEY. He has spoken to me already in the Row; I cannot escape from his pursuit. This conduct only confirms the scandal under which I am suffering.

NAT. And poor Tom is suffering as badly as you are.

KATEY. That's some comfort. What did he say of me?

NAT. "Sometimes," ses he, "my heart goes in for her, and then I feel as if I could take her in my arms again."

KATEY. Oh, why can't I pitch on one of those times.

NAT. "But arter that I gets skerry," ses he, "then I hates her, and I goes to the dogs."

KATEY. I'd go there too, with him, if he'd let me.

NAT. He is gamblin' away his fortune.

KATEY. So much the better. When he is poor he will come nearer to me.

NAT. He is making love to every girl he meets.

KATEY. I know it, but he has not settled down to one. Oh, dear, why can't he believe in me?

NAT. Ah, there now, if you had been a hoss, I could have given a warranty.

KATEY. If I could only make him believe me, I feel I could go down on my knees to him.

NAT. Ah! Hattitudes don't prove nothing.

KATEY. His heart must be as hard as iron, or my tears would have melted him.

NAT. Facts is waterproof, and on that 'ere occaision between you and Goodge, things didn't look sweet. Katey, when I heard on it, and then hopened that stable door, and saw you locked up there, well, it took all my faith in ye, and knowledge of your breed, to gie ye a clean bill o' health.

KATEY. There goes Goodge, the monster; oh, how I hate him. He has broken my life, ruined my happiness forever. [*She goes up a little L.*]

NAT. There she is, lamed for life, a confirmed case of nav'iclar in the heart. My poor gal, blisterin' won't do her no good. It is no use o' takin' such cases to the vet; she is nobbled, she is, scratched, and maybe will retire into private life in a paddock. [*Enter Bob L.1E.*] Hullo, Bob, what's up now?

BOB. Hullo, Nat. Haven't you heard? There's been a row.

NAT. Yes, you've got a notice in your peeper to that effect.

KATEY. Why, Bob, what have you been doing to your eye?

BOB. It wasn't me, Miss, it was Captain Goodge's lad. Him and me was at the club last night, waiting for our masters, and that's how we came to hear of it.

NAT. What?

Bob. Why, Goodge and his party set on my master last night, and sharped him at cards, but Lord Woodbie twigged and hexposed them, when up gets all four legs at master, and sets on him.

Katey. Oh, Tom!

Bob. "Come on," ses master to Goodge and Co., "I'll undertake to put you through the winding-up act," and before the spectators had time to take hodds, he set all four legs hexamining the carpet.

Nat. How do you know this?

Bob. I was there, and of course when me and Goodge's boy 'ad put up last night and littered down our horses, we had it out in our spare loose box; nine rounds comfortable and quiet, and Flying Scud a lookin' at us over the half door, amirin' that style of groomin'.

Katey. Was your master hurt?

Bob. Not he, Miss. When I accounted for wearing this cockade hon my heye, he larfed, tipped me a fiver to get it painted, a sov for Goodge's lad to square the doctor. Ah! I don't know why he ain't a royal dook, he have the heart of one. I suppose they'll settle the matter by what they call doolin', for I've got orders for the brougham to take master down to the Dover line, as it is there those ewents do come off, and I was carrying to Lord Woodbie a letter, but the young lady as the lord is sweet upon, took it. I shouldn't wonder but it is to ask him to hold the sponge.

Katey. What! My Tom going to fight a duel? They'll kill him! No, he shan't go! I'll cling to him; he may trample me under foot, but now I'll never leave him. Tom! Tom! [Business with Nat. Exit L.1E.]

Nat. You fat-headed bran mash, what did you tell her for? I've a good mind to put your other eye in mournin' for ye. [Business, and exit Nat and Bob L.1E.]

Scene 4: *Calais Sands. Enter Goodge, Moses and Mulligan R.U.E. or L.U.E.*

Mull. No sign of them yet. [Looks around]

Mo. Up to now he is invisible to the naked eye.

Goodge. They cannot have mistaken the place.

Mull. I'll look in this direction. [Exit R.1E.]

Mo. And I'll look in this. Jumping Moses, what's that?

Goodge. 'Tis your own shadow.

Mo. Oh, gracious goodness, to think I should ever live to be frightened by my own shadow. This is a dangerous business, Goodge. It puts my 'art in my mouth. [Exit looking before him L.]

GOODGE. After this affair, London will be too hot to hold me. I must disappear; after the Derby, I'll start for the gambling towns of Germany, and some new associates. [*Re-enter Mulligan R.1E. looks off R.*]

MULL. Here comes one of them at any rate. [*Re-enter Mo Davis*]

MO. It isn't him; it isn't Lord Woodbie. [*Enter Tom and Bob with pistol case R.*]

TOM. I regret, gentlemen, that through some error, Lord Woodbie has failed to appear.

MO. Then he will be posted as a coward through every club in London.

GOODGE. I presume he knew the hour and place?

TOM. I wrote to him, and he replied that he would meet me. [*To Bob*] You saw his lordship?

BOB. He said as how he'd attend to it.

MO. A pretty way to attend to it by stopping away.

TOM. By some accident he has missed the departure of the boat.

BOB. [*Aside*] I'm the haccident.

MULL. On such an occaision he would take a special train.

MO. Yes, he would have hordered a special train.

TOM. He may have done so, but he could not cross the Channel if he missed the steamer.

MULL. His own yacht lies at Dover; I saw it there.

MO. And I saw it, too. I took particular notice of the crew, two men and a dog.

TOM. Well, gentlemen, I think it probable that he has been induced to decline this meeting. I confess I used every argument to make him do so.

GOODGE. On what ground, sir?

TOM. Firstly, because he is a foolish boy; and secondly, because he is not obliged to meet a blackleg, nor stand up to risk an honorable life before a professional assassin.

GOODGE. Professional assassin! How dare you apply such an expression to me!

TOM. Because it best expresses the man who would attempt to pay his debts by murdering his creditors.

GOODGE. Beware, Mr. Meredith, beware! I owe Lord Woodbie nothing.

TOM. You're a liar, and your friends there know it.

MO. Jumping Moses! I know him to be a most honorable member of society. He vouldn't tell a lie on no account.

GOODGE. Why then do *you* wish to take his place?

TOM. Because you have stung the woman I love, and we believe in Yorkshire that the vermin rankles in the wound only as long as the vermin lives.

GOODGE. Your abuse shall not provoke me to meet you in his place. [*Julia on R.U.E.*] Nor does your bluster shield him from the brand of cowardice. [*Enter Julia dressed as Woodbie, comes down a little R.C.*]

TOM. Woodbie—

BOB. He has come to the post arter all.

MO. Wonders will never cease.

GOODGE. Come, gentlemen, we have lost enough time; measure the ground, Colonel.

MO. He vorks like a policeman, don't he? [*Bob crosses with pistol case to Goodge, Mulligan, passes from R.1E. to L.U.E. and places handkerchiefs*]

GOODGE. Your weapons are loaded, I presume?

TOM. I beg you, my lord, not to pursue this affair. This man is unworthy to meet you.

GOODGE. Lord Woodbie should have thought of that before he insulted me. I am here to meet his challenge; if he fails to meet me, I'll treat him as the boy you wish to make him out. I've brought my horsewhip.

JULIA. [*Imitating Woodbie's voice*] Proceed!

MULL. My man stands yonder; I have placed handkerchiefs at the distance. There is no choice of light, I think. Place your principal quickly, for look yonder, there is a movement on the pier, and we may be interrupted.

TOM. [*Having given pistol to Julia, places her L.U.E.*] I shall permit only one exchange of shots.

GOODGE. One will be enough. [*Takes place R.1E.*]

MULL. [*L.U.E.*] Is all ready? Will you give me the word?

TOM. No! [*Down 1E.*]

MULL. Then I will. On the word "three," gentlemen, you fire together.

MO. Hold hard; let me get out of the way. The bullet might go through him into me.

MULL. Now, gentlemen, are you ready? Now! One, two, three. [*Goodge fires*]

TOM. Woodbie has not fired. [*Runs up to Julia. Julia staggers to Tom's arms*]

BOB. He is falling!

GOODGE. He has it; he has it! [*Goes R.*]

MULL. Away wid you, quick. [*Exit Mulligan and Goodge R.1E., followed by Mo*]

TOM. Woodbie, speak! Where are you hurt? [*Enter Lord Woodbie L.*]

WOOD. [*Down R.C.*] Am I too late?

ALL. Woodbie! Who, then, is this? [*White Lime on*]

JULIA. [*Throws off hat*]   I am not hurt, Cecil, I—
ALL.   Julia!

QUICK ACT-DROP

ACT III.

SCENE 1: *Neat chamber in Nat Gosling's London lodgings. Julia discovered on sofa, Katey attending her. Nat with them. Table with physics, bottles, etc.*

KATEY.   Come, dear, just take this, and you'll be right in no time.

NAT.   It'll put you as right as a trivet.

JULIA.   Thanks, friends, thanks. I'm really not hurt, only this pain in my shoulder.

NAT.   The doctor said it was only a flesh wound.

KATEY.   Nothing serious! But, oh, how delightfully romantic, and all for the sake of the man you love. Oh, what wouldn't I give for a chance to be shot for Tom.

NAT.   For shame, Katey, for shame!

KATEY.   Grandfather, if it would do Tom any good, I'd have my arm shot off.

NAT.   What fond creatures these women are.

KATEY.   Perhaps he'd know that I loved him, then—and—and—

NAT.   And then p'raps he'd marry you.

KATEY.   Oh, Grandfather! [*Blushing*]

NAT.   And a nice thing it'd be to marry a one-armed wife. I wonder how the babbies 'ud get on when they wanted nursing.

KATEY.   Oh! Go along, do!

JULIA.   What has become of my uncle?

NAT.   After the duel, Goodge left before he discovered that it was you he had been firing at. You were brought over in the mail boat by Mr. Tom and Bob Buckskin, and brought here till it was decided what was to be done.

JULIA.   I hope that Mr. Meredith has done his best to hush the matter up; no good could come of its being made public.

KATEY.   Not a word has been said, or the newspapers might have made columns of it.

JULIA.   I wouldn't have it made known on any account. [*Bob knocks at door L.*]

BOB. [*Calls outside*]   Nat, are you at home?

NAT.   There's Bob Buckskin.

KATEY.   Come in, Bob. [*Opens door. Enter Bob*]

Bob. 'Um d'ye do, Miss. Hope you're better.

Julia. Oh, it's nothing.

Nat. Calls a bullet in her shoulder nothing. Some of our bold militia would declare on for a pension for half as much.

Bob. She ain't got it there now, has she?

Katey. No, no! The doctor extracted the bullet, and said that with perfect quiet, it was only a question of a few days before she'll be able to get about again.

Julia. I'm so sorry I shan't be able to go to the Derby, I should so like to see it.

Nat. Yes, Flying Scud is going to win in a canter.

Bob. That's a moral; a dead certainty.

Julia. I should like to send a message to my uncle that I'm comparatively unhurt.

Nat. Oh, he knows all about it; I sent him a message as soon as the doctor left. I knew your uncle very well, Miss, I saw him only yesterday on business, and have to see him again today about a horse.

Julia. My uncle knew nothing of my taking Lord Woodbie's place, and had he done so, would have done everything possible to prevent it.

Nat. Well, he may be your uncle, Miss, but I'm afraid he ain't twenty-two carat.

Katey. Hush, Grandfather! Hush!

Bob. Well, always speak of a man as you find him; and if he ain't a regular scorcher, I never met one.

Katey. How rude of you, Bob.

Julia. Believe me, friends, my uncle is not so bad as he appears to be. He has been led away by his companions, Captain Grindley Goodge and Mr. Davis.

Nat. Very likely, Miss, but you know the old adage, "Birds of a feather flock together."

Bob. Some of these days I'll let Mr. Jumping Moses have it, and if I get about him, he won't have many feathers left on him to flock with anybody.

Nat. Bob, if I have any more of such horrible sentiments, I'll have you bound down to keep the peace.

Katey. [At window] Good gracious, there's a carriage drawn up to our door, and an old lady and a young gentleman have got out of it.

Nat. P'raps it's Mrs. Soursawkins, the greengrocery woman, calling with her son about a bottle of embrocation I promised for the boy's leg; he strained himself at football.

Bob. [At window] It ain't Mother Soursawkins, it's too much of a swell.

KATEY. Why I do believe it's young Lord Woodbie.

JULIA. *[Starting]* Lord Woodbie; Cecil here!

BOB. And the old lady is his mother, Lady Woodbie.

NAT. Quality visitors, by jingo! *[Loud knock and ring heard]*

JULIA. Can she be coming here to upbraid me?

NAT. Will you go to the door, Katey, or shall I?

KATEY. I'll go, Grandfather; you stay here. *[Exit L.]*

NAT. Now what can bring them here? *[Bob whispers to Nat]* Yes, I shouldn't be surprised a bit. *[Whispers to Bob]* D'ye think so? Well, that would be nuts to crack.

BOB. Well, you see if that ain't a very good guess at it.

NAT. I only hope that it may be so. *[Katey re-enters door]*

KATEY. Lady Woodbie and her son wish to see our visitor, Miss Julia.

NAT. All right, Katey, only remember the doctor's orders, she wasn't to be upset on no account. *[Enter Lady Woodbie, followed by Lord Woodbie D.L.]*

LADY W. You will excuse this unceremonious visit, I'm sure. *[To Nat]* Where is she?

NAT. *[Points to Julia]* Here she is, mum—leastways I suppose you're enquiring after Miss Julia?

LADY W. The generous girl who risked her life to save that of my son.

BOB. *[To Nat]* There, what did I tell you?

NAT. You're as good as a horicle.

LADY W. *[Goes up to sofa]* Miss Latimer, I have already wronged you; I did not know your truly noble disposition. I thought you a scheming woman, endeavoring to entrap my son's affections for the sake of his fortune. I humbly beg your pardon. Will you forgive me?

JULIA. Oh, Lady Woodbie, how can you ask me such a thing? I am afraid that for Cecil's—I beg pardon—Lord Woodbie's sake, you speak so to me.

WOOD. Dear Julia, my mother at last knows you for the dear good girl that you truly are, and it is by her own wish, and not by my solicitations, that she is here.

LADY W. I know all; I have heard everything. You knew of the projected duel, and for my son's sake, you kept the matter secret, and took his place on Calais Sands. You risked your life to save his mother from a life-long misery. From my heart I thank you.

JULIA. I am grateful to you, my lady, for your kindness, which shall never be forgotten by me. All I hope is, that Lord Woodbie will not seek to meet Captain Goodge again.

LADY W. My son has now solemnly promised that he will not meet the man.

WOOD. Unless it be to tell him what I think of him—

LADY W. You must not be so impetuous, Cecil.

WOOD. All right, mother, I'll endeavor to bottle up my sentiments.

LADY W. And now, Miss Latimer, I have something of the greatest importance to say to you.

NAT. Shall we retire, mum?

BOB. Yes, shall we go outside on the mat?

LADY W. No, no, remain here, my good friends, for I should like you to hear what I am about to say. I have cruelly wronged this young lady by my suspicions of her, and I should like her and you to know that I am truly sorry for it.

JULIA. Do not again allude to it, my lady, I beg.

LADY W. My son, Cecil, knows what I am about to say. When he first spoke to me of marriage with you, I did all in my power to oppose it. Now I ask you to grace our family by becoming a member of it. I ask you to honor me by accepting my son's hand.

NAT. [*To Bob*] Well, hang me, if the old lady ain't been and popped the question. I wonder what sort of a Leap Year this comes in?

LADY W. Your answer, Julia?

JULIA. Oh, my lady, what answer can I make?

WOOD. Say that you will marry me by special license, and that you'll come with me to the Derby tomorrow and see Flying Scud win the blue ribbon of the turf.

JULIA. But the doctor?

NAT. Doctor "Cupid" is the best physician in the world.

SCENE 2: *Mulligan's rooms. Enter Mulligan and Mo Davis. Mulligan crosses back and forwards.*

MO. What's your caper?

MULL. Oh, man, the divil's luck, and the worst of it is on us.

MO. Vy, how's that?

MULL. Sure it wan't Woodbie at all we shot at Calais, but that poor girl of mine, who took his place.

MO. Vat! Julia dead!

MULL. No, praise be to Heaven, scarcely wounded. Goodge's bullet only scratched her arm, and she has hardly a mark. But, by the blood of the

Mulligans, it might have been worse. I have heard from Katey Rideout, that Julia is progressing favorably at Nat Gosling's lodgings.

Mo. Hush, here's Goodge. [*Enter Goodge L.1E*] Well, what's the state of the market?

GOODGE. [*Throwing tissue*] There's the latest betting. How do you like it?

Mo. [*Reads tissue*] "5 to 4 on Flying Scud."

MULL. Oh, it's a misprint.

Mo. "7 to 2 against Voltigeur; 4 to 1 against Rasper; 4 to 1 against Locomotive," taken freely.

GOODGE. Now, gentlemen, Woodbie having escaped my bullet through Julia's romantic folly, if Tom Meredith's horse wins the Derby, where shall we be?

MULL. Well, I should think in Australia within three months, feeding sheep.

Mo. I'll be sold for my weight in cat's meat.

GOODGE. It's popular opinion that our horse, Voltigeur, isn't in it with Flying Scud, and Meredith's horse will win as sure as the sun shines. If so, every penny we have staked will be lost.

Mo. Oo! Vat'll become of me? Oo, jumpin' Moses, vy didn't the measles carry me off when I was young and innocent?

MULL. What's to be done?

GOODGE. I'm for squaring the jockey. Who's the boy that gets the mount?

MULL. There's no dependin' on the honor o' thim boys; they'll be takin' your money and throw you over. I've been robbed fifty times that way.

Mo. Don't! O—o—o! I vos treated shameful dis mornin'. I'm all over from it.

GOODGE. You don't know whom we have to deal with. After the affair on Calais Sands, Julia was taken to Nat Gosling's lodgings by Tom Meredith. I went there to make enquiries about her, and got into conversation with old Nat Gosling. He is feeling very sore about Tom Meredith's behavior to Katey, his granddaughter. Julia has escaped with a scratch on the shoulder; I saw the doctor, and he says she'll be out in a couple of days, more frightened than hurt.

Mo. Vell, if I got a bullet in me, I should die of fright.

GOODGE. Don't I tell you it only skimmed her shoulder?

Mo. Vell, I think if it only skimmed me anywhere, it 'ud be more than enough. Oh, jumpin' Moses!

MULL. But what were you going to say about Flying Scud and Nat Gosling?

GOODGE. Well, I was going to say that he scarcely ever leaves the horse; that he almost lives in the stable. Last Christmas he got in six-months feed, and sleeps on it. The water the animal drinks is tested daily with litmus paper, and there's special police dotted round the park where Flying Scud takes his morning gallop.

Mo. It's worse than Sebastopol to get into.

GOODGE. So I thought to myself, why does old Nat stand by Meredith so strongly? When that snob found himself master of my fortune, he threw over Katey Rideout and broke off with her. Nat must want to serve him out for that, so I boldly proposed an offer; he hesitated; at last he consented to call on me here today. Now I propose that we run him with an offer of two thousand pounds, and knock him off his legs.

MULL. Two thousand pounds!

Mo. Say! Wouldn't he take something off for his revenge? He gets that in.

MULL. But where are we to get the money?

GOODGE. By one bold stroke for fortune. As Woodbie would not lend us the money, we have borrowed his name on account for the two thousand pounds.

Mo. On another bill. Lawyer Quail has advanced the money on it. He wants to get a slice of the young lord's ruin.

GOODGE. We shall be sure to take it up tomorrow after the race, so there's no risk of discovery.

MULL. Is there no fear of being found out?

Mo. No, no! Goodge is the best forger I know. Besides, as I said, it's sure to be taken up.

MULL. Yes, it's sure to be taken up.

Mo. So long as we aren't taken up, I don't mind.

GOODGE. I've just come from Quail's office, and asked him to accommodate us by cashing Lord Woodbie's acceptance. Of course he hadn't got the cash in the place, but promised to go and get it from the bank. You go round there and get the money; you'll be back in ten minutes.

Mo. There's a something about it that I don't like.

GOODGE. Nonsense! You'll get your share, won't you?

Mo. Vell, where is the forged document?

GOODGE. [Takes it from pocket-book] There it is.

Mo. The signature is beautiful; I can scarcely tell it from Lord Woodbie's own writing. Captain, you're a clever fellow, you deserve to be transported.

GOODGE. What?

Mo. I mean promoted with an award of merit. You write beautifully. You're a credit to the schoolboard. I say, suppose old Quail wants any receipt for the money?

Goodge. Oh, just endorse the bill, or give him any receipt he likes. Don't be frightened, man—we shall be all one thing or the other after the race. We've gone too far to think of sliding back now.

Mull. Come along, Davis, I'll go with you.

Mo. Yes, and you'll endorse the bill.

Mull. Oh, it won't do for Quail to see me in the matter. You're his client.

Mo. Oh—oh! Jumpin' Moses, if it's found out.

Mull. You didn't see our objections till just now.

Mo. I don't think I sees 'em now. I vos thinking of myself; I vosn't thinking of you. Ain't there no other way?

Goodge. None! If we are to share the plunder, we must first divide the risk; but there is no risk.

Mull. None at all. It will sure to be taken up.

Mo. That's what we shall all be if it ain't. [*Knock L.*]

Goodge. Hallo, here's Nat. You go out the back way, both of you, while I admit him. Get back as quickly as you can.

Mull. We shan't be many minutes. [*Exit Mo and Mulligan R.1E.*]

Nat. [*Outside L.*] Does Captain Grindley Goodge live here?

Goodge. Step this way, Mr. Gosling. [*Enter Nat*] I asked you to visit me this morning, because I wish to explain to you how sorry I am that my little attentions to your granddaughter have injured her so much. But why will she not let me square the matter? Come, if she is a little fool, you are a sensible fellow.

Nat. I am sir, uncommon; try me.

Goodge. Although Meredith has jilted Katey, you stick to him and his fortunes. Now this is not natural; so I said to myself, "I think I see Nat's little game." Oh, you are a deep one.

Nat. Oh, ain't I, so deep that I can't see to the bottom of what you mean. Just tell me what I've been a-doin' on.

Goodge. You've been quietly betting against the Scud.

Nat. Oh!

Goodge. You are going to sell the race tomorrow.

Nat. Ah!

Goodge. And while you feather your own nest, you revenge yourself on Meredith.

Nat. Revenge is sweet, ain't it?

Goodge. Have I guessed right?

NAT. What surprised me was that you didn't come before now, and make me comfortable, instead of trying it on with the stable boy. Wot's your offer?

GOODGE. I and my partner have laid heavily against your horse. We can afford to buy him off at two thousand pounds. My bets are nearly all with Meredith. If I win—I recover my estate, and then I promise you Katey shall be mistress of the old Hall—I will marry her, I'll make her my wife.

NAT. Two thousand pounds for me, and Katey to be made Mrs. Goodge.

GOODGE. Such a marriage will set matters right.

NAT. When can I have the money?

GOODGE. Immediately. Wait here, and I will go and bring my friends with it at once. [*Crosses L.*] May I say done?

NAT. Well, yes, I think you may.

GOODGE. [*Aside*] What a fool I've been to think he was not open to an offer. Moral: Never suspect a man of being honest. My fortune is safe now. Meredith, I have you under my heel. Where can Mo and Mulligan be? [*To Nat*] Just wait here a minute, Nat—I'll be back directly. [*Exit R.1E.*]

NAT. Two thousand pounds! Ah, it's a heap of money. Well, it's curious how horses do spile men—they're worse than women. There ain't in Nature a hanimal that's more nobler, more honest and hinnercent as an 'oss, but he's the cause of more meanness and dirt in the human 'eart, than all the female sex put together. [*Enter Goodge, Davis and Mulligan L.1E.*]

GOODGE. Well, Mr. Gosling, here we are, you see. These friends of mine would like to have your advice on the race tomorrow. They'll pay a good price for it.

NAT. Advice as is advice, means money. I am one of them as advertises to sell the names o' winning horses. Put a bushel of such winners in a sieve, ge 'em a shake, where are they? [*A pause*] Nowheres!

GOODGE. You sell the horses that lose, eh?

NAT. Ah! Them's my pick.

GOODGE. I've been hinting to my friends that you could sell us a safe loser for the Derby. Say Flying Scud, for instance; we'll give the price.

MULL. And he must be made safe.

MO. And we must see that he's comfortable.

NAT. Ah, I thought as you'd like to take the 'sponsibility on it off my hands.

GOODGE. Not that we doubt your honor.

MULL. and MO. Oh, no!

NAT. Werry good! Now here is the key of his loose box. You know the road to it well enough—you've been smelling round there long enough to count hevery 'air in his tail.

GOODGE. And here's the money. [*Takes notes from Mo and gives them to Nat*]

NAT. That's business.

GOODGE. How shall we get at the horse?

NAT. Just before daylight, the veterinary is a-comin' to fix his plates—now two on ye must get yourselves up to look like Jack Meadows and his man—I'll pass ye, and once you're inside, why if Flying Scud wins, it's your fault—ain't it?

MO. If he wins after I've fixed him, I'll heat him, hoofs and all.

NAT. No cruelty, mind.

MO. He'll catch nothing more than a slight cold that will make his coat stare, that's all.

NAT. Arter that, Meredith must win with him, if he can.

ALL. Aye; ha, ha! If he can!

NAT. I'll do my best, mind ye, and if ye get in a hole after all—

GOODGE. We'll forgive you.

NAT. That's your sort.

MULL. Our fortunes are made. [*Exit R.*]

GOODGE. [*Crossing L.*] And Meredith is broken, for tonight the favorite will be nobbled. [*Exit R.*]

MO. Yes, he'll have a severe attack of the vishy washy villy vobbles. [*Exit R.*]

NAT. Will he? Well, I shouldn't be surprised if some of you will have an attack of the washy willy wobbles before you've done.

SCENE 3: *Front scene on road to stable. Enter Bob, Jerry and Ned Compo with stable lads L.1E.*

JERRY and OMNES. Tell us all about it, Bob.

BOB. Well, give a chap time to breathe.

NED. Ah, you've got too much flesh about you, Bob, to breathe comfortably.

BOB. Have I? Well, it ain't got nothing to do with you if I have.

JERRY. You ought to try Doctor Skinner's mixture, that 'ud bring you down.

BOB. I've had gallons of it.

NED. I fancy chloride of lime and Condy's Fluid mixed with a little benzoline and Mrs. Allan's Restorer would do him a world of good.

BOB. Yes, it might prepare me for another world.

JERRY. Bob, tell us about Nat Gosling, Mo Davis and the rest.

OMNES. Yes, tell us, tell us!

BOB. Well, first and foremost, there's a-going to be a fashionable wedding in high circles and society—Colonel Mulligan's niece, Julia Latimer, is a-going to marry young Lord Woodbie. I was present when the consent was given, and Katey and me is a-going to be one of the bridesmaids, and I'm going to be the best man.

JERRY. Well, if you're going to be the best man, some of the others must be rather rum 'uns.

BOB. If you insult me any more, Mr. Jeremiah Cobbler, I shall be under the painful necessity of giving you a smack in the jaw.

JERRY. What?

BOB. You heard what I said, a smack in the j-a-w.

JERRY. Oh, you will, will you. You'll have to go into training first.

BOB. [*Threatening*] What?

JERRY. [*Squaring up*] Eh? [*Business*]

NED. Come boys, don't quarrel.

JERRY. Well, what did he want to say he'd smack me in the jaw for?

NED. Now, Bob, tell us all about Nat and the shufflers.

BOB. Well, after the bit of a bother on Calais Sands, Miss Julia left her uncle's house, and came to Miss Katey at Nat Gosling's lodgings. Captain Grindley Goodge came there after her, and got talking matters over with Nat Gosling, and I believe there's a bit of business on. [*Mysteriously*]

NED. Business! What sort?

JERRY. I thought Nat Gosling wouldn't mix up with such a set.

BOB. Oh, leave Nat alone, he's got his head screwed on the right way. [*Nat whistles outside*]

JERRY. Hush, I hear Nat's whistle.

BOB. Then he can tell ye himself what's up. [*Enter Nat L.IE.*]

NAT. Well, Bob, have you told the boys?

BOB. Some of it, but not all.

NAT. Now lads, to make a long story short, I've sold the race tomorrow. Goodge and his party have tipped me two thousand pounds to let them nobble Flying Scud, and I've got the money, and have promised them the key of the stables.

JERRY. Why Nat, all the stable is on the favorite.

NED. We all know, Nat, that Mister Meredith didn't behave fair and square to your granddaughter, Miss Katey, but we didn't think you'd take such a revenge as this. Howsomedever, I'm going to ride Flying Scud, and it'll be a fair race. I'll ride to win, and it wouldn't be twenty thousand pounds that would stop me putting Scud first past the winning post if he's the best horse in the field.

JERRY and REST. Bravo, Ned! Stick to that!

NAT. Ned Compo, I know'd a man as lived in Oundle in Northamptonshire as made his fortune—and d'ye know how? by minding his own business. You mind yourn, and let Nat Gosling, the oldest man in the stable, speak.

JERRY. Go on, Nat, let's hear the finish of it. What have you got to say?

NAT. Well, boys, as observed afore I was took up short, I've promised the key of Flying Scud's stable, and two o' them will be here tonight to fix the favorite.

JERRY. Nat, Nat, I couldn't have believed it of you.

NAT. Will ye shut up till I've done? I promised 'em the key of Flying Scud's stable, but didn't promise the Scud should be in it when they came. Now there's another horse, Voltigeur, a regular outsider, that's supposed to make the running for Tom Flyer, that's been backed heavily by Captain Goodge, Mulligan and Mo Davis. His stables are at the end of the yard. Dick Purvis has had to go home, and there's the key of his box. Voltigeur is the very image of Flying Scud—as like as two peas. You two [*pointing to Jerry and Ned*] go and bring it down to our stables, change the horse cloths, and let those chaps nobble their own fancy horse, instead of the pride of our stables. What do you say to that, boys, eh?

JERRY. What! Let 'em nobble the wrong horse?

NAT. Precisely! And then put them in the hole they intended for us. And as for the money I've got from 'em, it shall be fairly shared by every lad in the stable.

JERRY and OMNES. Hurroy! "Old Boots" for ever!

NAT. [*Looking L.*] There they are at the end of the lane. You go and meet 'em, Bob; don't bring 'em to the stable for about ten minutes or a quarter of an hour. Tell 'em it ain't safe for 'em to come about till we're quite ready for 'em.

BOB. All right, leave 'em to me. [*Exit L.*]

NAT. [*To Ned and Jerry*] You go and fetch Voltigeur; here's the key.

JERRY. Right you are, Nat. Come along, Ned. [*Exeunt L.*]

NAT. [*To rest*] You go to the yard and keep a sharp lookout. [*Stable lads exit R.*] And now, Master Goodge and Co., I wonder how you'll like being caught in your own trap. Tread Tom Meredith under your heel, will yer? Not while Nat Gosling is on this side of the turf. Give Flying Scud an attack of the wishy washy willy wabbles? Not if I know it, not if I know it. [*Exit R.U.E. Re-enter Bob with Goodge, Mo Davis, disguised, L.*]

Bob. This is the way to the stables, gents, but you'd better wait in the lodge for about a quarter of an hour; some of the stable boys are about, and it 'ud be just as well to give 'em time to get out of the way.

Mo. Right you are. Goodge, you look spiffin; a regular business-like cut about your jib. I declare, your mother wouldn't know you.

Goodge. Stow your chaff, Davis, I'm in no humor for it. If we miss the game we have in hand, it will be rather serious, for I'm ruined.

Mo. So am I—so are we all—we're all ruined. But there ain't no chance of anything going wrong. Haven't we parted to two thousand quid? Only fancy, two thousand thich 'uns to be left alone with a gee-gee a couple of minutes.

Goodge. If Nat Gosling acts on the square, one minute will be quite enough for me.

Bob. Now, gentlemen, we'd better get inside the lodge and wait.

Mo. All right, my dear. It's rather cold; have a drop of this. [*Offers flask*]

Bob. No thank you, sir, no thank you. You may drug your horses, but you don't drug me.

Mo. Oh, jumpin' Moses! What a lot of suspicious people there are about.

Goodge. Well, come on, Mo, the sooner the job is over, the better I shall like it.

Mo. And the longer we are over it, the verser I shall like it. [*Business: Mo going to drink out of bottle. Goodge takes it from him and pockets it*]

Goodge. None of that just now.

Mo. Oh, ain't he selfish? Wants it all himself. [*Exeunt R.1E.*]

SCENE 4: *Stable yard by night. Illuminated village in the distance, palings round loose boxes. Jackson discovered watching. Nat whistles outside.*

Jack. Hallo! Who's that? [*Whistles repeated*] Is that you, Nat Gosling? [*Enter Nat through gate*]

Nat. Yes, it's me. If I told ye it was somebody else, you wouldn't believe it.

Jack. I was expecting the farriers, and thought it might be one of 'em.

Nat. All right, you needn't wait now. Go and look if you see any signs of the farriers on the road.

Jack. Right you are, Nat. [*Exit through gate*]

Nat. I wonder whether Flying Scud's awake? [*Unlocks half door*] Ah, there he is—come over, my beauty. [*Business: with horse's head*] Thought to hocuss ye, did they? Well, we shall see, we shall see. Wants to give ye

a dose, do they? Well, what's good for Flying Scud can't be bad for Voltigeur. Talk about diamond cut diamond, or a Roland for an Allover!—why
it ain't in it. They'd give yer wishy washy willy wobbles, would they? I'll
wash 'em inside out before I've done with 'em. [*Jerry gives peculiar whistle
outside*] Hallo! There they are. [*Imitates whistle*] All right, my pippins, the
coast is clear. [*Enter Jerry and Ned leading the horse, Voltigeur, through
gate*]

JERRY.   Here ye are, Nat, this is Captain Goodge's horse, Voltigeur. We've
managed it. The stable boy is asleep. [*Village clock strikes in the distance*]

NAT.   Hark! Time's up! They'll be here in a quarter of an hour, or less.
Good evening, Voltigeur, sorry to put you to any inconvenience, but we
shall just trouble you to take Flying Scud's place in the stable for a few
minutes, and after your master's physicked you, you can go back to your
own stable.

JERRY.   Come along, Nat. Is Scud ready for the change?

NAT.   All serene, my beauty. [*Music. Nat brings Flying Scud out, and
Jerry with Nat change the two horse cloths on the two horses*] Now put
Voltigeur in Flying Scud's stable, and put the Scud in the spare box. Good,
good! Now we'll see who'll have an attack of the wishy washy willy wobbles.
Watch, boys, at the end of the lane, and when you see Goodge and Moses
disguised as farriers coming, give me the signal.

JERRY.   Right you are, Nat. Come on, Ned. [*Exeunt through gate*]

NAT.   Now they can come; I'm ready for them. [*Opens half of stable
door*] They thought to get at ye, did they? [*Repeat business with horse's
head*] They thought I'd sell you. I'd rather sell me life. See here now, and
listen to your ould nuss. The heye of all civilization is on ye this day, and
you know it. You're as vain as a peacock, and as pooty as paint. They'll
come to spile you, my dear; and arter their cookery, they'll expect to find
you strip tomorrow, and show a coat like a stubble field. Ay! but you will
come out like satin in the sunshine. I kin the faces they'll pull at that. Then,
my cock-a-wax, you'll pace among the admiring crowd, moving like suthin'
between a woman and a steam engine. That's when the ring will feel it. I
hear 'em at it now. The odds arisin', and bilin' over. Then you'll take your
gallop, my pippin, and when they sees your loopin' stride, they'll put settlin'
day afore their heyes in the biggest kind o' print. Now we're at the post.
Be quiet—no pullin'—steady! Down goes the flag—easy! Now ye knows
what's in ye. Wait on Rasper. Keep a heye on Locomotive. Round ye go,
shakin' off ruck, and takin' of it easy till the turn where I showed yer.
Then Ned will let yer go, and then go it. Locomotive is shook off like
a flea. Don't ye hear the outsiders saying, "Yalla! Yalla wins!" And the

edicated, a cryin', "Flying Scud!—The Scud ahead!" as ye go? My heart gets in my mouth. Rasper is close behind; ye may feel his pipes, as he puts on a spirt at the finish. He gains your quarter; Ned calls on ye; ye quit him like a bullet, and pass the post, held hard. Four lengths ahead; time—quickest on record. There's your programme! If ye falls short on it, never put your nose in my face again. [*Puts horse back. Enter Goodge and Mo Davis disguised R.1E.*] Show Mr. Meadows Flying Scud's box. He's come to 'just his plates.

Mo. [*Aside to Goodge*] That's the crib. I've been takin' stock of the lodgings, and know the jography.

Goodge. All right. [*Enters the box R.*]

Mo. Here's my patent fixer—here it is. That will make his coat stare just for a day or two, eh? [*Exit into box*]

Nat. Ah! and it will make you stare for a year or two, or I'm mistook. Let's see what they're arter. [*Looks into their box*] Who is that at the head of the hoss? Oh, that's Davis. 'Tother one is going over his plates. Take keer; Voltigeur is 'andy with his heels—he'll ketch ye a wipe in a minute. The fust thing you'll know, you'll know nothin'. [*Re-enter Goodge and Mo Davis bringing on horse Voltigeur. They drug him on stage*]

Goodge. There now, stand still!

Mo. 'Old ye head still, can't ye? There, that'll do ye a lot of good. Oh, jumpin' Moses! He's bit my finger.

Goodge. He's got it! Our fortunes are made!

Mo. We've nobbled the horse. We've nobbled the favorite. [*Dancing with glee*]

Nat. [*Aside*] Yes, and I've nobbled you!

Scene 5: *Front scene near Epsom Downs. Crowds of people, such as frequent races. Thimble riggers, Negro minstrels, vendors of race cards and dolls, vans, tents, drags, costermongers' carts, etc. Woodbie and Julia in a phaeton. Negro minstrel song is going on. Enter gipsy who tells Julia's fortune, while two cockneys are taken in by the thimble riggers. Enter policeman. The thimble riggers decamp. This scene should maintain several natural episodes in pantomime during the dialogue. A murmur outside. Enter Lord Woodbie and Julia accompanied by Lady Woodbie.*

Lady W. Come, my dear, this is the way to the course. We shall find our carriage just beside the stand.

Julia. Lady Woodbie, I hope some day to be able to prove my gratitude.

Wood. Gratitude for what? For making me the happiest fellow alive? When the preliminaries are all settled, there will be nothing to delay our marriage.

Lady W. Ah, my dear boy, you are so impetuous.

Wood. Everything is prepared for our departure to the Continent, and won't we have a jolly honeymoon? [*Enter Jerry L.*]

Jerry. A word with you, my lord.

Lady W. Come, my dear, this way to our carriage. [*Exeunt R.*]

Wood. Ladies, I'll join you in a few minutes. Well, my lad, what is it?

Jerry. Mr. Meredith's compliments to you, sir, and he wants you to know that Captain Goodge's horse, Voltigeur, is took bad; can't run; in fact, scratched. He's anxious about you, as he's afraid you might be backing it, seeing as how you used to be so thick with the price.

Wood. Thanks! But I haven't backed it for a penny. All my bets are on the favorite, Flying Scud.

Jerry. And it's as sure to win as if it had already passed the post. [*Enter Captain Goodge*]

Goodge. Ah, good day, Lord Woodbie. Glad to see you looking so well.

Wood. You will oblige me, sir, by considering we are not on speaking terms.

Goodge. Oh, indeed! Not on speaking terms, eh?

Wood. I have promised my mother, Lady Woodbie, never to speak to you again.

Goodge. Quite right! Always do what your mammy tells you. Poor boy, you're not old enough to think for yourself. You ought to be ashamed of yourself.

Wood. I hope I shall never be ashamed of taking my mother's advice.

Goodge. Yes, you were always a favorite with the ladies. It isn't every fellow that can get a woman to go out and fight his battles for him. Thank goodness for the honor of old England, it isn't every *milksop* that can persuade a poor girl to dress herself in male attire and risk being shot to save her so-called lover's life.

Wood. Why you infernal scoundrel! Do you dare to insinuate that I knew anything of—

Goodge. Oh, of course you knew nothing about it. [*Changing tone*] It isn't likely. There isn't a man in the club but shall know all about it, and your cowardly behavior. Lord Woodbie, you knew perfectly well that Julia was going to take your place.

Wood. [*With suppressed passion*] Captain Goodge, you're a liar! [*Strikes him with glove in face*]

GOODGE. I'll horsewhip you on the course, in the presence of your friends. [*Enter Tom Meredith*]

TOM. Oh, no you won't! For if you try it on, I'll break your neck.

JERRY. And if he doesn't care to soil his hands by contaminating them with your lavender water body, I'll see what I can do. [*Squares up*]

GOODGE. So, you cowardly cur, you've got your bullies close at hand to protect you.

TOM. Come along, Lord Woodbie. Remember your promise to your mother.

WOOD. Yes, but I—

TOM. Come, come! No more words! Follow me!

GOODGE. Yes, take him to his mother. Get his mother to mind him. Tie him to her apron strings for safety—but that would be rather awkward—perhaps the old lady doesn't wear aprons!

WOOD. Why, I'll— [*Business. Tom gets Lord Woodbie off*]

JERRY. [*To Goodge*] I'd give five pounds just to have you in our back yard for ten minutes. [*Exit. More variety business introduced here. Enter Mulligan L.*]

GOODGE. There's a report that there's something wrong in the crack's stable. The betting is down to even, and three to two against him. [*A cheer outside*]

MULL. What's the matter now? [*Enter Mo Davis L.U.E.*]

MO. Oh, dear! Oh, s'elp me! Oo—Oo!

GOODGE. What are you dancing about?

MO. There's been a mistake. I don't know! Eh! Voltigeur is scratched—he's amiss!

GOODGE. Who cares?

MO. Yes, but Flying Scud is—is—

GOODGE. What, man? Speak! [*A cheer outside*]

MO. You hear? He is as clean as I am—cleaner—nothin' the matter with him. We're done!

GOODGE. It is impossible! Damnation, man! You didn't give him the physic, then?

MO. Yes, I did.

GOODGE. He didn't swallow it, then?

MO. Yes, he did.

GOODGE. Then it didn't work.

MO. I didn't go along vid it to see. [*Enter Tom Meredith with super L.1E.*]

TOM. I'll bet three to one on Flying Scud! Three to one in hundreds.

Super. Done!

Tom. Done, and again.

Goodge. No; enough on.

Tom. He's a picture! Thanks to old Nat, he never peeled in such form as he does today. [*Cheers outside*] There! That's at him, again. The public could eat him up every bit.

Mo. [*R.*] So could I. I'd bolt him whole if I vos along wid him.

Goodge. [*Aside*] There has been some villainy here.

Mo. We are the wictims! I'm a wictim!

Goodge. We can't get at the horse, but we can get at the jockey. Ned Compo is the lad. I'll fix the boy. Come with me. [*Exeunt Goodge and Mo Davis L.1E. Variety business and introductions, five niggers ending with chasing the welcher. Enter Nat L.U.E.*]

Nat. Now, sir, I've come for orders; how's the lad to ride?

Tom. Give him your own advice, Nat, I can't improve on it. I think we have nothing to fear; let him ride as he may.

Nat. Nothin' is sure till it has happened.

Tom. Let him take the lead then, and keep it.

Nat. He can last, but won't give thirty shillings in change for a sovering. [*Bell rings outside*] There's the "clear the course." Ah, the old blood begins to tell inside me; my werry back gets lithsome, and I feel the old jockey amovin' in me strong. [*Business. Enter Bob running L.U.E.*]

Bob. Where is he? Where's Nat?

Nat. Here I be. Wot's up?

Bob. Oh, lor'! Here's a go—oh, sir, Ned, sir, Ned Compo—

Tom. Well?

Bob. He's been and took bad, sir.

Nat. Took bad? How?

Bob. All over, sir. Down at the mouth. Here he is. [*Enter crowd with Ned very pale*]

Ned. Oh, Lord! Oh, dear!

Nat. Wot's up?

Ned. 'Tain't what's up, it's what's down. I'm nobbled.

Tom. What d'ye mean?

Ned. I jest took a small drain of brandy as a gent offered me—wery kind he was—and a moment arter, I couldn't keep my saddle.

Nat. By jinks! They couldn't fix the horse, so they got at the jockey.

Mo. [*Aside*] Grindley Goodge, for a thousand. [*Bell outside*]

Nat. Oh, dear—Oh, mussy me! The warmints; they've ruined ye, Tom; and my beauty can't run.

ALL. Shame! Shame!

NAT. [*Suddenly*] Yes, he shall, by jinks! I'll double on 'em all yet. Peel the colors off that boy; gi' me his cap. [*Throws off his overcoat*] I ain't rode a race for five and twenty years. [*Enter Katey L.1E.*]

KATEY. Oh, Grandfather, what are you going to do?

NAT. Do, girl? I'm going to ride Flying Scud for the Derby. I'm four pounds overweight, but a pound or two won't count 'tween me and him. [*Re-enter Goodge and Mo Davis L.*]

GOODGE. The favorite can't win.

NAT. [*Dressed*] Can't he? But he will, though.

Mo. Who will ride him?

NAT. I will! "Old Boots!"

CROWD. Hurray! Hurray! [*Exit Nat L.U.E.*]

MULL. The old man is crazy.

TOM. I am ruined—he can't have it in him at his age to pilot such a dare-devil animal. [*Cheers outside*]

GOODGE. [*R.*] How d'ye feel now, Meredith?

TOM. I feel like an honest man. How do you feel?

GOODGE. Rich as a pie!

WOOD. There they go! By Jove, the old fellow is in the saddle. [*Cheers*] The crowd recognize him—hark how they cheer. [*Cheers outside*]

KATEY. He's up and off; but will he ever be able to stick on?

CROWD. Now then, make way a little. Where are you shoving to? [*Bell. Cheers. A row and a fight, during which a tent is knocked down on one side and the carriages, etc., are moved off at the other so that the whole course and spectators, grandstand, etc., become visible. The police enter. Order is reestablished. Bell rings*]

CROWD. There they are. There, they are off. No, they ain't. Yes, I tell yer— see! Which is him in front—black and tan cap? That's Kettledrum colt. No —yes! Where's Nat? Where's the favorite?

GOODGE. He's nowhere! Look! He will be off in a minute.

Mo. I vish he may break his neck. Oh, my inside is going it. Keep an eye on him.

MULL. Green and black is ahead. They'll never catch him. They're down in the hollow.

KATEY. Oh, Mr. Meredith, it is all Grandfather's fault, sir, if you are ruined.

TOM. Katey! If I could see into your heart, and know the truth! I'd rather win you than the Derby, but that is impossible.

KATEY. Alas! [*The crowd have turned and now watch the open course at the other side*]

ALL. Here they come! Here they come! Rasper is in front! Rasper! Rasper! No, Locomotive! [*The cloud of horses and jockeys appear*]

GOODGE. Locomotive and Rasper, neck and neck. Confederate, third. The favorite, a bad fourth.

TOM. Ay, but held—hard held. Now the old man is creeping on them. See! He catches Confederate, and passes.

CROWD. Rasper wins! Rasper wins! White and white!

TOM. The favorite for a thousand, even.

GOODGE. Done! Done!

TOM. Look! He collars Locomotive! Well done. Good race; good race! He's at Rasper's quarters! Now for it! Well done, Nat! Nat forever!

CROWD. Rasper! Flying Scud! Yalla wins! Rasper wins! Flying Scud! White! Flying Scud! Yalla, yalla! Hurray! Hurray! [*Immense tumult. The grandstand is seen to flutter with hats and handkerchiefs. The crowd surge and sway in the distance. A number is seen to go up in the distance on the post. Renewed cheers. The course is flooded with the crowd*]

TOM. No. 9! Flying Scud! [*Frantic cheers. Enter policemen surrounding Nat, who is mounted on Flying Scud and is on his way to the weighing room. Mo Davis appears very ill in one corner, Goodge, Mulligan and Chousir in another, stamping with vexation*]

TABLEAU

ACT IV.

SCENE 1: *Mulligan's lodgings. Goodge, Mo Davis and Mulligan discovered.*

MO. Oh, jumpin' Moses, what's to become of us? We're like the poor little "Babes in the Wood," only there's three of us.

MULL. By the blood of the Mulligans, we're cornered. Our creditors will swarm on us like bees on a treacle cask, and I shall be disgraced. *Me,* the descendant of the Prince of Gath-na-cush, in a direct line with the Mulligans of Castle Mulligan; our noble blood is disgraced forever.

GOODGE. Oh, damn your blood.

MO. Yes, damn your blood. Vot's the good of blood; it won't get us out of this schermozzle. Oh, dear! Oh, dear! I never vos in such a scrape before. Vot's to be done? Vot's you going to do?

GOODGE. Our only chance is immediate flight. We must get away from England at once.

Mo. Right you are! I'll go to the Argentine. I want to see my old friend, Jabez, and if once I get over, they'll never bring me back again.

Goodge. Why, you fool, we haven't got enough money to get so far.

Mo. Then let me go on a steamer as a poor little stowaway, in among the coals and bilge water. Oh, why didn't my mother put me in a pail when I was born?

Mull. It's no use talking, gentlemen, we must proceed to action at once. Julia has left me, and I have nothing now to live for. [*Weeps*]

Mo. Go on, crocodile, what are ye snivelling for? Look at the crocodile's tears running down the end of your nose.

Mull. Well, if they'd try to get down to the bottom of your nose, they couldn't.

Mo. Dat's right, dat's right, go on, abuse my nose now, just 'cos you can't pay your debts. Oh, this is an ungrateful world. I'm too good for it.

Goodge. Yes, you ought to have been an angel. Pity you haven't got a pair of wings.

Mo. And these are the men I once thought my friends. As Nebuchadnezzer said at the battle of Vaterloo, "And you, Brutus, go; never more be ossifer of mine."

Mull. What it comes to is this: how much money have we?

Goodge. Well, in the safe at our retreat at Lambeth Road, we've got about a hundred and twenty pounds.

Mo. Ve must divide it. Tell me how many times three times go into a hundred and twenty. Fifty—forty—thirty—seven. No, I vos never no good at figures. I'll have the hundred, and you shall have ten apiece; then I'll go to the Argentine, and throw myself on the mercy of the glorious republic; and when I'm settled down, I'll get up a subscription to send for you two to come over to me, and then we'll set up a branch establishment over there. D'ye see?

Goodge. We'll divide fairly, forty pounds apiece, and then take our chance. It must be done at once; tomorrow will be too late.

Mo. Yes, it's a hold saying, and a true one, "That a bush in the hand is worth two in the bird," and "Never put off till today, what you can do tomorrow."

Goodge. Chuck it, Mo Davis, and let us settle details with Mulligan.

Mo. Dat's a nice way to speak to me after all I have done for you.

Mull. Well, go on, what do you propose?

Goodge. Well, I think it would be best to— [*Knock heard at door*] Hush! What's that?

Mo. P'raps it's the man called for the taxes.

MULL. [*Looking through keyhole*] It's Quail, the lawyer.

GOODGE. Open the door; we must brazen it out.

MULL. Come in, Mr. Quail, come in. [*Enter Quail, with him two clerks who remain at door*]

GOODGE. To what are we indebted for the honor of this visit?

QUAIL. I daresay you can guess.

GOODGE. I haven't the slightest idea.

MULL. Perhaps you have called to ask my instructions concerning the little bit of property I thought of buying in the borough.

Mo. Or perhaps to ask us to take some shares in the new company which is being floated to acquire the very prosperous walk stalls and oyster barrows in the borough, and amalgamate them with the lady's trotter baskets in Drury Lane. I'm told it's a sure certainty to pay twelve and a half per cent.

QUAIL. No, gentlemen, that is not my business. I have just heard that the bill I discounted for you bearing Lord Woodbie's name, is a forgery. I give you twelve hours to find the money, and provide for it.

Mo. [*Looking at watch*] Excuse me, Mr. Quail, I can't stop; I've got to see a man about a dog. I forgot all about it till just now.

QUAIL. Excuse me, Mr. Davis, but you mustn't leave the room.

Mo. I'm a hinnocent party, Mr. Quail. Upon my word and honor, I knew nothing about it. I hope you didn't think me capable of such a thing as having anything to do with a forged bill. I can scarcely write my own name, let alone anybody else's.

QUAIL. You forget, Mr. Davis, that I have been your confidential solicitor, and I know quite well what you are capable of. Gentlemen, I have no desire to proceed to extremities; all I want is my money. Your conviction would do me no good, and would not pay me back the cash I have advanced you, but I must protect myself. If the forged bill remains in my office twelve hours longer, I shall present it to Lord Woodbie, and you know what that means.

GOODGE. Yes. Seven years!

Mo. [*Fainting in Mulligan's arms*] Seven years!

GOODGE. Very well, Mr. Quail, since those are your terms, we'll try and find the money.

QUAIL. Then you confess the forgery?

GOODGE. As you seem to know all about it, I may as well do so. It was written in a moment of indiscretion. Mulligan suggested it, and I drew it up.

Mo. There, you hear him say I had nothing to do with it. [*Looks at watch*] If I don't go, that man will sell the dog to somebody else.

QUAIL [*To Goodge*] Is this true?

GOODGE. Mo shared in everything with us. He came with Mulligan to your office to get the money.

Mo. Oh, hark at him! Where will he die when you go to?

QUAIL. Well, just step across to my chambers. And to prevent any possible difference of opinion hereafter, if I give you these twelve hours to find the money, you must give me the undertaking to do so in that time.

GOODGE. Come along, then. [*Aside to Mulligan*] In twelve hours we shall be out of the country. [*Going L.*]

Mo. Oh, I wish somebody would lend me the key of the Bank of England for ten minutes.

SCENE 2: *Front Street. Enter Nat and Lord Woodbie followed by Tom Meredith.*

TOM. I congratulate you, your lordship. I believe Miss Latimer to be one of the best girls that ever drew the breath of life.

WOOD. Thanks, Tom, thanks. I know I have your best wishes.

NAT. There was a time when Master Meredith thought the same of Katey, but all that's changed now.

TOM. No one more bitterly regrets it than I do, Nat.

NAT. Ah, I suppose that some day you'll be getting married to some fine lady of quality; then Katey will break her heart and die off like a flower, and I shall retire into private life until the Great Master of Life's course rings the saddling bell for me to weigh in and go up aloft.

TOM. Give me your hand, good, honest Nat, and believe me when I say that whatever Katey's feelings may be for me, mine towards her never change. Heaven knows that I love her as much as ever, but after what I saw with my own eyes, heard with my own ears, she could never become my wife; not that I shall ever marry another. I love her too dearly to ever think of such a thing.

NAT. Drat my old breeches if I can make it out. Human beings is funny things; I think I can understand hosses better.

WOOD. Here come Julia and Katey, accompanied by my mother. [*Looks at watch*] They are before their time. [*Enter Lady Woodbie L.U.E. with Julia on one arm, Katey on the other, followed by Bob. Bob crosses over to Nat after touching his hat to Meredith and Lord Woodbie*]

LADY W. Ah, Cecil, we are here rather earlier than I expected. I got my shopping at the stores done much quicker than anticipated. And while I was thus engaged, those two girls got comparing notes and talking over old times. Julia has told Katey something that you told her recently, Cecil, and if my surmises are correct, the clouds may be lifted from Mr. Meredith's life, and sunshine will once more gladden his path.

NAT. Oh, my lady, what do you mean? A voice seems to whisper to me that it's something to do with my Katey.

LADY W. Quite right. It has a great deal to do with Miss Katherine.

WOOD. Why you don't think it possible that she was the young girl that was locked up in the stable?

LADY W. But I do, though. She was telling Julia about her sad estrangement with Mr. Meredith, and I have not the slightest doubt that when you have told them the story you told us recently, all will be understood. Speak, Cecil.

NAT. Oh, speak, sir, you're lifting me off a hoverflowing coal-sack on to a feather bed.

WOOD. Well, I told my mother and Julia that some time ago at Doncaster, I came into Flying Scud's stable to escape a shower of rain, and to hide the tears that an interview with Julia had caused. That was when she refused to become my wife.

JULIA. Ah, but you didn't ask me properly, you know. [Coyly]

NAT. Go on—I remember meeting you as you came out.

TOM. I seem to have some recollection of it, too.

WOOD. I climbed up a ladder into the hayloft, and there overheard a cowardly attempt on the part of Goodge to force his attention on a girl, who evidently wished to repel him. I was unable to get down without attracting their attention, and was obliged to hear everything that took place. Hearing somebody coming, he told her she could get away by a side door, but instead of showing her the way out, he locked her up in Flying Scud's stable, and was afterwards arrested for an unpaid tailor's bill before he had time to release her. The bailiffs took him away with the key in his pocket. Since then he has done everything to try to make her appear guilty, but, on my word of honor, she is innocent.

TOM. Katey! Katey, how I have wronged you. [Embrace]

NAT. Oo—raw! Oo—raw!

CECIL and JULIA. Julia! Cecil! [Embrace]

NAT. Oo—raw, again! Oh, I can't stand it. Bob, embrace me. [Business]

BOB. Here! 'Old 'ard! I ain't a lovely female.

NAT. I couldn't help it, Bob. It's too much for me.

BOB. Here comes old Quail, the solicitor. How would you like to embrace him?

TOM. And you'll marry me now, Katey?

KATEY. Tom, Tom, I've loved you all the time.

NAT. Bless you, my chickabiddies, bless you!

LADY W. There'll be two weddings now, instead of one.

NAT. P'raps the clergyman will make a reduction in taking a quantity. [*Enter Quail L.U.E.*]

QUAIL. Excuse me, Lord Woodbie, but my business is urgent and most important.

WOOD. Yes? What is it?

QUAIL. I don't know whether I ought to speak in the presence of this young lady. [*Indicating Julia*]

WOOD. My affianced wife. [*Introducing her*]

QUAIL. Yes, your mother has told me all, but Miss Latimer is the niece of one of the parties implicated in a most unpleasant business.

JULIA. My uncle? Colonel Mulligan?

QUAIL. The same, madame.

JULIA. I can almost guess what you're about to say. Please speak without reservation.

QUAIL. [*Hands paper to Lord Woodbie*] That document is, I presume, a forgery?

WOOD. [*After looking at it carefully*] I regret to say it is. The signature is very like mine, but I never saw that bill before.

QUAIL. Written by Captain Goodge, accepted by Mo Davis, and endorsed by Colonel Mulligan.

JULIA. If my uncle is guilty, and a forger, let him suffer for what he has done. I have shielded him from the law too long already.

TOM. What is the amount?

QUAIL. Two thousand pounds.

TOM. Allow me to look at the bill. [*Does so*] You shall be paid, Mr. Quail; please regard this debt as being purchased by me.

QUAIL. But the paper is not worth the stamp that's on it.

TOM. I'll buy it. I shan't miss it out of my winnings on the Derby.

QUAIL. Well, if you're willing to buy with your eyes open, I'll sell. [*Hands him bill*]

TOM. And now, Grindley Goodge, I'll show you no mercy. The law will protect you against your racing debts, but with this proof of your forgery, escape is impossible.

QUAIL. Escape! Ah, that's it! I gave them twelve hours to find the money, but they have all three escaped, and I have put the police on their track.

TOM. We must go to the nearest magistrate, and obtain a warrant for their apprehension.

QUAIL. I'll take you to one; there's no time to be lost. Your presence will be necessary, my lord, so come. [*Exeunt L.*]

NAT. I feel twenty years younger.

BOB. And I feel two stone lighter.

NAT. Lord Woodbie is a trump.

BOB. And so is Meredith.

NAT. My Katey isn't to be scratched after all.

BOB. And Miss Julia has weighed in all right for the Matrimonial Stakes.

NAT. And what do you think of the old woman, Bob?

BOB. Why, she's another trump. Some of these high and mighty people have got their hearts in the right places after all.

NAT. This Captain Goodge put my darling Katey in a hole, but now we've got him in one, and before we let him out, he'll have to make a clean breast of it.

BOB. Well, if he's going to make a clean breast of it, he'll want a main drainage all to himself.

NAT. Follow me, Bob, let's be in at the finish. [*Exit R.*]

BOB. Well, this is a wind-up to a windy day. That Katey is a rare plucked 'un; a girl that is a werry 'ard 'un to meet. Like a sound hoss; you don't see 'em every day. Marry her, I should think he ought to. He ought to marry her once a month to his dying day. [*Exit L.*]

SCENE 3: *The garret. Table R.H., covered with a cloth; door L.H. Large safe. Enter Mo Davis.*

MO. Nobody saw me come in; vot an escape I've had. I'll lock the door hin'ards, and take the key out, so's there's no time to lose. Vere is my duplicate keys? Here they are. There's Goodge's, and here's Mulligan's—now for mine. Ah! [*He opens safe*] Here's the money. [*Takes it out*] All right; one hundred and twenty pounds. I'll start for Southampton by the next train, and get aboard the first ship leavin' for anywhere. The police vill be alive tonight. Bless me, what a sqveek I've had. [*Going. The door is tried*] Vot's that? [*Recoils*] Bless me 'art, there's somebody—oo—whish—dey is talking. 'Tis Goodge—oo—oo—here's a go! [*The door is violently shaken*] Oo—jumpin' Moses, here's another hole! My life is a honeycomb. Vere can I hide till he is gone? [*He creeps under the table. The door is burst open. Enter Goodge*]

GOODGE. I had no time for ceremony; in a few hours, the hunt will begin. I must secure the money at once. Where is my key? I must force the other locks. What! [*Sees the safe open*] Damnation! Someone has been here. Yes, the money is gone—not a penny left. Betrayed! Robbed by one of those

infernal associates of mine. Who could it be? Not Davis—he is safe in
Quail's hands. It was Mulligan! There is another room yonder—he may be
in there. [*Crosses R.D. Exits*]

Mo. He's gone—now's my time. [*Enter Mulligan with pistol case D.F.*]
Oh! [*Disappears under table again*]

MULL. If ever I come across that villain, Goodge, I'll pay him off. Poor
Julia! And to think that I was accessory to such a thing. I can never show
my face in Piccadilly again. A hansom cab would refuse me a fare. I'll borrow the few pounds here, and start for America. [*Turns and sees the safe*]
The divil! What's this? The safe open? The money gone! I've been robbed
by one of them blackguards, friends of mine. [*Re-enter Goodge R.D.*] It
could not have been Davis. It was Goodge!

GOODGE. [*Seeing Mulligan*] Ha!

MULL. [*Seeing Goodge*] Ha!

GOODGE. You Irish vagabond!

MULL. You cockney thief! [*Crosses to L.*] I left a hundred and twenty
pounds in the safe. You have taken it out.

GOODGE. You vile perverter of the truth, it was you that took it. You mean
thief! Give me half that money!

MULL. Disgorge your plunder, and share it like a gentleman. [*They seize
each other*]

GOODGE. Stand back! [*Releases himself and runs to pistol case*] Stay! You
pretend you have not on your person the contents of the safe. I know that
you have.

MULL. And I am certain that they are safe in your pocket.

GOODGE. Take that revolver, then, and I will take this; let the survivor
search the one who falls.

MULL. Done! I'll do society a service if I swing for it.

GOODGE. [*Standing behind table*] Are you ready?

MULL. [*R.H.*] One—two—three! [*They fire. The table begins to heave
and roll about. Enter Nat, Woodbie, and Quail. Nat advances, and with
Goodge lifts the table. Davis is discovered on his hands and knees, shot
behind. They help him up*]

Mo. Oo—oo—I'm killed! [*They seat him in a chair; he springs out of
it. Enter Tom with Bob, Jerry and detectives*]

TOM. Arrest these men!

GOODGE. You won't take me without a struggle for it. [*Business. Secured.
Six supers, two to each*]

Mo. Mr. Meredith, you'll be sorry for this. I shall instruct my solicitor to
commence an action against you for defamation of character.

GOODGE. I have yet to learn that a man can be treated like this for a few racing debts.

TOM. You're wanted on a charge of forgery, not only on this bill, which you deluded Mr. Quail into discounting, but those which you paid into the bank, thinking to escape before they reached maturity.

GOODGE. So it seems more a matter of personal enmity.

TOM. It's clearing off old scores. You have tried to ruin me, and I see no reason to spare you now. The game is played out, and the victory is mine. [*Enter Woodbie with Julia D.L.E.*]

MULL. Julia here! Forgive me, Lord Woodbie, I'm ashamed to look an honest man in the face.

NAT. [*D.L.*] How do you feel, Captain Goodge? Ain't you ashamed to look an honest woman in the face?

GOODGE. Who do you mean? I've never said a word against Julia.

NAT. No, but you did against my Katey. [*Leading Katey over at door*] Look at her! Lord Woodbie has told all he overheard in the stables, and Tom Meredith is going to marry Katey after all.

GOODGE. I confess there's not a word of truth in anything I ever said against her. She was too good for me. If she had loved me, I might have been a different man.

JULIA. There you're wrong, Captain Goodge. A good woman may save a weak man, but she can only share the fate of a bad one.

KATEY. Can't you let him go, Tom?

TOM. Yes, I'll let him go—to *transportation*.

MO. Oh, dear! Oh, dear! It's a good thing my mother's dead; dis dreadful blow would have killed her. It's all through mixing with bad companions. Vy didn't I join the "Band of Hope" ven I was young?

WOOD. I congratulate you, Tom. Flying Scud has turned out to be a four-legged fortune to you.

TOM. Yes, I shall make pots of money with him yet. Nat, we've entered Scud for all the great races of the year.

NAT. Hush, you're telling them where to lay their money. You're giving me away. You'll spoil my advertisements in *Sporting Life*. Let 'em apply to me, "Old Boots." Oh, I forgot, they paid their tips as they came in. Well, I don't mind telling you, that our hoss is engaged to run over the course every night this week. Take my advice, back him; and tell your friends they won't go far wrong if they put a bob or two on "Flying Scud."

CURTAIN AND FINIS

MERCY DODD;
Or, PRESUMPTIVE EVIDENCE

MERCY DODD;
Or, PRESUMPTIVE EVIDENCE

THERE is a slight confusion in the establishment of the name of this play, both because of its double title, and because of the existence of an earlier drama by Buckstone called *Presumptive Evidence,* which stayed on the boards of English and American theaters for many years. It is clear, however, that *Presumptive Evidence* was the title used for the performances in London at the Princess's Theatre beginning May 10, 1869; and that *Mercy Dodd* was chosen as its name for the production in Philadelphia in 1874.

The play did not enjoy a great measure of success, but it is interesting to us for its introduction of another Boucicault sensation scene—an exterior-interior setting showing Sir Bertie Buckthorne's library, a balcony overlooking the adjacent garden, and a large tree, a limb of which overhangs the balcony and thus gives access to the room; by some device the balcony collapses when Sir Bertie and Bobby Saker struggle over the possession of an important document, and men and timbers crash to the earth. Of interest also, is the character of Brassey, one of those flinty-souled detectives who never forgets a ticket-of-leave-man's face. Judging from the review in the *Illustrated London News* for May 15, the final curtain "was rather too sentimental for a certain portion of the audience," and certainly we feel a similar reaction when reading the dénouement seventy years after the first performance.

Most prominent in the cast at the Princess's was Madame Celeste, who played the rôle of Josephine Dubosc; Parselle appeared as Sir Bertie Buckthorne, F. G. Neville as Reginald, Miss Louisa Moore as Sybil, Mr. J. G. Shore as Matthew Dodd, Miss Emma Barnett as Mercy Dodd, William Rignold as Will Coveney, Dominick Murray as Bobby Saker, and F. Moreland as Brassey.

The source of the play is undoubtedly *Le Courier de Lyons,* but the treatment of the material is completely different from Charles Reade's adaptation of the same play in *The Lyons Mail.* A privately printed text bearing Boucicault's name on the title page was used in preparing this edition of the play.

F. T. C.

CAST OF CHARACTERS

SIR BERTIE BUCKTHORNE, *a Kentish landlord*

REGINALD, *his son*

SYBIL LENNARD, *his niece*

JOSEPHINE DUBOSC, *his housekeeper*

MATTHEW DODD

MERCY DODD, *his sister*

WILL COVENEY, *alias "Portland Bill"*

BOBBY SAKER

BRASSEY, *a detective*

A RAILWAY PORTER

SYNOPSIS OF SCENES

The scene lies chiefly in Kent, on the estate of Sir Bertie Buckthorne, and at the present period (1869).

ACT I. SCENE 1. THE KISSING-GATE
        SCENE 2. THE SPONG LANE
        SCENE 3. THE TURRET CHAMBER (EXTERIOR AND INTERIOR)

ACT II. SCENE 1. A ROOM IN DODD'S FARMHOUSE
        SCENE 2. A SHRUBBERY, PART OF THE GARDENS OF THE HALL
        SCENE 3. THE ROOM IN DODD'S HOUSE, AS BEFORE

ACT I.

SCENE 1: *The Kissing-Gate. A lane crosses the stage in front. A fence or hedge separates it from the fields beyond. R.H. in this fence is a gate leading into a wooded lane seen in perspective, R.H., at the end of which Dodd's farmhouse is perceived. Fields of reaped corn stretch away to the center distance. On a rising ground L. is seen Buckthorne, an Elizabethan mansion, surrounded by gardens and preserves, the seat of Sir Bertie. Sunset. A golden haze tinges all the landscape. Mercy Dodd is seated on the stile, C. Bill seated on a wheelbarrow near her.*

MER. [*Holding a spelling-book*] Come, try again! do not be dispirited.

BILL. I shall never learn, miss, I have begun too late.

MER. There is no such time in life. How old are you?

BILL. I don't know 'zactly. I was born on a doorstep in London, cradled in the gutter, and left there. Bless you, miss, I never know'd no mother 'cept the parish pump! No father ever give me a night's lodging, unless it were the p'leece magistrate.

MER. Do you mean that you have ever been confined in prison?

BILL. Off and on all my life!

MER. What for?

BILL. Trespass! As I grow'd up I found the world belonged to other people, and I'd no business anywhere in it. Prison! I believe you! What d've call living outside in the streets o' London? Vot's the difference atween them an' the yard of a penitentiary? There's the hiron bars and the spikes just the same between me and the world inside, vether the hiron keeps me hout or keeps me hin—vot's the odds? The streets is only a out-o'-door prison for such as me.

MER. Hush! You must forget that life, Bill. You must never mention it amongst our people. Your existence commenced when you first arrived here at the farm.

BILL. Ven you found me lying in the road-side ditch, yonder, took down with typhus—off my 'ed I wos—and ven I woke up von mornin', and found myself in a nice, white, clean bed, and in a nice, white, clean room—so different, oh! so full of sunshine—I tried to move—but I couldn't—bein' as weak as a baby. I shut my eyes, and I ses—I'm dead—and this here must be—what-d'ye-call-'em?—Heaven—I've heerd on. I opened 'em again, and there was your face bending over me. There's one on 'em, I ses—that's a hangel—and so it wos. Lord, miss, I didn't know where I had got to!

MER. You had got into a new existence—you were born into a nice, clean, white, new life, Bill.

BILL. That's it—and I'm just six months old! and, as I owes this life to your trouble over me, you're my mother!—and the fever was my father, I suppose.

MER. Very well. In that case you must be obedient to your elders; so take your book, and learn the lesson I set you.

BILL. I'll try, miss; but the book don't talk like you do! What you say I never forget. The book don't care whether I learn or no! Ain't there no way of comin' by learnin' except by workin' for it, like this?

MER. How do you mean?

BILL. Nobody never steals it, do they? Ah, no! o' course not. But the rich people, they ain't obliged to do spelling and all that?

MER. Yes, they are.

BILL. I thought they might 'a kep someone to do it for 'em. I'll go sit in the dry ditch yonder, where you first found me, and I'll try to get this into me. May I come to you, miss, when I can say it?

MER. Yes. [*Exit Bill*] Poor fellow! [*Enter Sybil behind Mercy, she places her hands over her eyes*]

SYB. Who is it?

MER. A goose!

SYB. No!

MER. A duck then!—a wild duck—called Sybil Lennard.

SYB. At your usual occupation, eh? Were you teaching that boor, or listening, all patience, to some selfish rustic complaint?

MER. Have you come to spend the evening with us?

SYB. No. My uncle wishes to see your brother about some repairs to be done at the Hall. Is Mr. Dodd at the farm?

MER. I left him with the harvest men in the field. But where is your uncle, Sir Bertie?

SYB. Yonder he comes with Madame Dubosc. I became so fatigued keeping pace with his feeble steps that I took a run to rest myself.

MER. How devoted an attendant Madame Dubosc has proved to her old master!

SYB. She is more like the keeper of a lunatic than a servant. I cannot tell whether he regards her with fear or with affection.

MER. She has been so many years in the family—it is natural that she should have established a great influence over an ailing and aged man. She is necessary to his life.

SYB. He never resists her, except on one subject.

MER. What is that?

SYB. His son.

MER. Reginald! [*Enter Sir Bertie and Madame Dubosc*]

SIR BER. Miss Dodd, I heard a name upon your lips which is never uttered with my permission within my hearing nor under my roof. It is banished, like its owner, from Buckthorne.

MER. I do not think that course likely to reclaim your son.

SIR BER. I do not ask your approval of my conduct, Miss Dodd.

MER. No. You ask me to conform to your humor.

SIR BER. If you please.

MER. Well, I do not please. I respect you too much to make myself agreeable to your faults.

SIR BER. You are a good girl, Mercy. But there is not a drunkard, a vagabond, or a hussy in the parish whose vices do not establish a claim on your regard. Your heart seems to be a refuge for the moral destitute.

JOS. That will do, Sir Bertie. I beg you will not pursue the subject, Miss Dodd; the doctors forbid him to dwell on any matters tending to irritate or excite him. [*Enter Dodd, over the stile*]

DODD. Good evening, Sir Bertie. It is a good sight to see you abroad. Why you look hearty, sir—you will be taking the field again—you will be riding to cover before Christmas.

SIR BER. Never again, Matthew. Ah! the next ride I shall take will be to a cover where the Grim Huntsman waits me, and the pack are tombstones, Dodd.

JOS. Change the conversation, Sir Bertie, if you please. You forget the object of your visit here.

SIR BER. True. The balcony outside my bedroom window—the turret chamber, you know—is crazy; it must be repaired.

DODD. I remember the architect condemned it two years ago. I thought it had been attended to.

SIR BER. There was something else, Josephine, what was it?

JOS. The brewery.

SIR BER. Oh, yes. I saw in this morning's paper that the Great Weald of Kent Brewery Company has failed.

DODD. I regret to say it has.

SIR BER. And the directors are accused of fraudulent practices.

Dodd. I believe they have been guilty of dishonest conduct.

Sir Ber. But your name is amongst the list of directors!

Dodd. Yes, unfortunately.

Syb. Oh! Matthew, I mean Mr. Dodd, surely they do not—they dare not —attribute such a crime to you! Mercy, do you hear? How can you stand there so unmoved, when he is accused?

Mer. Misfortune cannot ruffle me; and I know he is secure from all else.

Dodd. I do not know how far the errors of these men may involve me in their ruin—but surely it cannot involve me in their shame. Things have gone wrong with me for some years past, as you know, Sir Bertie. I borrowed large sums of you, for which you hold mortgage over my bit of land here. I was tempted to go into this brewery company, thinking to retrieve my losses, and you see the result.

Sir Ber. This affair may entail more serious consequences than you anticipate. Leave us, girls, I wish to speak in private with your brother. Mercy, we'll rejoin you at the farm. I will take a cup of tea from you if you will give me one.

Dodd. [Going up with Sybil] Do not look so pale, Sybil. [Aside] I must see you.

Syb. Tonight, at the Spong Lane Gate—will you come?

Dodd. Yes.

Syb. At the usual hour?

Dodd. Yes. [Exeunt Mercy and Sybil. He watches them]

Sir Ber. [Aside to Josephine] There—I promise not to excite myself; but this poor, honest fellow does not know that warrants have been applied for against the directors of this company. He will be arrested.

Jos. If he is wise, he will leave England, and remain absent until the storm blows over.

Sir Ber. He is honest enough to stay and face it. I must not tell him of his peril. [Dodd advances] Dodd, I have an estate in Canada which came to me a bargain. It shall be yours at cost price. It is a fortune for one like you.

Dodd. It will be a new lease of life.

Sir Ber. I shall not ask you to pay for it until you have won its purchase-money out of the soil. Can you start at once?

Dodd. Nothing detains me but the settlement of my affairs here.

Sir Ber. Leave those in the hands of my solicitor. Your sister Mercy is a first-rate man of business.

Dodd. Agreed, Sir Bertie.

Sir Ber. Precede us, Josephine; I will take Dodd's arm. [Aside to her] The poor fellow is perhaps in need of ready money—let me have a word in private with him. [*Josephine goes towards the Kissing-Gate; Sir Bertie speaks rapidly aside to Dodd, while she is going through the gate*] Come to me tonight to the Hall—come secretly—at ten o'clock—here is the key of the turret-door—you know the old staircase. [*Gives him a key*] I must see you alone—no one must know—no one—d'ye hear?

DODD.   I will come. [*They follow Josephine, who, having passed through the gate, waits; they go out. Enter Reginald. He looks after them. He then beckons off and calls*]

REG.   Here, my good fellow— [*Enter Saker*] You see that lady with those two gentlemen?

SAK.   Yes.

REG.   Follow them. Find an opportunity to give her this card privately; you understand? There's a shilling for you. Bring me her answer to the public house on the green.

SAK.   The Four Swans?

REG.   I will wait there till you come. A verbal answer will do. [*Exit*]

SAK.   [*Whistles, looks after Reginald until he is out of sight, then reads*] "Mr. Reginald Buckthorne." Here's some writing. "All right! I am here. The Spong Lane at half-past eight o'clock. Reginald." [*Sings*] "Meet me in the lane, love, when the clock strikes 'arf-past height." Vell hevery von to his taste, but if I'd my pick o'them gals, I'd choose the young'un from the Hall. Meet me at the gate! What game are they up to?—to be give to the old'un on the wink! 'Arf-past height! I'll be punctual. I might pick up somethin', Lord knows I want it bad enough. [*Re-enter Bill looking on his book*]

BILL.   There now, miss, I think I know it now.

SAK.   Bill Coveney!

BILL.   Saker!

SAK.   Portland Bill, as I live!

BILL.   Hush—what brings you here?

SAK.   Well, you don't seem over glad to see a cove! You recollect I got two years for that 'ere business in the Strand?

BILL.   Yes; your time is not out.

SAK.   After a twelvemonth in prison I got round the chaplain—shammed sick, and came over the doctor, and between 'em they got me a ticket. I'm out on condition I don't return to our old haunts in London. I can't make a living here in the country. But what's all this here rig? You are on a lay, Bill—take me in—halves, old pal!

BILL.   Yes, Bobby, I'm on a lay, and I'll tell you what it is.

SAK.   It's a big thing, I'll pound it. You've a sperrit above petty larceny.

BILL. All our lives, Bobby, you and me have spent together, from the day when we slept in one another's arms to keep one another warm, under a hempty vegetable cart in Covent Garden Market.

SAK. Or in the summer in Hyde Park on the grass.

BILL. We never saw a bit o' the country except there, or in the squares, where they put the green fields in a pound for straying into town. We was London sparrows, Bobby, you and me.

SAK. Ony not half so vell off, nor so quarrelsome.

BILL. It wos a foggy life, that wos. We didn't see more'n a day ahead; livin' from hand to mouth, and wery little in either. We never seed, never know'd nothin' beyond. Did we?

SAK. Never wanted to.

BILL. Vell, Bobby, one day fortin brought me here. I wos off my hed, I believe, and as I didn't know right from wrong, I did right for the first time in my life. I awoke in this place one mornin'. The people about me didn't know what I wos, and so they treated me as if I wos an honest man. It wos so new to me—I—I—

SAK. What?

BILL. I liked it. Then the life here seemed so safe, so free, so fresh. I took it in, I floated on it. It was like a glass o' cool water after wakin' from being drunk; it was what I never know'd afore—it was rest. Then they gave me work to do—work, Bobby—not like town-work, but lazy, quiet, easy. I say, old fellow, it ain't half sech hard lines to be an honest man, as it is to be a thief!

SAK. Wait till you get a chance. Come, Bill, this won't do. You are fishing in this quiet swim, and you don't want me to put a line out along side o' yourn. You have your eye on a big haul. Shares, Bill, shares!

BILL. Yes, we always did share, and so we will now. Here's my wages for three months, paid me today, six pounds ten shillings. Take the fiver, Bobby, and leave me in my new life. All I ask is, that you won't betray me, and I won't betray you.

SAK. Done! You always wos a queer one, Bill.

BILL. That's your way, Saker; this is mine. Good-bye.

SAK. Good-bye, Bill. [*Saker gets over the stile. Bill goes off by the Kissing-Gate*]

SCENE 2: *The Spong Lane. The boundary wall of Sir Bertie's park crosses the back. Enter Brassey.*

BRAS. It has just gone nine. I suppose it is too late to get this warrant signed tonight. Yet, if I could have obtained Sir Bertie's signature, I might have executed it on this here Mr. Dodd, and took him back to London by midnight train. But these country magistrates take their dooties mighty easy; so I must wait till morning. [*Enter Dodd*] Good evening, sir! This is Buckthorne Chase?

Dodd. Yes; that is the park wall.

Bras. Ah! I suppose it is too late to call there on a little bit of business. I believe he's magistrate here, and I want him to sign this paper—mere formality, sir. I'd like to get home to London tonight, if I could.

Dodd. I am Sir Bertie's land agent and transact all his business. I shall see him this evening, and obtain his signature for you, if you please.

Bras. Well, sir, this is lucky. There's the paper. I'm stopping at the Four Swans, in the village. [*Gives Dodd the warrant*] I may expect it returned in about an hour?

Dodd. I'll bring it to you myself.

Bras. Oh, sir! I would not trouble you; I'll call for it. [*Enter Sybil*]

Dodd. There is my card, then; I shall be at home at half-past ten. Good night! [*He gives Brassey a card*]

Bras. Good night, sir! [*Aside*] Oh, he's got a little affair on hand!—all right! [*Exit*]

Syb. How my heart beats! Dear Matthew! Surely my uncle will help you out of this dreadful misfortune?

Dodd. He has done so; but I must leave England—and at once!

Syb. Leave me?

Dodd. It is right I should, Sybil. I have tried the battle of life, and I can't hold my own with my fellow men. I have no right to own a woman until I have won a home for her. My wife must not pity me as you do—she must respect me.

Syb. And do I not? Oh, Matthew, are you not worth any woman's love?

Dodd. But that is not enough, dear. I must be worth her food, her raiment, her shelter.

Syb. My uncle would never let us want.

Dodd. No other man shall maintain my wife!

Syb. Matthew, you don't love me! I've seen that for a long time.

Dodd. Oh, Sybil!

Syb. Oh, yes—you do—you do—forgive me; but why do you sacrifice me to your pride? If you are going away, I will go with you. Take me—take me! You must feel now I love you.

Dodd. Indeed I do—for you cannot see how ungrateful such a step would be. Reflect.

Syb. I can't—I can't.

Dodd. You owe everything to your uncle. He still thinks that Reginald may reform and marry you. Hope never quite abandons a parent's breast. He cannot relinquish that darling project of his life, formed when he adopted you and brought you and his son together.

Syb. Nor can I relinquish the darling project of mine, which you formed when you brought my heart and your breast together.

Dodd. Hush!—someone is coming down the lane.

Syb. I don't care; I am too occupied to hear, and too happy to look.

Dodd. Let us enter the park—I will walk with you to the Hall. [*Enter Saker, whistling. Exeunt Dodd and Sybil*]

Sak. A pair of lovyers! I flushed half a dozen like 'em as I come along. One pair perched on a stile, talkin' loud—them was beginners. Another pair sat in a hedge—they wos whisperin'. Then two more walkin' opposite sides o' the road—sulking. And the whole place looks so quiet, so hinnocent. Why, it's wuss nor the Regent's Park. Not finding a young woman of my own, I couldn't help being ashamed of it. This is the Spong Lane. The old 'un said she'd come. Here's some one—'tis he! There's a dry ditch yonder, where I can lie hid. I hope there ain't no nettles. [*Exit. A pause. Enter Reginald, smoking a cigar*]

Reg. The hour has struck. She is not here. How long is she going to keep me kicking my heels here? [*Listens at the gate. Looks through the keyhole*] This is a pleasant game for a son and heir to play—scouting like a thief round his own house and grounds. [*The gate opens. Enter Madame Dubosc. She looks round*]

Jos. Reginald!

Reg. I have obeyed your summons, you see. On receiving your letter at Boulogne, I crossed over by the first boat.

Jos. You did well.

Reg. Yes; you have got both father and son under your thumb, haven't you?

Jos. Oh, Reginald! have I ever used my power for any purpose but for your sake? have I ever cultivated my influence over your father for selfish ends?

Reg. You have been a trump, as far as I am concerned—the queen of trumps.

Jos. No! the knave! for I have robbed your father to supply your extravagance.

Reg. Not until I had borrowed from you the total of your savings! I didn't mind giving the old man a commercial crisis; but when I reflected that

I accepted your little bit of cash, you won't believe me, but I've felt my face burn and my blood boil with shame.

Jos. Why—oh, why?

Reg. Because I had squandered the wages of a servant. I have plundered my nurse!

Jos. Your servant, your nurse, who has loved you more dearly than if you had been her own child!

Reg. What the devil you ever saw in me to be fond of, I can't imagine! When I was a boy I gave you no encouragement, nevertheless you always stood between me and blame. What a young demon I was! to you especially. I don't see I have improved much with age.

Jos. Whatever you are, I am yours with all my heart and life!

Reg. What have you brought me over here for? You know I am in great danger if my creditors knew of my presence in England.

Jos. Last week your father had a severe relapse; the doctors informed me that his life is in daily peril.

Reg. So he wants to be reconciled to his son and heir?

Jos. No. He made a will, by which the estate is left to Sybil.

Reg. But he can't do it, the estate is entailed!

Jos. But he can do it; he has done it, there is no entail; no, the estate is left to her, together with thirty thousand pounds—his savings during sixteen years past.

Reg. Did he confide all this to you?

Jos. No; but I have a duplicate key to the iron safe in his bedroom. I opened it, I read the will, and I counted the money!

Reg. What a haul! I say, Josephine, when I was a boy, I often climbed the old elm tree that grows so near the turret that from its upper branches one can step on to the balcony of the room.

Jos. What do you mean? Would you steal the money?

Reg. I don't see any other way I am likely to finger it, and he would not prosecute his own son.

Jos. No, no, not that!

Reg. There, don't be a fool. I was joking—really, I was. After all, the money is mine—that is, it ought to be, by-and-by. What's to be done?

Jos. You must marry Sybil.

Reg. There's no difficulty about that.

Jos. Yes, there is. She is in love with Dodd.

Reg. Dodd! Confound him! 'Twas he set his sister Mercy against me. I tell you, Josephine, that but for him and his infernal interference, that girl might have made me a better man. A canting hypocrite! I'll be even with him yet!

Jos. You are even with him—he is ruined. Complete your revenge by taking from him the woman he loves.

Reg. Will she consent?

Jos. Yes; for she owes everything to your father; so does Dodd. Neither will consent to build their lives out of the ruins of others.

Reg. Oh, won't they? Why not? What do they owe me?

Jos. Nothing. They owe it to themselves; but you need not try to understand what that means. It is called self-sacrifice, and is the weakness of those who love deeply and feel keenly. You never met with it.

Reg. Yes, I did once. I lost fifty pounds to a friend at billiards—a young cad he was. I suppose I looked rather pale over it. He remarked it, for he said, "I say, old fellow, do you know it gives me so much pain taking money I have won at play, I wish you would consider that we have been playing for love." What an idiot! It never pained me to pocket a bet; but, to do him justice, this fellow was so young. Perhaps he became a man of the world later in life.

Jos. Never. He remains that sort of fool always.

Reg. What's to be done?

Jos. You must remain here, in the hope that he may pardon you, and cancel that deed. You must be at hand to seize the relenting moment.

Reg. If he dies unforgiving—

Jos. Then—I—I must—destroy the will, and say he did it in my presence.

Reg. But how about the money?

Jos. As heir-at-law you can take possession promptly.

Reg. And so it falls to me!

Jos. Hark! the village clock is striking the quarter to ten. I must return—good-night.

Reg. Have you no money to spare?

Jos. None—I sent you my last shilling—how much do you want? I can borrow it.

Reg. Oh! in that case borrow as much as you can.

Jos. Sybil has some money.

Reg. Sybil! what's the use of making a fool of a fellow like that?

Jos. She will lend it.

Reg. D'ye think I have not cleaned her out long ago?

Jos. Oh!

Reg.   There—never mind—don't be annoyed that you can't get it out of her. By-the-bye, she might screw it out of the governor. Yes, manage that between you. Good-night.

Jos.   Be ready to appear on the scene when your father permits me to recall you; it is your last hope—obey me, and the will will be destroyed—your fortune will be restored.

Reg.   You are my guardian angel.

Jos.   Good-night. [*She kisses his hand*] Good-night. [*Exit through the gate*]

Reg.   Devilish odd woman that. Not a bad sort; but too fond of her own way. That kind of thing won't do with me, I can tell her. If I become master of Buckthorne, she will have to turn out. [*Exit. Saker re-appears*]

Sak.   Thirty thousand pounds locked up in an iron safe in a bedroom! Which bedroom? An old elm tree grows near the balcony; that will mark it. [*He draws out a jemmy*] Here's a skeleton key; I never travels without. Let us try it on this lock. [*Goes to the gate*] No! Unnecessary violence is against all the true principles of art. I can get hover the wall and leave no tracks. [*Exit. Scene draws*]

Scene 3: *The turret chamber. A window on one side, outside which is a dilapidated balcony, beyond this the branches of a tree. A fire burns in a grate, R.H. Saker appears in the tree, steps on the balcony, and looks through the window. Tries in vain to push it open, sticks some pieces of gummed linen on the pane, then breaks it gently; the strips of linen prevent the glass from falling; he puts in his arm and opens the window. He enters, looks round, recognizes the safe. Goes to the door, R.H., opens it and listens. Closes it quietly. Returns to the safe, and commences operations. He is inserting the jemmy, when he stops, listens, and then steps behind the curtain of the window, which he draws so as to conceal the broken pane of glass. Enter Sir Bertie and Josephine. She bears a lighted candle which she places on the table.*

Sir Ber.   I think I have everything I require for the night. [*He sits at table*] It is nearly ten o'clock. Good-night.

Jos.   It is long, Sir Bertie, since I have passed a good night. How is it with you? Do no evil dreams disturb your rest?

Sir Ber.   I would they were dreams! Alas! they are realities. At Reginald's birth I committed a crime—for him I have robbed my niece of her inheritance—and Heaven has appointed my own son its avenger!

Jos.   Is he so much to blame? You taught him to believe that he was heir to this estate. You educated him to be an innocent impostor, that the old name might not die out in the county. You wronged him even before he was born. You have deceived him through life!

SIR BER. And he has taught me repentance.

Jos. If you have much to pardon in him, has he not something to forgive? I do not defend—I plead for him. I do not say he deserves less than the worst you can inflict, but oh, sir, do not reveal the secret of your life and consign him, nameless, to a disgrace for which you are responsible—if not for his sake, for mine. Repay my services, reward my attachment with his pardon!

SIR BER. If Sybil will consent to marry him, all may be reconciled. Let him endeavor to secure her regard.

Jos. But you have banished him from your presence and from hers.

SIR BER. Let the scoundrel come back, then. He is here, I suppose? [*Sir Bertie unlocks the safe*]

Jos. Yes; near at hand, awaiting your permission to return. He is all submission and repentance.

SIR BER. I'll see him on one condition. He shall no longer be deceived about his position. This will, executed a few days ago, contains my confession. He shall read it, and know at once his past and his future. If he can gain Sybil, he becomes my heir, and that deed may be destroyed. More than this I may not concede.

Jos. More than that I do not ask.

SIR BER. Good-night! I beg you to leave me now; I am weary.

Jos. Good-night, sir. [*Exit*]

SIR BER. [*Rising, locks the door after her, then goes to the safe*] This money is not secure here. I am all anxiety to get it out of my possession.

SAK. [*Aside, peeping out*] I can oblige you, guv'nor—now's my time!

SIR BER. There are those in the house who have their eyes on this money.

SAK. [*Aside*] Yes, there are, and who mean to have it. A tap over the 'ed with my jemmy will square him, and— [*A knock is heard at the door*]

SIR BER. 'Tis Dodd! [*A second knock*] Yes! [*He goes to the panel door*]

SAK. [*Regaining his hiding place*] Vot a many wisitors! Can't they leave a poor old inwalid gentleman in quiet? At his time o' life it's unfeeling!

SIR BER. [*Opening the door*] Dodd! Hush! Come in. [*Enter Dodd*] Did you come unobserved?

DODD. Yes, I believe so. But why all this secrecy?

SIR BER. I wish to confide to your charge a sum of money, my savings of many years, laid by for Sybil. Here it is—thirty-four thousand pounds.

DODD. Have you kept so large a sum of money by you?

SIR BER. No; but it was invested in my name. I wish it to be secured in hers—safe from—from—

Dodd. From whom?

Sir Ber. From Reginald and Josephine. Hush! Take it, Matthew! no one will know you have it—you are my executor. You will not rob the poor girl —as some would—as some have done!

Dodd. I do not like the trust, sir; besides, I am leaving England.

Sir Ber. So much the better; take it to Canada, invest it in Colonial securities. It will be out of their reach there—there it is. [*Gives him the money*]

Sak. [*Aside, looking out*] Oh, Lord! the old willin—wot's he arter? He's a-robbin' me.

Dodd. [*Aside*] Here is another obstacle to my marriage with Sybil, but for her sake I cannot refuse the trust.

Sir Ber. That is off my mind—good-night!

Dodd. Here is a paper, sir, which requires your magisterial signature. [*Gives him the warrant*] Some county business I suppose—I did not inquire —I found the man hanging round the gates.

Sir Ber. [*Reading*] What's this—why, this is a— [*Aside*] Bless me, what does this mean? [*Aloud*] I—I cannot sign this until I have seen this person. Where is he?

Dodd. Waiting at my house.

Sir Ber. At your house?

Dodd. Awaiting my return.

Sir Ber. Send the fellow here.

Dodd. Tonight?

Sir Ber. Yes; tonight! and oh, Dodd, I have been reflecting. You agreed to start for Canada at once.

Dodd. I am prepared to do so.

Sir Ber. If you go by the mail train tonight to London, reach Liverpool tomorrow evening, you will just catch the steamer for Quebec.

Dodd. Tonight!

Sir Ber. Why not—to please me? You need not tell Mercy the extent of your journey. Say you are going to Liverpool, and may be absent three weeks.

Dodd. Agreed, sir!

Sir Ber. Farewell, then, and God speed you for a worthy, honest fellow!

Dodd. Farewell, Sir Bertie, and Heaven keep you! [*Going*]

Sir Ber. Stay. I'll light you down. [*Aside*] I'll detain the officer until the train has gone and he is safe. [*Exit with candle, following Dodd*]

Sak. [*Emerging*] He's got clear off with my money. [*Examines the safe, pulling out books, papers, etc.*] Not a screw left! What's this? The will! Ecod! the old gent's confession as he is a-goin' to destroy. This may be worth somethin'—a family secret—here goes! [*He creeps back to the balcony. Re-enter Sir Bertie. The candle is extinguished and broken*]

SIR BER. He is gone. I saw him out of sight. I let fall my candle— [*He sees the shadow of Saker thrown by the moonlight across the floor, as he climbs over the balcony. He stands gazing at it*] What is that!—the shadow of a man! [*Goes to the window*] Ah! a thief escaping! [*Seizes Saker*] Help! help!

SAK. [*Under his breath*] Leave go, you old fool: and hold your cursed noise! [*A struggle. The balcony gives way beneath their united weight. They disappear*]

ACT II.

SCENE 1: *A room in Dodd's farmhouse. Mercy discovered at a table, writing, near her stands Bill Coveney.*

MER. [*Counting money*] Sixty-four pounds, four and six-pence. You will take this money and pay Stokes. Get his receipt.

BILL. Yes, miss. I beg pardon, but when I carried down Mr. Dodd's portmanteau to the station last night, he told me as how you and he was going to leave the farm here.

MER. It is true, Bill.

BILL. Do you go far away, miss?

MER. Very far away—we go to Canada.

BILL. Ah! a good bit of a walk from here, I suppose?

MER. Three thousand miles across the sea.

BILL. You might as well be transported. Ah! it don't matter to you where you go. You carry yourself with you, and Canada will be as happy a place as this is, when you get there. But what's this here going to be like when you are gone?

MER. Why, Bill, that is a very pretty compliment.

BILL. Is it? I shouldn't ha' known it unless you'd told me. I wasn't thinking of you though.

MER. No?

BILL. No. I was thinking of myself, what's to become o' me? Three thousand miles! I'd not mind the miles, if it worn't for the water. Ain't there no way round?

MER. No, Bill. I am afraid we must part. The gratitude you feel for the service we have done you more than repays us.

BILL. Gratitude? Yes, that's a sort of fear, ain't it? I'd a dog once that would face any living thing, but cowed when I looked at him. I often wondered why: now I know—he was grateful, like what I am. And when I was sent to—I mean when we was parted—he set to and died, all out o' gratitude.

MER. It is quite new to me to inspire fear.

BILL. It is new to me to feel it—you are the only person as ever made me tremble; and the kinder you speak, the worse I get. [*Turns aside with emotion*]

MER. [*Aside*] Poor fellow! he little suspects what is the matter with him! He is making love without knowing it—and betraying his heart like a child. [*Enter Brassey*]

BRAS. Good morning, miss.

BILL. [*Aside*] Brassey—the officer! [*Turns quickly away*]

BRAS. Mr. Dodd ain't at home, I suppose? [*Looks after Bill*]

MER. No, sir. He went to London last night.

BRAS. Ah! about the time he brought me that message from Sir Bertie to go up to the Hall. Why he must have started just after I left.

MER. Yes! Stay, Bill, you are forgetting this money.

BRAS. Rather sudden his departure, wasn't it?

MER. Very.

BRAS. Quite unexpected! You could not oblige me with his address in London, could you?

MER. No, sir; he left no direction. [*She goes up*]

BRAS. Thank ye, miss. [*Still keeping his eye on Bill, says aside to him*] Don't we know one another?

BILL. I never seed you before.

BRAS. I've got your face stowed away in some corner of my mind, or else you are very like somebody I know.

BILL. Am I? Well, if you owe him anything, you can pay *me*.

BRAS. Where did you pick up that chaff? 'tain't grown in these parts.

BILL. No! we have it down fresh every day from London.

BRAS. Well! if I don't know you, you seem to know me.

BILL. 'Cause you can see I don't want to improve your acquaintance.

BRAS. [*Aside*] They are all in this business. They pretend they don't know what happened at the Hall last night. They are close as oysters. [*Enter Sybil*]

SYB. Where is Matthew? Why has he not been to the Hall this morning?

MER. He left home last night.

SYB. Before the accident?

MER. What accident?

SYB. Have you not heard? Sir Bertie fell from the window of his chamber, and was taken up insensible.

MER. When did this happen?

SYB. At ten o'clock last night. We heard the crash when the balcony gave way, and his cry for help. On breaking into his room we found his iron safe open—its contents strewn about the floor. They say that a large sum of money has disappeared, which Madame Dubosc declares was deposited there.

MER. Do they suspect that a robbery has been committed?

BRAS. They more than suspect it, miss—they feel sure of it.

MER. But by whom?

BRAS. By your brother.

MER. My brother!

SYB. By Matthew! Who is mad enough to conceive such an idea?

BRAS. I am, begging your pardon.

SYB. And who are you?

BRAS. Joseph Brassey is my name, ladies, police officer. [*The women start back—he looks at Bill*] He ain't surprised. There, I was sure you knew me.

BILL. Score one—and go on.

BRAS. Perhaps, ladies, you ain't aware that Mr. Dodd was with Sir Bertie in his room last night at ten o'clock?

SYB. It is impossible.

BRAS. It is true, miss, nevertheless. At nine o'clock I gave this warrant to your brother—a warrant for his own arrest. I little thought, when he offered to get it signed, that I was employing the very man I was in search of. At ten o'clock this same paper was found on the floor of Sir Bertie's bedroom, amongst the contents of the iron safe.

SYB. Was Matthew absent from home last night at the hour he mentions?

BILL. No, miss! he was here along with me in—in the cow-shed.

MER. No; he was not here; he was absent; but—I thought he was with you, Sybil!

BILL. So he was, miss; only I thought you would not like to own it.

SYB. He was not with me. I was at home by a quarter past nine.

BRAS. [*To Bill*] It's no use; they don't understand your play—they are trumping all your tricks.

SYB. Of what is he accused?

BRAS. That depends; if Sir Bertie dies of his fall, it will be murder.

MER. Do you mean that my brother is suspected—

BRAS. Of disposing of the old man out o' window, to conceal this robbery.

MER. Oh, thank Heaven! This is too horrible to render suspicion possible.

BRAS. [*Producing the jemmy left by Saker in the room*] Have you never seen this article of furniture in your brother's possession? This party can explain to you its use, I dare say.

BILL. It's a James! Whew!

MER. I have never seen it.

BRAS. Perhaps not; for I have reason to think he was assisted by an accomplice in this affair; and that accomplice was a professional.

BILL. [*Aside*] Saker! I spot the game! Saker's in it!

SYB. No one will listen to a conjecture so ridiculous. It is only your ignorance of Mr. Dodd's character that renders it pardonable in you.

BRAS. Then why ain't he here to answer for himself? [*Enter Dodd*]

DODD. He *is here!*

SYB. Matthew! [*Runs to him*]

MER. My dear brother!

BILL. Lord, sir! what brings you back?

DODD. A telegram, which I read in the newspaper this morning, headed "Accident to Sir Bertie Buckthorne—alleged robbery and murder—description of the suspected assassin."

BRAS. That's my telegram, sir, I drawed your photograph, so nobody could mistake you. I sent it by lightning, and made every reader and every traveller in England a detective. You knew that. You found yourself headed off in every direction. It is a downy move, though, to come straight back; that's a facer I didn't expect.

DODD. Do not tremble so, dear Sybil; you have nothing to fear. You have charged me, sir, with a revolting crime—the murder of a defenseless old man, my benefactor. Who are you?

BRAS. Who am I?—as if you did not know! You forget the warrant you took last night to Sir Bertie—this paper; that told you who I am.

DODD. I never even looked at it. I handed it to him, unread by me.

BRAS. Oh, you did see him then?

DODD. Yes; I saw him in his chamber at ten o'clock, by his own appointment.

BRAS. Ahem! What's his game now? He's throwing down his cards on the table!

BILL. That's another facer you didn't expect!

DODD. I constitute myself your prisoner.

BRAS. I have not the formal authority to take you away.

DODD. You have taken my character away without authority. Do you think I'll leave that in your hands to deal with behind my back? No, I have come to face you, and when you drag my name, you must take me. I'll not let you out of my sight. [*Seizes Brassey by the collar*]

BRAS. Why, the man is taking me into custody, I believe!

DODD. Yes, I am.

SYB. Be calm, dear Matthew. No one suspects you.

BILL. See here, you had better apologize.

BRAS. Well, sir!—either you are a very hardened man, or a very unfortunate one. I'll give you the benefit of the doubt. If you will lie quiet here, I'll take this business in hand; I'll get at the bottom of this mystery. Leave your character with me; if you ain't guilty, it shall come to no harm.

DODD. Agreed—on those terms I release you, and will await your investigation. You will find me by the bedside of my old friend and master. Let us go to him, Sybil. Come, Mercy. [*Exeunt Dodd and Sybil*]

MER. Your business, sir, does not lie with honest men, and the truth puzzles you. If you will be kind enough to believe my brother, it will save your time. [*Exit Mercy*]

BILL. [*Aside*] Now for Saker—if he's atop of the earth, I'll find him! [*Exit*]

BRAS. If this fellow is innocent, who is guilty? That Frenchwoman and the son may have done the trick, and then tried to fasten it on—no—they are too earnest in their rage. [*Enter a railway porter with a portmanteau*] What's that? Oh—Mr. Dodd's luggage arrived from the station—leave it there. [*Exit porter*] I wonder if it contains anything to assist me in. [*Looks round, and pulls out a bunch of keys*] Let me see. [*Examines trunk*] Oh! the simplest lock I ever see—this pick will do—why, it's a baby. [*Opens the trunk—examining*] Nothing there much! what's here—a pocket-book, and notes—phew! thousand-pound notes, one, two, three, four. Why, here's above thirty—the stolen money! Lord—what a face that fellow has! Now this ought to be a lesson to you, Brassey, never to believe in any man, woman, child, or nigger. I'll pound this cash—no—better leave it here—and set watch on the premises. So—now to lock up this trunk. [*He locks the trunk*] Oh! he was anxious to get into custody, was he? I'll not keep him waiting long. [*Exit*]

SCENE 2: *A shrubbery, part of the gardens of the Hall. Enter Josephine, followed by Reginald.*

JOS. Here, in this part of the garden, we may speak unobserved.

REG. Josephine, I can see by the faces of the servants that they suspect I had some hand in last night's work.

JOS. Yes, they do; and I confess—

Reg. You shared their belief. Give a dog a bad name! I have enough to answer for, but not this—not this!

Jos. You forgot that you proposed to steal the money; and who but yourself had any interest in taking the will? What good to take the will unless your father were rendered powerless to make another?

Reg. Murdered, you mean! But he lives, and he can prove—

Jos. Nothing: his mind is shattered—his reason may never be restored.

Reg. Appearances are against me; yet I am innocent. [*Enter Brassey, R.*]

Bras. You are, sir; and I'll undertake to prove it. Good morning, mistress. You will excuse me, sir. You know I came down here on another affair, but got mixed up in this matter, and followed it up more for pleasure than in the way of business.

Jos. I allowed you to examine the premises this morning. Have you discovered how any person could have entered Sir Bertie's chamber?

Bras. Yes, by the tree that grows under his window. There are marks on it where the man climbed.

Jos. Ha! [*Looks at Reginald*]

Reg. Do you know that man?

Bras. Yes, I do. He is the best imitation of a honest man I ever see. He's a hoptical delusion! I was a child in his hands. What a face!

Reg. Whom do you mean?

Bras. Mr. Matthew Dodd.

Reg. Dodd!

Jos. Impossible!

Bras. There, whenever I goes into a case like this, where mystery hangs over who did it, the first question I ask is "Who is the most unlikely person to suspect?" and that's the one I begin with.

Reg. What proof have you?

Bras. Plenty. I found the missing money in his trunk.

Jos. And the will?

Bras. I forgot to look for that; but do not fear—we shall take the whole of the plunder in one haul.

Jos. Why did you not arrest him?

Bras. I prefer that Mr. Reginald shall apply for a warrant on my evidence, so if I take him on this charge, it clears that gentleman.

Reg. I thank you for your consideration, and I shall not forget to reward your success.

Bras. Success is its own reward, sir, to them as loves their art. I love a thief as some loves a fox. I'd preserve 'em if I had my way. I've a tooth agin this fellow though, for he made a fool of me—that I can't forgive till I'm even with him. Now, sir; if you please, I am ready to accompany you.

Jos. Stay, Reginald. [*To Brassey*] We shall follow you. [*Exit Brassey*] We are lost—we are in Dodd's power.

Reg. In his power?

Jos. Yes. He has read the will—he knows.

Reg. What?

Jos. That which enables him to defy you—to make his own terms. We are bound hand and foot by the secret divulged in that accursed paper.

Reg. What secret can bind me to protect him, and make me his accomplice in this crime?

Jos. You must let him invent what tale he may; you must pretend to believe his exculpation, and leave me to deal with him.

Reg. Yes, I am to play the puppet, and you are to pull the strings. By some such scheme you held my father in subjection, but don't hope to rule me. [*Going*]

Jos. Where are you going?

Reg. To the Hall.

Jos. Matthew Dodd is there—he will order the servants to shut the door in your face—you have no right there. Go, if you will, and ask him why—he can tell you.

Reg. No right in my father's house!

Jos. No more than I have.

Reg. Is this the secret?

Jos. Yes; and by its discovery I have held Sir Bertie in my power. Many years ago he loved a young woman beneath him in station. He deceived her.

Reg. The old story.

Jos. Yes—the very old story; but the end is not so old. Your father's young wife died in giving birth to her first child, who survived her but a few hours.

Reg. What do you mean?

Jos. She died in that very room where Sir Bertie now lies, and there the bereaved man knelt beside their remains. He did not hear the footstep of a woman who mounted the private stair—he did not know that she stood by his side bearing in her arms a newly born child—his illegitimate son. She called to him—he rose—and pointing to her dead rival he said—"You are avenged; there is my retribution!" The woman whispered, "No, not retribution only—but reparation!" and taking up the dead infant, she replaced it with her own living offspring.

Reg. And I am—you mean—that—'tis a lie! You may have extorted this romance from the dotage of a crazy old man; but who will believe it?

Jos. You will—you do—your heart shakes in your breast as I speak! Cease, then, that grimace you intend for a smile—it does not deceive me.

Reg. Why have you concealed this secret from me until now?

Jos. Why? because I would have had you innocent of all share in this crime. But now it is no longer mine alone. The will—your father's—contains the confession which makes you an outcast. The estate goes to Sybil Lennard.

Reg. Curse the estate! Give me your hands. [*Taking them*] Why do you confess to me one-half your secret only? Look me in the face! Why do you fear to avow the rest?

Jos. Reginald!

Reg. You are that woman of whom you spoke, and I—I—am your son.

Jos. [*In terror*] No, no! Do not believe me! I have lied—the story is all false! Forgive me! You are not mine—you are the heir!

Reg. Your whole life convicts you. Who but a mother would have borne with me as you have done. [*Embracing her*]

Jos. No, no, Reginald, you are not—you are not my son! [*Saker appears behind them*]

Sak. Oh, yes, he is, ma'am.

Reg. Who are you, fellow?

Sak. I'm the cove as done it. 'Twas me as stole the will; and 'tis me as has got it—for sale.

Jos. You?

Sak. Yes, me! I didn't mean as this old gent should get hurt—but he would pitch on his 'ed, though I showed him how I comed on my feet.

Reg. And you dare to confess—

Sak. Well; I wouldn't ha' come so sharp to the p'int, but as I sat in the ditch there, listenin' to the old lady, I heerd all she said to you, and she put it so strong, and showed me how snug I'd got you under my arm—ses I, Bobby, you have got the gentleman in chancery, take it out of him.

Jos. Was Dodd your partner in this affair?

Sak. No; he worn't in the swim along with me. He come by the side door, private, arter you, ma'am, had gone out; and the old gent—he gave him the notes under my werry nose, he did. He said as how you two was werry like to bone 'em if you got a chance, and he was no match for either of you—let alone both.

Jos. Dodd received them in trust for Sybil?

Reg. Then he is innocent.

SAK. No, he ain't. If you only let Brassy alone, he's bound to make him guilty. He's sweet on the gentleman—he believes in him, and once a p'leece gets a hidea atween his teeth, you might as well get a bone out of a dog's mouth.

Jos. We have no choice, now, but to deal with this ruffian.

SAK. That's me!

Jos. Or give him up to the police and accept the issue.

SAK. Don't accept that, whatever it is.

Jos. How much do you ask for the paper you stole?

SAK. Now that's business! I can't make a figure afore I consult my pardner.

REG. Your partner?

SAK. Yes, there's two of us in it. Here, Bill, come out; it is all right. Me and Bill goes halves in every game. [*Enter Bill*]

Jos. Are we in the hands of these wretches?

SAK. Don't be afeared, ma'am—you are safe enough. If things go wrong, I'm in for the assizes—you only lose what you never had, nor wasn't likely to get.

REG. [*Aside to Josephine*] The fellow is right. Dodd will be compelled to refund the money, out of which we can pay these fellows to destroy the will. They could not molest me in the future without proclaiming their own crime. We are safe. [*Aloud*] Where are you to be found?

SAK. At the Four Swans.

REG. Meet me there in an hour. [*Exit with Josephine*]

SAK. Wot's it to be, Bill? Two thousand won't hurt him! That's one thousand apiece.

BILL. It is a big fortin'—enough to set up for an honest man upon.

SAK. We'll go to America—over there we can afford to hold our 'eds high.

BILL. So high, maybe, our heels won't touch the ground. Where have you hid this will, Bobby?

SAK. [*Looks round and then*] Here it is. [*Hands it to Bill*] It's short, ain't it?

BILL. Yes; and this piece of paper is worth thousands and thousands of pounds, maybe.

SAK. Yesterday you shared your money with me. I'm above keeping your half of my fortin' from you, whatever it is. We've always shared like pals and pardners, ain't we?

BILL. So half o' this here belongs to me?

SAK. A fair half.

BILL. [*Tears the paper in half*] There—there's your share, Bobby, and this is mine.

SAK. What are you doing of?

BILL. One-half is no use without the other.

SAK. Do you doubt me?

BILL. Not a bit; but I mayn't like the terms you make—you sell your half—let me make the most of mine. [*Going*]

SAK. You ain't going to betray me?

BILL. Betray you! you know me better.

SAK. There's no knowing what weakness comes over a man when he goes in for reform. Then you mean that, after this, we don't row the same boat any longer?

BILL. Till death, Saker; but I must take the helm. [*Exeunt*]

SCENE 3: *The room in Dodd's house, as before. Dodd and Mercy enter.*

DODD. He is still insensible, still unable to bear witness to my truth. I feel the evidence against me creeping like the folds of a serpent slowly round my limbs. I see how my most innocent acts may be turned into convincing proofs of guilt.

MER. The truth will prevail, Matthew. I have no fear. [*Enter Sybil*]

SYB. Nor I. After you left, and as I stood beside my uncle's bed, holding his hand, I felt a gentle pressure, and his lips moved. I heard my name. Oh! I feel sure he recognized me.

DODD. Heaven grant he may be restored to us! [*Enter Reginald and Brassey*]

REG. I have come in to make you a proposition. You were about to leave this country—well, you are free to depart. We accept the explanation you have given of your interview with Sir Bertie, that his fall was the result of an accident.

SYB. I knew that Reginald could not entertain any doubt on the subject.

MER. Stay, there is something behind this liberality.

REG. We accept this version of the facts, provided you will restore at once the money you took from my father's safe.

SYB. The money he took!

REG. I use the mildest term. Come, Mr. Dodd, I presume you will not deny that you have in your possession a sum of thirty thousand pounds, or more, which I do not suppose you will allege was given to you on that occasion?

DODD. I allege nothing. I deny your right to question me.

REG. I do not question you; I state a fact. The money is in your trunk. I beg you will not oblige me to prove it by force.

MER. Matthew, is this true?

SYB. No! How can you ask?

DODD. It is true, Sybil. The money is there—and it is yours. It was confided to me by your uncle in trust.

BRAS. You have a deed then to prove this?

DODD. No; he trusted to my integrity.

REG. The integrity of a man against whom a warrant for felony was found in his chamber, awaiting his signature: a fugitive from justice!

BRAS. It was a fine move though, to endow the young lady with the plunder, knowing it would come round to him again through her. [*Enter Bill and Saker*] Come, Mr. Dodd, there's a door left open for you; be advised. There's only this case against you, for it seems they have caught your two directors in that brewing company, and the fugitives have disgorged; so you are clear of that business. Follow their example, sir, in this case, do! Take my advice, and the next train for Liverpool.

DODD. I will not confess that I am guilty of this dastardly act; nor will I surrender this girl's fortune, for it was placed in my hands that it might not fall into yours.

BRAS. You will get no one to believe that story, sir; and, unfortunately for you, there was no witness present to corroborate your statement. Here is my authority to arrest you for felony. I am sorry to put it into execution.

BILL. You are mistaken—there was a witness present last night, who heard and saw all that he has stated.

SAK. [*Aside*] What's he a-going to do?

BILL. There was a man concealed in the room, who had entered it by the window, and was there when you came in by the door.

SAK. [*Aside*] Is he going to sell me?

BILL. 'Twas he who stole the will, who was engaged in a struggle with the old man when the balcony gave way, and they fell.

REG. [*Aside*] Betrayed!

DODD. Who was there?

BILL. I was.

ALL. You!

BILL. I expected to get the money, but I saw it slip between my fingers, just as Mr. Dodd has stated.

SAK. [*Aside*] He's on a lay!

REG. Is he mad?

MER. This cannot be true. This man was here at the moment he avows that he was present at the Hall. You are deceived by him; he is incapable of the act of which he accuses himself.

BILL. I beg your pardon, miss. It's you have been deceived by me. Mr. Brassey here will tell I am quite capable of it. My name is William Coveney, *alias* Portland Bill. There's my written character. [*Hands a paper to Brassey*]

BRAS. I thought I knew you, my lad. [*To Reginald*] It's quite true, sir. [*To Dodd*] This man is a licensed convict; there is his ticket-of-leave.

MER. A licensed convict!

SAK. [*To Bill, aside*] What's your little game, Bill? What are you to get for this?

BILL. [*Aside to him*] Fourteen years—d'ye want halves?

BRAS. This fellow is the accomplice of his master—I have thought so from the first. This is a bold game to secure a great stake.

MER. Stay, sir, may I speak with this man? [*The rest withdraw*] You did not commit this act—you must know I am aware of that.

BILL. It don't matter much to me whether I did or not, but it matters a good deal to you, whether your brother is had up for felony.

MER. Then it is to save him you do this?

BILL. A prison is nothing to me, 'specially after you are gone. It's the best place for me. I can't go back to my old ways now. You've put a stopper on that.

MER. And you were willing to spend your life in a prison for my sake?

BILL. Either with you for life, or alone for life. If I can't follow your heel like a dog, chain me up. I ain't fit, I don't want to go free!

MER. [*Aside*] He loves me; when I reached out my hand to save a poor drowning creature, I did not see the slippery stone on which I placed my foot was his heart. [*She goes away, and sits, leaning her face in her hands*]

SAK. [*Aside to Bill, giving him the torn paper*] There is my half of the risk. Square this business with the heir—he will pull you through—he must.

BILL. Thank ye—Saker [*goes straight to Sybil*]—there, miss, is something that concerns you. [*Hands her the two parts of the will*]

SAK. What is he after now? [*Enter Sir Bertie and Josephine behind*]

SYB. [*Reading*] What is this? A letter addressed to me by my uncle. [*Reads*] "My Dear Niece—The confession I am about to make of the life-long injury I have done you—"

REG. Stay. That is the paper stolen from the safe. It was not intended for you.

SIR BER. Yes it was—it is. Read, Sybil, read.

REG. My father!

Dodd. Restored to us!

Sir Ber. Restored to his senses, Matthew, in more ways than one. Read, Sybil, I insist; and retain the proofs that confirm you heiress to my estate.

Syb. And your son?

Jos. [*Taking Sybil aside*] He is also mine.

Syb. And I am then heiress of Buckthorne; and he, Reginald, my cousin, is—

Jos. A nameless outcast!

Syb. [*Tears the paper*] Not by my consent. Dear uncle, the fortune you gave to Matthew for me is more wealth than we desire. Would you add to it that content of heart, without which wealth is poor? Forgive Reginald—let him bear your name worthily, and inherit your estate. I have an estate there [*pointing to Dodd*] in which I beg you to invest my life.

Sak. [*Aside to Bill*] The old gent ain't noticed me yet. Ain't there no way I can get out?

Reg. I understand your generosity, Sybil. I wish I could feel that I deserve it. [*To Sir Bertie*] Will you let me try to regain my place beside you? [*Sir Bertie shakes hands with Reginald. Reginald kisses the hand of Sybil, shakes hands with Dodd*]

Jos. [*To Mercy*] Will you help him to regain it? You can do so. He loved you; he loves you still. Your influence will redeem him.

Dodd. But what is to be done with this man who has confessed to the crime of which I was accused?

Sir Ber. I never saw him before in all my life; my opponent was a shorter person. I could not distinguish very well in the dark.

Sak. No, of course not.

Sir Ber. But the other man seems more like the figure.

Sak. What! Mr. Brassey!

Bras. No, sir—he means you.

Sak. Me? good hevings!

Sir Ber. But I could not swear to his identity.

Sak. No, sir, I never had any. Thank ye, sir. I'm very sorry you was hurt, but that warn't my fault. [*Bill nudges Saker to be quiet. Saker retires a little*]

Dodd. What motive induced you to plead guilty to this crime.

Bill. There worn't no other way to get you off except to take your place. A year or two in prison would be nothing to *me*. I'm used to it; but a week in the House of Detention would ha' killed you. [*Dodd shakes his hand*]

Sir Ber. Nature intended you for a better man.

Syb. Then let us give nature a chance. You were going to occupy that farm in Canada, and there to recommence your fortunes. Let this poor fellow take your place abroad and begin the world again.

Sir Ber. Well said, Sybil.

Sak. [*Aside to Bill*] Take me with you—halves—old pal,—halves.

Dodd. You accept?

Bill. Yes, sir. Heaven bless and reward you both for the thought. I'll try and show you ain't deceived in me. Good-bye, Miss Dodd. Ah, she turns from me now, but by-and-by you will learn, miss, that your goodness warn't quite wasted on the poor devil you picked out of a ditch—and—and—made a man of.

Jos. [*Aside to Mercy*] Mercy, did you hear me? Will you take Reginald by the hand and preserve his life, as you have done that of this poor fellow?

Mer. [*Aside to her*] No, I cannot, Josephine! Heaven has awarded me another mission, and I will not leave it half fulfilled. It has confided an erring soul to my charge to lead towards eternal life, and it shall not relapse. I will follow that man!

Jos. You love him then?

Mer. Yes.

Bill. [*Approaching Mercy and kneeling*] Won't you say good-bye, miss —won't you?

Mer. No! [*He is about to rise, she puts her hand on his shoulder*] Stay there—we may not part. A higher power has bound us together, and has devoted me to you!

Bill. [*About to rise*] To me! to me!

Mer. Stay there. Yes—you would have saved my brother by a supreme sacrifice; thus I repay the debt he owes you—'tis all I have—my life!

CURTAIN

ROBERT EMMET

ROBERT EMMET

IN a letter to his brother dated Monday, December 16, 1878, Augustin Daly wrote: "Yesterday I was taken by Mrs. Wood for a call on Frank Marshall. . . . He is at work now on a play for Irving—on the subject of Robert Emmet; but the managers and authors both are queer fish in this country." The sequel to this information appears in Townsend Walsh's *Career of Dion Boucicault,* and I believe that no better introduction can preface *Robert Emmet* than a quotation from that important biography.

"This play had something of a history. Early in his career and shortly after his tenancy of the Lyceum Theatre in London, Henry Irving was imbued with a desire to portray upon the stage Ireland's patriot-martyr. The actual facial resemblance of Irving to Emmet, his physique and bearing, all suggested the Irish patriot; while the tragic story of Emmet, his romantic love for Sarah Curran, his union with Michael Dwyer, that epic figure in Irish history, seemed rare material for a fine and strong play. Frank Marshall was commissioned to undertake the work, and was rewarded by payments amounting to some six hundred pounds. But just as Irving, after announcing his intention to present the play, was consummating the details of the production, he received a gentle reminder from the British Government that Robert Emmet would be *persona non grata* just then in London. The troubled period of the Land League and agrarian violence had set in, Ireland was in a political turmoil, and an Irish play with so patriotic a figure as Emmet for its hero, and so potential an actor as Irving to incarnate Emmet, might cause untold 'ructions.' Moreover, Irving ran the risk of being credited with something more than a purely dramatic interest in such a character. So, in deference to the wish of the Government, the project was abandoned.

"Frank Marshall's uncompleted manuscript remained on the shelf till, one day, the idea came to Irving that perhaps his old friend and manager might make some use of it. He turned it over to Boucicault, who rewrote it, reshaped it, 'boucicaulted' it, and produced it in Chicago. A more inopportune time for the trial of any play could not have been chosen. It was the night of Grover Cleveland's first election to the Presidency, and the city was in a state of feverish suspense and excitement. The next President of the United States was a matter of timelier import than the tragedy of Robert

Emmet. So the play did not get an attentive hearing, and Boucicault, losing all heart in it as a 'drawing card,' never revived it."

On the first page of the *Robert Emmet* manuscript deposited in the William Seymour Collection at Princeton, Boucicault had listed the characters, indicating his preference for the actors who should play them, and commenting, "I have underlined the seven parts that are peculiar and very particular." It is interesting to note that all these players appeared in the original cast. The play opened on November 5, 1884, at McVicker's Theatre, Chicago, with Boucicault as Michael Dwyer, his son, Dion, as Andy Devlin, his daughter, Nina, as Tiney Wolfe, Joseph Haworth as Robert Emmet, Gus Reynolds as Quigley, Joseph A. Wilkes as Major Sirr, Donald Robertson as Captain Claverhouse, Helen Leigh as Sarah Curran, and Mary E. Barker as Ann Devlin.

Another performance on the preceding day, November 4, 1884, is recorded in the *Era Almanac* for the Prince of Wales's Theatre, Greenwich, England.

F. T. C.

CAST OF CHARACTERS

ROBERT EMMET

MICHAEL DWYER

LORD KILWARDEN, *Chief Justice of the King's Bench*

LORD NORBURY

RIGHT HONORABLE JOHN PHILPOT CURRAN

CAPTAIN NORMAN CLAVERHOUSE

MAJOR SIRR

ANDY DEVLIN

MICHAEL QUIGLEY

PATRICK FINERTY

FATHER DONNELLY

BRANGAN

SARAH CURRAN

ANN DEVLIN

TINEY WOLFE

LADY KATHERINE YORKE

ENGLISH OFFICERS AND SOLDIERS, IRISH SOLDIERS, PEASANTS AND CITIZENS, LINK-BOYS AND FOOTMEN, A DRUMMER, JURY, BARRISTERS, JAILERS, ETC.

SYNOPSIS OF SCENES

ACT I. SCENE I. RATHFARNHAM, NEAR DUBLIN. A GARDEN

SCENE 2. A STREET IN DUBLIN

SCENE 3. A ROOM IN DUBLIN CASTLE

ACT II. SCENE I. THE COTTAGE AT BUTTERFIELD LANE

        SCENE 2. A GORGE IN THE MOUNTAINS NEAR THE SCALP

        SCENE 3. THE CAMP AT THE SCALP

        SCENE 4. A ROOM IN THE HOUSE OF MRS. EMMET

        SCENE 5. COLLEGE GREEN AND THE HOUSES OF PARLIAMENT

ACT III. SCENE I. A ROOM IN THE VICE-REGAL LODGE, PHOENIX PARK

        SCENE 2. ANN DEVLIN'S COTTAGE IN BUTTERFIELD LANE

        SCENE 3. GLENMALURE

        SCENE 4. THE INTERIOR OF FATHER DONNELLY'S—A SMALL CHAPEL

        SCENE 5. THE YARD OUTSIDE FATHER DONNELLY'S HOUSE

ACT IV. SCENE I. THE COURT HOUSE, GREEN STREET

        SCENE 2. A PRISON

        SCENE 3. THE BULL INN

        TABLEAU—BRANGAN'S WHARF, RING'S END, NEAR DUBLIN

        TABLEAU—THE YARD OF KILMAINHAM

ACT I.

SCENE 1: *Rathfarnham, near Dublin. A garden; night; on the R.H. is a house; the windows are lighted. A low wall across stage at back; a door in it L. of C. Shrubs R.H. up stage; spades, a scythe and garden tools R. against wall. Music.*

Enter from the house, coming from the back, Ann Devlin; she looks around with caution, then crosses to door on wall; listens; then recrosses to C. towards house; calls.

ANN. Miss Sarah! [*Enter Sarah Curran from the house*] Spake low.
SARAH. Is he there? [*Crosses to door L.C.*]
ANN. I don't know—rightly! I hear two voices whispering outside.
SARAH. He always brings some trusted follower with him to stand on guard during our meeting. It may be Dwyer, or Quigley.
ANN. No; it is a strange voice. [*Two knocks at door*] Whist! that is not his signal. Go outside awhile until I see who is in it? [*Sarah runs back into the house; Ann opens the door. Music ceases. Enter Major Sirr; his scarlet uniform is covered in a long cloak; his face is shaded by his hat*]
ANN. What do you want?
SIRR. I want a word with your master.
ANN. He is engaged entertaining a party of friends at dinner.
SIRR. His friends must excuse him. I bring this summons from the castle. [*Hands her a letter*]
ANN. [*Taking it, reads superscriptions by the light from the hall*] "To the Right Honorable Philpot Curran, on his majesty's service."
SIRR. That business brooks no delay. See that it reaches him quickly. [*Exit Ann into house. Sirr goes rapidly to door in wall. Quigley and three men enter*] You three fellows pass round to the porch of the house; don't show yourselves until you are called to act. [*Exeunt the three officers behind the shrubs and off R.U.E.*] You are certain the man we seek will present himself here tonight?
QUIG. Never fear. Shure he's afther sendin' me ahead of himself to see the road is clear. He is hidin' now sumwhere widin' cast of my voice. He won't show up until he gets the offis from Miss Curran. Her maid, Ann Devlin, raps three times agin that dure in the wall. He will answer wid one rap; and she opens it.

SIRR. And lets our bird into the trap? Return to your post outside.

QUIG. More power, Major. [*Exit door in wall. Enter Curran from the house, with the letter opened in his hand; he is in full court dress*]

CUR. You are the bearer of this letter from the lord justices? Be good enough to precede me to them. I follow you at once. Tell their lordships I am at your heels. It is mighty provoking to be called away at such an hour. [*Re-enter Ann; with his coat and hat*] Where is my daughter?

ANN. In her room, sir. [*He takes his hat and coat*]

CUR. Explain to her the motive of my departure. She will see my guests cared for during my absence. [*Music. Exit into house, followed by Ann*]

SIRR. Your daughter, Mr. Curran, will entertain a guest here tonight that I'll take care of! [*He disappears behind the shrubs C. Re-enter Ann from house*]

ANN. [*Looking round*] He is gone. [*She crosses to door, then knocks three times; a pause; one knock is heard; she opens it*] Who is there?

QUIG. [*Appearing*] Meself.

ANN. Quigley! Did you see a strange man lavin' this dure awhile ago?

QUIG. I did. Shure I was houlding his horse for him while he was in here. Who was he?

ANN. A messenger from the castle! [*Re-enter Sarah*]

SARAH. Has he come? [*Enter Robert Emmet; he wears a long blue coat*]

ROBT. Sarah!

SARAH. Robert! [*Embracing him*]

ANN. [*To Quigley*] Stand aside. [*Exit Quigley, by door in wall. She locks the door after him*] I'll wait in the hall beyant, and watch over yez. I'm not aisy in me mind tonight. [*Exit*]

ROBT. You tremble in my arms. You should fear nothing when so sheltered! Or is it the chill night air? Let me protect my treasure. [*Wraps his cloak around her*] So! Its folds may retain the sweet warmth of your form. Sit there—let me hear your voice and look into your eyes. There are tears in them.

SARAH. They are for my father whom I deceive. They are for my love, that I hide away as if it were a shame! During your long absence in France, he constantly urged me to receive the addresses of lovers to whom I could offer no objection, excepting that there was another here in my heart; my old, old playfellow to whom I had given my life long, long ago. You came back at last, but in secret, concealing from everyone your presence in Ireland. What is this enterprise in which you are engaged?

ROBT. It is one in which the fortunes and lives of others associated with me are involved; all we possess is staked on an event which will be assured within the next few days. Till then be patient, dear one!

SARAH. Be it as you will! But I feel it is all so gloomy around us. Oh, for the honest daylight when I can show the love of which I am so proud; you have placed a crown of jewels on my head—the emblem of a girl's nobility, but I may not wear it openly!

ROBT. Oh, my love! what if we fail? What if I become broken in fortune? a fugitive from my home? an exile from my country?

SARAH. You have no fortune but my love; you cannot be bankrupt there; you have no home, but my heart; no country but my arms; how can you be a fugitive or an exile? [*Re-enter Ann*]

ANN. Get him away quick for his life! Major Sirr with his following are searching the house.

ROBT. [*Rising*] Major Sirr! here!

ANN. 'Twas himself was in it a while ago! away wid ye! [*The three men at back appear, Ann seizes the scythe and as they try to intercept Robert's escape by the door in the wall, she sweeps it round as if mowing at their legs*] Stand back! or I'll make twins of any one of ye. [*They retreat. Sarah runs to the door and vainly tries to turn the key*]

SARAH. It's rusted in the lock. I cannot turn it. [*Enter Major Sirr, R. at house, standing on step; he points a pistol at Robert*]

SIRR. Robert Emmet. In the King's name I arrest you. [*Emmet retreats to L. Sarah runs between Sirr and Emmet, and taking off the cloak holds it out so as to hide her lover*]

SARAH. Unlock the door. I can't.

SIRR. Stand aside, girl! [*As he advances, she advances to meet him. He tries to pass her, but she swiftly throws the cloak over him and the pistol, while Robert succeeds in escaping by the door; Sirr disengages his arms, and replaces the pistol in his belt*] The man you have aided to escape is the leader of a rebel movement that threatens this city with bloodshed and plunder. His confederates are watching his signal on the Wicklow Hills. The woods and bogs of Kildare are alive with them. You will have to answer for the blood that will flow from the streets of Dublin into the Liffey this night.

SARAH. Let there be oceans of it, rather than one drop of his. [*Enter Norman Claverhouse, his sword is drawn*]

NORM. I was seeking for you, Miss Curran! Nae sooner your gude father had excused himself and left us, than a posse of black devils, savin' your respect, raided the hoose wi' whingers and pistols, searchin' everywhere. Even your ain rooms wor no sacred from their conseederations.

SIRR. My men have their warrant, Captain Claverhouse, for what they did.

NORM. And I had mine, for dhrivin' them before me from the premises.

SIRR. I shall report your interference in this matter to the authorities at the Castle. [*Beckons to his men*] We tracked a leader of the rebel movement to this house, to which he comes nightly, and in secret. We found him at the feet of that lady. By her assistance he escaped. But within ninety days he will be at the foot of the gallows. Good-night.

ANN. Bad-night to you, you prowlin' kite!

SIRR. Never fear, Ann Devlin. I'll get you in my clutches some day, and then I'll make it hot for you, my beauty! [*Exeunt officers at door*]

ANN. Never fear, Henry Sirr, the devil will get yer in his clutches some day, and then he will make it hotter for you, my dandy. [*Exit Sirr; he carries Robert's cloak on his arm. Ann locks the door after him.*]

SARAH. Leave us, Ann. [*Exit Ann*]

NORM. Miss Curran, I have made no disguise of my feelings toward yourself; and your father encouraged me to hope that, one day, I might persuade you to share my name; for I have loved you verra-verra dearly!

SARAH. I—I know it.

NORM. Was it true what that man said about you?

SARAH. Yes!

NORM. You love this—other one?

SARAH. Ever since I knew how to love. I am sorry for you, Norman. I tried very hard to care for you, as my father wished me to do, but this other one returned—and then I knew I had no heart to give you.

NORM. You could na help it more than I can help loving you. If I canno' reap the harvest of your life, I can assist in bringing it home. I can ha' some share in your happiness. It seems your lover that meets you here is implicated in this rebellion?

SARAH. He told me that he was engaged in some secret enterprise, but until now I did not suspect its nature.

NORM. Before tomorrow it will be known in Dublin that, concealed in the house of the Right Honorable Philpot Curran, his majesty's attorney general and member of the Privy Council, the police discovered the rebel leader.

SARAH. My father is innocent. He had no knowledge, no suspicion of his presence here. I—

NORM. Will he protect his honor behind his daughter's shame?

SARAH. What can I do? Oh, Norman! help me to shield him from the consequence of my guilty folly!

NORM. It is a cruel task you put upon me, Sarah. There is no way but one. You maun gae to this lover tonight. You must fly from your home. Seek him out.

SARAH. Go to him?—to Robert?—to Mr. Emmet?

NORM. Aye, if that be his name. Bribe him wi' yerself to abandon this cause. Take him away beyond the seas. Your flight will clear your father from any suspeecion and will explain the presence of Mr. Emmet in the house! 'Tis hard on me to say the words; it is verra bitter, dear. Before this night is past you must bear my rival's name.

SARAH. Oh, Norman, Norman! You deserve a better woman than I am. [Calls] Ann, Ann—my hat and shawl! She will accompany and protect me.

NORM. No; I will! I will never quit your side until you are Robert Emmet's wife. [Enter Ann]

NORM. Where does he lodge?

ANN. In my father's cabin—Butterfield Lane. I'll meet you there, and bring with me what things she will need.

NORM. Come!

ANN. [Looking after them as they go out at garden door] Every step she takes she treads upon his heart and he lets her do it. If Dwyer found I was fond of any other boy, he'd squeeze the life out o' my throat; and I'd love him all the bether for killin' me! I'd die happy.

SCENE 2: *A street in Dublin. Enter Quigley.*

QUIG. [Calls] Finerty—Pat. Finerty—Pat, ye divil, are ye there? [Enter Finerty]

FIN. Is it yerself, Mike? Well, what luck?

QUIG. Is he here? Has he come back?

FIN. Who?

QUIG. Emmet.

FIN. Come back! D'ye mane to tell me he was not tuk?

QUIG. No; bad luck to it!—he escaped.

FIN. Did he show fight?

QUIG. No; but he showed two pair of heels. The thrap was all right, and baited wid the girl. The Major's following—ten blackguards, not including him nor meself—wer in an' around the house when I led him along fair and aisy into the middle of them.

FIN. How did he escape from thim all?

QUIG. Divil a know, I know! for, shure I could not shew in it. I was outside in the lane, houlding the Major's horse, stooping down wid my ear close agin the dure, when I heard Sirr's voice calling on him to surrender. The dure flew open. I felt a fut on me back, and before I could rise a cry, Emmet was in the saddle, and out of sight.

FIN. Bad cess to the chance! Won't we lose the reward for his capture— a hundred pounds—that the Major promised should be paid to us tonight at the Castle?

QUIG. Why not? We led thim to the bird; we gave thim a fair shot; if they missed it we are not to blame. Whist! may I never—but is not this himself? [*Enter Emmet*]

ROBT. Quigley, you saved my life! That horse you held ready for me at the door was a godsend! Without it, the men stationed in the lane to inter- cept me would have made me prisoner. How did you escape?

QUIG. While they were afther yer honor I made off, aisy enough. I rode straight to our depot at the Bull Inn where I left the animal in charge of Andy Devlin. [*Go to C. Enter Andy*]

ANDY. More power, sir. I've got him safe in the stables. Your honor was wantin' a purty baste to carry himself to Wicklow Hills tonight where the boys are expectin' you.

ROBT. We won't be there by midnight. We hold a council of war to decide on our plan of action. I have prepared them to submit to the staff the manifesto to the people, the list of our forces and place of action. Surely, I placed them in my breast. I cannot have lost—no, no! Where can I have placed them? If lost, and they should fall into the hands of—Ah! my cloak! They were in a breast pocket. I left it with Miss Curran. Run, Andy—quick to Rathfarnham—for your life; find your sister, Ann; get from her the cloak; bring it to Butterfield Lane, where you will find me.

ANDY. Will I take the Major's horse, sir?

ROBT. No; the manner of my escape is known, and search is doubtless being made for the brute. He will be looked for and recognized.

ANDY. Awow! I left him wid Larry Fox and a pail of white paint. By this time the bast wud not know himself, for he's got three stockins and a bald face on him. Whoo, yer sowl! The Major will want another mount. I'll sell him this one tomorrow if yer honor's afraid to back him.

ROBT. Be off, you imp, and be careful of the papers. [*Exit Andy*] This thoughtless act of mine might undo us all. He who undertakes the business of a people should have none of his own. Quigley—Finerty—you will be present tonight at the camp. The hours are pregnant with our cause. We cannot tell at what moment it may spring into life. [*Exit*]

QUIG. Pat, yer sowl! Our fortune is made! It is not one hundred pounds, but a thousand pounds, I am goin't to claim for this night's work.

FIN. A thousand pounds, Mike? What for?

QUIG. For the list of our forces; for the plans of attack; for all the pur-tiklars of the whole business.

FIN. I see. You mane we should follow Andy Devlin and seize the papers on him?

QUIG. No. The cloak was tuk away by Major Sirr. He has it now! But we never dhramed what a prize lies hid in the pocket of it. Tare alive, Pat!—is not a thousand too little to ax for all this? The lists, Pat! and all the names in Emmet's own handwritin'—ho, ho, big names!—men o' quality—that no one suspects. Put them down at ten pounds a head!—tottle them up like onions on a sthring. Then the plans!

FIN. It's little enough, indeed, to pay min like ourselves; for, afther all, when you think of it, sure it is the counthry itself that we have for sale.

QUIG. Be jabers, Pat, it is not everybody that has got a counthry to sell! [Exeunt]

SCENE 3: *A room in Dublin Castle. Lord Norbury and Lord Kilwarden seated at table, R.H., examining papers. Tiney Wolfe looks in at door.*

TINEY. May I come in?

KIL. Yes, if you will not stop very long.

NOR. I must overrule the objection. Stop as long as you please.

TINEY. Lord Norbury, you deserve a kiss for that.

NOR. Offering bribes to the Bench is an awful offense!

TINEY. You know, papa, we promised to call at the vice-regal lodge tonight. Shall you be detained here very long?

KIL. No, Tiney. We have some important business to transact with Mr. Curran, we expect at any moment.

NOR. I think, Kilwarden, you may leave this matter to me to settle. Your daughter is weary.

TINEY. You are very kind to consider me.

NOR. Who would fail to consider you? Had I so sweet a loving a child beside me I should be, perhaps, as good a man as your father is, my dear. [Enter Curran]

TINEY. [Running to him] Oh, Mr. Curran, I am so glad you have come! How is Sarah?

CUR. Complaining, Tiney. Complaining very badly, indeed.

TINEY. Oh, I am so sorry! What is her complaint?

CUR. That she sees so little of you.

TINEY. There is very little to see. Papa, dear, may I spend the evening tomorrow with Miss Curran?

KIL. Yes, dear; I'll lend you for a few hours.

TINEY. What will you charge for the loan?

KIL. A dozen big kisses which you will bring me back. Keep them fresh on your lips. There, run into the next room and amuse yourself while we despatch our business.

TINEY. [*To Curran as she goes out*] Don't keep him very long. [*Exit*]

CUR. The summons to attend your lordships found me at dinner with some friends. What has happened? Has a French expedition landed at Kerry? Has the British fleet broken into another mutiny?

KIL. The danger is much nearer home.

NOR. These depositions sworn this afternoon contain disclosures of an alarming condition of affairs in the adjoining counties of Wicklow and Kildare.

KIL. Dublin is threatened; two thousand men are now under arms, and are marching on the city.

CUR. Two thousand jackasses! I don't believe a word of it. These government spies are purveyors of mares' nests, and make a market of your fears! My lords, the revolutionary spirit of Ireland was broken in 'ninety-eight, and was buried three years ago, when the Act of Union swept our leading men cross the channel and into the British Parliament. It was a crafty measure for it left the body of the people without a head. I have just passed through the streets; the city is asleep and not dreaming of disturbance.

NOR. But these affidavits are very precise.

CUR. If the Government supports a host of spies, the rogues are bound to encourage your fears, and keep them alive! Whom do they pretend is at the head of this new insurrection?

KIL. Robert Emmet.

CUR. What? Robert? the son of my old friend, the doctor? Why, the boy is in France, and has been there for months past. Had he been in this country, mine is the first house he would have visited. [*Enter Major Sirr*]

SIRR. He is here in Dublin. It is strange you should profess ignorance of his whereabouts, when he is a daily visitor at your house, where I found him in your daughter's company an hour ago.

CUR. You found him in my house?

SIRR. By virtue of a search warrant issued by the Privy Council! While you were entertaining your friends at dinner, she was entertaining her lover—

KIL. Silence, sir! You forget you are speaking to a father.

SIRR. When treason-felony is abroad, I forget everything but my duty.

CUR. What evidence do you bring to sustain this infamous charge?

SIRR. Come forward, Mr. Quigley. Step this way, Mr. Finerty. [*Enter Quigley, followed by Finerty, who carries Robert's cloak*] This man [*points to Quigley*] is associated with Emmet, and is his trusted follower.

QUIG. 'Twas meself guided him to Mr. Curran's house awhile ago.

CUR. May I ask what office you hold besides that of traitor?

QUIG. I'm colonel in the army of the Irish Republic.

KIL. Your face is familiar to me. Were you not on your trial for murder before me last year?

QUIG. It was my brother, my lord, you hanged that time. It wasn't me.

CUR. And on no better evidence than the croak of this jailbird, you violated my house?

QUIG. Never fear, if it is evidence you want, I hould a crop as fine as you ever handled. Here is Emmet's cloak that he left behind him in your garden, and in the pocket we find these papers. Wait now! [*He takes some packets of paper from the pockets of the cloak, and hands them to Sirr*]

SIRR. [*Examining them*] Lists of the commanding officers and of the insurgent force in Kildare.

QUIG. You'll find my name among the first on the list. [*Sirr passes the paper to Norbury; he and Kilwarden examine it*] Here's another one. [*Sirr takes it*]

SIRR. Plan of attack! Points of check. Lines of defense. This seems to be a well digested conspiracy to seize the city of Dublin. [*Passes the paper*]

QUIG. Divil a less! And it's short work we would make of you, Major, to begin with. You're the tit-bit our pikes are hungry for.

CUR. I must have some proof better than this to satisfy me that the son of my old friend and schoolmate, Dr. Emmet, is associated with these ruffians.

FIN. Maybe this bit o' writing will open your eyes. [*Hands a letter to Curran who reads it silently. Enter Tiney at back. She stops and listens*]

CUR. My God! it is true!

QUIG. Aha!

CUR. This letter is written by my unhappy child to Mr. Emmet, and it confirms all you have stated.

SIRR. [*Taking the letter from Curran*] It will form an interesting episode in the case—let us see what she says.

KIL. [*Putting his hand upon the paper*] Major Sirr, have you a daughter?

SIRR. I have.

KIL. So have I. [*He tears the paper. Tiney falls*]

CUR. I ask your lordships to acquit me of all complicity in a knowledge of this business.

NOR. Be assured, we do so heartily.

KIL. We are convinced of your ignorance in the matter.

SIRR. 'Tis more than I am.

CUR. I am glad to have secured your evil estimation, sir; it entitles any gentleman to the respect of this community.

SIRR. I hold his majesty's commission.

CUR. So does the hangman! Good-night, my lords! [*Exit*]

KIL. There can be no doubt that we stand in presence of a formidable conspiracy.

NOR. The country is in danger.

QUIG. And no lie in it.

NOR. What do these wretched men propose to do, to accomplish?

SIRR. They propose to seize the Castle of Dublin where a guard of seventeen men forms at present its sole defense; to carry off the lord-lieutenant to their camp on the mountains, there to hold the person of his excellency as a hostage and proclaim the Irish Republic.

QUIG. One and indivisible.

NOR. What is to be done?

SIRR. These men hold offices of trust and command under Emmet—they are in our pay. The military must be called out promptly and secretly posted where their fire can sweep the streets of Dublin. Then Quigley and Finerty will give the people Emmet's signal to rise, and before he can arrive with his troops to control the mob, the regulars will make short work of the crowd.

KIL. You cannot proceed to use force until the people commit some breach of the peace.

QUIG. Oho! be aisy. We'll get the pikes to work. Maybe I'd redden one o' them myself in the blood of some man—a big one—whose death would raise a howl.

KIL. This is horrible! [*Tiney rises and listens*]

NOR. Egad, Kilwarden, such means were successfully employed five years ago in '98.

SIRR. We must bring rebellion to a head.

QUIG. And save your own?

FIN. Thrue for ye, Mike!—and we'd like to know the price of heads now.

QUIG. Yes. What's to be our reward for the crop we bring?

SIRR. What do you claim?

QUIG. That's the chat! We want a thousand pounds for Emmet's and fifty apiece for each other head we bring to the dock. [*Tiney leans weeping with her face in her hands against the wall*]

FIN. An' we'd like to see a little ready money down on account.

SIRR. [*Handing them a roll of notes*] Count that. [*Finerty and Quigley eagerly bending over table. L.H. Counting money*]

NOR. You expect the insurgents when they find the first outbreak is defeated will become discouraged? will desert and regain their homes?

SIRR. No! They will come here—ha! ha! 'Twill be a race among such men as those—[*points to Finerty and Quigley*] who will get here first to betray their leaders.

QUIG. Thirty-two—thirty-three! Divil a doubt about that. Thirty-five—hi! hi!

NOR. [*Commencing to write at table R.H.*] Lord Kilwarden is now on his road to the vice-regal lodge. He will submit to his excellency the measures you propose to precipitate the outbreak, by the help of our agents amongst the mob. I will draft your plan, Major, if you will repeat the particulars. [*Miss Wolfe advances and stands beside Lord Kilwarden*]

SIRR. [*Turns and sees her*] Miss Wolfe!

KIL. Tiney!

QUIG. [*Counting*] Fifty-eight, fifty-nine!

TINEY. Go on; don't mind me.

NOR. Affairs of state cannot be discussed before you.

TINEY. I see that you hesitate and look at each other as though the affairs of state were guilty things to which a father could not listen in the presence of his child. You dare not unfold your thoughts before her. Is it not so?

NOR. You are not old enough to judge—

TINEY. My father is, and he said it was horrible. You see, papa, I over-heard what those men proposed. Forgive me if my heart comes to your side and pleads to stand by yours. You taught the motherless little child how to be worthy of your name and of your race. She was nursed on your breast. Let her now give you back the teachings of your love. Have no share in this infamy. Set your honest face against it.

SIRR. Are we come to this? that the chief justice of Ireland cannot share our councils without an appeal to a schoolgirl.

TINEY. Nor can he preside on the bench over trials for conspiracy and murder planned here and executed by his compliance.

KIL. Lord Norbury, I will take charge of these papers. They will explain, if they do not justify, my resignation of the office I hold under the crown. Come, Tiney, let us go. [*He embraces her*]

QUIG. [*Counting money as Kilwarden and Miss Wolfe go out*] Ninety-five, ninety-six. There's four pound short in this pile!

ACT-DROP FALLS.

ACT II.

SCENE I: *The cottage at Butterfield Lane. Enter Ann Devlin. She carries a small valise; she looks around, advances, and feels for the table, on which she places the valise; then returns to the door.*

ANN. Come in, Miss. [*Enter Sarah and Norman*] Wait till I fetch a light from the kitchen; maybe I'd find a sod o' turf alive in the fire there. [*Going out L.*] I must feel my way in the dark.

SARAH. So am I, Norman, feeling my way in the dark!—in doubt and in fear.

NORM. There's no doubt between right and wrong—no fear where there is love.

SARAH. Can you not see the position in which I place him?

NORM. I can. I wish I were in his place. [*Re-enter Ann with light*]

ANN. I heard him moving overhead in his room. He is there. My brother Andy will soon be here wid the outside car, to take the masther to the mountains; for the camp is moved to the Scalp, and the boys are hungry for himself. [*Sarah sits at table*]

NORM. The Scalp!—Why, that pass is within sight of Dublin. Is rebellion so close to us?

ANN. Close! It looks up out of every cellar and down from every garret windy in the city. It runs in the gutters, and sweeps like the blast through the alleys and the lanes! You are breathing it—and you don't know it, nor feel it. Whist! I hear the masther comin'. Will I send for the priest, Miss, and bring him here?

SARAH. No! [*Rises quickly*] Is it not enough that I present myself in so unmaidenly a manner? What will he take me for?

ANN. For betther or for worse! The sooner the betther; the later, the worse for you both. There's Father Donnelly lives at Cabinteely, convaniant to the road from this to the Scalp. You can stop there an' wake him up. The business is short and sweet, and no delay. When it is over the masther must hurry to the boys in the mountains; he is expected there by midnight.

NORM. By that time he must be on the seas. Oh, that I were at the bottom of them, while you and he were passing over me to a happy life!

ANN. He is here! [*Enter Emmet. He is dressed in the Irish uniform*]

ROBT. Sarah—in this place! Who—what—brought you here?

NORM. I did, Mr. Emmet. Permit me to present myself, that I may spare Miss Curran some embarrassment. I am Norman Claverhouse, Captain in His Majesty's Ninety-third Highlanders. I was a guest in Mr. Curran's house tonight, when Major Sirr arrived with a search warrant. [*Taking Sarah's hand*] In the absence of our host—her father—I took the liberty of driving the Major and his posse from the place; and as her rejected lover I now bring her to the only man who can repair the injury this night's business may do to the name of a lady to whom we are equally devoted.

ROBT. Are you aware, sir, to whom you have rendered this service?

NORM. I have rendered this service to her who owns my life.

ROBT. Do you know I am one whose name men whisper fearfully; an outlaw, whom to see and not to betray is a crime; a rebel, whom to serve is a capital offense?

NORM. I only know that she loves you—that makes me at once your foe and your accomplice.

ROBT. Martyrs have died in the flames who had not in their breasts so brave a heart; for they fell assured of paradise, while you suffer, renouncing your hopes of heaven. Let me feel your hand in mine; the other on my shoulder. So; I had rather be thus ennobled than feel the sword of a king there.

ANN. [*Aside*] Well! 'Tis mighty hard on women that one girl should have two such lovers, and waste one o' them like that.

SARAH. He brought me to your side; he bade me seek the refuge of your arms—it is all the home I have now. Hide me from myself, for I am ashamed of what I do.

ROBT. We shall be married tonight; and if forthwith this gentleman will further extend his good offices, he will conduct you to my mother's house, where you will find the home I dare not enter.

NORM. Why not?

ROBT. Because I would not bring over it the cloud that now obscures my life! Because I would not make those I love the sharers of my fate!

NORM. You must quit that life for her sake. Tonight after your marriage, you will leave Ireland and take her with you.

SARAH. Not for my sake, but for your mother's—for your own.

ROBT. You ask me to abandon the cause into which my voice has drawn thousands of my fellow-countrymen; to desert them in the field on the brink of battle; to play the executioner, and leave them headless. Oh, it could be done so easily, for their trust in Robert Emmet is so blind! Bribed with your person, he can leave the fools in the fell-trap baited with his lies—to perish—as you know, sir, they will perish—like helpless dogs flung into the lion's den. Eternal scorn would point its finger at the deed!—and say the hand that Emmet gave to Curran's daughter was full of Ireland's blood; in the breast on which she rested was the heart of a renegade; and the name she shared was blasted with dishonor!

NORM. You are so occupied with the peril in which your honor stands that you overlook hers. What matters it if her name be scathed with shame, if yours shall live unblemished? You say that you would not make those you love sharers of your fate; yet you would make her so! You would not bring the cloud that obscures your life over theirs, yet you would have her live in its shadow!

ROBT. God, who knows my heart, have mercy on me, and direct me what to do!

SARAH. [*At his feet*] And *you*, who know my heart, have mercy on *me!* —and on us both! Have mercy on my love, that now pleads for itself at your feet. Oh! I am helpless to persuade him; I ask him to spare his life that is my own—my own—all I have in this world.

ROBT. Sir, have you no council to offer us?

NORM. Yes; marry her! Follow your mad career; stop here, and I'll find myself within three months heir to your widow!

ANN. [*Aside*] O Michael Dwyer! If it wasn't for your ugly mug, that I'm so fond of, that fellow might make me a Scotchwoman any day that was plazin' to him. God bless him! [*Enter Andy*]

ANDY. Where the masther?

ROBT. Here!

ANN. What makes you so pale, dear?

ANDY. Bad news. I put the Major's horse into a car; for it's not between shafts they would be on the look for him. [*Pointing to Norman*] Who's that?

ROBT. Never mind him.

ANDY. 'Tis the coat on him that bothers me.

ANN. I'll go bail for what's behind it; go on, alanna!

ANDY. Divil a sowl was in your house, miss, when I got there; so I turned back. As I drove past Portobello Barracks, two men came out and hailed me, axed me to take them quick to Island Bridge. Be jabers! me heart stud still as they climbed outside the car, for one o' thim was Major Sorr himself—jauntin' behind his own horse.

ROBT. You heard what they said?

ANDY. Maybe I didn't cock my ear! "We've got him now," ses he; "he's pounded! The papers—the whole bag of insurgent thricks is in my hand.

There's the list of their members; the names of their leaders; the plans of attack—all in Emmet's own writin',"' ses he, "not to spake of his man and pestol," ses he.

ANN. His what?

ANDY. 'Tis what he said—"his man and pestol to the people."

ROBT. Manifesto!

ANDY. It's all the same to me!

ROBT. But these papers were in the cloak I left with you.

SARAH. Sirr carried it away with him.

ROBT. Betrayed! Betrayed!

ANDY. That's what the Major said. "Tomorrow them papers will be published in the *Morning Journal,* and the news that Emmet has betrayed his followin' and sowld out o' the business. The Government has his own handwritin' to show for it. That news will put down the risin' quicker than all the horse, foot and artillery in the country could do it," ses he.

NORM. Fortune stands your friend. By this mischance your cause is lost.

ROBT. Aye! Is it so!—so!—so! I'm trapped and caught! Now, by Saint Patrick, they shall find my foot upon their necks, choking the lie in their throats, before their black hearts have time to give it flight. Tomorrow, you said, they begin their work; tonight I shall begin mine. Before the sun rises on Dublin, a thousand men, now camped at the Scalp, shall descend upon the city and seize the Castle. Our drums will call the people to arms, and then at their head I'll meet this calumny.

SARAH. Robert, I beseech you—

ROBT. It is too late, Sarah—too late! I have no choice but to vindicate my life; ask him.

NORM. He is right.

ROBT. Andy Devlin!

ANDY. That's me.

ROBT. What men have we within call?

ANDY. Three, your honor, in the loft outside, and one howldin' the horse.

ROBT. Give them the signal. [*Andy goes out to the door and whistles*] I must ask you, sir, to pledge your honor that what has passed here in your presence will be held sacred by you.

NORM. When I leave this I shall make my way straight to the Castle, and report to his excellency every word of it.

ROBT. I knew you would. [*Four men appear at the door*] Reilly, you will stand guard with your men over this house until sunrise. Then, and not till then, you will liberate this gentleman. He is your prisoner for the night.

NORM. What a release! I am obliged to you.

ROBT.   Ann Devlin, you will take Miss Curran to my mother's house in Stephen's Green; your brother Andy will drive you there. Farewell, my own one. I will bring you back a name you will be proud to wear [*he holds her in his arms*], or leave you a memory worthy of your love. Pray for me, Sarah!—It is not my will, but God's, that parts us now. Farewell! [*He embraces her. Exit*]

SARAH.   [*Falls on her knees as Robert leaves*]   God bless and guard my love! [*Scene closes in*]

SCENE 2: *A gorge in the mountains near the Scalp. Enter Quigley, meeting Brangan; both in uniform.*

QUIG.   Well, how are things workin' in the camp?

BRANG.   Finely; the boys are getting wild as muzzled dogs! There's no howldin' them.

QUIG.   The sight of Dublin lyin' asleep beyond there is mate and dhrink to fellows starvin' for a fight! What news of Dwyer?

BRANG.   He is lying still in the Devil's Glen, waitin' till he gets the offer to join us wid four hundred Wexford men.

QUIG.   You must cross the hills tonight. Tell him that Emmet has sold us all, body and bones, to the Castle. They are goin' to make him a lord, an' rise him to a big place at coort—tell him.

BRANG.   Stop that—enough! When I get as far as that in the lie, Dwyer will shut my mouth forever.

QUIG.   There's no lie in it; look at them sheets; they are fresh and wet wid the ink from the Castle press. Rade them! [*He hands him a small handbill*] There's our secret plans, the roll-call of our leading min, and the divil an' all, printed from papers in Emmet's own handwritin', on show in Major Sirr's office.

BRANG.   Have you seen them?

QUIG.   Sure, any one can see them. They will be cried for a hapenny tomorrow at every corner in the city, from Ring's End to Kilmainham. He has turned approver agin us.

BRANG.   Tare alive! I did not think he would go do a thing like that!—taking the very bread out of our mouths. He's as bad as one of ourselves. The boys will go wild when they hear this. O wurra! is it for this we have been drillin' and marchin' and starvin' for weeks past! 'Tis mighty hard upon us, entirely so it is!

QUIG.   Go amongst them; tell them so! Tell them the Bank of Ireland must pay for it. It is full wid the poor man's money—the rints he has paid to the landlords! Then there's the city itself. Let us have a hack at it. Them Dublin tradesmen are castle-fed pigs, rowlin' in goold.

BRANG. A bowld dash at them would fill our sacks, an' we could be off to the hills and bogs before them redcoats could fall in, or them dhragoons could saddle up.

QUIG. That's the work! Go you among the men; scatter them bills among them; I'll get a howlt of the officers. We will court-martial Emmet—break him. What do we want, anyhow, wid a general? Cock him up, and here's the end of it. Let aich county folly its own leaders, and divil take the hindmost!

BRANG. I'm wid ye, Quigley. I was light porther for awile at Goggins', the jewellers, in Dame Street; I know the place in the shop where a handful of diamonds is kept that would buy a barony in Roscommon.

QUIG. To work! Brangan—to work!

SCENE 3: *The camp at the Scalp. Shed or ruined cabin R.H., which serves as headquarters; rude hovels are scattered over the hillside; watch-fires, around which figures are lying and pikes are piled; Dublin and the bay are seen below, in the distance; night; the city is sparkling with lights. Finerty, Duggan, and Mahaffey are in this cabin; groups of men in green stuffs uniform are drinking, smoking, etc.; laughter. Chorus.*

FIN. Ordher in the camp. How can the Council of War know what it is talking about if you blackguards don't howld your prate.

ALL. Thrue for ye, Pat. We'll be as quiet as oysthers. Three cheers for the Council of War.

M. MAGAN. I wish there were less council and more war. [*Enter Quigley*]

QUIG. You shall have your wishes. Your officers will debate wid open dures before you all. For why should we dale wid your lives, and never let on to you a haporth about the business?

ALL. He's right; thrue for ye. Hurroo!

QUIG. I have come from Dublin where the people are lookin' out for ye. There's not a windy below there but howlds an impatient face, cursing your delay. Every ear is open for the thramp of your feet an' your cry "to arrums!"

ALL. Hurroo for Dublin!

QUIG. Aisy, boys. You'll be there soon enough; I'll go bail. [*Finerty and the officers have brought out of the shed a barrel, on which they place the hatch door of the cabin, so as to form a table; two buckets, a basket, and a three-legged stool. The officers sit*]

FIN. Colonel Quigley will take the chair. [*Offering him a stool with only one leg*]

QUIG. I'll wait till I take one in Dublin Castle.

ALL. Hurroo!

QUIG. Ordher! Men of Kildare, your time has come! Boys of Wicklow, you have waited long enough! Dublin is waitin' for you like a bride, and widin two days from this she whill be in your arrums. You men from the County Meath will howld the Phoenix and the Lodge. James Hope, with eight hundred men from the County Down, is on his way from Drogheda, and will seize the Custom House. So much for the North. The Kildare boys will take the Castle.

ALL. We will! Down wid the red and up wid the green.

QUIG. Finerty, wid a guard of honor, will bring the lord-lieutenant on an outside car, and lodge his excellency in our camp here. Wicklow boys, you will take the Bank of Ireland.

ALL. Hurroo!

M. MAG. Begorra! Wicklow has the best of it.

QUIG. Here is a list of the officers of the crown, the ministers, and all the big men. They will be on our hands. What's to be done wid them?

FIN. A few executions to begin wid might have a fine effect.

QUIG. It would make our cause respectable.

M. MAG. There's old Norbury! I'd like to see his mug in the dock.

QUIG. And a jury of convicts drawn from Kilmainham in the box.

FIN. And before me on the bench.

ALL. Whoo! [*Tumult outside*]

QUIG. What's going on there?

M. MAG. Maybe 'tis only a fight.

QUIG. Can't they fight peaceably, without making a row? [*Enter a crowd of men, with Brangan; some of the men have the bills in their hands. Brangan hands papers to the officers and to Quigley*]

BRANG. News from Dublin! Emmet has turned his green coat. It was lined with red all the while. He has sowld us.

ALL. Oo!

M. MAG. Emmet a thraitor! [*Takes the papers from Brangan*]

QUIG. The proofs are plain enough.

M. MAG. 'Tis a black lie, and you know it!

QUIG. If you weren't a woman, I'd make ye put down them words on paper and ate them.

M. MAG. Where did you get these bills?

BRANG. Where?—I—I did—I got them.

M. MAG. You haven't a lie ready. See! they stick together; for the ink is wet. You got them at the printer's! What took you there? You knew what dirty scheme was at work in the Government office. Spake up. [*Seizing Brangan*]

BRANG. [*Falling on his knees*] Oh! Oh! I know this grip.

M. MAG. Would you whist. [*Aloud*] Is this all the proofs you have agin him?

QUIG. If Robert Emmet is not a traitor, why is he not here? [*Emmet enters*]

ROBT. He is here!

M. MAG. You may go now! [*Releases Brangan, who crawls away amazed. All the men slowly retire to R., behind Quigley and Finerty, leaving Emmet alone with Mother Magan, L.H.*]

ROBT. Why do you turn your faces from me? Speak, men!

M. MAG. They have heard you have turned approver, to save your skin and fill your pockets.

ROBT. Who accuses me?

FIN. That print.

ROBT. [*After looking at them*] I scorn to fight with lies. That they are so needs no words, for I am here. Quigley was with me when the thieves robbed me of those papers, and now they charge me with selling to them what they stole.

QUIG. 'Tis all one how they got the information; we are betrayed. Now they are ready to meet and to crush us.

ROBT. No, the documents they stole shall serve to deceive them; they shall fall into the trap they set for me. Tonight, before their troops can be moved, we shall swoop down upon Dublin.

QUIG. Tonight?

ROBT. Relying on this information, they will be unprepared.

QUIG. What can we do with a handful of men?

ROBT. With a handful of men Bonaparte put an end to the Reign of Terror and released France; with a handful of men Cortes conquered Mexico; with a corporal's guard Cromwell cleared the House of Commons, and founded the first English republic.

M. MAG. Thrue fur ye; but they were men—not jailbirds, like Quigley and his gang of thieves.

QUIG. Mother Magan, you will make me forget your sex.

ROBT. What would these men have?

M. MAG. They want six hours' free quarters in Dublin for pillage and for plundher, then afther pikin' a few grandees, they would skip.

RoBt. Let those amongst ye that are of this mind assemble round him yonder, so let me count how many honest men there be here who will stand by our cause and by their country. [*The men go to the R.H., and stand behind Quigley, Finerty, and Brangan*]

M. Mag. There's only one honest man in the crowd, and, be jabers, that's a woman!

RoBt. [*After burying his face in his hands*] God forgive me for having done this thing! I have been self-deceived by my love for this helpless people —children of misery—by my blind devotion they have been brought to this infamous extremity. Let the penalty be mine alone; let no blood but mine be shed; accept my young life in expiation of my foolish faith. My friends—my countrymen! I go hence—to Dublin—alone, and in this uniform—the badge of treason; I carry with me that flag—the emblem of rebellion; I go with my life to redeem yours; to offer my hands to the chains, my head to the executioner! [*Some of the men cross to Emmet's side*] There is yet time to retrieve your errors, and to make your submission. Put off those uniforms; bury them out of sight; and seek your homes quietly by unfrequented paths and by night!

ALL. [*Murmuring*] No! No! We'll stand by your honor to the death. [*Some more men join Emmet's side*]

RoBt. If you stand by me you must march as children of Erin, as united Irishmen, whose one hope is freedom; not as banditti, whose sole object is plunder. The green flag that led our countrymen at Fontenoy under Sarsfield has never been dishonored, and it shall not be so under Robert Emmet, so help me God! [*The rest of the men, uttering loud cries, join the crowd around him, some kneeling at his feet*]

Quig. This is mighty fine, but it comes too late; two hundred biys from Kildare left for Dublin an hour ago. The divil himself could not stop them now.

M. Mag. No, but Michael Dwyer could! His men, five hundred strong, the bodyguard of Emmet, are posted at the foot of this hill, wid orders to shut the road.

Quig. Michael Dwyer is at Glendalagh!

M. Mag. You lie, Quigley! He is here. [*He removes his bonnet and wig*]

ALL. Hurroo!

Dwy. [*Striding across to R.*] Now I am ready to ate the words Mother Magan spoke to you a while ago.

RoBt. Hold, Dwyer! I'll have no fighting amongst you.

Dwy. Divil a fear o' that! Is there, Quigley? Give me your hand. [*He takes Quigley's hand*] By this and by that, by signs on your face that I never mistook yet, and by the pulse in our hearts that spake to one another in this grip, I know that I will die by your hand, or you will die by mine. [*Shakes his hand*] Now, masther dear, I'm ready for your orders.

Robt. Lead three hundred of your men by Enniskery and Rathmines; enter the city on the south by Harcourt Street; your point is Stephen's Green; be there by two o'clock. Who commands under you?

Dwy. Phil Maguire; he is howldin' the Kildare boys below there.

Quig. Maguire!—the man is dumb.

Dwy. Thrue fur ye, so he can not turn informer. But he is mighty talkative wid his hands; don't get into any argument wid him.

Robt. Let Maguire unite the Kildare men with the rest of your Wexford boys, and sweep around, entering the city by James's Gate; rouse the liberties, and occupy Thomas Street by St. Patrick's.

Quig. The Kildare troops are under my command; they will not march without their officers.

Dwy. Oh, be aisy! You will be there at their head beside Maguire; he'll take care of you.

Robt. My men will march by Slellorgan and Brunswick Street; our point is College Green. Thus our forces, eleven hundred strong, penetrating the city on three sides, will meet at the Castle. Before sunrise Dublin will be ours; the citizens will awake to find Ireland a republic, and our people numbered among the nations of the world.

All. Hurroo! To Dublin!

Robt. Fall in! [*Repeat of the chorus, which the men fall into now; the scene closes in*]

Scene 4: *A room in the house of Mrs. Emmet. Enter Curran and Lord Norbury, preceded by a servant.*

Cur. Be good enough to inform Miss Curran that her father is here and desires to see her. I believe she is in this house. [*Enter Ann Devlin. Exit servant*]

Ann. She is here, sir; sitting by the bedside of Mrs. Emmet.

Cur. You were the companion of her flight.

Ann. No; she had a guard of honor all the way, and with him she left her home.

Cur. Your master, doubtless?

Ann. No; betther still. It was the lover you gave her—Captain Claverhouse.

Nor. My nephew! I can not believe it! Where is he?

ANN. I left him asleep by the fireside of Robert Emmet, where he is passing the night. Your honors look surprised to find young people have hearts, and hearts will have their own way. Two years ago you gave your daughter to young Emmet. Then you took her from him, to give her to young Claverhouse. You see she knew her own mind, if you didn't know yours, and that's the way of it. [*Enter Sarah*]

CUR. Are you aware what you have done?

SARAH. Yes, father. I have become the bride of a rebel, and to rescue and protect your house from any suspicion I left it, when my presence there became a reproach.

NOR. My dear child, the man for whom you have made this useless sacrifice, betrayed by his own followers, is already doomed to an inevitable and ignominious death.

SARAH. He knows it, and will face it if it comes to that.

CUR. Is it my gentle Sarah, my daughter that speaks.

SARAH. No, father, it is the outlaw's wife; forgive me if I have been true to myself. When your nephew, my lord, discovered how it was with me, he told me how I should vindicate my falling honor and my own heart; he stood by my side while I obeyed his counsel. Do not mistake my misfortune for my fault, and believe me, it was for your dear sake I was moved, not for my own.

ANN. [*Who has been looking from the window*] There is a carriage at the door.

NOR. It is mine; it brought us here.

ANN. There's a mighty big crowd gathering round it; I'll go see what they want. [*Exit*]

NOR. The rogues want six months in Kilmainham, or a visit to Botany Bay.

SARAH. Be advised, my lord, and escape to your country house at Cloncilla. Emmet knows that Major Sirr has possession of the plans of the insurrection, and already he has changed them. [*Cries outside*]

NOR. [*Running to the window*] The square below is full of the mob. What do they want?

SARAH. Hark! [*Cries of "Norbury!" "Norbury!"*] Do you hear? They want you. [*Re-enter Ann*]

ANN. Bar the door; make fast the shutters on the ground floor; let loose Master Robert's wolf hound and load the two blunderbusses in the hall.

CUR. What is the matter? What brings the people here?

ANN. All Dublin is awake tonight, and on foot. The air is full of growl and the rumbling of a storm. It wanted little to make it burst. They saw your liveries standing at this dure, and that invited the lightning. [*Blows heard below, and cries; smashing of glass*]

CUR. They are attacking the house.

ANN. Divil a doubt of it!

NOR. What do they want?

ANN. Your life—no less.

CUR. Are they mad?

ANN. Aye! wid joy; for they say Emmet is entering Dublin from King's End and Rathmines, while Michael Dwyer, wid five hundred men, is at James's Gate. [*Enter servant, who whispers to Ann*]

NOR. Before help can arrive they will wreck the house, and we shall perish.

ANN. The girl says they have brought up a load of straw that they are piling agin the dures and windies below; there's no fightin' agin fire.

SARAH. Leave me to defend you. [*She goes to the window; cries and shots; she advances on to the balcony, and raises her hand; silence*] Men of Dublin—my name is Sarah Curran, and I am the bride of Robert Emmet.

ALL. Hurroo! Long life to ye! God bless ye both!

SARAH. This is my husband's house, his mother lies sick beside me; take that straw and lay it down carefully on the road, that her sleep may not be broken by the noises of the street. My father, John Philpot Curran, is here; he came in that carriage to see me; he will return home in it.

Cry. Three cheers for Curran!

SARAH. No! Be silent, and respect the rest of Emmet's mother. Good night to you all. Begone! [*She closes the window*] You are safe, my lord. Ann and I will escort you by the back premises and the stable lane to Dawson Street, where we shall find a car. Meanwhile my father will enter your carriage in the presence of the crowd, and drive home. Come! [*Exit Curran, preceded by a servant, R. Ann, Sarah and Norbury L.*]

SCENE 5: *Scene changes to College Green and the Houses of Parliament. Crowds of people; sellers of fruit, ballads, etc.; college lads; coal porters; a blind fiddler.* Here's yer hot pitaties! Oysthers hot—hot! Cherries ripe, all ripe, a hapenny the stick! [*Enter Andy*]

ANDY. Here's the last new song, "The night before Larry was stretched"; "The Duke of York was a damned bad soldier."

ALL. Ha! ha! ha!

ANDY. [*Sings*]

> "The Duke of York was a damned bad soldier,
> From Dunkerque he ran away!"

Here comes Counsellor Flood and Hussey de Burgh. Three cheers, boys, for
them that stood up for the people! [*Enter two gentlemen*]

ALL. Long life to de Burgh. Hoo! Hurra! [*The gentlemen bow and pass
out*]

ANDY. Here's Sirr. Three groans for the Major—the drum major. [*Enter
Sirr*] I wish I had the drummin' of him.

ALL. Yah! oo!

ANDY. [*Sings*]   Now Major Sirr
>   He is a cur,
>   And his kennel is the Castle, etc.

ALL. Ha! ha! ha! [*Exit Sirr*]

ANDY. A groan for the Castle hack.

ALL. Yah! [*Song, Andy. Enter Quigley, Finerty, and Brangan*]

QUIG. We gave Maguire the slip in Patrick Street. How many of our boys
followed you?

FIN. A score maybe. They are close by.

QUIG. That's enough! [*He addresses the crowd*] You, Brangan, go by
Crafton Street and raise the cry "To arms!" You, Finerty, by Dame Street;
call on the people to turn out. Never fear; there's two regiments under arms,
wid four pieces of artillery in the Castle yard, so look out for yourselves
when you hear the rumbling of the guns. [*To the crowd*] Min of Dublin,
the hour has come! The boys from Wicklow, Wexford, and Kildare are
amongst ye, well armed and ready to sthrike for Ireland! Down with the red
flag, up wid the green!

ALL. Hurroo! hurroo! [*An attack is made on the shops, which are broken
open. The carriage of Lord Kilwarden, in which Kilwarden and Miss Wolfe
are seen, is driven on, preceded by link-boys and running footmen. The
crowd surround it. Kilwarden is forced by them to descend*]

KIL. My good friends, you do not know me. I am Kilwarden, chief justice of the King's bench.

QUIG. Then you are the man I want. [*Thrusts a pike into Kilwarden*]
That's for my brother that you hung! [*Tiney utters a cry and tries to intercept the blow. Enter Emmet and Dwyer*]

FIN. Let the cub go wid the wolf.

ANDY. [*Wrenching the pike from Finerty*] Would you kill a girl?

ROBT. Who has done this? [*Raising Tiney, who has fallen on her father's body*]

DWY. [*Seizing Finerty*] I have him.

ROBT. Tie him to the College rails, and let him be shot.

KIL. [*Raising himself*] No, let no one suffer death, excepting by due process of the law. Where is my child—my child?

TINEY. Oh, papa! my dear papa! [*He drops dead out of her arms; Robert holds her sobbing to his breast*]

ROBT. The coward who struck this good man planted his steel in the bosom of his country. Ireland was murdered by that blow!

ACT III.

SCENE 1: *A room in the vice-regal lodge, Phoenix Park. A large opening, C. curtained; large lattice window at back, C.; the inner room is a bedroom— toilet R., bed L.; in front room, door R.H. of opening; door L.H.1E.; candles burning on toilet table; small lamp on table next bed; Tiney in bed L.C.; music heard in distance; Lady Katherine Yorke enters door R.H., creeps toward bed; she is in ball dress.*

TINEY. I am not asleep, Katie.

LADY K. You naughty girl; the doctor said that sleep was the only medicine to restore your health.

TINEY. I have been listening to the music from the ballroom. Come sit by me and tell me all about it; who were there? with whom did you dance?

LADY K. [*Sitting on bed*] Oh, if the Earl knew I steal in here every night to keep you awake with my chatter.

TINEY. Tell your papa you are trying to make me forget mine. Oh, Katie, you have brothers, sisters, mother, father—but he, my darling, was all I had in the world.

LADY K. Is there no one who could teach you to forget him better than I can?

TINEY. What do you mean?

LADY K. You speak as you sleep; I can hear you from my bedroom, yonder. There is one name constantly on your lips.

TINEY. What name?

LADY K. Let me whisper it—"Robert."

TINEY. I don't know anyone of that name.

LADY K. Are you sure?

TINEY. Quite sure. [*After a pause*]—Oh, yes; I forgot.

LADY K. Aha!

TINEY. Our under coachman! It was he that drove the carriage on that horrid night.

LADY K. A coachman! Oh, you cruel Tiney, to crush all my hopes of a secret romance. [*Goes to toilet and begins to take flowers from her hair*] Oh! here is my bouquet! Let the flowers be your bed-fellows!

TINEY. How sweet they are! Here is sweetbriar, and here are violets. Oh, they bring the green fields and hedge rows to my bedside; who gave you this?

LADY K. Our new under-secretary—Sir Barry Clinton.

TINEY. Is he handsome?

LADY K. Very.

TINEY. How nice?

LADY K. Very! and so clever! He has only been here a week, and he has already made his mark.

TINEY. On your heart, Katie?

LADY K. Nonsense; papa says he will be a distinguished man.

TINEY. How often did he dance with you?

LADY K. Well, he undertook to teach me the new German dance that is becoming quite the rage in London—it is called the waltz.

TINEY. Is it as a dancing master that he has made his mark?

LADY K. No! it was while we were waltzing that Barry told me—

TINEY. It has come to "Barry" already, has it? and he has only been here a week—oh! Katie!

LADY K. Don't interrupt me.

TINEY. Go on; I'm shocked!

LADY K. It seems that my Barry has succeeded in a great affair in which the police and Major Sirr have failed. Everybody believed that the dreadful young man Emmet had escaped to France. Barry has discovered that he has never left Dublin; he has been here all the while, concealed in a cottage in Butterfield Lane. [*Tiney sits up in bed*]

TINEY. Is—is he taken?

LADY K. Not yet; they will arrest him tonight. What have you done with the hairpins?—oh, here they are! It seems that Barry was out fishing this morning at Dunleary; the boatman he employed, a fellow named Rafferty, tempted by the reward of eight hundred pounds offered for the capture of the rebel, told him where Mr. Emmet lay in hiding, and that his boat had been hired to take the fugitive across the Channel to France. Rather shabby of Mr. Rafferty, but it will make my Barry's fortune. There—now I'll slip on my dressing-gown, and come back to bid you good-night. [*Exit*]

TINEY. Tonight! She said "tonight he will be taken." They will kill him, and I am helpless to save him. Oh, what can I do? He would have saved papa—he would have killed the man who murdered my darling—and I can do nothing!—[*wrings her hands in despair*]—nothing! Oh, how tenderly he spoke to me. I felt the tears on my neck as he held me to his heart, and the eyes that shed them will be closed forever. His sweet face is ever present there—there—above mine. Oh, I know now whose name I spoke in my sleep. [*Re-enter Lady Katherine, dressed in a wrapper*]

LADY K. There, I come to bid you good-night. I will put out the lights. [*She extinguishes the candles. The moonlight falls through the window on the girl and over the bed*] I declare, she is asleep already. Oh, what a weight off my conscience that is. Good-night, sweet angel! [*She takes the lamp, and draws the curtain so as to close in the recess, then goes out quietly, L.H. door; stage dark; after a pause, the face of Tiney appears between the curtains; she enters; she is dressed in a long peignoir; she tries to walk, but falls, kneeling near door R.H. in F.*]

TINEY. Oh, Merciful Father in Heaven, bear up my poor weak limbs! inspire my failing body with your will! grant me strength to reach him who saved my life! take it now, and let me die at his feet! [*She raises herself feebly, feels her way by the wall to the door—opens it—listens, and then creeps out. Scene changes*]

SCENE 2: *Ann Devlin's cottage in Butterfield Lane; Robert seated at table C.; Ann asleep by fireside; Andy lies across the door.*

ROBT. Betrayed by knaves! deserted by cowards! tracked and hounded like a wild beast! It is the inexorable fate of all the saviors of the people! Oh, ye spirits! you immortal band of heroes who suffered for your faith! Bodyguard of Him who died for the human race! Accept into your ranks the humble life of one, who, loving his native land not wisely, but too well, followed in your footsteps upward to the Throne where sit the Eternal Trinity of Truth, Light, and Freedom! [*He rises*] Men will call me visionary, a rash fool, and dupe. Ah! had those on whom Bonaparte relied failed him in the pinch! Had Washington misplaced his trust amongst traitors, these monarchs of men might have stood as I do now! An outcast! downfallen! the scoff of the world! The wood of which Fortune shapes a throne, is ready at need to build a gallows! [*Two knocks at door in F., followed by a whistle; then a third knock*] It is the signal! [*He opens the door. Enter Dwyer, who steps over Andy*]

Dwy. Is that the way he kapes watch over yur honor while I am away? Wait till I wake him up. [*Raises his whip*]

Robt. [*Staying him*] Don't be hard on the boy. For three nights, while they hunted us from garret to cellar, he has had no rest. Let him sleep! What news?

Dwy. Wexford is ready and willing. Kildare, Carlow, Waterford and Kilkenny are waiting your word.

Robt. [*Sits at table*] Ay! So they told Lord Edward in '98! but what followed?—treachery in his camp—disconcerted plans—mutiny amongst the leaders—confusion—drunkenness and plunder amongst the men—havoc, panic, and despair. I will not give the signal for bloodshed!

Dwy. It is for your honor to say. [*He puts a shawl over Ann*]

Robt. Why should you continue the fight?

Dwy. Maybe because it's all I am good for! Sure I'm only a dog at your heel, to watch for your bidding, and do it without axin' why.

Robt. My brave Dwyer, had I only five hundred men like yourself, I'd bid the world stand by to see our people made a nation! But our enterprise is beset with pitfalls—we are walking on a bog—the ground under our feet is rotten.

Dwy. Then save yourself. If you go on hanging 'round this place, you will lave your life here. [*Sits and lights his pipe*]

Robt. I will leave Ireland tomorrow.

Dwy. Why not tonight? Joe Rafferty's hooker is lying in Dunleary—she will fly wid your honor to the French coast like a saygull.

Robt. Are you sure of Rafferty?

Dwy. Am I sure of my own sisther's son?

Robt. This letter from Miss Curran appoints a meeting tonight at Father Donnelly's, at Glenmalure; he has consented to perform the ceremony of marriage between us—thence we go direct to France.

Andy. [*Who has risen, and listens at the door*] Whist! there's a strange footfall in the lane! it stops at the gate! [*Dwyer puts down his pipe, brings out a pistol and a short iron bludgeon*]

Ann. [*Waking*] Did your honor call me?

Dwy. Hould your prate.

Andy. 'Tis mighty queer. I believe it is only a dog, for it has got no footsteps at all. [*Looks through keyhole*] Hould your breath! It is here, close agin the dure.

Dwy. Throw it wide. [*Andy throws open the door. Tiney is leaning against the post*]

Robt. Miss Wolfe! [*Runs to her and brings her down*]

ANN. Here at this hour. She is perished with cold. We heard you were lying ill at the Lodge.

TINEY. So I was. 'Twas there, an hour ago, I learned that you were hiding here. They know it. They will come here tonight to arrest you.

ROBT. Who could have betrayed us?

TINEY. A man named Rafferty, whose boat you are to take at Dunleary.

DWY. Blood alive! My sisther's son—my own flesh.

ANN. Michael! For the Lord's sake, don't look so white.

DWY. 'Tis Joe's winding sheet you see in my face.

ROBT. And you rose from your bed to come here?

TINEY. Yes.

ANN. Not on foot? [*Kneels beside her*]

TINEY. I dared not take a car. Look at my dress—I must lock like a banshee. The carman would have driven me to Swift's hospital for the insane. [*She laughs*]

ANN. Without shoes on her feet.

TINEY. It is so.

ANN. See how they bleed.

TINEY. I did not feel it. [*She faints*]

ROBT. She has fainted.

ANDY. [*At door*] A crowd of men have stopped at the fut of the lane. One is on horseback.

DWY. [*Blowing out the light*] If they are on the sarch, a light in the house at this hour will guide them. [*Goes to the door. Looks out*] It is the Major.

ROBT. Sirr? [*Andy runs to L.H. door. Looks out*]

DWY. Quick, sir; you have ten minutes before they can reach us.

ANDY. I see lights on this side. They are all around us.

ROBT. Is there no escape?

ANN. Yes; the ould well by the shed outside. Hide yourselves in it. Down with yez, all three. There's not a fut of wather there. They will only find me here, and this poor sick child. Never mind us.

DWY. She is right. Come, sir. [*Exit Robert with Dwyer*]

ANN. Don't lave that coat there. [*Points to Robert's overcoat*]

ANDY. [*Taking it up*] The Major will get his horse back afther all. Bad luck to the baste he'll tell on us, for he's stabled in the shed. Whoo! Wait a bit. [*Puts on the coat*] I'll back him an' take a flier through the crowd o' them. I may as well be shot as hung. So here goes for which. [*Exit L.H. door*]

ANN. Poor child. This night will kill her. [*Two blows on the door*]

SIRR. [*Outside*] In the King's name open this door.

ANN. [*Turning*] In the devil's name—pull down the latch. [*Enter Sirr, followed by sergeant and soldiers*]

SIRR. Who is the owner of this house?

ANN. I am, for want of a fetther.

SIRR. A man calling himself Ellis lodges here.

ANN. He does.

SIRR. Where is he?

ANN. There is his room—help yourself.

SIRR. Go search the place. [*Exit sergeant and two soldiers*] I told you that some day you would fall into my hands, and here you are.

ANN. Here I am, sure enough.

SIRR. What girl is that? Stand aside! Miss Wolfe! What brings her here?

ANN. She brought a sportin' message that the hounds would meet here early in the mornin', and here you are. [*Re-enter sergeant and soldiers*]

SIRR. Not there—what is this—a letter in the handwriting of the man we want. The ink is still wet on the pen. He has been here within the last ten minutes. Will you tell us where your lodger is?

ANN. How would I know? It is no business of mine where he goes. [*Sirr goes up to the door*]

SIRR. We'll sharpen your wits. Prepare a rope there. [*Speaks off at the door*] Tilt back that car, with the shafts in the air. Haould it so, some of yez. That will sarve for an elegant gallows to suit this woman. [*She struggles with the soldiers who would seize her; they present their bayonets so as to keep her prisoner against the wall*] Will you confess now? I'll give you two minutes.

ANN. You are not the priest. I have nothing to confess. [*They seize her*] You may murder me, you cowards, but not one word about him will you get out of Ann Devlin. Now do your worst.

TINEY. [*Recovering*] Ann! Where are you?

ANN. Good-bye, Miss.

TINEY. Release that woman! If you hurt a hair of her head, I will denounce the infamous plot you planned in Dublin Castle in my presence. It was by the hands of your accomplices my father fell. Assassin! Assassin! [*Cries outside; shots; Sirr runs to the door*]

SIRR. My horse! Stop him! Cut him down! 'Tis Emmet. Shoot. [*Runs out followed by the soldiers, who release Ann; Ann bars the door. Enter Emmet and Dwyer. Tiney runs to Robert. Scene closes in*]

SCENE 3: *Glenmalure. Enter Quigley.*

QUIG. Mind how you step across that single bit of road. This way, Miss. [*Enter Sarah*]

SARAH. Are we near to Father Donnelly's?

QUIG. You may see his chapel there beyant.

SARAH. You are sure Mr. Emmet received my letter?

QUIG. Never fear, Miss.

SARAH. Then I will ask you to leave me here, and return to the car at the foot of the hill where we shall join you.

QUIG. More power, Miss. [*Exit*]

SARAH. There was no way but this to save him. [*Exit. Quigley returns*]

QUIG. There she goes straight into the thrap! [*Enter Sirr*] He! he! There will be a gay weddin' tonight at Father Donnelly's!

SIRR. Go to the Enniskerry road. See the men are posted there, so as to close his escape that way. I'll take with me twenty rank and file to surround the house.

QUIG. [*Going R.*] More power! be jabers we'll put the net securely over him this time. Whist! look here! d'ye see them two shadows creepin' down the side o' the hill?

SIRR. They are cattle, maybe!

QUIG. Cattle on two legs, Major! they are makin' straight for the priest's house.

SIRR. They must be two of our fellows that got astray.

QUIG. Divil a man you had that could foot the hillside like them two. Look now! the big one is in the moonlight! 'Tis Michael Dwyer! and his follower is Andy Devlin! Whoo! yer sowl! we'll bag the whole covey!

SIRR. Hark! I hear the hoofs of a horse!

QUIG. And so does Dwyer! Ye see—he stops to listen!

SIRR. Yonder comes a man riding a piebald!

QUIG. 'Tis your own baste, Major! and Emmet himself is across him! 'Tis yourself is in luck, sir, this night.

SIRR. You are right; the two fellows have joined the horseman, and they are going together towards the house. [*Claverhouse, outside, sings verse of Bonnie Dundee*]

QUIG. What is that!

SIRR. The officer in command of the detachment sent to assist me in this capture. Confound the fool, he will betray our presence.

QUIG. And scare the game. [*Enter Claverhouse*]

SIRR. Do you always sing, sir, when you are in sight of danger?

CLAV. No; sometimes I smoke.

SIRR. You are betraying our presence to the foe we are in pursuit of.

CLAV. British troops always betray their presence. D'ye want us to skulk?

SIRR. Captain Claverhouse, you see those three men yonder, standing before that house?

CLAV. I see two men and a half.

SIRR. Then you see Robert Emmet and Michael Dwyer.

QUIG. And the half is Andy Devlin; but he's a half that can tackle a whole one as big as yourself.

SIRR. You see your duty before you? it is to place your men so as to surround and command those premises, and to make prisoners of all we find there. Are you prepared, sir, to perform that duty?

CLAV. Needs must, sir, when the devil drives.

SIRR. Do you mean that for a joke, or an insult?

CLAV. Both; and I hope you mean to resent it. This is a convenient spot, and there's no time like the present. Are you agreeable?

SIRR. Duty before pleasure, captain. After we have lodged our prisoners in Kilmainham, I'll take a walk with you in the Phaynix, if you are so minded.

CLAV. [*Aside as he goes out*] How can I warn him of his danger? [*Exit L.*]

SIRR. Follow me! [*Exit R.*]

QUIG. [*Looks around*] There will be hot work when they try to tackle Dwyer. Where will I find a safe hidin' place convenient to see it all? There's a clump of bushes that looks well out of harm's way. [*Goes R.; recoils*] It is movin'! 'tare an 'ouns! there's somebody inside! maybe he's got his gun fixed on me! [*Creeps off L.H. Enter Finerty very pale*]

FIN. Stop!

QUIG. Don't shoot!

FIN. 'Tis meself, Finerty.

QUIG. I thought it was one of Dwyer's men; what brings you here?

FIN. I'm nearly dead. I dare not show in the streets of Dublin. I'd be killed. The people say I sould the life of Emmet. So I was hidin' here when Dwyer's men caught sight of me, and have been huntin' me like a rat. I believe I know every hole in these hills.

QUIG. Are Dwyer's men about here?

FIN. An hour ago they were here as thick as flies, but they vanished over the hill towards Dernamuck.

QUIG. They were scared by the redcoats; but now himself is here, there will be wigs on the green before sunrise. Pat, this is no place for us. I've got the car below here. I'll take ye back to Dublin where you will get safe lodgin' in Kilmainham until we get the reward, and then we'll show Ireland our heels.

FIN. The sooner the betther. [*Going*] After we pocket our pay, I'll go to America and take some other name.

QUIG. Be jabers, Pat, but that will be mighty hard on the man whose name you take. [*Exeunt*]

SCENE 4: *The interior of Father Donnelly's—a small chapel is seen L.H. through an arch in the wall, facing audience; a large bay-window R.H.; door R.H.; fireplace L.H.; candles are lighted in the altar in chapel; door L.H.3E. at entrance to chapel.*

SARAH. [*At bay-window*] I thought I heard the sound of a horse in the road.

FATHER D. You are listening with your heart.

SARAH. Oh, father! I can hear nothing else! Fear and hope possess me, that my being feels like one great pulse! Now, do you hear! my ears do not deceive me! [*Enter Robert*] Thank Heaven!

ROBT. Do so, with all your heart on which I come to rest! for mine is well nigh sped! I have none for further struggle! I have slighted your love for a wanton infatuation! My other love has betrayed and deserted me; I come to you for forgiveness, for comfort, and for peace! [*Enter Dwyer*]

DWY. Get to work, your reverence! there's something wrong! for I told Maguire to meet me at Stony Creek beyant, but the hillside was as bare as a bog—not a sign of one of my people to the fore. [*Exit Father Donnelly*]

SARAH. What do you fear?

DWY. There's somebody in the mountains tonight besides ourselves and the grouse; as I came over Glenmalure I did not hear a cock crow, nor a plover cry. [*Enter Andy with gun*]

ANDY. I found your gun in furze bush as you said, and this beside it. [*Shows a pike broken in two pieces*]

ROBT. What is it?

DWY. A letter to me from Phil Maguire. Did you mind how them pieces lay?

ANDY. I did.

DWY. Which way did pike end point?

ANDY. To Tallaght.

DWY. There are redcoats there, and in power o' them, or Phil would not have shown his heels. How did the shaft lay?

ANDY. Pointing to Dernamuck.

DWY. He has gone there to join two hundred men in the Glen of Emall.
How will I let on to him that I am here?

ANDY. I lighted the furze bush before I left.

DWY. Andy, me bouchal, asthure ye were—you are worth your weight
in one-pound notes. Bar the dure! [*Andy looks out before closing the door*]
How did you get here, Miss?

SARAH. On an outside car.

DWY. Who drove ye?

SARAH. Quigley.

DWY. Ah! Did he know your business here, and that his honor was to
meet you?

SARAH. Yes.

DWY. We are trapped! You guided the redcoats! You little knew you
had their escort behind you all the way from Dublin.

ROBT. I cannot believe Quigley capable of such dastardly treason. [*A shot
is fired outside*]

ANDY. Ah! [*Pulls to the door*] Quick, Mike! help me to pull down the
bar! [*Dwyer runs up and bars the door*]

DWY. [*Aside to him*] Were you hit?

ANDY. It is nothing.

DWY. [*To Robert*] Do you believe it now? [*Re-enter Father Donnelly
in his vestments*] Get into the chapel, your reverence, and take the lady; the
walls are thick—you'll be snug then! Oh! if we can only howld out for an
hour!

ROBT. We cannot hold it for a quarter. They will soon break in the door.

DWY. Not while I stand here. [*Three shots*] Andy, blow out the light
there! it guides their fire! [*Andy blows out the light; Robert draws Sarah into
the chapel*] Now, Andy, we'll take a hand in the game! Let us see how it
lies—there's a crack in them shutters! [*Andy and Dwyer enter the bay-
window behind the curtains. The scene changes*]

SCENE 5: *The R.H. flat revolves and comes down oblique, enclosing L.H.
side of stage, showing a yard enclosed by a low stone wall; the R.H. flat
serves as exterior of house with porch; the wall is lined with soldiers; Sirr
amongst them. Enter Claverhouse.*

CLAV. Stop firing! Who gave the order?

SIRR. I did.

CLAV. Mind your business, and don't presume to take my command. [*To drummer beside him*] Roll! [*Drummer gives a sharp roll on drum*] Father Donnelly—we are under orders to search your house, where we have information Mr. Emmet is concealed.

SARAH. 'Tis Norman!

CLAV. We call on you in the King's name to open your doors that we may do our duty! if you refuse, we must employ force! and if resisted, our directions are to destroy your house and chapel and bring you prisoners to Dublin! [*The door opens: Father Donnelly appears in it, dressed in his vestments*]

FATHER D. Strangers came to my door and claimed my ministry; I led them to the foot of the altar. God forbids I should violate that sanctuary as you would have me do! You will do your duty to your Master, as I shall do mine to Him whose commission I bear. [*He retires and closes the door*]

SIRR. Now, captain, as we have no time to lose, pour a couple of volleys into the rat-trap, and set fire to the stable beyant—that will fetch them out.

CLAV. There is a lady there.

SIRR. We do not regard the sex of a viper when we crush it—so with rebels.

DWY. Oh, Phil Maguire! why arn't you widin call?

ANDY. Maybe he is, but is waitin' for your ordhers.

ROBT. Sarah—I cannot sacrifice this noble old man. I cannot wreck his house and consign him to prison. I will surrender.

SARAH. No! no! death here, with us together! [*Clings to him*]

ANDY. [*Aside to Dwyer*] Michael, listen hither, my arm is broke; that first shot did it. 'Tis no good. If we are tuk, it is a dog's death by the rope on the next tree.

DWY. That's it.

ANDY. Stand by me, while I show you o' thrick to draw their fire; and when they have emptied their guns, make a dash over the wall and through their line; gain the hills, and before they are through wid ourselves, you will be back wid Maguire and his men.

DWY. What are you going to do?

ANDY. Lave me alone. Kiss me, Mike, for Ann. Lend me your gun—be ready now for the rush! [*He throws open the door—entering the yard*] Hurrah! Ireland forever! [*He fires*] Come on, boys! [*A volley is fired at him; he staggers forward crying*] Now, Mike, now! [*Falls*] tare alive! off wid ye, before they can load agin!

DWY. Andy! Andy me boy! what have you done?

SIRR. Down with him! 'Tis Michael Dwyer!

ROBT. [*Entering*] Hold! I surrender!

ANDY. No! no!—no surrender! I hear the thramp of the Wexford boys! [*Whistles from behind every rock, and up the valley appear crowds of insurgents. Dwyer and Robert raise Andy*] Ha! they are comin'! [*Enter Sarah and Father Donnelly*] Ha! ha! ha!—the redcoats fell into the trap! I laid for them! I emptied their barrels, and the masther is safe! Sure, it is not for me you are crying, miss? God bless you, I'm good for nothing. Don't waste a prayer over me, your riverence; I'm not worth it. I ax your pardon for dyin' like this, and thrubblin' you all. Kiss me, Mike! I believe I—am goin' now! 'Tis asier than I thought! [*Dies*]

TABLEAU

ACT IV.

SCENE I: *The court house, Green Street; the trial of Emmet; Norbury on the bench; jury; barristers; officers; public.*

NOR. Prisoner at the bar! You have heard the evidence brought against you by the crown. You have been found guilty of a treasonable conspiracy to betray your country into the power of our common foe, the French. With this infamous object you provoke an insurrection, and became an accomplice in the most brutal murder of Lord Kilwarden, chief justice of the King's bench. To these and divers other capital charges you have offered no defense. It is needless for me to impress on a man of your high attainments and position the baseness and infamy of such crimes. What have you now to say why judgment of death and execution should not be awarded against you?

ROBT. [*After a pause*] My lord; why judgment and execution should not be passed upon me, I have nothing to say. If I were condemned to suffer death only, I should bow in silence to my fate. A man dies—but his memory lives. Your sentence that delivers my body to the executioner shall not deliver my soul to the contempt of generations to come. You charge me with being the emissary of France. It is false! I would accept from France, for my country, the same assistance in our struggle for independence that Franklin obtained for America. But were the French, or any other foreign nation to come here as invaders, I would meet them on the shore, and if compelled to retire before superior discipline, I would dispute every inch of Irish soil, every blade of grass; and my last entrenchment should be my grave! I did not seek to free Ireland from the tyranny of one foreign power—Great Britain—to deliver her unto the bonds of another. Had I done so, I would have earned the execration of the country which gave me birth, and to which I would have given freedom.

Nor. Mr. Emmet, you must confine yourself to showing cause why judgment should not pass upon you; instead of doing so, you are broaching treason the most abominable.

Robt. I am showing cause, my lord, why the judgment of the world should not condemn me to a more shameful ignominy than the scaffold; why the calumnies you have uttered should not rest upon my name. If I stand at the bar of this court and am forbidden to vindicate my motives, what a farce is your justice! If I stand at this bar before you, and dare not vindicate my character, how dare you assail it? Does the sentence of death condemn my tongue to silence, when it would defend that immortal part of me which must survive; and is the only thing—God help me!—I can leave to those I honor and love, and to the people for whose sake I am proud to suffer? You have charged me with the murder of Lord Kilwarden; I would he were sitting there to judge me now, to sweeten death as he, deplored the sentence he was bound by law to pronounce. If I call on God to witness that I had no share in that foul deed—it is because I have no other witness to testify in my defense. [*Tiney rises, crosses over to the dock and gives him her hand*] My sweet child, do you absolve me?—would I had died in your father's place!

Nor. He who lets loose the storm is responsible for the havoc in its path.

Robt. My enterprise failed; had it been otherwise, your lordship might have occupied my place here at this moment, and I, yours!

Nor. Have you done, sir?

Robt. You are impatient for the sacrifice, my lord!—bear with me awhile, I have but few more words to say, and these, not to you—but to my people. See! For your sake I am parting with all that is dear to me in this life— family—friends—but most of all with her—[*Sarah rises with a cry*]—the woman I have loved. [*She goes to him*] My love—Oh! My love! It was not thus I had thought to have requited your affection! [*He kisses her*] Farewell! [*Curran receives her as she faints*] Farewell! I pass away into the grave. I ask of the world only one favor at my departure. Let no man write my epitaph, for as no man who knows my motives dares now to vindicate them, let not prejudice or ignorance asperse them; let my tomb be uninscribed until other men and other times can do justice to my character! When my country shall take her place amongst the nations of the earth—then—and not till then, let my epitaph be written! I have done. [*Murmurs in the court*]

THE CRIER. Silence in the court—while his lordship the judge passes sentence of death upon the prisoner at the bar. [*As Norbury assumes the black cap, the scene closes in*]

SCENE 2: *A prison. Enter Finerty—followed by Quigley.*

QUIG. It is done at last. He is condemned.

FIN. When is he to die?

QUIG. Tomorrow mornin'.

FIN. That's a short day.

QUIG. Long enough for Dwyer and his boys to pull down Newgate, to get him out.

FIN. It will be a hard nut to crack.

QUIG. And they will find it a blind one. They will draw it blank, for Emmet will lodge here tonight.

FIN. Here? in Kilmainham?

QUIG. The police say there's not a turnkey in Newgate that is to be trusted. They would throw open the prison doors to the people.

FIN. Are you sure of the jailors here? One of them gave me the offer awhile ago. He is one of Dwyer's men—the place is full of them.

QUIG. Kilmainham will be held tonight by a company of redcoats; meanwhile, a special warden has been appointed to watch the prisoner and sleep with him in his cell.

FIN. I hope they have picked a sure man?

QUIG. They have. One I recommended. Yourself.

FIN. Me?

QUIG. That's to be your duty this night.

FIN. But sure I can't stay here. The vessel that was to take you and me across the says to America will sail at daybreak.

QUIG. You axed the Government to put you in here for protection. You could only be admitted as a prisoner, and a warrant for your release must be sent from the Castle before they can let you out. Be aisy; I'll take care of you.

FIN. And the money—the reward—it is due.

QUIG. And will be paid tonight.

FIN. To you?

QUIG. To me! Who else?

FIN. Where will it be paid? Will Sirr bring it here?

QUIG. No; he will meet me at Brangan's wharf at Ring's End.

FIN. Furninst the spot where the ship lies moored and ready to sail! Quigley, you wouldn't go back on me, and run off wid my share of the reward?

QUIG. Pat, I'm sorry for you; but the polis have found out that you tuk a hand in the killin' of Crawford.

FIN. You were there, and helped.

QUIG. Then they say you were the man that murthered Kilwarden.

FIN. 'Twas yourself!

QUIG. They dare not let you go.

FIN. Not let me out? Do you main they are going to keep me here a prisoner?

QUIG. Until the next batch is transported to the penal settlement in Botany Bay. You are in for life, Pat.

FIN. Quigley, you are jokin'.

QUIG. 'Tis a sorry joke. I brought the ordher from the Castle, and left it at the gate as I came in.

FIN. The ordher to kape me here? I won't believe it.

QUIG. You see that dure? I am goin' out of it, just try to lave this place along wid me, and you *will* believe it, maybe; good-bye, Pat. [*Exit. As Finerty follows him, a jailor appears and stops him*]

FIN. It is true! Oh, the villain! the—the traitor! and to think while I am caged here, he will be sailin' away wid my money in his pocket, and a grin on his mug. Oh! no! no! not so fast misther Quigley. Aha! two can play at your game. [*To the jailor*] Come here! 'twas you gave me the offis awhile ago; give me your hand. You know this Wexford grip? I am one of your-selves—mind me now. I'll give you a paper; it is for Michael Dwyer, and must reach him, say widin an hour. Lend me your back to write it. [*He takes a pencil and note-book from his pocket and writes*] "Quigley will meet Major Sirr tonight at Brangan's wharf, Ring's End—there to receive the price of Robert Emmet's head. Patrick Finerty." You have heard, and you know what's in it; don't delay a minute. [*Gives him the note. Exit jailor, closing door, locking it*] Ha! ha! so, I have set the dog to watch the rathole. [*Enter Claverhouse*]

NORM. Are you the warden charged with the care of Mr. Emmet?

FIN. So I am tould.

NORM. I am the officer in command of the men detailed to protect the jail.

FIN. I know your honor well.

NORM. They are preparing the cell in which he will pass the night—you can keep watch in the corridor.

Fin. Thrue for you, sir! The less he sees of me the better for us both. [*As Finerty goes to the door, he suddenly retires and conceals himself behind it as Robert, accompanied by two turnkeys, enters. He is manacled*]

Norm. Remove those chains. If these walls are not responsible for the prisoner's safeguard I will be so. [*They remove the chains*] See! They have cut into his wrists; they bleed.

Robt. It is nothing! [*Finerty escapes. The turnkey retires*] Are you on duty here?

Norm. Yes.

Robt. So am I. We are prisoners both! You to watch and to guard; I to await my release. Yours is the more painful office.

Norm. I bring you a visitor. Will you see him?

Robt. Whom?

Norm. Mr. Curran.

Robt. Ah! With all my heart! [*Norman goes to the door*] For it owes him a debt. [*Enter Curran*] Oh, sir! I know I have done you a very severe injury—greater than I can atone for with my life. Let my love for your daughter plead for me. Do not turn away. Do not let a man with the coldness of death upon him feel any other coldness.

Cur. Robert, my poor boy, I would hide my weakness from you. God forbid I should turn away from the son of my old friend—the child who has played about my knees!

Norm. We have no time for bletherin'. Why don't you tell the lad what has been done for his sake.

Cur. Miss Wolfe and my daughter have been with the lord-lieutenant pleading for a commutation of your sentence. I urged my own claim on the Government for many and valuable services. His excellency was much moved by their prayers, and, at last, in consideration of your youth and your distraction, he yielded so far as to receive your petition to the crown for its mercy, to be forwarded to London. [*Hands Robert a paper*]

Norm. I have seen my uncle, Norbury. He will back the prayer.

Cur. Meanwhile execution will be stayed.

Robt. [*Reading to himself*] "To the King's Most Excellent Majesty. The humble petition of Robert Emmet, a prisoner lying under sentence of death." [*Reads the rest in silence*] Oh, sir! This is a beggar's petition for life! for life at any price. What shall I say? What answer can I make to those angels of love and pity. I see their pleading faces, their sweet eyes blinded with tears, lifted to mine. I see the sweet, childish mouth of Tiney trembling with her tender supplication! Yet between my kisses I would say I cannot crawl to the foot of the throne and sue for pardon. My country is my accomplice! Shall I indict her by confessing my penitence? Ah, sir, you may call me mad. It may be so. Call me rash. The fool of vain hopes. Tell his excellency I am sensible of his goodness, but I cannot accept a few dishonorable years as the price of my life to come.

Cur. You refuse the royal clemency?

Robt. No! I will accept so much of it as his majesty may grant to one so poor as I am. I ask to face the death of a soldier. Let me stand before a platoon of brave fellows, and wearing the uniform of my country, let me fall like a man, and not die by the rope like a dog.

Norm. Thankee, sir; thankee! I'm proud o' ye! 'Tis a shame to waste a mon like yersel'.

Cur. Must I take back this answer to his excellency? [*Enter a turnkey who speaks with Norman at back*]

Robt. I have staked my life, and have lost the game. It is a debt of honor, and as such must be paid within twenty-four hours. [*Smiling, as he offers Curran his hand*] You see, sir, it takes all I have in the world to meet the claim.

Cur. Give me some ground to plead upon. Will you not promise to forsake the cause that has betrayed you?

Robt. Ask me to forsake your daughter, and be foresworn to my love. Bear with me, sir—and let me live out my life—what is left of it is full of her. Her dear image is before me. I have no other care—no other thought—this is the eve of my wedding-night. I lie down in my grave to dream of her until I wake to meet my bride at the altar of heaven. Tell her I wait her there.

Norm. Your cell is ready.

Cur. Farewell, Robert, my son.

Robt. God bless you, sir; for that word—farewell! [*Exeunt Robert with turnkey. R. Curran and Norman L.*]

Scene 3: *The Bull Inn, a low class public house of the period. It occupies a cellar, approached by a short flight of steps, R.H. in F., door leading to street. Doors R. and L. Secret door, L.H. in F. Tables R. and L., at which men are drinking, smoking clay pipes, and two are playing at cards. Enter by secret door, Dwyer.*

Dwy. Boys! attention! There is brave work to be done this night; listen to this! [*Reads paper*] "At eleven o'clock Quigley will be at Brangan's wharf, Ring's End, to receive from Major Sirr the reward agreed wid the Govern-

ment as the price of Robert Emmet's head. Signed Patrick Finerty." What
d'ye say should be this black traitor's reward?

ALL. Death!

DWY. That's enough. Lave the payment of the debt to me. [*Enter Ann
Devlin*]

ANN. Dwyer, are you there?

DWY. Is it yourself, Ann? Did you see the Major?

ANN. Yes; and I followed your bidding. But oh, Mike, 'tis a terrible thing
you axed me to do.

DWY. What did he say?

ANN. He is close behind me, wid a guard of soldiers at his heels.

ALL. Redcoats! comin' here? [*Tumult*]

DWY. Order! fall in! If there's any one of you dares not thrust his life in
the hands of Michael Dwyer let him fall out! The dure is open to him; the
road is clear. This woman wid a man's heart in her breast, is worth a boat-
load of your cowardly carcasses. Hark! I hear the thramp of the soldiers;
they are comin' here to this place! There's time to escape by that dure to
the house in Marshalsea Lane that backs on this; you can save your dirty
skins that way! Be off still! Be quick! When a man has no heart left, and he
loses his head, he takes to his legs.

ANN. Don't be so hard upon them, Mike. They mane to stand by you.

ALL. Ay! Ay! never fear!

DWY. Go back to your pipes then, and to your games! and lave me alone
to play mine! [*The men resume their places at the tables. A sergeant and
soldiers appear at the door; they enter. Enter Major Sirr*]

SIRR. This is the Bull Inn? [*To Ann*] Beware, woman, how you trifle
with us. You have laid information that this place is a depot of concealed
arms, and the resort of rebels.

ANN. Yes.

SIRR. The Bull Inn, though poor, bears a good name.

ANN. The pikes and guns are stored in the house in Marshalsea Lane
that backs on this. There's a secret passage between the two. D'ye see that
row of pegs? pull the third one. [*Points back to the secret panel*] Pull it
down. [*A sergeant approaches the row of pegs, and pulls it down; the secret
door opens*]

SIRR. Sergeant, take your file of men in there and report what you find!
[*Exit sergeant with all the soldiers but two that remain on guard*] So far,
good! Now you promise to deliver into my hands the person of a leader of
the insurrection, for whose capture the Government has already offered a
reward of five hundred pounds; there are only three rebels worth that sum.

I am here by your agreement to put the head of this man in my hands—to whom do you refer? Where is he?

ANN. Where is he? [*She struggles with her emotion*] No! no! I—I can't do it—Oh Mike! it is more than my heart can bear.

SIRR. You said "Mike"—you cannot mean Michael Dwyer?

DWY. That's what she does mane! and I am he! [*Advances and faces Sirr*]

SIRR. You—Michael Dwyer?

DWY. Himself.

SIRR. If you are he, we met at Vinegue Hill when I put a bullet in your throat.

DWY. I believe the compliment was returned at Bally Ellis, when I put a pike in your ribs.

SIRR. We are quits. [*Offers his hand*]

DWY. [*Taking it*] Not until you get me where Robert Emmet is now! [*Re-enter the sergeant with two men*]

SIRR. Lads, have you found the arms?

SERGT. We have, sir; the place is full of them.

SIRR. And this woman has betrayed you?

DWY. This woman is my wife that was to be, and she obeyed me; I wanted to sell my life; she made the bargain. Have you the money there?

SIRR. Here it is. [*Offers it to Ann*]

ANN. [*Repelling it*] No! no!

DWY. Give it to me. [*He receives the money from Sirr*] There, boys, divide that between yez. 'Tis what the Castle says Michael Dwyer is worth. They came here wid me to rescue Emmet. Those are keys to every gate in Kilmainham. You seventy redcoats there wouldn't be a mouthful amongst two thousand undher my command. The turnkeys are united Irishmen. There are eight hundred prisoners, like wild bastes, behind your bars, hungry for liberty and your death.

SIRR. Then why did you not attempt this release?

DWY. Captain Claverhouse ordhered the irons off him and shared wid him his own quarters in the prison, taking only his word not to escape, and Emmet will kape it. That's why we failed. These arms are no good now. I give them up and sell my life on condition no other shall be taken. [*Sits on a keg*]

SIRR. And if I refuse your terms?

DWY. You won't do that.

SIRR. Why not—you are in my power.

Dwy. I'll show you why not! I am setting on a hundred weight of gun-powder [*He strikes in the bung of the cask; the powder flows out*] Patsey, lend me your pipe. [*The soldiers make a move for the steps*]

Sirr. No, stop.

Dwy. We are not afraid of death, and this way will save law costs.

Sirr. I accept your terms—the men can go.

Dwy. You give your word not one of them will come to harm?

Sirr. Will you rely on it?

Dwy. Yes. I know a man when I've fought wid him! You will kape your word. Go home boys, paceable, and tell the rest outside there's nothin' more to be done—this time. Good-bye, God bliss you. [*Exeunt the men*]

Sirr. Sergeant, march your men back to the Castle. You can leave me here. [*Dwyer leans over Ann, who has been seated L. crying*] Michael Dwyer, here are two passes to America by the vessel that lies off the north wall and sails tomorrow at daybreak. Take Ann Devlin with you. You are free.

Ann. Oh, Major, do you main it? Mike, d'ye hear what he says?

Dwy. I do, Ann, but I want more than that, or nothing. Read that paper. [*Sirr reads it apart, handed to him by Dwyer*]

Sirr. It is true—we meet there in an hour.

Dwy. The money will be paid in gold?

Sirr. Gold and silver.

Dwy. 'Twill be quite a weight.

Sirr. Yes, I'll take it on a car.

Dwy. I'll dhrive yer honor. 'Twill be quite convanient for me and Ann to get aboard the ship, and I've a trifle to pay Quigley before I go. So when your business is done you can lave me wid him.

Sirr. I understand. Bring the car to the Castle yard at once, I will be there to meet you. [*Exit*]

Ann. Michael, what are you going to do to Quigley?

Dwy. As sure as God made us both, one of us will go to render his life account up there tonight. Come. [*Scene closes in*]

Tableau: *Brangan's wharf, Ring's End, near Dublin; a rude shed; a flight of steps, L.H.; a door, L.C. in flat, looking out on the river; a boat appears at door; Quigley looks around—strikes a light, and lights lamp on table, L.C.; chair and keg.*

Quig. St. Patrick's is after strikin' eleven. It is time for the Major to come. This boat will save me to get aboard the ship! There she lies! 'Tis time I got away out o' this country. That's too hot to howld me. Whist! I heard the wheels of a car! Ay! it stops! [*Goes to door L.C.*] It is mighty dark; there comes a lanthorn! 'Tis himself! [*Retires to R., and closes door in flat. Enter Sirr with lantern, followed by Dwyer carrying bag. Dwyer has a huge carman's coat; a beard conceals his face*] I thought you would come alone.

SIRR. And carry half a hundred weight of coin? Lave the bag there, my man, and go mind your horse. [*Exit Dwyer with lantern*] Now, sir, count out your money. [*Quigley seizes the bag*]

QUIG. [*Counting*] He! he! oh, but there's nothing in life so sweet as that sound of coin. [*As he counts*] Your honor promised me two free passages for myself and Finerty to New York.

SIRR. You will get them when you are done your count there, never fear.

QUIG. I knew you would be as good as your word, sir. There's three hundred—how they shine! [*Opens his vest, takes from his waist a belt; Major Sirr rises and after walking up and down, exit L.; Quigley continues*]

QUIG. There's two hundred more! Ho! ho! I'm in luck! [*He puts the money into the belt. Enter Dwyer, without his beard or coat; he takes the seat recently occupied by Major Sirr*] Fifty—seventy—eighty—a hundred—six hundred—and I see there's two hundred more! [*He sweeps it all into the belt, and buckles it around his waist*] There's no knowin' what kind of a crew I will find aboard that ship; and if they knew what cargo I had in my hold, it is a poor chance I'd have to land it. So [*buttons his coat*], 'tis a heavy load; but it gives a lightness to my heart. Now for the passes, and good-bye, Major! [*Dwyer advances his hand as he takes Quigley's hand, Quigley looks up; their faces meet; the candle between*] Mother o' mercy! It is a ghost!

DWY. I tould you Quigley that some day I would die by your hand, or you would die by mine; that day has come.

QUIG. Would you murdher me, and rob me afther?

DWY. It would be no murdher to kill a rat! It is not your money I want, it is your life! Keep the price of blood! There are the passes, and there [*throws two knives on the table before Quigley*] choose one of these—they are alike! [*Quigley takes the knives and examines them by the candle; suddenly he blows the candle out, and springs on Dwyer, who, leaping to one side, avoids him*]

DWY. Egorra! I forgot the blackguard I was dalin' wid! [*As he dodges around the table, he meets the chair in which he had been seated; he seizes it, and holds Quigley at bay; he calls:*] Ann—Ann avourneen! come! [*Ann appears at door L.H. with lantern*]

ANN. What's the matter?

DWY. All right—stand there and give us a light!

Ann. Kill him, Mike! kill him! [*Holds the light above her head*]

Dwy. Never fear!

Ann. Will I help you?

Dwy. No; I'll be equal to the dirty work. Come on, Quigley! Are ye afeerd of an unarmed man? Don't be bashful! why a rat would make a better fight. [*As Quigley makes a rush at him, he claps the chair over his head, which appears through the legs and rails, while his arms are pinoned to the back legs and side rails*] The rat is in the trap! [*He pins him against the wall; holding him then with one hand, he seizes his throat by the other*] D'ye remember the grip?

Quig. Mer—mercy!

Dwy. I don't hear what you are saying! Spake up, man! [*Quigley drops the knives*] That's right, be aisy now; you are goin' into the Liffey, where the price of blood will take you to the bottom. So, he's gone to where he will meet Masther Robert tomorrow—to where I must answer one day for what I have done tonight. Now you can help me, Ann, to poison the tide. [*She opens the door at back; he throws Quigley out; they get into the boat and disappear; the shed is drawn off; the river appears; they are in the boat; a vessel with lights burning is seen about a quarter of a mile away*]

END OF TABLEAU

Last Tableau: *The yard of Kilmainham. Muffled drums are heard. Enter Sergeant with a file of men, followed by Norman Claverhouse and Emmet.*

Robt. So! this is the place! and this is my last day. Look! the sun never lighted a brighter one! Do not be cast down, my friend. If I had fallen in the strife of battle, it would not have been a more glorious ending. I sought no other. You promised me to see my mother this morning, and bring to me her blessing. Have you seen her?

Norm. No, Robert, for you will receive your blessing from herself.

Robt. She is coming to see me?

Norm. No; you are going to see her.

Robt. She—she is dead?

Norm. She died last night.

Robt. My sentence killed her! God forgive me! Well, I go to seek her pardon! [*A bell tolls; a black flag on the flag-post is seen to rise half-mast high over the prison*] Is that the signal? Ay, I see it is. [*Takes off his coat and cravat*] Sergeant, accept this watch; let it remind you of this hour. [*Takes out his purse*] You brave fellows will accept these few pieces—they are useless to me now. [*Gives purse to sergeant*] Let me be buried in my uniform, and with this portrait, that has lain for years upon my heart; tell her it was pressed to my lips when I blessed her name with my last breath; tell her to be happy. [*Bell tolls; Norman falls in his arms weeping*] Come, come, do not let your tears unman me. Men! you have your duty to perform—do it bravely, as I have done mine! This death is a boon, not a penalty! It is an honor to fall before you! and I receive your salute over my grave! I am ready!

SERGT.   Right wheel, march! [*The file of men wheel round and exeunt R. The sergeant re-enters and stands R. Robert embraces Norman tenderly*]

ROBT.   This for Sarah, and this for Tiney. [*Kisses him twice farewell. He goes up L.C. to the wall of the prison; stands a moment as if in prayer, then pressing the medallion to his lips, he extends his left arm in which he holds his cravat*] God bless my country! [*He drops the cravat; a volley is heard; he falls on his knees, his hand on his heart; the shots strike the wall, and show where they have scarred the masonry. Small clouds of dust fall to the ground. The black flag is raised. Bell tolls. Stage dark. Norman stands with his head averted. The wall behind Emmet slowly opens. A vista of pale blue clouds appears. The figure of Ireland clothed in palest green and with a coronet of shamrocks in her hair descends slowly; and bending forward when she reaches the spot behind Emmet, she kneels. Two children at her feet, R. and L., draw slowly back the body of Emmet until his head lies looking up into her face*]

TABLEAU

THE END

FALSE SHAME
AND
THIRTY YEARS

AMERICA'S LOST PLAYS

VOLUME II

A series in twenty volumes of hitherto unpublished plays collected with the aid of the Rockefeller Foundation, under the auspices of the Dramatists' Guild of the Authors' League of America, edited with historical and bibliographical notes.

BARRETT H. CLARK
GENERAL EDITOR

Advisory Board

ROBERT HAMILTON BALL, QUEENS COLLEGE

HOYT H. HUDSON, PRINCETON UNIVERSITY

GLENN HUGHES, UNIVERSITY OF WASHINGTON

GARRETT H. LEVERTON, FORMERLY OF NORTHWEST-
ERN UNIVERSITY

E. C. MABIE, UNIVERSITY OF IOWA

ALLARDYCE NICOLL, YALE UNIVERSITY

ARTHUR HOBSON QUINN, UNIVERSITY OF
PENNSYLVANIA

NAPIER WILT, UNIVERSITY OF CHICAGO

A complete list of volumes, with the names of plays contained in each, will be found on pages 107-8 of this volume.

FALSE SHAME

AND

THIRTY YEARS

Two Plays

BY WILLIAM DUNLAP

EDITED BY ORAL SUMNER COAD

INDIANA UNIVERSITY PRESS

BLOOMINGTON

Requests for authorization of the use of any of the plays in this volume on the stage, the screen, or for radio or television broadcasting, or for any purpose of reproduction, will be forwarded by Princeton University Press to the proper persons.

CONTENTS

INTRODUCTION

IN THE spring of 1796 William Dunlap, casual portrait painter, occasional playwright and part owner of a china store, was induced to purchase an interest in the Old American Company, which, with headquarters at the John Street Theatre, New York, was one of the two principal theatrical organizations in the United States. Dunlap took this step partly in the hope of substantial monetary returns and partly that he might be in a position to bring out his own plays, but he was also influenced by a desire to develop a truly moral and artistic stage in America. The painful realization was soon thrust upon him, however, that money could be more readily lost than made in the theatrical business and that New York playgoers felt no irresistible impulse to witness his original dramas or to lend their support to a truly moral and artistic stage. But, once a partner in the concern, he was unwilling or unable to withdraw, and indeed within two years he found himself sole director and manager of the New York theatre. To stimulate his languishing box office he almost immediately turned to the translation and production of the most popular plays by the European sensation of the hour, August Friedrich Ferdinand von Kotzebue. "The German Shakespeare," as his admirers sometimes labelled him, did not meet with Dunlap's unqualified approval. The American took exception to his false philosophy and his unsound moral standards, but he recognized his genuine skill as a craftsman and he could not ignore his equally genuine drawing power. It should be said, however, that Dunlap expurgated his originals freely and left some of the more objectionable plays untranslated.

The manager's first adaptation from Kotzebue, *The Stranger,* based on *Menschenhass und Reue,* was brought out at the recently built Park Theatre on December 10, 1798. A year and a day later his fifth translation, *False Shame; or, The American Orphan in Germany,* was produced at the same house. The cast was as follows:

Baron Flachsland	Joseph Tyler
Captain Erlach	John Hodgkinson
Wieland	Thomas A. Cooper
Vicomte de Maillac	John Martin
Frelon	Gilbert Fox
John	Joseph Jefferson

Baroness Flachsland	Mrs. Hodgkinson
Adelaide	Mrs. Lewis Hallam
Emmy	Ellen Westray
Madame Moreau	Mrs. Charlotte Melmoth

On the opening night *False Shame,* according to Dunlap's account in *A History of the American Theatre,* "was performed with the utmost success. . . . This play, without scenery or decoration, by the plain dialogue and natural character, supported the theatre this, the second season of the author's direction. As in the case of 'The Stranger,' it ran through the whole winter." While stating that the entire piece was well acted, the translator praises in particular Ellen Westray and John Hodgkinson: "Her youth and beauty contrasted finely with Hodgkinson's figure and manner, which were so well suited to the veteran German officer who had borne her when an infant from the flames of Charleston—the exquisitely natural playing of both —made an impression never to be forgotten, and rendered the comedy useless to the theatre of New-York when they ceased to perform the parts."

For some reason Dunlap's version of *Falsche Scham* was never published, although various American editions have been attributed to him. The play in English was printed three times in this country: at New York in 1800, at Charleston in 1800 and at Newark in 1801. But an examination of these editions proves that all three are exact reprints of the anonymous British translation published at London in 1799. Dunlap's rendering shows no trace of obligation to this English version and in fact, although not without awkward phrases, is a considerable improvement upon it in smoothness and colloquial ease. Except for the omission of several unimportant speeches or parts of speeches, which are cancelled in the manuscript and hence omitted in the present edition, he follows his author quite closely. Two characters undergo a change of name: the daughter Minchen becomes Adelaide, and von Hugel, the country gentleman, becomes Wieland—probably as a gesture of respect toward the recent novel of the translator's closest friend, Charles Brockden Brown.

The wave of prosperity in the New York theatre for which Kotzebue was responsible was only temporary, and early in 1805, after a brave struggle, Dunlap was forced to declare himself a bankrupt. He now resumed his former profession of painting and almost completely abandoned playwriting until 1827, when the manager of the new Bowery Theatre requested him to provide a series of plays to compete with those being offered at the Park. In his own words, he received "meager compensation for poor commodities." The second of the three plays thus produced was *Thirty Years; or, The*

Gambler's Fate. It is a translation of a then famous French melodrama, *Trente Ans ou la Vie d'un Joueur,* written by Prosper Goubaux (who sometimes employed the pseudonym of Dinaux) and Victor Ducange, and produced at Paris in 1827. In an English translation by H. M. Milner called *The Hut of the Red Mountain; or, Thirty Years of a Gambler's Life,* it was given the same year in London. On November 15, 1827, the play appeared at the Park Theatre in an entirely different translation called *The Gambler's Fate; or, Thirty Years of a Gamester's Life,* also ascribed to H. M. Milner. On February 22, 1828, Dunlap's competing version was brought out at the Bowery and was repeated over a dozen times in the course of the year. The following incomplete cast was listed in the newspaper advertisements:

George St. Germain	George H. Barrett
Warner	Thomas Archer
Albert	Mrs. G. H. Barrett
Amelia	Mrs. Charles Gilfert
Mrs. Birman	Mrs. William Jones

Of the three translations, all of which seem to have been independently made, Dunlap's is much the closest to the original. He leaves unchanged the names of the characters, except that he substitutes St. Germain for de Germany, and he follows the outline of events carefully until the very end, where, perhaps to satisfy poetic justice, he causes George to kill Warner and himself instead of allowing them to be seized by soldiers in the midst of the burning cabin. Although the dialogue is not translated with literal exactness, it is faithfully rendered except for some condensation, especially in the longer speeches.

The title-page of the manuscript bears the double name of *The Gambler's Fate—Thirty Years or The Life of a Gamester.* But the newspaper advertisements refer to the play as *Thirty Years; or, The Gambler's Fate;* hence that name has been adopted for the present edition.

In preparing these manuscripts for publication I have dealt somewhat freely with certain details of composition. In matters of spelling, capitalization and punctuation Dunlap seems to have been governed chiefly by caprice. It is not merely that he violates many of the canons of modern usage but that he is notably inconsistent with himself. Consequently I have taken the liberty of introducing such changes as would result in a reasonable uniformity of practice, while retaining in a modified degree some of his peculiarities, such as an extreme fondness for the dash as a mark of punctuation. Slight changes have also been made in the stage directions, likewise in the interests of uniformity. The language of the dialogue, however, has not been altered in any way, even by the correction of an occasional error in grammar. The text as here printed for the first time is a literal reproduction of what gives every evidence of having been the prompt copy, and therefore the acting version, of both plays.

It is perhaps worth pointing out that the manuscript of *Thirty Years* is only partly in Dunlap's hand. The second act is clearly his, but the first and third acts are in a more delicate script. Two sheets bear the signature of A. Gilfert (Mrs. Charles Gilfert) written diagonally across in a chirography very similar to that of the first and third acts, suggesting that the leading lady may have helped the translator in making a "fair copy" of his play. The manuscript of *False Shame* is entirely in Dunlap's hand and is a beautiful specimen of penmanship throughout.

ORAL SUMNER COAD

LIST OF PLAYS BY WILLIAM DUNLAP

The Modest Soldier; or, Love in New York
  Written 1787; unacted; unpublished
The Father; or, American Shandy-ism
  Acted September 7, 1789; published 1789
  Revised as *The Father of an Only Child* and published 1806
Darby's Return
  Acted November 24, 1789; published 1789
The Miser's Wedding (sometimes called *The Wedding*)
  Acted May 20, 1793; unpublished
The Fatal Deception; or, The Progress of Guilt
  Acted April 24, 1794; published as *Leicester* 1806
Shelty's Travels
  Acted April 24, 1794; unpublished
Fontainville Abbey
  Acted February 16, 1795; published 1806
The Archers; or, Mountaineers of Switzerland
  Acted April 18, 1796; published 1796
The Mysterious Monk
  Acted October 31, 1796; published as *Ribbemont; or, The Feudal Baron* 1803
Tell Truth and Shame the Devil (translated from *Jérôme Pointu* by A. L. B. Robineau)
  Acted January 9, 1797; published 1797
The Knight's Adventure (revised by John Hodgkinson as *The Man of Fortitude; or, The Knight's Adventure*)
  Acted June 7, 1797; published under Hodgkinson's name 1807
André
  Acted March 30, 1798; published 1798
The Stranger (translated from *Menschenhass und Reue* by A. F. F. von Kotzebue)
  Acted December 10, 1798; unpublished
Sterne's Maria; or, The Vintage
  Acted January 14, 1799; unpublished
The Natural Daughter
  Acted February 8, 1799; unpublished

The Temple of Independence
  Acted February 22, 1799; unpublished
Lovers' Vows (translated from *Das Kind der Liebe* by Kotzebue)
  Acted March 11, 1799; published 1814
Count Benyowski (translated from *Graf Benyowski* by Kotzebue)
  Acted April 1, 1799; unpublished
The Italian Father
  Acted April 15, 1799; published 1810
Don Carlos (translated from *Don Carlos* by J. C. F. von Schiller)
  Acted May 6, 1799; unpublished
Indians in England (translated from *Die Indianer in England* by Kotzebue)
  Acted June 14, 1799; unpublished
The School for Soldiers (translated from *Le Déserteur* by L. S. Mercier)
  Acted July 4, 1799; unpublished
False Shame; or, The American Orphan in Germany (translated from
  Falsche Scham by Kotzebue)
  Acted December 11, 1799; unpublished
The Robbery (translated from *Clémentine et Désormes* by Boutet de Monvel)
  Acted December 30, 1799; unpublished
The Wild Goose Chace (translated from *Der Wildfang* by Kotzebue)
  Acted January 24, 1800; published 1800
The Force of Calumny (translated from *Die Verläumder* by Kotzebue)
  Acted February 5, 1800; unpublished
The Virgin of the Sun (translated from *Die Sonnenjungfrau* by Kotzebue)
  Acted March 12, 1800; published 1800
Pizarro in Peru; or, The Death of Rolla (translated from *Die Spanier in
  Peru* by Kotzebue)
  Acted March 26, 1800; published 1800
The Stranger's Birthday (translated from *Die Edle Lüge* by Kotzebue)
  Acted April 23, 1800; unpublished
Fraternal Discord (translated from *Die Versöhnung oder der Bruderzwist* by
  Kotzebue)
  Acted October 24, 1800; published 1809
The Knight of Guadalquiver (sometimes called *The Spanish Castle; or, The
  Knight of Guadalquiver*)
  Acted December 5, 1800; unpublished
Abaellino, the Great Bandit (translated from *Abällino, der Grosse Bandit*
  by J. H. D. Zschokke)
  Acted February 11, 1801; published 1802

The Soldier of '76
Acted February 23, 1801; unpublished
Abbé de l'Épée (translated from *L'Abbé de l'Épée* by Jean Bouilly)
Acted March 9, 1801; unpublished
Where Is He? (translated from the German)
Acted December 2, 1801; unpublished
The Merry Gardener (translated from the French)
Acted February 3, 1802; unpublished
The Retrospect; or, the American Revolution
Acted July 5, 1802; unpublished
Peter the Great; or, The Russian Mother (translated from *Die Strelizen* by J. M. Babo)
Acted November 15, 1802; published 1814
The Voice of Nature (translated from *Le Jugement de Salomon* by L. C. Caigniez)
Acted February 4, 1803; published 1803
The Good Neighbor (translated from the German of A. W. Iffland)
Acted February 28, 1803; published 1814
The Blind Boy (translated from *Das Epigramm* by Kotzebue)
Acted March 30, 1803; unpublished
The Glory of Columbia; Her Yeomanry!
Acted July 4, 1803; published 1817
Bonaparte in England
Acted December 19, 1803; unpublished
The Proverb; or, Conceit Can Cure, Conceit Can Kill
Acted February 20, 1804; unpublished
Lewis of Monte Blanco; or, The Transplanted Irishman
Acted March 12, 1804; unpublished
The Wife of Two Husbands (translated from *La Femme à deux Maris* by Guilbert de Pixerécourt)
Acted April 4, 1804; published 1804
Nina (translated from *Nina ou la Folle par Amour* by Joseph Marsollier)
Acted December 31, 1804; unpublished
Alberto Albertini; or, The Robber King
Acted January 25, 1811; unpublished
Yankee Chronology; or, Huzza for the Constitution!
Acted September 7, 1812; published 1812
The Battle of New Orleans
Acted July 4, 1816(?); unpublished

The Flying Dutchman
  Acted May 25, 1827; unpublished
Thirty Years; or, The Gambler's Fate (translated from *Trente Ans ou la Vie
  d'un Joueur* by Prosper Goubaux and Victor Ducange)
  Acted February 22, 1828; unpublished
A Trip to Niagara; or, Travellers in America
  Acted November 28, 1828; published 1830
La Perouse (translated from *La Perouse* by Kotzebue)
  Unacted; unpublished
Forty and Twenty (original or translation?)
  Unacted; unpublished
Robespierre (original or translation?)
  Unacted; unpublished

PLAYS DOUBTFULLY ATTRIBUTED TO DUNLAP

The Africans
Blue Beard; or, Female Curiosity
The Corsicans; or, The Dawning of Love (translated from Kotzebue)
The Count of Burgundy (translated from Kotzebue)
Fiesco (translated from Schiller)
Rinaldo Rinaldini
Self-Immolation; or, Family Distress (translated from Kotzebue)

FALSE SHAME;
Or, THE AMERICAN ORPHAN IN GERMANY

CAST OF CHARACTERS

MEN

BARON FLACHSLAND, *A Counsellor of State*

CAPTAIN ERLACH, *His Friend*

MR. WIELAND, *A Country Gentleman*

VICOMTE DE MAILLAC, *An Emigrant*

FRELON, *His Valet*

JOHN, *The Baron's Gardener*

WOMEN

BARONESS, *The Baron's Second Wife*

ADELAIDE, *His Daughter by his First Wife*

EMMY, *An Orphan*

MADAME MOREAU, *The Baron's Sister*

THE SCENE, UNCHANGED THROUGHOUT THE PLAY, REPRESENTS A PART OF THE BARON'S GARDEN.

ACT I.

*The stage represents a part of the Baron's garden. On the R.H. side is a
hedge coming down the stage towards the audience and terminating in an
arbor R.H. On the other side stand two high linden trees with their branches
entwined and overshadowing a grassy bank. R.H. a watering pot with water.
John is discovered upon a garden ladder, singing and trimming the hedge.*

JOHN. Useless shoots here and everywhere. I wish they were as well
trimmed everywhere as here. Oh, if I could but go to work among our family
with my shears, snip snap, how the heads should fly! I would soon prune off
the suckers which now draw the wholesome juices from my master's noble
stem. [*Descends and comes forward*] Poor Baron! Formerly, joy was the
perennial growth of our garden; it flourished without nursing, and gaily
bloomed in every corner; but now they have drawn a hedge round about my
good lord, so thick that not a beam can pass through. The business grows
worse and worse every day. We can see it in the Baron's looks. He fades
like a Viola Matronalis on which insects continually gnaw. [*Enter Emmy
with knitting work. L.H.*]

EM. [*As she passes slowly over the stage*] Good morning, John.

JOHN.   Good morning, dear young lady. Out in the garden so early? There
is a heavy dew fallen; you must take care or you will wet your little feet.

EM. [*Having crossed over*] The sun shone in at my window and enticed
me down. [*Exit R.H.*]

JOHN. [*Looking after her*] A lovely little flower—and hides itself in the
grass, like a ripe strawberry. Heaven preserve it from sweet-toothed sparrows. Adelaide is good too. Oh yes, very good; but she imitates the Baroness,
her stepmother, too much, and perhaps we shall soon be only able to say,
"She *was* good." [*Ascends the ladder and goes to work. Enter Frelon
U.E.L.H.*]

FRE.   *Bon jour, Maitre Jean.* [*John turns and looks at him, smiles contemptuously and then continues his work; Frelon goes close to him and
halloos*] Halloo! Are you deaf?

JOHN.   What's the matter?

FRE.   I say, *bon jour, Maitre Jean.*

JOHN. And I say, Go to the Devil. I am an honest old man, and he that speaks with me must speak German. Do you understand me, Mounseer *Bon Jour*?

FRE. *Maitre Jean,* always growling, *Maitre Jean.*

JOHN. The cuckoo is called *Maitre Jean.* My name is *Jahn* [*Pronounced very broad, Yawn*]. Stand farther off with your French jabber, Mounseer *Bon Jour.*

FRE. Yawn! Yawn! So brays the ass.

JOHN. So I hear.

FRE. *Maitre Jean* sounds better.

JOHN. Sounds? Aye, with a Frenchman sound is everything. Anything is good that sounds well. I should thank you, Mounseer Clingclang, to leave me in the same good company that you found me. Leave me with the old German Jahn. [*Works and sings*]

FRE. *Maitre Jean, avec permission,* leave off singing. You have a bad voice.

JOHN. Who hinders you from removing out of the sound of it?

FRE. My master has ordered me to wait for him here.

JOHN. Go stand among the peas and frighten the sparrows, and then you may boast of having been useful once in your life.

FRE. Your jests are truly German.

JOHN. He that eats German bread must expect to hear German truth.

FRE. [*Fanning himself*] It will be very hot today.

JOHN. Go to the ditch and bathe; there is nothing cooler than mud.

FRE. Apropos, that ditch must not remain there.

JOHN. [*Starting*] What?

FRE. I say, that ditch must not remain there. [*John looks at him contemptuously, then turns away, works and sings*] When my master is married to the daughter of the house, the Lady Adelaide, who by the bye is a damned fine girl, things will be put in a very different train I can assure you; this Dutch garden will soon wear another face.

JOHN. Your master? Marry the Lady Adelaide?

FRE. Yes, the Vicomte seems very much inclined to forget what he owes to his illustrious ancestors.

JOHN. But my Lady Adelaide will never forget what she owes to herself.

FRE. *Mon ami,* my master is accustomed to turn the heads of the ladies.

JOHN. Yes, they must be turned when they suffer him about them.

FRE. Respect, *Maitre Jean*; it costs me but a word, and my master will cause you to be disgraced.

JOHN. Indeed!

FRE. Upon the whole, I very much doubt whether my master will keep you in his service.

JOHN. So?

FRE. You may be endured perhaps in what concerns the kitchen garden, but, *mon ami,* you are totally destitute of taste.

JOHN. Aye?

FRE. These trees, these hedges, these tulip beds, may be well enough in Holland, but they do not suit *us*; *we* admire the grand, the striking, the surprising—hermitages, tombs—

JOHN. This is too much.

FRE. You are old, *mon ami.* You have seen little worth seeing. *Il faut lui passer son ignorance.* You may still remain here as undergardener, but we must send for a Frenchman to remodel things; a delicious man! Ah! *Maitre Jean,* you shall go to school to him.

JOHN. I, go to school. [*Steps off the ladder*]

FRE. He will soon revolutionize the garden. The low shall be high and the high shall be low. Out of the miry ditch he will make a bath of Diana and out of the old hot-house a Chinese pagoda.

JOHN. Pagoda! Aye! You damned wind-bottle! [*Seizes the watering-pot and begins to sprinkle Frelon's legs*] Bath of Diana! Ha!

FRE. [*Skipping about*] *Maitre Jean, Maitre Jean!* what do you mean?

JOHN. The bath of Diana, Mounseer *Bon Jour.*

FRE. Stop, I tell you, stop!

JOHN. If it don't please you creep into the pagoda. [*Drives him about the stage. Enter Baron Flachsland L.H.*]

BAR. John, what are you doing?

JOHN. Sprinkling weeds.

BAR. Know'st thou not in whose service the man is?

JOHN. [*Half aside*] Oh, yes! Like master like man.

FRE. [*Drying his legs with his handkerchief*] *Maitre Jean* is very jocular.

BAR. Where is your master?

FRE. Probably still at the ball, my lord.

BAR. [*With a forced smile*] Bravo! This is dancing indeed.

FRE. About daylight he sent me away, and ordered me to wait for him here.

BAR. [*Affecting an air of carelessness*] Without doubt the Vicomte will conduct my lady home.

FRE. I flatter myself, my lord, that my master understands life.

BAR. Was the Baroness—I mean the company—merry—?

FRE. O my lord! The Baroness dances *comme un ange,* and my Lady Adelaide *comme un zephyr.*

BAR. Was the company numerous?

FRE. Oh, very, my lord, very! I saw the Baroness about midnight surrounded by a circle of *beau monde.*

BAR. [*Stifling his uneasiness*] If she does not take cold in coming home.

FRE. She has sent the phaeton back, my lord; Monsieur Wieland offered his carriage.

BAR. [*Much relieved*] Wieland! Is he in town? That rejoices me.

FRE. He came yesterday evening in full gallop; jumped from his horse and flew to the ball.—*Ventre-saint-gris! Maitre Jean* has so besprinkled me, that I must beg permission to change my shoes and stockings. [*Bows and exit R.H.*]

BAR. John, what is the meaning of the trees being chained together with flower-garlands in the lower part of the garden?

JOHN. It is done by order of the Baroness. All the flowers are cropt from their stocks. Not a rose left to perfume the air.

BAR. What is it for?

JOHN. How should I know? She is going to give a thing—the wind-bottle there that just skipt away named it in French, and Mounseer Rosat, the friseur, has translated it for me; it is called—ha, ha, ha!—a dancing breakfast. The cooks have been at work all night making kickshaws and the girls rubbing chocolate.

BAR. [*With forced indifference*] So!

JOHN. Aye, aye! For the last two years there has been so much noise in the garden, that the nightingales have all flown away.

BAR. Well, well, good old man, we will be satisfied as long as Content builds her nest with us.

JOHN. Yes, yes, Content is a lovely little bird, but it sometimes disappears as suddenly as the swallow. [*The Baron sighs but seeks to hide it*] Do not take it ill of me, my lord; I am an old grey servant. I stood by and devoutly looked on when you were baptized. As you grew you always wished to be by yourself; and when the neighbors' children played, you sometimes joined in their sports, out of complaisance to them, tho' you had rather have been alone, and at such times you looked just as you look this morning—I mean no ill, my lord; you understand me.

BAR. [*Smiling*] If the neighbors' children had such claims upon my complaisance, how much more has a dearly loved wife!

JOHN. But that which is easy to the boy, may be a hard task to the man. The young tree bends, the old tree breaks. When one has jogged on peaceably in the same path, every day for a quarter of a century, one is not willing at the end to make a side-spring.

BAR. I see thy meaning. But my wife is young; I am already past forty, and must therefore double my complaisance. [*With warmth*] And does she not deserve my utmost confidence? So good, so excellent!

JOHN. She is very well, if she would not meddle with the garden.

BAR. How now, old man! In what does she trouble thee?

JOHN. Alas, my good lord, the garden is *my* paradise. My father, God bless him! laid it out; I was born and brought up in it, and except a few years which I passed in Holland to perfect myself in the art, I have scarcely set my foot over the door. Each little fruit tree has been propt by my hand, and those great trees which my arms can now scarcely encircle, I can remember when twigs. I was thinking *thus:*—behind the meadow is a little grassy place—scarcely perceivable—there stand some birch trees by the garden wall —there where I smoke my little pipe of an evening—

BAR. Well? Go on?

JOHN. There thought I thus to myself: if thou askest the favor of the good Baron, he will let thee be buried in this spot.

BAR. It shall be so! Good old man!

JOHN. Yes—but pardon me, sir—who knows how long the birch trees shall stand? The Baroness designs many alterations. The wall shall be torn down and the meadow planted with young trees. Here will she lay out a winding path, and there a wheatfield, and yonder a Mount Parnassus—and how do I know but my birch trees may stand in the way?

BAR. [*With warmth*] Thy birch trees shall nobody touch.

JOHN. Who shall protect the poor birch trees, when even these lindens shall not be spared?

BAR. Which lindens?

JOHN. [*Pointing to the trees*] Do you no longer know your foster-children, my lord? You and your sister, my young Lady Phillipina, planted them on the birthday of your dear good mother.

BAR. Oh, I remember it well!

JOHN. At that time you were both children, hardly as high as this rose bush. Your sister a little taller than you. After you had planted the scions in the earth, you stretched out your little hands and joined them over the twigs and kissed one-another. And your mother wiped her eyes and said to me: "John, take care of the little trees!" And I have done it faithfully. They have become a pair of fine proud trees! And now shall I cut them down?—No, that can I not! My heart would smite me and my hands would tremble, if I should lift the axe against one of these trees.

BAR. Who asks of thee to cut them down?

JOHN. The Baroness says that if one sits there in the bower, the linden trees obstruct the view of the village.

BAR. Never mind. Nobody shall touch the lindens. It is my command.

JOHN. Very well, my lord. Now let the Devil touch them, if he dare.

BAR. Let them stand and entwine their arms and kiss each other to the sound of each murmuring breeze, when my sister and myself shall sleep far beneath the green turf. Let no one touch them; they are all that remain of my sister.

JOHN. Alas, yes!

BAR. But the Baroness knew not that. Mark, John. My wife knew nothing of that.

JOHN. Possibly not. Yesterday was the first time she mentioned it. I believe that skip-about vicomte of a Frenchman puts such things in her head. He was with her, and capered and played tricks around her, treading down here a cucumber and there a strawberry vine. I think the Baroness values him highly.

BAR. [*With stifled feeling*] Think'st thou?

JOHN. He is always by her side.

BAR. He has the reputation of being an agreeable companion.

JOHN. He can chatter, it is true, and so can his Mounseer Valetchamber. He boasts already of connexions—

BAR. [*Hastily*] What connexions?

JOHN. I may not even repeat. Neither do I believe a single word of the matter.

BAR. [*Aside*] So! Already in the mouths of the domestics. John! [*He checks himself suddenly*] Enough, John. I have disturbed you in your work. I could not sleep this morning, and thought to be the first in the garden.

JOHN. The first! Oh no. Miss Emmy has been here this half hour.

BAR. Emmy!—Where is she?

JOHN. There she sits with her knitting work. There by the rose-bushes. [*Pointing R.H.*]

BAR. [*Calling to her*] Good morning, Emmy! [*Enter Emmy R.H. John moves his ladder back, working, and at length disappears. U.E. R.H.*]

EM. Good morning, dear father, I did not know that you were up already.

BAR. Neither knew I it of you, or I could have spared my caution in passing your chamber door. What will you give me if I bring you glad tidings?

EM. Give? You jest. To give to you would be but to return your gifts. What have I that comes not from you?

BAR. From me? By no means, my child. You are indebted to me for nothing but the roof which shelters you. For every thing else does my whimsical friend refund to the uttermost farthing, out of his scanty stipend, a poor lieutenant's pay.

EM. Can he pay for your fatherlike love of me?

BAR. For that do *you* richly repay me, dear girl. You accustom me to the sweet thought that I possess *two* daughters. Indeed I might almost become jealous when I think, that I must this day divide with another my dearest claims on your heart.

EM. This day?

BAR. Erlach will be here.

EM. Erlach? Today? My preserver! My noble benefactor! At last? After eight years of absence! But certainly, dear father, will he come?

BAR. So he writes me in his usual laconic style, a letter of three lines. I confess the news has surprised me, for it is not Erlach's fashion to pay visits at the beginning of a campaign.

EM. I can scarcely remember his face or figure. Oh, I wish he were already here. I will go to meet him. Which way must he come, dear father?

BAR. That is more than I can tell. My good Erlach seldom encumbers his epistles with place or date. This is his letter. [*Takes it out and reads*] "By this comes the money for Emmy's board; and next Tuesday myself." That is all.

EM. Truly but few words, yet they bear the stamp of benevolence. From whence should he snatch time to write? He must act. Is it not so, dear father? He holds that hour for lost, which carries not a good deed from his hand into eternity.

BAR. The tender Emmy becomes warm—

EM. O sir—

BAR. It gives me pleasure, my child.

EM. He drew the poor Emmy from under the smoking ruins—he divided with her his scanty and hard-earned pay—Can I think on these things and not weep? He has my heart entire and undivided!

BAR. And deserves it. I wish it may be thy lot, dear girl, to cure him of his aversion to thy sex. And truly the more I consider it, the more reasonable appears the hope. What think'st thou, Emmy? The man has been long known to thee; his figure, alone, hast thou forgotten; even in *that* there is something noble. Do you give me your permission to become a matchmaker?

EM. You jest, dear father. But do you know that your jest tends to cherish a romantic extravagance which has occasionally haunted my little head for sometime past?

BAR. Now, my dear little American, let me hear it.

EM. When on a fine evening I have stole away from your cheerful circle, to walk alone in the dark beech-alley, then have I built castles in the air; then have I thought *how* I might repay my benefactor, might make the evening of his life serene—but I am a foolish talkative girl.—Happily for me, here they all come from the ball. Dear father, you have seen my soul unveiled,—I must run from the eyes of those who are coming. [*Runs off L.H.*]

BAR. Do they come at length?—But not to me!—A *déjeuné dansant* entices them home! [*Enter Wieland and Adelaide U.E. L.H.*]

AD. Good morning, papa! Yet I had better say "good night" and lay my ear on my pillow.

BAR. Are you tired?

AD. To death!

BAR. Mr. Wieland, I rejoice the more in seeing you here, as I should hardly have dared to expect it at this season.

WIE. You are right, my lord, the country at this season affords so many occupations and so many enjoyments—

AD. Now, well may we compliment you, on leaving all behind, to dance a country dance with me.

WIE. If my society was of any value, I might flatter myself with having deserved the compliment.

AD. Excessive modesty is vanity. Would you believe it, dear papa, this young gentleman who always used to stand in the corner and *look* on when others danced, at last in consequence of my high and sovereign command took the bold resolution to stand up as my partner in a country dance, upon condition that after having figured up to the top, he should have liberty to sit down if he found the dance too difficult. I expected nothing less than a perfect clown of a partner whom I should have to lead this way and push that and throw everything into confusion; instead of which he flew with me through the ranks as if he had been a pupil of the great Vestris. Pray, sir, why did you always stand aloof as if you were lame?

WIE. I am not accustomed to dancing in public; and your city gentlemen seize every opportunity of turning us rustics into ridicule.

BAR. False shame is the only fault I ever could find in my young friend.

AD. But that is not all, papa. At table I sat near him and filled his glass for him and was very attentive to him I'll assure you, and, whether it was the wine or my politeness which inspired him, Heaven knows, but the mute Mr. Wieland became so talkative, and spoke so reasonably, and discoursed so interestingly, that I almost forgot we were in the temple of Folly. For Heaven's sake, sir, why are you in general so covetous of words?

WIE. Because in large companies I find myself apt to say foolish things.

AD. My dear sir, why that is the very use of large companies: they are public marts where each brings and exhibits his folly with impunity. What would be modesty in the smaller circle, would, in the great world, be false shame. There our clothes must shine and our words sound; at home, we require warmth from apparel and instruction from conversation.

BAR. [*Who has been looking about with uneasiness*] Where did you leave your mother?

AD. She thought you were still in bed, and hastened to your chamber that she might awake you with a kiss.

BAR. Was she alone?

AD. Alone indeed! As if it were possible to get rid of the Vicomte de Maillac!—Unless indeed one was to order the footmen to turn him out of doors, or dip him in the horse-pond.

BAR. Was he with her, then?

AD. Not properly with her, but behind her. When they find you are out, they will come down hither in the garden.

BAR. There they come already. [*His countenance brightens and he hastens to meet his wife. Enter Baroness and Vicomte de Maillac L.H.*]

MAIL. Ah ha! *Monsieur le Baron, nous voila!*

BAR. Good morning, my love! Have you been well entertained?

BAR:SS. Tolerably so, my lord. Have you missed me?

BAR. My heart misses you ever.

MAIL. Very gallant, a genuine French turn, upon my honor.

BAR:SS. I will not leave thee the whole of this day for that speech. I have invited about two dozen friends; we will breakfast there in the alley under the beech trees and imagine ourselves in Pyrmont.

MAIL. Ha, ha, ha! Bravo! The Baroness has most delicious ideas.

BAR:SS. [*Curtsying*] My ideas thank you.

MAIL. Sincerely, ladies, I came to Germany with very low expectations. They had given me a horrible idea of the German ladies. A girl of fifteen, said they, blushes for shame, if she is obliged to take off her gloves, and sticks her hands under the dinner table; she sits mute and imbecile near a man of the world or turns away, whispers and titters in the ear of one of her unmannerly companions; a girl of eighteen always has moist eyes, swims in a sea of sensibility, affects to be in love, and calls it constancy to her lover when she treats a stranger with rudeness; a woman of twenty thinks she proves her immaculate virtue by drawing back and childishly pouting when a young man approaches and says a handsome thing in her ear; a woman of five and twenty—

Bar:ss. *Basta,* my lord vicomte! or we shall send you to Hanover, to the man who has written such a scandalous book on our sex.

Mail. I will write an encyclopedia against his book; and if ever I see my native country again, woe to the babbler who permits himself to make a single *bon mot* derogatory to the German ladies.

Ad. Soon may the maidens of Germany carry you to the grave, that they may deck with garlands the tomb of their poet.

Mail. It may to be sure be objected to my book in praise of German civilization, that it is the French emigrants who first began to polish the nation, and that the Revolution which has caused so much misery in the South, has been the means of extending taste and cultivation to the North.

Ad. You are perfectly right, my lord vicomte. An ordinary German maiden, who obeyed the impulses of nature, would laugh in your face on hearing such a speech; but I, who already feel the mild influence of your polished society, am so perfectly a courtier, as to make you a curtsy and—run away. [*Running off L.H.*]

Mail. Ha, ha, ha! Bravo!

Bar:ss. Adelaide! where are you going?

Ad. To seek Emmy. Bless me, mama, do you not know that the greatest joy a young lady brings home from a ball is the unestimable privilege of talking about it for eight days after? Emmy must hear all. [*Exit L.H.*]

Mail. [*Starts and puts his hand on his shoulder*] Bless my soul! What was that? A rain drop?

Bar:ss. Certainly not. The sky is serene, and smiles propitiously upon our intended pleasures. Though we are in a state of sin we shall not be driven from the garden.

Mail. I know not what you may think, my lady—but look—look, sir—look, my lord—there is certainly a wet spot on my new frock.

Bar:ss. Probably a dew drop from the trees.

Mail. It is so, my lady. I am happy to recollect that you yesterday pronounced sentence of death on those damned high lindens.

Bar. Let me, my lady, be a petitioner for their reprieve.

Bar:ss. Are they dear to you?

Bar. Unspeakably dear!

Bar:ss. I knew not that.

Bar. I and my poor sister planted those lindens.

Bar:ss. Thy sister, my lord! Hast thou a sister?

Bar. I had a sister. God knows whether she still lives.

Bar:ss. And you never said a word of it to me.

Bar. Forgive me. I feared to open old wounds.

Bar:ss. But I never heard one of your family speak of her.

Bar. My family, from false shame, avoid to mention the name of my poor sister. She, contrary to the wishes of her parents, loved a young merchant from Lyons. She became culpable in their eyes and fled. It is now two and twenty years that she has been dead to us. The greater part of my family have forgot her. I will never forget her!

Mail. Lyons? Lyons? I am myself from that neighborhood. Yes, yes, the Lyonese are dangerous fellows among the ladies.

Bar:ss. [*Caressing her husband*] Dear my lord, I am frightened to think what a deed I was upon the point of doing. From this moment do I take these lindens under my protection. My lord vicomte, I hope your frock will pardon me.

Mail. Without jesting, my lady, I shall be obliged to change my dress.

Bar:ss. [*Smiling and tapping him on the shoulder*] Nothing can recommend you to us ladies so much as the noble occupation of the toilette. But I forget that mine awaits me.

Bar. Dare I offer my arm?

Mail. Fie, *monsieur le baron!* That would be German indeed. You will permit—[*Offering his arm*]

Bar:ss. My lord vicomte, I have not been long enough your pupil; the German wife still pulls me at times by the gown. [*Takes her husband's arm*] We shall soon meet, gentlemen.

Bar. [*Going out*] I will be with you again immediately. [*Exeunt Baron and Baroness L.H.*]

Mail. Bravo! A good German anecdote, upon my soul!

Wie. I must pity the French if such scenes are so rare as to be anecdotes with them.

Mail. What else should they be? Fit subjects for Florian's novels or Arnaud's "Epreuves du sentiment." [*Wieland shrugs his shoulders*] You shrug your shoulders, sir, ha? I must tell you that your manners do not please me.

Wie. That is my misfortune.

Mail. Upon my soul, the teaching of this people is rather a hopeless task. Precept or example, wit or reason, all is equally vain! They sit and look on, like a novice at first entering the school of Monsieur l'Epée, the celebrated teacher of the deaf and dumb.

Wie. I had rather resemble the unapt scholar than the unasked teacher.

Mail. But that must not be, sir. At your age and with your figure, a man may say anything. You have good teeth, you must laugh. You have good eyes, you must stare. You are well made, but you are not master of those negligent movements of the body which fascinate the eyes of the women. The waving line, sir, the waving line is the line of beauty. A young man should always be on the wave—sometimes with the arms—sometimes with the legs—sometimes with the whole body—

WIE. Unfortunately I was brought up in the military school.

MAIL. Yes, yes, that one may easily see. It will cost some trouble to make you flexible.

WIE. It will.

MAIL. Meanwhile, *mon cher ami,* if you will trust yourself to my guidance—

WIE. You do me honor.

MAIL. But upon one condition though.

WIE. What is it?

MAIL. I have observed that you cast a presumptuous eye upon the Lady Adelaide.

WIE. Presumptuous?—Yes, it is indeed presumptuous to love so charming a maiden!

MAIL. You love her then?

WIE. I know no shame in avowing the noblest feeling of my heart.

MAIL. To herself?

WIE. I know not, sir, by what right—

MAIL. By what right? *Parbleu!* I will marry her.

WIE. So will I.

MAIL. She is rich, handsome, witty—

WIE. She is good, reasonable, amiable—

MAIL. I will make her a vicomtesse.

WIE. I will make her happy.

MAIL. Both cannot have her.

WIE. Perhaps, *neither.*

MAIL. *Entre nous,* my good friend, let us speak reason.

WIE. Willingly, if it will not incommode your lordship.

MAIL. Adelaide must be my wife.

WIE. I must wrestle for the prize notwithstanding.

MAIL. Not when I promise you that after marriage, I will not incommode you in the least.

WIE. I do not understand you.

MAIL. *Au contraire,* you will oblige me very much if you will become my wife's cicisbeo.

WIE. That is a business not taught in the military school.

Mail. You may love, sigh, and languish as much as you please. You need not even wait for the end of the honeymoon. The *l'ami de la maison* shall always be welcome.

Wie. Your most obedient. [*Takes off his hat and bows ironically*]

Mail. But until the nuptials, I must beg of you to keep at a greater distance.

Wie. It grieves me that my obstinate heart—

Mail. But I beg it, sir. Do you understand me? The tone in which I beg will sufficiently show you what impression a refusal must produce on me.

Wie. The path of true love, like the path of honor, is broad. The candidates for fame or for happiness may walk by the side of each other. And certainly, he who is so conscious of his merits as you, Mr. Vicomte, can have nothing to fear.

Mail. [*Ironically*] Fear? Oh no! But it is my way—a caprice of mine—I suffer no rival.

Wie. Only this time. You will permit—

Mail. No. I permit nothing, sir, nothing at all!

Wie. That sounds a little dictatorial.

Mail. You will force me to speak a rougher language.

Wie. The Lady Adelaide may determine this difference.

Mail. I take no lady as an umpire as long as I wear a sword.

Wie. I do not admire knight-errantry.

Mail. So much the worse for you, when we come to break lances.

Wie. My sabre has long been ground down to a peaceful sickle.

Mail. Permit me the sooner to advise you to retreat from a scene in which your part would not be the most brilliant.

Wie. Underparts are not always unprofitable.

Mail. You persist then in your obstinacy. [*Wieland shrugs his shoulders*] Although I in plain language say, that one or other of our necks must be broken.

Wie. I hope not.

Mail. You have nothing to hope, sir.

Wie. I am willing to consider this whole scene as in jest.

Mail. Jest, sir! Hell and the Devil! I feel that your infernal coldness makes my blood boil.

Wie. I pray, my lord vicomte—

Mail. Sir, you pray in vain; you quit the field or draw your sword.

Wie. I would very unwillingly—

Mail. [*Ironically*] That I perceive, sir. You have probably never seen any blood in the military school.

WIE. Well, then, since you positively command—[*Puts on his hat*]

MAIL. I still leave you the choice.

WIE. It is impossible for me to renounce Adelaide. [*He very coolly takes a pair of gloves from his pocket and deliberately draws them on*]

MAIL. Stop, sir. I hold it my duty as a nobleman and a man of honor, to inform you, that I was taught the art of fencing by the greatest master in Europe.

WIE. I thank you for this generosity but it comes too late. [*Draws*]

MAIL. In confidence, *mon ami,* the precise reason of my emigrating from my native country, was that I had the misfortune to kill in single combat all the staff officers of my regiment.

WIE. *Tant pis pour moi!* I acknowledge the danger and tremble. [*Puts himself in posture for fencing*]

MAIL. [*Drawing back*] How, sir? What? Now? Would you in earnest—

WIE. Perhaps you only jested. [*Advances on him*]

MAIL. You do not consider where we are.

WIE. It is certainly not the place.

MAIL. The place! Certainly not! That is my only reason for not drawing, sir. Forbid it, Heaven, that I should make a field of bloodshed of a spot rendered sacred by hospitality. On the frontiers, sir, on the frontiers, there will I pass my sword through your body, and escape. [*Exit R.H. hastily*]

WIE. [*Sheathing his sword*] And such a man dares pass and repass the doors of the Baron Flachsland. Thus is many a fool suffered because he is a good dancer, or because he holds out his hands when a lady would wind off her thread. With women, foolish men and foolish fashions enjoy equal privileges; they bear the one and suffer the other, and four weeks after laugh at both. The proverb, "Tell me thy company and I will tell thee who thou art," is not applicable to women, for we find lapdogs and fools in the company of the most reasonable among them. [*Exit L.H.*]

ACT II.

Wind instruments are heard at a distance L.H.U.E. playing country dances. Enter Captain Erlach R.H.

ERL. So ho! They lead merry lives here. [*Walks up and looks towards the music*] Hats, headdresses, feathers, dancing and card playing!—all jumbled together in most delightful confusion. [*Comes forward*] That is not *my* way. This, I suppose, is what they call summer amusement. And does my old friend suffer such disorderly doings in his garden? What am I to think of this? Perhaps it is his daughter's wedding-day. If I could only meet a servant who would whisper in his ear, "Erlach is here!" I will not go nigh yon scene of confusion. Rather would I go to the inn and read in the almanac. Halloo there!—Good friend!—Is not this old John? [*Enter John L.H.*]

JOHN. Aye!—What!—Gadzooks!—Mr. Lieutenant!—or may be Captain by this time—

ERL. All's one for that, John, if I am only welcome.

JOHN. Oh! how will my lord the baron rejoice!

ERL. Has anyone here time to rejoice over an old friend?

JOHN. Sometimes he complained that you wrote so seldom.

ERL. That same writing, John, is not my way.

JOHN. And that one never knew where you were.

ERL. Why should he complain of that? I cannot bear that friends should be every moment writing assurances of their eternal attachment to one another. Friendship is a thing that speaks for itself and understands itself; besides a friend is not a girl that one adores today and laughs at tomorrow. Apropos of girls! How does my Emmy do? Is she grown a fine tall maiden?

JOHN. Tall and handsome and good. A rose—a centifolia—

ERL. That rejoices me. There is company here, I see.

JOHN. Alas, yes! [*Shaking his head*]

ERL. Thou likest it not, old man?

JOHN. I am not used to it, sir.

ERL. And thy master?—Formerly it was not his way.

JOHN. Ah! Mr. Captain, things are strangely changed here.

ERL. How so?

JOHN. The Baroness—

ERL. What?—What Baroness?—I hope he has not—a second marriage—

JOHN. Did you not know that? More than two years ago.

ERL. Indeed! I am sorry to hear it. And he is deceived—it serves him right!

JOHN. A good lady, but too lively, too gay—it seems to me like two queen bees in *one* beehive; too much humming—too much swarming—

ERL. Go call the Baron hither to me. But do it secretly, that it may cause no gaping.

JOHN. I understand. [*Exit L.H.*]

ERL. Is it then with marrying as with drinking? Intoxication gives the drunkard a headache, yet scarcely is he sober again before he grasps the glass. No, Erlach! thou hast done many a stupid thing in thy life, but marry wilt thou never; that is not thy way. He who stands on the shore and sees how people exhaust themselves in struggling with the stream and yet jumps in—let him drown! [*Enter Baron. He rushes on with open arms L.H.*]

BAR. Erlach! My Erlach! [*They press each the other to his breast with silent joy*]

ERL. [*Struggling to suppress emotion*]   Old lad!—I am glad to see thee again! [*Shakes his hand*] *This* is true pleasure. Thou art become a little thin, otherwise still the same.—What?—I believe thou weepest?—Fie for shame!— [*Turns away to conceal his own tears*] How the gnats sting one!

BAR. I weep, yes! And thank thee that thou camest not to the company; *there,* I must have suppressed these sweet tears.

ERL. Must you so? Why then do you keep such company?

BAR. Of that another time. Let them play and dance. We have not seen each other for eight years. Dear Erlach, how has it been with you?

ERL. Well. I have obtained my discharge from the service as a captain.

BAR. Why so?

ERL. Because it no longer pleased me; and because an old aunt has died and left me her heir.

BAR. Thank Heaven! Now then we shall dwell together? Shall we not?

ERL. Indeed that was my intention, but—

BAR. What mean you?

ERL. Thou art married again as I hear.

BAR. To an excellent wife.

ERL. May be so. But this manner of living which I see around me—you know *me*—it is not my way.

BAR. Thinkest thou *I* like it?

ERL. Why do you suffer that which you can change?

BAR. I am twenty years older than my wife. Shall I refuse her the pleasures to which her youth has been accustomed?

ERL. You should have considered that sooner.

BAR. I loved—

ERL. If you talk of love, I have done.

BAR. Has Erlach still found no conqueror?

ERL. My friend, it is with love as it is with the smallpox; he who escapes it in his youth, seldom or ever gets it.

BAR. But it is the more dangerous if he *should* take it.

ERL. So much the more care must he take to guard himself from infection.

BAR. But in earnest, what could you do in your present situation more reasonable than to take a wife?

ERL. What?—Blow my brains out! That would be far more reasonable.

BAR. As much a woman-hater as ever.

Erl. If a man has a worthless wife, God knows it is bad enough, but if he is so unfortunate as to have a good one, it is ten times worse.

Bar. You are jesting with me.

Erl. Not at all, for if I had a good wife, I should love her.

Bar. So much the better!

Erl. So much the worse! A husband who loves his wife is the slave of his own heart. If she has a single wish beyond his power to content, though a trifle to her, it is to him a source of unceasing torment.

Bar. A good wife has no such wishes.

Erl. Don't tell me! Wishes are like dust, which penetrates to the most secret recesses of the house, though every door and window be shut.

Bar. But is blown away by love. Besides, matrimony has its joys.

Erl. Oh, yes! You look like an image of joy. Do you reckon yonder noisy scene among the joys of matrimony?

Bar. [*With a sigh*] That might be otherwise—

Erl. Come, come, my friend! Speak out! Where does the shoe pinch?

Bar. O good Erlach! there is more than one worm gnawing at my heart.

Erl. This manner of living is *one;* is it not so? Thou lovest peace? Thou wouldst fain retire to thy estate in the country?

Bar. For the love I bear my wife, I would go from one carnival to another. But the expense is too great. My purse will not hold out.

Erl. Why dost thou not tell her so?

Bar. I cannot. She was used to live thus in the house of her parents. Besides, when she was yet a bride, she asked in all the confidence of love, what was the amount of my income—"I wish to know that I may regulate my expenses accordingly," said she; "tell me sincerely."

Erl. And you did not?

Bar. I—excuse me, my friend, I was ashamed. "Live as you have been used to live," was my answer. "You shall never find money wanting."

Erl. And has it remained thus?

Bar. She has wished to know if she should diminish the expenses of our living—if a retired life would please me better. "My will shall be regulated by yours," said she.

Erl. But you?

Bar. I could not prevail upon myself to lay any restraint on her inclinations. I wished her to be as little sensible as possible, that she had married a man of forty.

Erl. That signifies, in other words, thou art ashamed of thy age.

Bar. It may be so.

Erl. And wouldst pass for richer than thou art.

BAR. It is now too late to revoke.

ERL. Reason never comes too late, though it be midnight when she knocks at the door.

BAR. All *that* might yet be well; my heart is not touched that my fortune is diminished,—but—

ERL. Still a *but?*

BAR. To thee, and thee alone, do I confess my weakness. I am tormented by jealousy. I am doomed daily to see a swarm of adorers around her—to be sure they are only coxcombs—but woe to the man who imagines that a coxcomb cannot poison his peace! The need of a something to trifle away time has reduced many a female's virtue to a trifle indeed!

ERL. Why do you not say this to her?

BAR. It is true, she has often said to me, "Do these butterflies give thee disquiet? Speak the word and in an instant I drive them away."

ERL. And you have as often answered—?

BAR. What I answered when I was a bridegroom: that my confidence in her knew no limits.

ERL. That signifies, again, in other words: thou art ashamed of thy jealousy.

BAR. Thou art right, dear Erlach.

ERL. Now what a damned thing is this *false shame!* There would not be one-half of the misery in the world which we now see, if men only understood themselves, only had the courage to speak boldly out, and tell where the shoe pinches. Here now stands a man who could be happy, whose wife asks nothing at his hands but confidence; she wishes to regulate her conduct by *his* will, to renounce everything which can give *him* disquiet; but he—he is ashamed, and is silent.

BAR. I feel myself wrong, yet have not courage to amend.

ERL. Well then I must occasionally lend you the courage of an old bachelor. Come, man, be of good heart! If thy wife resembles the picture which thou hast drawn of her, we will make a man of thee yet. Cheer up, man! A fig for the past, let us take care that the future is better; that's my way!—Now tell me, what is my foster-daughter about? Must I go to the company if I would see her?

BAR. You would in vain seek for her there.

ERL. That rejoices me. Between ourselves, brother, I intend well by that little girl. When she is grown up—

BAR. That is she already.

ERL. Nonsense! Impossible! She was only a child, so high, when I was last here.

BAR. Yet a girl will grow in eight years.

ERL. Be that as it will, she is still very young. Chance has thrown the poor orphan to *me,* and I will provide for her faithfully. I have neither child or family. She must still continue to call me father, and when friend Death challenges me to *his* dance, I shall leave her my purse in keeping.

BAR. Have you never heard anything of her family?

ERL. Not a word. But that's a matter of no consequence. *I* may as well be her father as anybody else.

BAR. Why not rather her husband?

ERL. Thou art mad.

BAR. Her joy at the news of your approach was almost the joy of a bride.

ERL. Indeed! Did it make her happy? Prythee make haste, and send her to me quickly.

BAR. I will. [*Going L.H., returns*] But you have ordered your trunk to be brought to my house?

ERL. Not yet, brother. You know *me.* I must first know if everything here goes according to my way.

BAR. My friend! my brother! I hope—

ERL. Go only now and send Emmy hither; the trunk will take care of itself. [*Exit Baron L.H.*] I must first know more of the new wife. The charming state of matrimony has given many a sleeping draft to friendship; and if it once comes to nodding it never wakes again. From the holy state of matrimony, good Lord deliver us! Poor Flachsland! Thou wouldst persuade me to marry? Thou?—a decoy bird in a trap-cage. Sing as thou wilt, I am aware of the birdlime. [*Enter Emmy, with outspread arms, running towards him L.H.*]

EM. My preserver! My benefactor!

ERL. [*Starts back, avoiding her caresses*] What!—Madam!—

EM. Do you no more know your own Emmy?

ERL. You? You, madam, my Emmy?

EM. Oh, why do you not speak to me as you formerly spoke?

ERL. Are *you* the same Emmy, that eight years ago was not higher than my cane?

EM. And could only lisp then, what now she feels.

ERL. Who sat on my knee, who—?

EM. The same whom you have overwhelmed with benefactions, yet repulse the expressions of her grateful joy.

ERL. [*Wavering between embarrassment and love*] Now—now if this is —I am heartily rejoiced—Art thou—you—? To the Devil with it—come here and let me kiss thee!

EM. That was the well known parental voice! [*She caresses him*]

ERL. [*Kisses her on the forehead, then looks at her with extacy*]   Girl, thou hast become tall and beautiful, thy eye is benevolent and thy whole appearance lovely. Indeed I know not how those feel who have children, but at this moment I would not give a kreutzer to have a daughter all my own. [*Pats her cheeks*] I feel so full of joy at the heart, and yet so strangely—do not laugh at me, because the water runs over my cheeks—this crying is not my way, I'll assure you.

EM. I?—I, laugh?—Never was my heart more moved—[*Weeps*]

ERL. Thou?—Dost thou weep?—Hark 'ee, Emmy—I cannot bear to see that—I shall go away again. [*She suddenly dries her eyes and smiles kindly on him*] So!—That's right, my dearest girl. With such a look you might stop a whole regiment when they were running to the charge! But now let us talk reasonably. Emmy, it cannot remain so—this familiarity between us cannot be.—No, it must cease.

EM. Why, my father?

ERL. To the Devil with it!—Why must you call me father? Do I look so old? Why, girl, I am eight years younger than the baron.

EM. Your benevolence—

ERL. What, again? [*Hastily*] Hark you, Emmy—[*Tenderly*] Good Emmy, be silent on that head; I must hear no more of that; it is not my way. However, if we must still continue our former familiar intercourse, let me be as a brother to you, an elder brother, a half-brother, by a first marriage.

EM. My heart needs no relationship to strengthen its love to you.

ERL. So much the better!

EM. You have written to us very seldom.

ERL. My teacher struck me over the fingers when I made crooked letters, and ever since I have had a great disinclination to write. But thou notwithstanding hast wanted nothing?

EM. Your goodness—

ERL. Pooh, pooh! We were not talking of that. I could do very little for thee when I had only my lieutenant's pay. But in future it shall be better. Fortune has become kind to us, Emmy; an old aunt,—Heaven bless her! has left us a very genteel estate. I have taken my leave of the army, and would willingly take up my winter quarters here with my friends.

EM. Oh, that is excellent!

ERL. Yes, but the manner of living here is not in my way. If this dancing and feasting goes on every day—however, the baron has already told me that you, dear Emmy, hate this tumult.

EM. Custom has made solitude dear to me.

ERL. Custom only? Not inclination? Not desire?

EM. You must not think the worse of a young girl, if she has sometimes looked on with a beating heart as the many colored crowd danced before her.

ERL. Why, then, do you not make one in it?

EM. Because it does not become me, because I am a poor orphan living upon the bounty of strangers, because—

ERL. Because?—Come, out with it. Let us hear all.

EM. Before you I will not hide my weakness. *Because* I dare not think in the brilliant circles of the great, that I can balance by inward worth the splendid appearance of my companions.

ERL. That is as much as to say, in other words, you are ashamed of your wardrobe.

EM. Not here, not in company with the wise and good; but you know upon what the world grounds its mistaken and superficial opinions.

ERL. Already, again, *false shame*. Dear Emmy, a maiden is nobly clad, when the vestments of innocence bedeck her. However, thou shalt want for nothing. I confess I like such an apron and pockets, it looks so domestic; but the pockets must not be empty. [*Attempts to put a purse in her pocket*]

EM. [*Very much frightened*] No! No!—For Heaven's sake not!—You have misunderstood me.—You humble me—I have more than I want—if you love me put up the money again.

ERL. Well, well, only be quiet. [*Puts up his purse*] I did not manage it well. Pardon me, I am too downright. The art of giving is the finest of the fine arts; but alas! I do not understand it.

EM. I intended to confess a weakness, and my words have assumed the appearance of effrontery. Am I not treated here as a daughter or a sister? How often have they pressed me to accept jewels and costly clothing of every kind. But they would ill become me. I still perhaps have parents living, who languish in poverty and misery, and shall I clothe myself in satins? I am perhaps only a common peasant's child, and shall I hang brilliants in my ears?

ERL. A peasant's child? No, truly that thou art not!

EM. [*Hastily and anxiously*] You know perhaps something of my origin?

ERL. Nothing, dear girl, conjectures—

EM. Oh, impart to me your conjectures! Tell me the history of my deliverance! When you left us, eight years ago, I was a child and did not understand it. I will assist you with the obscure remembrances of my infancy—I will describe to you the figure of my mother—perhaps she still lives! Gracious God! perhaps my mother still lives!

Erl. It is possible but not probable. We landed and surprised Charlestown in the night. Our people had overcharged themselves with drink and from soldiers became incendiaries. The town was soon in flames; the fire spread from every corner; those who escaped from the devouring element were cut down and trampled under foot. No command, no subordination. I unwillingly recall the remembrance of that night of Hell! I made myself hoarse with calling to the soldiery—the thunder had roared equally in vain. At length the day broke and cast its light upon the scene of multiplied horrors. Covered with blood and dust, begrimed with smoke and embers, the soldiers lay scattered among the ruins and snored. All was desolate and horribly still. As I clambered, sword in hand, over the smoking beams, I suddenly heard a low, soft plaint beneath me. I listened—I removed the glowing rafters and half-burnt planks, when behold! an infant's lovely face! The little eyes were fixed on mine and mournfully it cried, "Mother! where is my mother!" That helpless infant was thee, dear Emmy. Thy body half buried in the ruins, thy life had been saved but by miracle. I cleared away the rubbish as well as I could and one of your little hands becoming free, the first use you made of it was to waft me a kiss—the action touched me beyond expression! "Patience, poor worm," said I; "it shall yet be well with you." My servant was at no great distance; I beckoned him to me, we gave thee air, and drew thee unhurt to the day. I took you on my arm; you clung about my neck. "My mother!" you cried in English, "take me to my mother." "My mother!" you repeated in French, "to my mother"; and thinking I did not understand, you at last repeated in German, the same touching words.

Em. My mother!

Erl. "Who is thy mother?" I asked. "Here in the narrow street, the good woman in the yellow house." Alas there was neither narrow street or broad, neither house or woman. All my endeavors to discover something relative to you were in vain. With those who had escaped we had no intercourse. We were ordered on board our ships. What was to be done? Should I leave you behind among the burning ruins? I obtained my captain's permission to take you with me, for he was touched with compassion when he saw you—you were then such a little thing—that I cannot conceive, for the soul of me, how you have become so tall.

Em. Alas! and do you know nothing more?

Erl. [*Shakes his head*] We were fortunate enough to return safe to Europe, and you found a safe asylum in the house of my friend.

Em. Not even my name? Could I not lisp to you my name?

Erl. Your first name, Emmy. Therefore I hold you to be the child of English parents; but you spake French and German as fluently as you did

English, from which I conclude that you are of no common family. On your clothing was marked A.M.; nothing further do I know.

EM. Oh, if I were but there, in America! my native country! If I should see my parents, surely I should know them again. My father was a thin, brown man—and my mother—I shall never forget her figure! She looked so pale, and often wept—perhaps she weeps now still oftener than then—and I cannot mingle my tears with hers. [*She sobs*]

ERL. Cheer up, dear Emmy. I see the confused squadron sailing up the alley this way. Such tears are not for people who have just been sweating away in the dance the little feeling God gave them.

EM. I cannot now be cheerful. I pray your permission to withdraw. [*Exit R.H.*]

ERL. Lovely maiden! What a pity it is, that she has grown so tall and handsome. The heart expands not as formerly, and the familiar appellations, so dear in childhood, now die upon my lips. I will, however, order my trunk to be brought. [*Enter L.H. the Baroness, Adelaide, Wieland and Maillac*]

BAR:SS. Welcome, Captain Erlach! heartily welcome! I but this moment heard from my husband—

ERL. [*With cool politeness*] Have I the honor to see the Baroness Flachs-land before me?

BAR:SS. If you derive not more satisfaction than honor from my presence, I must add one more to the list of my disappointed wishes.

MAIL. Bravo! That was fine! A delicate turn 'pon honor.

ERL. Your wishes are very modest, my lady.

BAR:SS. We have been waiting for you a time which, to our expectations, has appeared an eternity.

ERL. So much the worse for me! He who is long expected, is commonly found much below expectation.

BAR:SS. A hundred and a hundred times have I asked how you looked? When I hear of persons who are interesting to me, I always endeavor to sketch to myself a figure corresponding to their character, but I commonly find that my portraits bear no resemblance to the originals. For example I have always painted you as a jovial man, with an open countenance, an aquiline nose and a hawk's eye.

ERL. Your most obedient, my lady.

BAR:SS. I would have laid any wager that you could not have looked from under so lowering a brow.

MAIL. Ha, ha, ha! Bravo!

ERL. A serene mind may sometimes place a lowering sentinel on the out-post, to deter intruders. [*Looking at Maillac*]

Bar:ss. But, Mr. Soldier, when friendship has determined to take a heart by surprise—

Erl. Only the heart of a fool can be taken by surprise.

Bar:ss. You are right; conquer, I would say—she fears not the guards who stand on the outposts. In short, I am resolved to become your friend that I may no longer be your rival.

Erl. Rival!

Bar:ss. Yes indeed, sir. Already, more than once has my whole heart been jealous of you. Not a day has passed on which my lord has failed to speak of you with the warmest enthusiasm. So passionate has been his desire to see you, that if I was of a suspicious disposition, I should have expected a second Chevalier d'Eon in the person of my husband's friend.

Mail. Ha, ha, ha! Bravo! Bravissimo!

Bar:ss. My lord vicomte, I release you from the obligation of applauding every thing I say.

Ad. Ha, ha, ha! Bravo! Bravissimo!

Mail. [*To Adelaide*] Little, mischievous devil, I shall punish you for that.

Ad. What? I suppose you will write verses again in my praise.

Erl. By and by it will be my turn to cry "Bravo."

Ad. [*To Erlach*] Will *you* bring the word into credit again?

Erl. Truly, beautiful unknown—

Bar:ss. How? Do you not know the daughter of your friend?

Erl. [*Starting*] This! This—little Adelaide—your pardon for the familiar expression—

Ad. If I must lose by it the intimacy of those I esteem, I shall for the first time regret that I have become tall.

Erl. You have indeed become tall and beautiful.

Ad. And can become red, Captain.

Erl. It is not my way to flatter. Beauty as well as fortune are hereditary. The wise think nothing of either.

Mail. Ah! Captain, she is as cruel as beautiful.

Erl. [*To Adelaide*] Probably a lover?

Ad. Yes, a piece of one.

Bar:ss. The Vicomte de Maillac, a French emigrant.

Erl. So, so; servant, sir.

Bar:ss. And this is Mr. Wieland, an honest country gentleman who lives on his farm.

Erl. That is my way. With this gentleman I am already allied; we Swiss are all born farmers.

BAR:SS. Captain, your arm. We must go to the company. You shall there become acquainted with titles innumerable.

ERL. I would rather you should conduct me to yonder bed of hyacinths; for there, after having stood to hear you call one a prince of the blood and the other Cardinal de Fleury, I shall at least be rewarded by their fragrance. [*Exeunt Erlach and Baroness L.H.*]

MAIL. The Captain is a little rude.

WIE. He is no summer-house. In such buildings Friendship may dwell in winter and rough weather.

AD. Shall we follow to the company?

MAIL. Sure, you jest. The comet never asks its tail if it will follow.

AD. Ha, ha, ha! Do you know that the tail of a comet consists of nothing but vapors?

MAIL. Of whatever you command.

AD. [*Casts herself negligently in the bower*] Well then, gentlemen, since it pleases you, we will remain here. But I have no desire to talk; I will be entertained. No matter what with.

MAIL. If I dared to profit by this happy moment, and speak of my love—

AD. No, no!—Do you not hear that I wish to be entertained?

MAIL. Perhaps you will command me to read to you? I have here a volume of Rousseau's "New Héloïse."

AD. That I dare not read; papa does not permit it. But tell me, my lord vicomte, why is your book called the "*New* Héloïse"?

MAIL. Probably a whim of the author's, for in the whole book I do not find a single word of any Héloïse.

WIE. [*Smiling*] Indeed!

AD. But certainly there must be some connexion.

MAIL. By all means.

AD. Héloïse must have been very handsome.

MAIL. [*Presenting his snuffbox*] I can have the honor of showing you her portrait.

AD. Is it like?

MAIL. As like her as one eye the other.

AD. You have perhaps seen her. [*Ironically*]

MAIL. No, not herself; she has been dead some years, but her uncle Fulbert I am very well acquainted with, an honest old owl enough. They have engraved him on copper.

AD. You smile, Mr. Wieland.

WIE. I take part in your pleasure.

AD. The uncle, my lord vicomte, is he a man of rank?

MAIL. A financier. As to family—but you know with such people we are not over scrupulous as to family. He keeps a good table and gives damned good wine.

AD. And Abelard?

MAIL. He was an *avocat au parlement* and acquired some reputation.

AD. Probably an old man by this time?

MAIL. Oh, no! In the prime of life.

WIE. [*Smiling*] Oh, yes, he cannot be more than six or seven hundred years old.

MAIL. How, sir?

WIE. At least, Bayle says that he was born in the eleventh century.

MAIL. What Bayle says is false, sir. Certainly I must know better than such an obscure fellow.

WIE. Bayle an obscure fellow!

MAIL. In short, sir, whoever accuses a man of my appearance, to his face of an untruth, is—

WIE. Sir.

MAIL. Betrays at least that—

WIE. What, sir?

MAIL. That he is no Frenchman. This Abelard is a man betwixt forty and fifty, that I assure you on my honor! You understand me? On my honor! Therefore the thing is decided. When a gentleman asserts a thing upon his honor, there can no more be said about it. But if you should still doubt, I am ready in the next meadow to lay before you the most conclusive of all arguments. [*Makes a slight bow to Adelaide, looks contemptuously on Wieland and walks off humming an air R.H.*]

AD. Why, that was a formal challenge?

WIE. So it appeared.

AD. And why do you not follow?

WIE. Because I know by experience that he has lighter heels than I have.

AD. It would be droll enough though if you were to fight a duel to prove Abelard seven hundred years old.

WIE. Men have often cut one another's throats for causes of as little consequence.

AD. Yes. Or become martyrs.

WIE. Obstinacy is a passion as well as anger; and passion only wants to be put in motion, no matter by what.

AD. That is a confession you should by no means make to a lady.

WIE. Why not?

AD. Because, thereby, you make our sex suspicious of the love of yours.

Wie. Did I speak of love?

Ad. Is not love a passion?

Wie. Not true love. It is an interior and intimate propensity, interwoven with our nature, to be pleased with the good and the beautiful.

Ad. I doubt if my sex will relish this definition. We are too fond of exciting passion, and making you men do stupid actions. Oh, what a flattering picture is Reason crowned with a fool's cap and prostrate at the feet of Beauty!

Wie. A picture in crayons. The fleeting bauble of a day.

Ad. Girls are seldom connoisseurs.

Wie. And do not wish to be.

Ad. Calumny, sir.

Wie. I wish you would submit the point to argument.

Ad. We carry our arguments in our hearts, men in their heads.

Wie. The head and heart should visit.

Ad. Visits are tiresome.

Wie. Or marry.

Ad. Marriages are still more tiresome.

Wie. That is not your real opinion. I will lay a wager that before you are seventeen you will defend the marriage state with all the warmth of a youthful bride.

Ad. Before I am seventeen! Forbid it Heaven! for in that case I must marry tomorrow morning.

Wie. That depends only on yourself.

Ad. On me! That's droll enough! As if one could say, "Today will I give away my heart."

Wie. Why not? Even as well as one can say, "Today will I not shut my ear to the supplicant; today will I make glad the unfortunate."

Ad. My reasonable sir, you overrate the worth of a maiden's heart.

Wie. I speak only of yours.

Ad. And of that you know nothing.

Wie. I, not know your heart! Then must the sweet remembrance of my childhood have flown without trace from my mind. Oh, where are those days of joy, when your father still resided at his country seat and lived in neighborly friendship with mine! When oft times the sportive Adelaide sought the first strawberries to carry to her father or flowers to make garlands for her mother's birthday. O Adelaide! do I not know your heart?

Ad. I never knew before that you were a poet.

Wie. [Chagrined] O my heart! Be mute! The expression of thy feeling is taken for a fiction!

AD. I begin to be afraid of you. Enthusiasm is catching.

WIE. Enthusiasm—I have been used to hear the pure effusions of nature and love so called. Therefore did I shut up my heart, but I threw not the key into the sea of the great world; I preserved it sacred for the ideal mistress of my hopes and wishes. A maiden would I seek to whom the man without ostentation is more worth than the fop who titters sneeringly as he skips by the plain country gentleman because he cannot dance; and classes at the luxurious board, the silent man with the fool. Alas! I thought I had found her!

AD. [*With embarrassment and tenderness*] And did you deceive yourself?

WIE. [*With enthusiasm*] No! No! I deceived myself not! This kind embarrassment proves a traitor and shows me your inestimable mind. Yes, with extacy have I often observed that when mingling in the confused noise of the gay world, the serenity of your forehead has been clouded with displeasure and disgust and that you became witty when you dared not be cordial and sincere. Oh, fly these deplorable circles, which are walls against reason, and cardhouses when opposed to passion. Where those call one another friends who cheat each other of their time; where the rich man pities the unfortunate while he shuffles the cards, and before the third trick, has forgot him; where selfishness marries interest, fear begets servility, and familiarity with vice hides its deformity. Fly, Adelaide, from this infected atmosphere to the seats of rural delight where each noble feeling awakes and becomes active in well doing. We are cheerful without cards, and conversable without calumny. We dare not be ashamed to love the oppressed, or fear to call him loudly rogue whose actions deserve the appellation. I possess but a little piece of land which I can call mine, but if to the blessing which industry, fortune and my own heart have given me, Adelaide will still add love, there will be nothing wanting to my little paradise but to be walled around with towering rocks that it may be inaccessible to envy.—Are you silent?—Does the lively Adelaide cast down her eyes and disrobe her nosegay of its leaves?

AD. I think, Mr. Wieland, that it is a proof of my esteem for you that my levity at this moment abandons me.

WIE. Your esteem is my pride, but love alone can make me happy.

AD. Before I answer you, avow to me sincerely—What part has my figure in your love?

WIE. Indeed, lovely Adelaide, on that point I have never examined myself.

AD. Do it then now. It is of much consequence for me to know. Should I have been the object of your choice if I had been ugly or deformed?—I demand a sincere answer upon honor and honesty.

WIE. Be it so. I would love you even if you were ugly, but I dare not assert that I should have so ardently sought, or so quickly recognized, the beauties of your soul if it had been shrouded in an ugly cover.

AD. And if now, suddenly, the smallpox should disfigure my face? Or if I were not that which I appear?

WIE. I am willing to take the hazard.

AD. You shall hazard nothing. She who can deceive an honest man, deserves not an honest man's love. [*She takes his hand*] I—Mr. Wieland—I esteem you highly—perhaps something more—but—

WIE. No but!

AD. I must confess to you—

WIE. That your heart is promised? [*Trembling*]

AD. My heart is free.

WIE. Well then?

AD. I am—I appear—

WIE. Oh, you are what you appear!

AD. No!—No!— [*The musicians, behind, play a dance. Adelaide is uneasy and embarrassed*] They are beginning to dance again.—Shall we go to the company?

WIE. Without deigning me an answer?

AD. Yes, yes, I will answer you—soon—but not now—this dance is a favorite of mine—come—come, you shall dance it with me.

WIE. I cannot possibly dance now.

AD. Indeed—the music is so inviting—you will not?—Pardon me then, I must find a dancer. [*Exit hastily L.H.*]

WIE. [*Looking after her with astonishment*] Is it possible! God! Is it possible! The avowal of the most tender love is forgotten at the sound of a miserable dance. An honest man has she found, but she goes to seek a dancer! Now then farewell, all faith in innocence and nature! Go, Wieland! Hide thyself under thy rustic roof! Water thy cabbage garden, and frighten away each singing bird from thy borders, that his song may not remind thee of this accursed dance! [*Exit R.H.*]

ACT III.

Enter Captain Erlach L.H.

ERL. Much eating and drinking, much laughing, and no true joy. He is not always glad who laughs. One laughs at his own wit, and, if he happens to be rich or great, the whole company force themselves to join in chorus. Another laughs at a *double entendre* which he alone finds out to be such, and then looks round upon the ladies to amuse himself with their embarrassment. Here a talkative mother recounts the ingenious tricks of her children and forces the hearer to mingle yawns with his laughter. There a chapter in the scandalous chronicle is discussed, and the laughter of malice poisons the blossoms on the trees. When they go home, my Lord A. says to my Lady B., "It was a delicious party! How we all laughed!" No, that is not my way.— My friend's wife seems to be, still, the most reasonable of the whole bunch. If she knew how her husband consumes away in secret—but a little patience and she shall know it. When we shall have lived a few months under the same roof.—A few months?—How, Erlach?—Couldst thou swim so long in this strange element?—Why not? Flachsland is my friend, and Emmy is— Why dost hesitate, old boy?—Daughter, sister, friend—it is all one which she is to me! It is enough that I bear her a hearty good will; and as I once drew her forth from under the ruins, so—yes, yes—a good girl—there is but one thing about her which displeases me: she should not have grown eight years older in my absence. [*Enter Emmy L.H.U.E.*]

Em. [*After looking here and there as seeking some one, sees Erlach*] Ah! You here, sir?

Erl. Yes, I am here, dear child. Were you seeking me?

Em. No, I seek—It is absolutely necessary that I speak with somebody who has hidden himself, I believe—Heaven knows into which bush he has crept. Your pardon. [*Curtsies familiarly and exit R.H.*]

Erl. Your most obedient servant! Now that was not so handsomely done of her. She might have spared a few minutes, and a few words, if it had been only to tell me that the weather is fine, or the leaves on the trees, green. Hum! Whom seeks she?—Who is this somebody?—And what has she that is so absolutely necessary to tell him?—Somebody?—That may mean a woman—but I will lay a wager it is a man. Aye, aye, Miss Emmy, is it thus? —Perhaps a secret of the heart?—Well, what is that to me?—How does it concern me?—If I was really her father she would not have dared to put me off with a bare "somebody"—and I think *I* have deserved so much confidence, that she might have said in passing by, "This somebody is called so or so." But so it goes when girls grow eight years older. [*Enter Baroness L.H.*]

Bar:ss. Do you seek solitude, Captain?

Erl. It is hard to find it here, my lady.

Bar:ss. Is that praise or censure?

Erl. I never dispute about taste.

Bar:ss. I understand. But I pray you, do not take that for taste which with me is only habit, and not seldom a burthensome habit.

Erl. What prevents your shaking off the burthen?

Bar:ss. My husband will have it thus.

Erl. He will have it thus?

Bar:ss. If I am alone with him, immediately he becomes anxious, and asks twenty times in an hour if I am not weary, if I will not ride to this place or that, and knows no rest until I let him have the horses put to.

Erl. And goes he with you?

Bar:ss. Seldom. Unless forced by my earnest entreaties.

Erl. What makes he alone at home?

Bar:ss. God knows. [*Sportively*] Perhaps he makes gold. At least, at my return he always receives me as if he had found a treasure.

Erl. Hum. I am sorry for it.

Bar:ss. How?—What are you sorry for?

Erl. To hear that my honest friend has learned, since our separation, the art of dissimulation.

Bar:ss. Dissimulation! How so?

Erl. At his years men are seldom so transformed.

Bar:ss. Speak more plainly.

Erl. I had rather hold my peace. We are yet strangers.

Bar:ss. Strangers? When my husband gave me a right to his love, he gave me a right to your friendship. To please my husband is my inmost wish. Indeed the difference of our years is great, nor was it Love that conducted me to his arms, but invited thither by Esteem, Love overtook and made me his prize. We have played no romance with one another. No lightning has inflamed us, but the unclouded sun of matrimonial felicity has warmed us through by degrees. In full confidence of my feeling this warmth, speak. And if still, after this explanation, my presence embarrasses you, I will place myself behind these trees, you shall forget that I am near, and in your soliloquy you need not spare me.

Erl. Bravo! That is my way. Those who think in this fashion I esteem highly, and to those whom I esteem highly will I speak the truth.

Bar:ss. Well then, begin.

Erl. How can a lady of wit and feeling suffer so many coxcombs about her?

Bar:ss. Alas! Captain, if we should banish the coxcombs, our circles would become very narrow.

Erl. The narrower the better. Reason and Joy are a pair of guests who pass by without knocking when they see light in all the windows.

Bar:ss. But Folly serves Reason as a foil.

Erl. She needs none, and if your husband has persuaded you that this manner of living is according to his wish, he has deceived you.

Bar:ss. That would grieve me.

Erl. He thinks this complaisance due to your youth.

Bar:ss. Then he little knows me.

Erl. He fears that you will find out—

Bar:ss. What?

Erl. That he is jealous.

Bar:ss. Jealous? You jest.

Erl. You will not think so when I assure you, for example, that during the last night his eyes were never shut; that his reveries tormented him unceasingly even till the morning hour;—when I tell you that he is obliged to collect his thoughts and compose his looks when he hears your coach driving to the door—

Bar:ss. I am astonished!

Erl. "It gnaws on my life," cries he mournfully; "in vain do I strive to master it."

Bar:ss. My God! What hinders his mentioning it to me?

Erl. False shame, the destroying angel of confidence.

Bar:ss. Well! I have left, until now, our company to the caprice of accident; in future he shall choose them himself. He shall every where be my conductor. Even this day shall he make out a list of those persons whose conversation he values—

Erl. The list will be very small.

Bar:ss. Not at all. There are here excellent and scientific men—

Erl. Yes, but the more there are of them the harder it is, for a man who is no Croesus, to receive them with hospitality.

Bar:ss. What would you that I should infer from your words? Flachsland is rich.

Erl. He was rich.

Bar:ss. How?

Erl. Nay he may still be called a man of property. But if his riches melt away as they have done the last three years—

Bar:ss. Sir! You frighten me!

Erl. Where the expenditures so far exceed the receipts—

Bar:ss. Is it possible!

Erl. He may perhaps soon be compelled to make use of that property which his children inherit from their mother.

Bar:ss. My God! Why has he not told me this?

ERL. False shame. He has long wished to retire to his estate in the country.

BAR:ss. Willingly! Willingly! Even yet this evening!

ERL. But he feared that to your youthful mind, the uniformity of a country life—

BAR:ss. Oh! how it grieves me, that my husband has not held it worth his trouble to learn to know my heart; that a stranger has had more confidence in me, than the man of whose love I am proud; that I should impoverish his children and rob him of repose; that I should squander away what father's care and mother's love had gathered together! Why did he not prove me? What right has he to believe that a swarm of coxcombs can give me more pleasure, than domestic quiet and the society of a reasonable man? O Captain Erlach, you men often reproach us with our weakness; it is not weakness, it is flexibility of soul, and it only depends upon you to bend and attach it to the amiable and the good. But you think that the love of women accords itself not with truth. You demand from them health of soul yet poison them with flattery—But I complain and reason when I should act. Your hand, Captain; you shall hear from me, and avow that I have deserved your confidence. [*With emotion and exit L.H.*]

ERL. Right—That is my way. If she keeps her word, then will I dwell here. But if I dwell here, that girl must alter her behavior—she must not run away from me—must have confidence in me—I wish to know however if she has found her damned somebody. [*Enter Wieland L.H., very thoughtful*] Here comes another who has escaped the gabbling, and wishes to gain the use of his ears again. Welcome, Mr. Wieland, I wish you joy.

WIE. Oh what, sir?

ERL. Of solitude. There are excellent people, who imitate nightingales; if there is too much noise around, they remain silent. When in yonder crowd, you seemed to be out of your right place.

WIE. In this at least I resemble the nightingale, that I am only in my right place when I am in the country.

ERL. You compliment yourself.

WIE. If my inclination to a country life does me honor, it is an honor I must share with every peasant.

ERL. Would that diminish its worth?

WIE. With many it would.

ERL. If you speak of such fools as yon French coxcomb who infects the air of this place, you may be right.

WIE. Oh no! of better than him—the best perhaps. That Frenchman for example—I dare not presume to make myself his judge—but he pleases.

ERL. Whom?

WIE. He enchants.

ERL. Whom?

WIE. [*With a sigh*] And is perhaps beloved.

ERL. [*Anxiously*] By whom?

WIE. By a maiden who lacks nothing of being perfect, but the uncommon faculty of seeing men's hearts, that she might choose *that* where *she* would be all in all.

ERL. And who is this maiden? As to the gentleman to whom she would be all in all, I guess him.

WIE. You guess him?

ERL. Yes. Without "the uncommon faculty of seeing men's hearts." But who is the lady?

WIE. Methinks that had been easier for you to guess, when I said expressly that she lacks nothing of being perfect.

ERL. Your most obedient. [*Aside*] He certainly means Emmy. [*To him*] And do you think she loves the Frenchman?

WIE. I must almost fear it.

ERL. [*Half aside*] Hum!—Can he be the "somebody" whom she sought so industriously?

WIE. [*Hastily*] How, sir? She sought?

ERL. A "somebody"—the Devil fetch him—and with such haste that she had almost ran over me.

WIE. Indeed!

ERL. She had an absolute necessity for speaking with him.

WIE. I am sorry that she seeks him in vain; about an hour ago a couple of young gentlemen called for him to ride with them.

ERL. [*Half aside*] A damned idler;—such a maiden—that has no fault under Heaven—but being too old—too old—

WIE. How too old? She is sixteen.

ERL. So much the worse! So much the worse! [*Enter Emmy R.H.*]

EM. [*On seeing Wieland*] Ah! Have I found you at last?

WIE. [*Surprised*] Me, madam!

ERL. [*Surprised*] He?

EM. I have been seeking you this hour.

WIE. I took a walk on the meadow, not daring to think that I could be missed.

ERL. *He* was then the "somebody" whom you sought?

EM. Yes, sir, I have something of consequence to say to Mr. Wieland.

ERL. Probably something secret.

EM. Emmy has no secrets from her benefactor; but it concerns a friend.

Erl. [*Feelingly*] So, so. I understand. To intrude is not my way. I shall learn the secret soon enough when I am bidden to the marriage feast. [*Exit L.H.*]

Em. I have a message to you, Mr. Wieland.

Wie. If it is a message of ill, as I presume it is, the person who sends it has at least had the kindness to choose a tender messenger.

Em. I hope to be a messenger of peace.

Wie. Peace presupposes discord, and I know not—

Em. You have said to my friend that you loved her.

Wie. True, madam. I am a simple country gentleman—I forgot it for a moment and Adelaide has deeply humbled me—I shall never forget it again.

Em. Humbled? That is a hard word.

Wie. The thing was harder than the word. She who rewards an honest endeavor to please with ignominy—she who would wantonly drag to the dance a man in whose eyes the tears of love stood trembling—does she not show him contempt?

Em. Condemn not too hastily, my good Mr. Wieland, or you may repent your rashness at the feet of my friend. Do you make no allowance for the embarrassment of a poor girl? What would you say if Adelaide heartily loved you, but only avoided a *certain* avowal for fear of diminishing her worth in your eyes?

Wie. [*Smiling ironically*] You presuppose a case—

Em. I presuppose nothing. There are things, Mr. Wieland, which our sex think of vast consequence, but which, happily, are not always so in the eyes of yours.

Wie. Speak clearer.

Em. You must know then, that Adelaide's foolish behavior arose simply from this—she was ashamed—notwithstanding that she was convinced of the necessity of confessing to you that she has a small defect in her shape. When an infant her nurse let her fall on the stairs. Her habit-maker has the skill perfectly to conceal it; but in the eyes of her future spouse, she would not appear more charming than she is. Now you have the key to the riddle. False shame prevented her from telling you this, herself. Now you know all; you know what you have lost in personal perfection, and gained in beauty of the mind. Softly whispered my friend in my ear, "Emmy, I love him! but let him guess that."—I have exceeded my powers. The next moment will inform me if I must repent my precipitation.

Wie. [*In ecstasy*] Is it a dream? Adelaide! Noble Adelaide! Where is she? Where shall I find her?

Em. Dare I ask—with what intention?

WIE. *Can* you ask?—She is my beloved! my bride!

EM. I expected no less of you. Go. But where she is I know not. Love must direct you.

WIE. Adelaide! Adelaide! [*Exit L.H.*]

EM. Go, seek the most delicate and lovely of maidens; but if I know her heart, you will not find her soon. Now, probably, again impelled by false shame, has she crept to some corner as a hiding place, and there sits and listens to each approaching step, and her little heart beats high when she thinks, "Now Emmy is speaking with him."—[*Sighs*]—What was that? Do I catch myself sighing?—Yet sure I am no envy moves in my breast at the thought of my friend's good fortune. No, no! But one may dare to confess to oneself that to be beloved by a worthy man, is truly enviable. Erlach appeared displeased when he left us. He did not think it right that I wished to be left alone with Wieland. Why so?—[*After a pause*] Emmy! Emmy! betray to no one what you now think. [*She sinks in a reverie on the bank. Enter Madame Moreau R.H. Her dress is poor but neat. She stops several times and looks mournfully around; at length approaches Emmy unperceived and examines her from head to foot with a mixture of emotion and curiosity*]

M:M. Pardon me, miss—

EM. [*Starts*] Ah!—[*Recovered*] Who—madam—who do you wish to see?

M:M. Am I in the garden of Baron Flachsland?

EM. You are, madam.

M:M. Perhaps you are his daughter?

EM. I wish I could say "yes" to that question. Will you speak with the Baron, madam?

M:M. It is my wish, if it is possible.

EM. Go with me, madam, I will conduct you to him.

M:M. Is he alone?

EM. I believe so.

M:M. If he is not entirely alone, please to request that he would come down hither in the garden, for the sake of an old woman to whom mounting up stairs has become painful.

EM. I will instantly deliver your wish.

M:M. Has he a family?

EM. One son, in the army; and one daughter.

M:M. And you are not that daughter? That is a pity!

EM. You are very kind, madam. How shall I mention you to the Baron?

M:M. A poor old woman, nothing more. I hope I am in a house where that title will shut neither door or heart against me.

Em. By that I understand that you already know the Baron. He will be here instantly, madam, for to the summons of the poor and the old he is never tardy. [*Exit L.H.*]

M:M. Indeed?—Alas, good child, confidence in mankind is a plant which is so sparingly watered by philanthropy, that its constant fate is to wither and die for want of sufficient nourishment. Yes, formerly he was soft and good, but then, also, he was young. Youth is tender and kind, but age hardens all things. And what dare I to hope from my brother, when my only son—? Be still! Hold thy peace, poor mother! Think that thou hast dreamed it, and tell not thy feverish dreams. Will he not be ashamed of me? The rich find relations in every quarter of the globe, the poor are only allied to misery. It will be better not yet to disclose who I am, but observe his behavior first—perhaps I shall be more welcome as an object of benevolence than if I demanded assistance for a sister, which might then be given as a burthensome duty. A man hastens this way through the beech alley. Are those the features of my brother William?—I think—yes—O God! How my heart beats—betray not thyself!—If once more obliged to fly from this house, where, where shall I find a grave? [*Enter Baron L.H.2E.*]

Bar. My foster-daughter has told me that you wish to speak to me. Wherein can I serve you?

M:M. I am an emigrant, my lord. I once had house and home, husband and children; I have now—nothing. Yet am I no beggar, my lord. In my youth I learned many things, intended by my indulgent parents as accomplishments and sources of pleasure; these may now, perhaps, procure me a piece of bread in my old age. I can sew and wash, cook and bake—perhaps, my lord, you may want a housekeeper?

Bar. It gives me pain, madam, to answer you in the negative.

M:M. Perhaps you have small children, whom I can instruct in French and English.

Bar. I have only one daughter, at home, and she is already grown up.

M:M. O God! And must I leave this house, too, without consolation!

Bar. That shall you not, madam. I have friends to whom I will recommend you, and in the meanwhile you shall fill a room in my house and a place at my table.

M:M. May God reward you for it with a heart ever glad! Oh, my friend did not deceive me when she promised me an asylum here!

Bar. Your friend? Perhaps you have a recommendation to me.

M:M. I am a native of Lyons, and was acquainted for many years with an unfortunate German woman—Phillipine Moreau.

Bar. God!—My sister!—Does she live?

M:M. She is dead.

BAR. Dead! [*Tears rush in his eyes; he turns away, leans against a tree and weeps*]

M:M. [*Aside with uplifted eyes*] He loves me still! There is still somebody in the world that loves me!

BAR. [*Advancing and looking straight forward*] The first news of her for twenty years.—She is dead!

M:M. She died in misery.

BAR. Oh, why did she so totally forget that she had an only brother?

M:M. She did not; but she was silent through shame. Often has she said, "Shall I present myself before my brother's eyes in rags? Will he not reproach me with my fault?"

BAR. Did she so little know the heart of her William?

M:M. "Shall I," she said, "only see my father's house again, but to learn that my good parents left me behind, their curse as my inheritance?"

BAR. Both father and mother with their dying breath blessed her.

M:M. Blessed her!—Did they bless her?—Oh, why can I not whisper these tidings of peace in the ear of my friend?

BAR. Long, long have I hoped that she would one day think of her brother, whom, as a boy, she so heartily loved.

M:M. [*Hastily*] Yes, yes, that she did! [*Collecting herself*] She has often mentioned her love of her brother.

BAR. With these trees grew my hope to see her again. Look, madam, these two lindens were planted at one time by our hands, the one by me, the other by my sister. Time has entwined their boughs together but torn from me forever the heart of my sister.

M:M. [*Much moved*] No, no!

BAR. Yonder bower our good mother planted but one year before her death. "I shall not live to see these twigs give shade," said she, "but perhaps thou may'st one day sit here with thy sister, and think of me." [*He turns to go to the lindens*]

M:M. [*In vain restraining her tears*] I can no more!

BAR. [*Embracing one of the lindens*] I envy our ancestors their sweet superstition. Fain would I believe that the spirit of my sister resides in this beloved tree.

M:M. [*Sinking on her knees*] My brother William.

BAR. [*Hastening to her*] God! What was that?

M:M. [*On her knees, her arms extended*] William! My brother!

BAR. [*Rushing to her arms*] Phillipine, is it thee?

M:M. It is me, my brother, reject me not!

Bar. I, reject thee!—[*Pause*]

M:M. Help me, William, lead me under the lindens which we planted on the birthday of our mother. We then embraced each other by the little twigs we had planted, and our mother looked down on us and smiled! Let me now in their shade press thee again to my heart and again will our mother look down on us and smile.

Bar. [*Leads her to the bank under the trees, embraces her, then looks upward with tearful eyes*] Mother! Partake of our joy! This moment of delight hast thou obtained for us from God!

M:M. [*Leaning her head on his breast*] Here let me die!

Bar. Here, by my side shall you recall the long flown joys of your youth. Here, leaning on my arm, shall you visit each tree from which we formerly gathered fruit, each grassy place on which formerly we used to sit. Then will I lead you up to the paternal mansion, will show you the chamber where you dwelt as a maiden, will point to you, "There stands the brown table on which we used to draw, and there the cupboard in which we deposited—" [*Looks at Madame Moreau and perceives that she is almost fainting*] You do not hear me!—Sister! This paleness!—For God's sake! Help! Help! [*Enter Emmy R.H. and John L.H.*]

John. What's the matter?

Em. The poor old woman is sick!

Bar. Help! She is my sister!

Em. Your sister! [*Assisting her kindly, she recovers*]

John. What? My young Lady Phillipine?

Bar. Yes, good old man. Oft with me have you bewailed her loss. Rejoice! We have her again!

John. *Have* we her again? Now God be thanked! Yet I never should have believed that in the December of my life so precious a flower would have grown to me. My Lady Phillipine, do you remember old John?

M:M. [*Giving him her hand*] Good John, livest thou still?

John. Aye, why should I not! And your godchild, little Margery, lives still, though Heaven knows she's none of the smallest now.

Em. Dear madam, shall I conduct you to the house? You will be more comfortable there.

M:M. No, my dear. The fresh air, and the view of those objects which surround me, are sufficiently medicinal—my heart drinks largely of the cordial.

BAR. If our love is thus reviving, oh, why did you not sooner return to our arms?

M:M. Forgive me, my brother! Forgive me, my beloved parents! Often when I had gained courage to overcome my shame, Fate threw obstacles in my way which were insurmountable. From hence I fled with my husband to his native place, Lyons. His parents were violently irritated at the introduction of a wife, for they had other views for him, and in consequence turned us from their doors. We resolved to wait a more favorable change of our fates from the all-reconciling hand of Time and by the scanty aid of a friend we emigrated to America.

BAR. To America!

EM. To America? May I ask in what town you settled?

M:M. In Charlestown.

EM. Charlestown!—Heavens!—[*Anxiously, with mixed hope and fear*]

M:M. [*Not perceiving Emmy's emotion*] The industry of my husband procured us a scanty support, but we loved each other, and were content. Heaven tied our band of love still faster, by giving us two lovely children, a son and daughter—

EM. A daughter!

BAR. Where is she?

M:M. Ah, William, ask me not! Heaven has punished me for the sorrows which I caused to my parents. The war in which America preserved her liberty by the sword, reduced us to beggary. Eight years ago we returned to Europe. Only the mother of my husband remained alive. She forgave him. We enjoyed once more a moment of rest, until the terribly tempestuous revolution of France again wrecked our fortunes. My husband was a warm patriot, and fell a victim to anarchy and avarice. My son—a poor deluded youth—emigrated to Germany with some French libertines of rank under the monarchy—. Alas, too well have they succeeded in making him a selfish, foolish coxcomb; and in stifling within him the feelings of nature and duty. I confess with confusion that he was the first person that met me as I approached the gates of this town.

BAR. This town!

M:M. Yes, he is here, I have recognized him; I have not even the little consolation of daring to doubt. In the company of a crowd of wild young men he rode close by me. "My son!" cried I, and threw myself on my knees. He heard my voice, he cast back a hasty glance and I saw the blood rush in his cheeks and the bridle tremble in his hand. "What is that?" I heard one of his companions ask. I stretched out my arms, "I am his mother," sobbed

I. Alas! he was ashamed of his kneeling mother. "The good woman is mad," he cried, and applied the spur to his horse.

Bar. Poor sister!

M:M. The avenging arm of Providence is on me. When I saw from afar the house of my parents, the whole sense of my guilt rushed on me, and then, even then, the Almighty sent my son before me, to reward me like for like. I murmur not. He who abandons father and mother, let him remain in old age deserted and childless.

Bar. But your daughter?

M:M. She died a miserable death!

Em. [*Hastily*] She died? Where? When?

M:M. Must I also relate this woe? The English and Hessians stormed Charlestown—

Em. [*Wildly*] The Hessians!

Bar. Go on! go on! dear sister!

M:M. In one terrible night was the town plundered and set on fire in every part. The inhabitants fled, I with the crowd, leaning on the arm of my husband, who carried our little daughter. The boy ran by our side. Before we had got clear of the town a falling roof o'erwhelmed my husband—the same moment the affrighted multitude rushed through the narrow pass and hurried me senseless out of town. It was not until two days after that I found my husband—but my darling, my Emmy was lost!

Em. Emmy!—Oh, for the sake of Heaven!—[*Casts herself on her knees before M:M.*]

M:M. What means this?

Bar. [*With a tremulous voice*] Sister—this maiden is also called Emmy —this lovely maiden was after the storm of Charlestown dragged forth from the smoking ruins—

M:M. Brother!—

Bar. Hast thou no mark by which to recognize thy daughter?

M:M. None but the impression on my heart.

Bar. What was her age?

M:M. Eight years.

Bar. The mark on her clothes A.M.

M:M. [*Almost shrieking*] Amelia Moreau!

Bar. It is her!

Em. My mother! [*She sinks on her mother's bosom; Madame Moreau falls powerless in her brother's arms; John sobs and dries his eyes*] Curtain drops.

ACT IV.

Enter Captain Erlach L.H. hastily. He stops suddenly in the middle of the stage and seems to consider. After some moments of deep contemplation, he strikes his stick violently on the stage as if he would say, "Yes, it shall be so," and is hastening away R.H. Enter Baron R.H., meeting Erlach.

BAR. Whither? Whither?

ERL. Off.

BAR. What's the matter?

ERL. Nothing.

BAR. Your behavior is singular.

ERL. Accursed be the hour in which I entered this house!

BAR. Art thou dreaming?

ERL. How long is it since you saw a fool? Look here—here stands one.

BAR. What fancies have found their way to your brain? We have been seeking you this hour past.

ERL. Me?—Nobody seeks me. To be sure, if I was a "somebody"—

BAR. At length we saw you on the meadow, striding backwards and forwards and gesticulating violently with your arms—

ERL. That's nobody's business but my own.

BAR. I hastened to tell thee—

ERL. I know all already.

BAR. Impossible. The unexpected discovery—

ERL. Peace! I tell you, I know all. The maiden is a bride? Is not that it? The bride of Mr. Wieland—is it not so?

BAR. Know you *that* so soon? *I* have but just been made acquainted.

ERL. There! there we have it! It *is* so. Good bye. I'm off.

BAR. Good God, what do you mean? Whither would you go?

ERL. Do you think I will stay to serve the wedding guests for a laughing-stock?

BAR. Erlach! My friend! I never saw you thus before.

ERL. No, you did not. Hark ye, Flachsland—I am, for the first time in my life, a fool! But it was ever my favorite maxim "to be nothing by halves."—I am a *complete* fool.

BAR. How can this alliance trouble you?

ERL. Man! man! torment me not!—Ask me not!—Are your senses so bound up in darkness that I must spell it to you letter by letter? I, yes I, that have just been reading you a lecture on false shame, and you may now reproach me with laboring under the same disease. Hark ye—you shall hear it, although I pull the words out of my mouth with tongs—I—damn it—it will choke me yet—I—I am—I am in love. [*Claps his hand on the Baron's mouth*] And now hold your tongue!—Hold your tongue for Heaven's sake!

BAR. You!—*You* in love!—Ha, ha, ha!

ERL. There we have it. He laughs at me.

BAR. Indeed, I am truly sorry. If I had only known it sooner—

ERL. You would have persuaded the girl to have me? Good digestion to you.—She shall never know it! And if you let a word about it drop from your lips, I will blow your brains out and the next moment my own!

BAR. Who could ever have suspected such a thing of you! At your age men seldom take the smallpox.

ERL. Very well.

BAR. But now let me tell you—

ERL. I know enough! I will hear nothing! Do me the favor to send for post horses.

BAR. How? You will not in earnest—

ERL. I pray you go!—And hark ye—if you know anywhere of a bottomless pit where there are no women, tell me of it. [*Looks towards R.H.U.E.*] Aye! there we have it! There she comes, with her modest demeanor and cast down eyes—I suppose she will ask me for my blessing!

BAR. Who? [*Erlach without looking points behind him*] I see nobody but Emmy.

ERL. Certainly. Ah, brother! What a pity it is that that girl should have grown eight years older!

BAR. Is it of her you have been speaking?

ERL. Of whom else should I speak?

BAR. The bride of Wieland—

ERL. You need not repeat that—I know it by heart already.

BAR. Ha, ha, ha! that is excellent!—Dear Erlach, I leave you alone with her. Ha, ha, ha! [*Exit L.H.*]

ERL. And *he* laughs at me. So it goes. Let a man fall in love, and every misfortune under Heaven befalls him. He will leave me alone with her? What? Shall I speak to her? No! I will go my ways. Farewell, miss! and if you should ever lie buried up to the neck in ruins again, I'll be damned if— Erlach! Erlach! nothing in the world should make a man swear. She comes nigher. What is that to me? If I should go now, she would think that I ran away from her. No, no, miss, it is not so dangerous. We will seat ourselves here in the bower. Perhaps she is seeking her dear "somebody" again. [*Sits in the bower and appears to be making figures with his stick in the sand. Enter Emmy R.H.U.E. She approaches slowly to the lindens and looks at*

them with melancholy pleasure; at length she entwines her arms around one
of the trees and sinks on her knees]

EM. Here did I weep my first tears of joy! Father of the orphan! I thank
thee!

ERL. [*To himself, with his chin resting on the head of his cane*] Yes, yes.
Here it was that she found him.

EM. My warmest wishes are fulfilled.

ERL. Warm wishes! Very improper for a girl of sixteen.

EM. Happy futurity!

ERL. That is still a question.

EM. My misery is all forgot.

ERL. Yes, and Erlach in the bargain.

EM. [*Rises and comes forward*] I must seek the noble Erlach.

ERL. At last comes my turn.

EM. How he will rejoice!

ERL. I doubt that.

EM. [*Turns and sees Erlach*] Ah! Are you there, sir?

ERL. [*Very coldly and without changing position*] Yes. Here I am.

EM. [*Sportively*] You have played the eavesdropper.

ERL. That's not at all my way.

EM. Do you already know—?

ERL. Oh, yes—I know.

EM. Has the Baron told you that—?

ERL. Yes, yes, the Baron has told me.

EM. But you take no part in my joy.

ERL. Oh, yes. To be sure. Why not? I, I wish you joy.

EM. So cold?

ERL. I cannot play the hypocrite. That is not my way. And to tell you the
truth, I think I might have expected to have heard sooner of it.

EM. Sooner? How could that be?

ERL. Why did you send me away? One can easily conceive what passed
between you.

EM. I do not understand—

ERL. So the world goes. Friendship engraves its rights on the heart as I
form these letters in the sand—a breath of love and all is puffed away.

EM. Can my benefactor condemn *this* love?

ERL. Oh, no. What is it to me? I have no vote in your choice.

EM. In my choice?

ERL. You love him—he is a man of good sense—family—property—

EM. He?—Him? What does this mean? We misunderstand each other.

Erl. Oh, no. Not at all. The Baron has told me that the *thing* with Mr. Wieland is all settled.

Em. Oh, yes.

Erl. Well then?

Em. What is that to me?

Erl. What is it to you? What the Devil should it be to anybody else if it is not something to you?

Em. I have grown up with Adelaide, we love one another as sisters, and so far I rejoice in her good fortune.

Erl. Adelaide? What has Adelaide to do with it?

Em. She is the bride.

Erl. Would you make sport of me?

Em. Forbid it, Heaven!

Erl. You spoke with Mr. Wieland?

Em. In Adelaide's name.

Erl. And gave consent?

Em. For Adelaide.

Erl. No—Was it so indeed?—In earnest?—And the pious gratitude with which you sank to the earth beneath these lindens—could friendship alone produce such extacy? Maiden! maiden! blessed then is he who shares your love!

Em. How came you to think of that?

Erl. Very naturally—by my poor soul! I feel myself so taken by surprise, and yet so much the better for it!

Em. Dear sir, you speak to me in riddles.

Erl. May be so. One half word from you and I solve the riddle.

Em. Your coldness—your astonishment—your extacy—it is well that we were without witnesses.

Erl. Why?

Em. [*Sportively*] A third person might have done you the shame—to have supposed you were in love.

Erl. The shame? Yes—yes, it is indeed a shame at my time of life.

Em. Rather say with your principles.

Erl. No farther insult, I pray you.

Em. How should I dare—?

Erl. To be ashamed to abandon foolish principles is false shame. And— to make short of the matter—have you perceived nothing?

Em. Sir! What?—

Erl. *Nothing* at all?

Em. Nothing.

Erl. A damned affair has happened to me.

Em. To you, sir? What?

Erl. Guess.

Em. How *can* I?

Erl. Only try. It is harder for me to speak than you to guess.

Em. If I was vain—

Erl. Well?—Go on.

Em. I should be tempted to believe—

Erl. Well?—Go on.—What?

Em. I am afraid you will laugh.

Erl. The Devil fetch me if I am in a laughing humor. Now what would you be tempted to believe if you were vain?

Em. That—that—but you must pardon me.

Erl. Only be quick! Be quick and I pardon everything.

Em. That—you love me.

Erl. So! At last it's out!

Em. Now you may laugh at me.

Erl. Now—*you* may be vain, dear Emmy.—Do you understand me?

Em. *Only* vain? The love of my benefactor would make me more proud than vain.

Erl. And the *benefactor* would gain as little by your pride as by your vanity. Ever benefactor, benefactor. I pray you, let me hear no more of it. If you think you owe me anything, pay me, and let us balance the account.

Em. I?—A poor girl like me!

Erl. Yes, yes. Those who are unwilling to pay, pretend poverty. You are handsome, you are good, you have an excellent understanding and a feeling soul,—yet—poor! poor!

Em. For all I *am* or *have* I am indebted to you.

Erl. Words, words! That is not what we are talking about. I perceive well you *will* not understand me. I am too old for you—too plain—out with it.

Em. That sounds indeed almost—

Erl. Like a proposal of marriage; it is so. Now we understand one another.

Em. [*After a pause*] You make this day the most noteworthy of my life.

Erl. So!—Now what does that mean? Yes or no?

Em. I esteem you highly.

Erl. Nothing more?

EM. A maiden seldom avows more. Had you not interrupted me you would already have known that since some hours there is a third person who shares with you the most sacred claims upon my heart.

ERL. Shares?—That is not my way.

EM. And that you must apply to my mother.

ERL. Your mother?

EM. The sister of your friend, who fled to America with her husband and there lost, in one unfortunate night, house, home and child.

ERL. Lost? How?

EM. Amelia Moreau is the name of the lamented child whom a brave man drew forth from under the smoking ruins of Charlestown. Amelia Moreau as a child was delighted with your parti-colored soldier's dress, but since she has been able to think has been more delighted to praise the generosity of her savior. Many, perhaps, would have saved the weeping infant from death and afterwards left it to its fate. [*With increased fervor*] But the man who for eight years has divided his scanty pay with *me,* poor orphan,—oh, for that can I find no expression of praise! Praise and fame may be the rewards for heroic actions, actions for the performance of which, scarcely one moment of intoxication is necessary. The noblest deeds are not the most brilliant. A great sacrifice is easier made in one hour, than a thousand smaller ones in a space of eight years—

ERL. [*Who has shown great impatience*] Are you nearly done?

EM. Not yet, sir—[*With the tenderest emotion*] Not yet, my friend—benefactor—brother—

ERL. Brother?—I understand you.

EM. No, you do not understand me. If my heart was engaged I would confess it with a sigh. I would say, "Noble man, pity me that I cannot love you!"—But God be thanked, my heart is free. Esteem and goodwill, friendship and gratitude—yes! these feelings will melt together in *one* and that *one* will be *love.*

ERL. Maiden, is this thy real intention?

EM. With an Erlach I need not fear precipitation. Without figure or ornament—without false shame—if a heart full of innocence, a grateful confidence, and the endeavor to become worthy of you, are worthy of your acceptance, I am willing to become your wife.

ERL. Maiden, [*Seizing her hand*] maiden, what do you make of me? I could sink down on my knees before you—if I had not so often laughed at kneeling. Here stand I now—wishing to speak—and cannot—mute before a creature—that eight years ago was not higher than this rose bush. But short and good—that's my way. It is done! You are my wife. Let them laugh at me now. [*Talking rapidly whilst he puts her hand confidently under his arm*] Yes, we will buy us a little country place in an Alpine dale, where the friendly sun shall shine on our cot, where aromatic herbs shall breathe health around us, and wild roses artlessly blossom like thy cheeks. There will we join in the dances of the free-hearted shepherds—Huzza! Erlach and his lovely wife! [*Catches her up and whirls round with her in his arms*]

EM. Dear Erlach, my mother comes.

ERL. Who? Thy mother? I had almost forgot that story. Is it then so? Forgive me if I do not at present ask how it comes to pass. It appears to me as if I and Emmy were alone in the world! "As if the rest of mankind were nothing more to me."

EM. Let us ask her blessing.

ERL. Yes, yes, that we will. [*Throws his hat and stick away, takes Emmy in his arms and carries her to meet her mother. Enter Madame Moreau L.H.*]

ERL. Your blessing, mother.

EM. Dearest mother! This man is my savior, my benefactor, and if you consent, my husband.

M:M. Is this the man to whom I owe my life's last consolation?

ERL. Nothing! Nothing! It is all paid. We have just come to a settlement of accounts and there is a very large balance in her favor.

EM. He asks me as his wife.

M:M. God! So many joys in one day! My blessing is with thee; follow thy wishes.

ERL. Come then to me! We have your mother's blessing, and if upright and honest we pass through the world, who shall deny us God's blessing?

M:M. Does my brother know—?

ERL. How should he? I knew nothing about it myself ten minutes ago. Bravo! Flachsland *my* uncle—as such he may dare laugh at me and the nephew will say not a word. Come, dear Emmy, let us take courage. We will boldly look the scoffers in the face.

EM. What have we to be ashamed of?

ERL. I, that I was two and thirty years a fool; and you, that you held it worth while to convert such a fool from his folly. [*Puts her arm within his and is going L.H. Enter Adelaide and Wieland L.H. arm in arm meeting them*]

ERL. Who comes there?

AD. A friend!

ERL. The countersign?

AD. Love and Hymen!

ERL. Bravo! Everything pairs. That is just my way.

AD. How, Mr. Captain? That was formerly not at all *your* way.

ERL. Other times, other customs.

AD. Marrying is a very old custom, I take it; and truly you stand there with Emmy and look very like—ha, ha, ha!—very like a bridegroom!

ERL. Yes, yes, there it is. Lavater has forgotten to give us the bridegroom's physiognomy, but a *woman* knows it at first sight.

AD. Emmy! Emmy! Who would believe that the man who entwines his arm so fast about thee is only thy foster-father.

ERL. What foster-father? Damn foster-father! She is my bride. And now laugh, laugh, I am armed against your raillery.

WIE. Truly you are. If we laugh, 'tis a laugh of congratulating joy.

AD. Little cousin, you say not a word.

ERL. What should she say? She has said *yes* and that's enough.

WIE. Bravo, Captain! *Enough* indeed!

AD. Often *too much*. How, dear aunt? Have you said *yes* too? Give this sweet tempered creature to an animal that is always grumbling, fault-finding and making a noise—

ERL. Emmy? Thou seest into my heart.

EM. Dear Erlach, it beats for me.

AD. O dear! Alack, alas, and a welladay! My poor friend! She is lost!

ERL. Let her prattle.

AD. The Captain is a second Caesar, he comes, sees and conquers.

EM. Have I known him then, only this morning?

AD. But what knows he of you?

ERL. Bah! When the spark falls in a powder-cask, in a moment all is in the air.

AD. "Bah!" I did not know that men's hearts were powder-casks. However, we should make the best of past things, and since it has gone so far, let this solemn curtsy say—[*Begins a formal curtsy and stops short with great vivacity*] No—that's worth nothing. Come here, my dear, dear Emmy! [*Puts a hand on each side of her head and kisses her heartily*] Do you understand me?

WIE. [*Giving his hand to Erlach*] Captain, I am heartily glad—

ERL. [*Shakes his hand*] That's right! A hearty German shake of the hand. This is the language of honesty and Switzerland. Now, children, when shall we be married?

WIE. Tomorrow.

ERL. Why not today?

EM. In about four weeks.

AD. In about a year.

WIE. Who shall decide?

AD. My aunt.

M:M. Take care of thyself, child, I always take part with the weakest.

AD. That is we maidens.

ERL. By no means!

WIE. Certainly not, as brides.

M:M. Ask my brother, here he comes. [*Enter Baron L.H.*]

AD. [*Runs to meet him*] Dear papa! the south wind has brought a terrible influenza into your garden. Everything pairs. Everything will marry.

BAR. So much the better.

AD. Our platonic Captain here, our grumble-head, our woman-hater—

ERL. Fine titles of honor.

AD. For more than thirty years has he been making an ice-house of his head, and heaping cold sentences one on the top of the other; but those blue eyes have pierced through the thick walls and the ice is all melted away.

BAR. So much the better.

ERL. [*Sportingly*] Yes, dear uncle, if you have nothing against it—

BAR. My *dear nephew,* you have more luck than you deserve.

ERL. The Spaniards sail to America for gold. I have brought from thence a treasure, beyond all comparison more precious—the innocent heart of a native!

BAR. I see with satisfaction that the gaudy swarm have fluttered away.

AD. The Baroness pretended headache, and one after another glided off.

BAR. Where *is* your mother? She alone is wanting.

AD. She has shut herself up.

BAR. Shut up? From us? What does that mean?

ERL. My sword to a shoetie, nothing ill.

M:M. She received me with the most heartfelt love; she appeared transported at my unexpected return. "Heaven," cried she, "pays me my reward beforehand! But, dear sister," she continued, "leave me a little while, one hour must yet pass before I can make you truly welcome; in one hour more, I hope to be worthy of this joy."

BAR. Inexplicable!

ERL. What will you give me if I put you on the scent? [*Enter John L.H.*]

JOHN. Ah! Good my lord! Good my lord!

BAR. What ails thee?

JOHN. I have been half a century in your service—

BAR. Well?

JOHN. When I was but a little boy, they put me here to cut up the weeds, long before you was born, my lord. Truly, I was then so little and so stupid, that I remember me once, I rooted out all the parsley and left the weeds standing.

BAR. Good old man, that happens daily among the children of six foot high. But why weepest thou?

JOHN. Because I now stand in danger myself of being rooted out like a weed and thrown over the wall into the street; and—indeed, my lord, although I am no peach tree, yet am I no nettle in your garden.

BAR. Who injures thee?

JOHN. Truly as yet they have spared me; but when one tree after another is cut down the axe must hit me at last. Mounseer Rosat the friseur, Mister Beefsteak the coachman, Signor Macaroni the cook, and Master Manstmann the porter are all very civilly dismissed.

BAR. How?

ERL. Ah ha! Bravo!

JOHN. One after the other is called in, receives a half year's wages and must make up his bundle. At present the meddling French mamsell is in the room, and when she is dispatched then perhaps comes my turn. But consider, my lord, I am an old tree and can no longer bear transplanting. Besides, I have little sprouts around me—what shall become of them?

BAR. Be without fear. Thou hast carried me in thy arms, and hast helped me to climb for many a bird's nest. As long as I live shall no one disturb thy nest, old man.

JOHN. A thousand thanks. Indeed, my lord, it is no sparrow's nest, one need not cover the cherries with nets on account of it.

BAR. But I do not understand—

ERL. You soon shall understand it. Here comes your noble wife. Out, out of the way! There will be a matrimonial scene played here which requires no witnesses. Come, let us see if the musicians have received *their* passport too. I hope not, for I want to dance today—and I *will* dance, though I dance to my own singing. [*Gives his arm to Madame Moreau. Exeunt L.H.U.E. all but the Baron and John*]

JOHN. My old woman sits in the bleaching place and sprinkles the linen with her tears. I must go to her; I must say, "Weep no more, old woman! As long as we live will a cabbage-head grow for us in this garden." [*Exit R.H. The Baron remains in deep thought and seems not to notice that he is left alone. Enter Baroness L.H. in a simple domestic dress*]

BAR:ss. [*Approaches him without noise and lays her hand on his shoulder*] So deep in thought, dear husband?

BAR. Yes, but I thought on thee.

BAR:ss. Indeed! And looked so gloomy.

Bar. Your appearance drives away every wrinkle, but those of old age.

Bar:ss. Domestic content can smoothe even the wrinkles of age.

Bar. Then must *I* look like a youth.

Bar:ss. Your hand on your heart. You deceive me. [*Seriously*]

Bar. How?—Do you doubt my love?

Bar:ss. No. But more appertains to a happy marriage than love.

Bar. *More* than love?

Bar:ss. Love decks the spring of life, and marriage the summer; but harvest time must also come to provide for a happy winter. O my lord, he who through present joy forgets to sow the seeds of confidence, how shall he dare in harvest time hope to gather domestic happiness?

Bar. [*Smiling*] What means this poetry?

Bar:ss. Poetry?—Yes, call it so. Poetry is the handmaid of Truth and must decorate her mistress.

Bar. The naked truth would I hear from your mouth.

Bar:ss. Very gallant. While you are disposed to say handsome things to me, permit me to ask—how do you like me thus?

Bar. The simplicity and neatness of your dress makes you charming.

Bar:ss. [*Smiling*] Handsomer than usual?

Bar. Far more handsome in my eyes.

Bar:ss. Why then do you every moment load me with costly clothing? Why do you force me to enter into every foolish fashion?

Bar. You go into company—

Bar:ss. But *must* I go into company?

Bar. For your own satisfaction—

Bar:ss. And who tells you, my lord, that I anywhere find more satisfaction than with you? I know that this simple dress becomes me better than the glitter of courts—I have done it only to please *you,* my lord. Discreet, unassuming—[*Roguishly*] in the folds of this simple dress, the dust of jealousy cannot lodge.

Bar. Jealousy?—I hope you do not hold me capable of jealousy?

Bar:ss. Why not, if you love me—?

Bar. But my confidence—

Bar:ss. Ah, there, there is the sticking place. O dear my lord! You feign confidence in me, and in secret torment yourself with the most frightful chimeras. Was I not right in saying that love alone suffices not to the happiness of marriage?

Bar. [*Embarrassed*] I—you do me injustice—

Bar:ss. No, no, my lord! I know all and spare you a confession. A painful *place* must be healed if possible without touching it. Let me however add, you yourself have thrust me forth into the gay world; you yourself have set open your doors to fools and coxcombs. You were afraid that your young wife would be weary of your house and your conversation. That was false modesty. And when I conformed to your wishes, then did strange dreams torment you in secret and you were ashamed of them. That was false shame. Man and wife should not even conceal from each other their dreams. A sign would have been enough for me. I should perhaps have laughed a little at you; but how willingly should I have sacrificed those worthless trifles to your peace! Oh, how many marriage ties have been sundered because the bands of confidence were not twined around *both* hearts! How many discordant flames are past extinguishing, because husband or wife kept the first spark secret!

BAR. [*Pressing her in his arms*] Noble, excellent wife!—forgive me!

BAR:ss. I do forgive thee—but only on one condition—that you will make it your pleasure, from this time, to take no step without *me*. When you write, I must sit with my knitting work near you; and when you have finished—we need not be sundered.

BAR. Thou rewardest instead of punishing me!

BAR:ss. Oh, but I have thought of a punishment for you. You wish to be in town; now I had rather be in the country. In three years, we have only been once on our estate—that is a crying sin! And for your punishment, you shall pass the whole summer with me there.

BAR. Caroline! That is too much!

BAR:ss. I cannot help you. And what is more, when there, you must content yourself with common fare, for I have dismissed our privileged poison-mixer, the cook.

BAR. I hear that you have undertaken a great alteration in the house.

BAR:ss. A formal revolution of state.

BAR. Your convenience will lose thereby.

BAR:ss. And my contentment thereby win. Husband! husband! must I also learn from a stranger, that the luxury which you daily recommended to me, was bought at the cost of your repose? That I robbed your children to pay for the means of chasing away a chimerical *ennui*?

BAR. Has Erlach then—

BAR:ss. Praised be Heaven that sent him to my salvation! Without *him* I should have continued to stagger on with the unsteady pace of intoxication, and have opened my eyes to the precipice too late. Unkind husband! And all owing to your want of confidence. You held women incapable of esteeming the worth of an honest man, unless, like the subjects of an eastern despot they always pay their court with full hands. Learn to know us better. A wife is prouder of a good husband, than of the most sparkling brilliants that ever blazed in her ears; she would rather, unnoticed, carry on foot the esteem of her husband, than without it glitter in a phaeton to catch the admiration of the crowd.

Bar. [*Throws himself at her feet*] Caroline!

Bar:ss. [*Smiling*] Dear my lord, for the first time I must remind you that —you are forty. Kneeling does not become you.

Bar. I have not known your worth! Forgive me!

Bar:ss. [*Raises and embraces him*] It is past. Now for a country life, and in a few years my prodigality will be forgot. Oh, how many a household goes to the ground, because the husband is ashamed to discover to his wife the true situation of his circumstances. My experience of today has so fully convinced me of this melancholy truth, that if I now stood before a numerous assembly, I would stretch out my arms to them and full of the spirit of philanthropy cry out to every father of a family, "Confide in thy wife! Thou now, perhaps, standest on the brink of a precipice; confidence in her may save thee! Banish *false shame,* that monstrous offspring of bragging and vanity! Confide in thy wife, thy friend, and thou wilt find consolation for the past, counsel and aid for the future!"

Bar. Wife! What a spirit of wisdom speaks from thy lips!

Bar:ss. I were indeed an ordinary wife, if love and duty could not inspire me.

Bar. I could be ashamed that a woman of five and twenty should teach *me* this lesson—but that would again be *false shame,* a vice which I banish for ever from my heart! From this day, like unto God, shalt thou see every secret of my heart; even such as would fain shun the light will I whisper in thy ear. If a weakness would hide itself, the remembrance of this hour shall drag it forth—that thou mayest kindly smile and pardon it.

Bar:ss. I thank thee, Heaven! It has succeeded! My husband is again mine!

Bar. Thine for ever! But, dear Caroline, do not think that my circumstances are so deranged, that there is a necessity for you to bury your youth in the country. I am still rich.

Bar:ss. Bury? To enjoy oneself and nature, men call burying. Well, be it so, and the nightingales shall sing my funeral dirge.

Bar. You are not used to solitude.

Bar:ss. For the sake of her husband, a wife can adopt a new mode of living with the same ease that she adopts a new fashion. A few years ago I thought no hat became me but a large one, and hats could never be large enough. Now, I find this fashion abominable, and can only be pleased with a hat that is small. So will it be with this. Four weeks in the country and the town life will appear like a great hat and I shall wonder how I could ever endure it.

BAR. Well then if you are in earnest—?

BAR:SS. Here is my hand on it.

BAR. I grasp it with extacy!

BAR:SS. Economy be our joy.

BAR. And repose in the bosom of my family.

BAR:SS. In the arms of love—

BAR. Seasoned by friendship—

BAR:SS. Embellished by nature—

BAR. Nearly lost through false shame—

BAR:SS. Through confidence regained—

BAR. [*Clasping her in his arms*] Never to be lost again!

BAR:SS. Never! [*Enter Erlach L.H.*]

ERL. [*Speaks entering, very angry*] Miserable, vile rascal! Whoever breaks his neck will deserve well from me!

BAR. What's the matter, brother?

ERL. I could hardly keep my cane from dancing about his ears.

BAR. Of whom do you speak?

ERL. Of the dearly beloved Vicomte de Maillac, my fine brother-in-law.

BAR. [*Astonished*] Thy brother-in-law!

ERL. Yes, the scoundrel has the honor of being Emmy's brother, and is ashamed of his poor mother. Even now skipped he into the garden. As soon as Madame Moreau perceived him, she exclaimed, "My son!" with a voice that would have melted a flint. The idle rascal started and seemed frightened; but his beloved shamelessness did not leave him in the lurch. "The lady is mistaken," snuffled he through the nose. We were all astonished, and every one explained the story to him in his own fashion. Emmy called him brother —and I, rascal! His mother, meanwhile, stood with trembling and uplifted hands, and seemed only to expect the signal for rushing into his arms.

BAR:SS. Unfortunate mother!

ERL. "Indeed it was always my wish," lisped out the damned monkey, "to be allied to the family of Flachsland, but if this is the only mode which they leave to my choice—" And then shrugged his shoulders, twisted himself like an eel in a mud-pond, and darted out of the gate. "Mister," called I after him, "of all the kinds of false shame that is the most shameful which makes a man ashamed of his own poor parents, because he has not courage to defy the miserable railleries of fools."

BAR. My poor sister! Where is she?

Erl. The maidens are striving to dry her tears. She comes hither. Behold how suddenly the grief of a mother bleaches a woman's cheeks. [*Enter Madame Moreau, Wieland, Adelaide and Emmy L.H.*]

Bar. [*Meeting Madame Moreau affectionately*] Good sister!

M:M. I pray you, brother, speak not of him; let no one speak of him more! You could only condemn him, and his mother could say nothing in his defense. Indeed it is far gone, when a mother's love must be mute!

Em. [*Caressingly*] You have still two children.

M:M. The lost is always the most loved.

Bar. Is there then no day without clouds?

M:M. Pardon me—I will not murmur. God has given me so much to-day! Alas! what was I but a few hours ago! Come to my arms, dear children. [*Takes Erlach's hand and leans upon Emmy*]

Erl. My hand, mother—I will make you forget your son.

Bar:ss. What! Do I see our woman-hater converted?

Ad. Sudden conversions are not the surest.

Erl. Miss Wisdom, learn from me, that love makes exceptions to all general rules.

Ad. But when a man has so often sworn eternal hatred to all women—

Wie. To women, but not angels.

Erl. Right, Mr. Country Cousin!

Ad. [*To Wieland*] Sir, it stands written, you shall only have eyes for me. Take example by my father. He has been married these three years, and see how his eyes are rivetted to my mother.

Bar. Seek you to resemble her. She has made me today the happiest man in existence!

Wie. I deny it!

Ad. Bravo! I give you credit for that. What says Captain Benedict?

Erl. I will prove it false—I swear it and kiss the book. [*Kisses Emmy's hand*]

Bar. Erlach, my friend, we go to the country!

Erl. Amen!

Bar:ss. Thank him, my lord.

Erl. Hush! Do not betray me.

Bar. A friend thanks not with words.

Erl. Come, boys and girls, let us be merry! Here is an honest little flock together that no angel dare be ashamed to mingle with. You have had many a drinking song today at the table; now to please me join in a song of joy. [*Goes to side scene L.H.U.E.*] Gentlemen, please to play "Joy, Brightest Spark from Heaven!" [*The music behind the scenes plays. The Baron takes*

the center of the stage, his wife leaning on his right, his sister on his left arm.
To this group Erlach and Emmy link themselves on the left side, Wieland
and Adelaide on the right, and standing arm in arm, sing]

ERLACH.

Joy, brightest spark from Heaven,
Daughter of Elysium, come!
Vice has fled our blissful garden,
Virtue here has found her home.

BARON.

Let him who in the game of life
Hath gained the prize like me—
A friend—a true and loving wife—
Join in our jubilee.

CHORUS.

Joy, brightest spark from Heaven,
Daughter of Elysium, come!
Vice has fled our blissful garden,
Virtue here has found her home.

CURTAIN

THIRTY YEARS;
Or, THE GAMBLER'S FATE

CAST OF CHARACTERS

FIRST DAY

Mr. St. Germain

George, *twenty-five years of age*

Warner, *twenty-six years of age*

Dermont, *forty-five years of age*

Rodolph Dericourt, *twenty-two years of age*

A Magistrate

An Officer

Valentine, *thirty years of age*

Servant at the Gaming House

Banker

Amelia, *sixteen years of age*

Louisa, *thirty-five years of age*

Servants, Gamblers, etc., etc.

THE ACTION OF THE FIRST DAY PASSES IN 1790.

SECOND DAY

George, *forty years of age*

Warner, *forty-one years of age*

Dermont, *sixty years of age*

Rodolph, *thirty-seven years of age*

Valentine, *forty-five years of age*

Amelia, *thirty-one years of age*

Louisa, *fifty years of age*

BOY, COMPANY, SOLDIERS, SERVANTS, ETC.

TIME—1805 SCENE—Paris

THIRD DAY[1]

GEORGE, *fifty-five years of age*

WARNER, *fifty-six years of age*

ALBERT, *twenty-one to twenty-two years of age*

BIRMAN

A TRAVELLER, *thirty to forty years of age*

AMELIA, *forty-six years of age*

MRS. BIRMAN

GEORGETTE, *eight to ten years of age*

SERVANTS, PEASANTS, VILLAGERS AND SOLDIERS

FIFTEEN YEARS HAVE PASSED BETWEEN THIS DAY AND THE PRECEDING.

THE ACTION TAKES PLACE IN BAVARIA ON THE ROAD TO MUNICH.

---

[1] At this point a few pages are missing from Dunlap's manuscript. Consequently the passage from the beginning of the Third Day to the point marked by note 2, p. 92, is a literal translation made by the editor from the French text.

FIRST DAY

SCENE 1: *Saloons in a gambling house, illuminated. Time, midnight. At the bottom of the stage a table surrounded by gamblers, who are in continual motion.*

BANKER. Play on, gentlemen. [*Warner advances*]

WARN. Twenty thousand francs and two hundred *louis d'ors!* Bravo! [*He displays the money*] Success to the gaming table! Two hours ago I was a beggar. But I leave the table too soon. Fortune is with me—I must—[*Enter Rodolph R.H.; speaks entering*]

ROD. Heaven is just! I have deserved my punishment! Ruined! Ruined!

WARN. So, so! My friend Rodolph has lost. What's the matter? You don't seem pleased with Dame Fortune.

ROD. You mistake, sir. I have reason to rejoice that I am cured of the worst of diseases—the love of play!

WARN. The usual tone of a losing gamester.

ROD. It was you, sir, who enticed me to this accursed place. I have seen and experienced all its abominations. I have lost twenty thousand francs, one-third of the fortune acquired by my father in a life of honorable industry. But I rejoice! I have had the film removed from my eyes. I know the secrets of this detestable place and I know—you.

WARN. My good fellow, be more philosophical—I will demonstrate to you—. But here comes one with whom I must make you acquainted.

ROD. George St. Germain! Not a word—do not mention my name in this house. [*Retires. Enter George L.H. hurried and wiping his forehead*]

GEO. At last I am here! Warner—the hour?

WARN. Midnight.

GEO. Cursed chance! I reckoned upon this night to retrieve my fortune! You know that I have lost thirty thousand francs, but you did not know that the money had been entrusted to me by my father to purchase the diamonds for my intended bride. You may therefore conceive that I must have money, cost what it would. And I have been in the pursuit—Old Pinch the broker had gone to his country seat—I followed—but here I am!

WARN. Why did you not apply to me? I have been in luck!

GEO. How could I know that? I have succeeded—I got jewels from the infernal usurer, which I have, like Jupiter, metamorphosed into a shower of gold. [*Shows louis d'ors*]

WARN. It is a shower which will gain you all your wishes.

GEO. Shall I pursue the same mode, as last night? By the bye, it cost me a thousand *louis d'ors*.

WARN. I have thought better of it. This way—follow my instructions and you shall break the bank. [*They retire up*]

ROD. Unfortunate young man! The fiend has full power over him!

GEO. Thank you, best of friends! Fortune, give me one-half hour! And I am the happiest of men, of lovers and of husbands! [*Exit*]

WARN. Success attend you. [*Comes forward L.H.*] He wants diamonds for his bride—I saw a superb set in the hands of Madam Sarabec, left doubtless as security for a supply to one of the pigeons of the house. [*Goes to a table and writes*]

ROD. What plot is he now maturing?

WARN. [*Folding a billet*] Waiter! [*Waiter enters L.H.*] Instantly take this to Madam Sarabec above stairs.

WAIT. I know, sir. [*Exit L.H.*]

WARN. Yes, you know. Ah, my friend Rodolph, you should have become acquainted with George St. Germain; he is the finest fellow in Paris and will soon be the richest.

ROD. How so?

WARN. He is on the brink of marriage with a charming girl with an immense fortune.

ROD. You are acquainted with the family.

WARN. I made George what he is—I brought him out.

ROD. I understand. But it is said that his father, M^r. St. Germain, is a man of strict principles and manners.

WARN. He is like all old grumblers. But thanks to my address, the old fellow, who is too infirm to leave his armchair, believes us to be two young saints. In the mean time George draws freely on futurity and I negotiate his bills, knowing that tomorrow we touch the bride's fortune.

ROD. And she is in the secret?

WARN. No, no! Left an orphan at the age of ten, she has been brought up in the family of M^r. St. Germain. She has an uncle, whom they expect to the wedding—he has just returned from the Indies or Mexico or somewhere or other. He has given his consent and all is ready for tomorrow morning. But the calm of wedlock will soon be changed to a storm. George is full of fire

and cannot bear restraint, and the innocent Amelia is all softness and senti-
mentality—they can't agree.

Rod. Do you fear this?

Warn. Fear it? Ha! ha! ha! If the wife is unhappy a friend must console
her.

Rod. Wretch!

Warn. But here am I talking while George is pushing his fortune for the
recovery of his bride's diamonds. I must watch over him.—If you play tonight
I will put you in a way that can't fail. I will see you again. [*Exit L.H.*]

Rod. Into what an abyss is St. Germain rushing and he sees it not! Why
do I stay in this place? [*Is going L.H.; returns*] A stranger—I blush to be
seen here. As I live it is M^r. Dermont of Marseilles, a correspondent of my
father's. He, in such a place! I must avoid him and observe George St. Germain. [*Exit L.H. Enter Dermont, his hat in his hand*]

Der. This is the first time in my life that I have seen the interior of a
gambling house.

Wait. [*Advancing from within*] Your hat, sir.

Der. Thank you, my friend, I had rather keep it.

Wait. It is not the custom of the house, sir.

Der. Well, well. [*Gives it*]

Wait. [*Gives in return a number*] Enquire for No. 113. [*Retires. A confused noise of many voices at the table. "Stop, gentlemen!" "The game is
done!" "Silence!" "It is false!" "Give back the money!" "That's the man!"
"Turn him out!" They drive out a gambler.*]

Banker. Play on, gentlemen, play on.

Der. And such is the place to which George St. Germain, the only son of
my best friend, the future husband of my beloved niece, comes nightly, to
sacrifice to the Demon of Gaming peace, fortune, and honor! I cannot yet
believe it; I have taken this mode of assuring myself and of witnessing—but
how shall I distinguish him among so many? It is now ten years since I saw
him—then a boy. I am ashamed to address any one. I breathe with difficulty
this impure atmosphere. [*Sits down. Warner advances from among the
gamblers; observes Dermont. L.H.U.E.*]

Warn. A provincial! A novice! [*Down on R.H.*]

Der. I must overcome my repugnance. [*Rises*]

Warn. Your servant, sir. [*Bowing*]

Der. Sir, yours.

Warn. You appear heated, sir—the air of these saloons is oppressive.
Waiter! Refreshments—quick! [*Enter Waiter L.H.1E. with refreshments*]

Der. You are too good, sir.

WARN. Permit me to help you—

DER. Nothing. This fellow is too civil. [*Waiter retires L.H.1E.*]

WARN. You appear to be a stranger here, sir.

DER. I am indeed.

WARN. Probably you do not know any one here.

DER. Not yet.

WARN. You will put yourself in the way of fortune?

DER. That is not exactly my intention.

WARN. You are right, sir. It is only by aid of an experienced friend that a stranger can prevent the having his heels tripped up. Here are fellows who can smell a *louis d'or* though ever so snug in the corner of your pocket. If you wish to try your fortune, however, I can put you in the way to do it without risk. My experience is at your service.

DER. Indeed!

WARN. Upon my honor. I take an *interest* in you, sir. What game do you prefer? I advise "Thirty and Forty"—the chances—

DER. [*Sternly*] Hold, sir! I did not come hither to take lessons in the infamous trade of a gamester. I equally despise—[*He is interrupted by a loud and confused noise R.H. Enter George. He breaks from them and advances; Rodolph with him*]

GEO. By Heaven, I'll tear these instruments of Hell to pieces!

ROD. George!—M^r. St. Germain!

DER. Yes! It is George St. Germain! [*The play ceases at the bottom of the stage. The gamblers are forward and the doors are closed*]

WARN. What's the matter? False dice?

GEO. I have lost all!

WARN. That's bad—but it is no reason—

GEO. All! I tell you all! All the money I brought with me—the twenty thousand you lent me—and sixty thousand more on credit! All! All! Why do not the powers of Hell crush to atoms these walls and their infernal inmates? May these infernal instruments be swallowed in an abyss of fire!

DER. Horrible madness!

WARN. Come, come! I thought you too much of a man to be overcome thus! What! Play the madman for the loss of a hundred thousand francs? I thought better of you.

GEO. Damn the money, sir! It is the infernal run of ill-luck that vexes me. Did any one before lose twelve times on the red? I divided my funds. I made twelve heaps of gold. One, two,—up to ten. Loss—loss—loss! I was astonished—but firm and cool. I played again on the red—again came up black—infernal black! I shuddered—my fingers left their marks in blood on my breast, but my face was unmoved. With a hand of ice and a smile on my lips I staked the twelfth heap—the last! It covered the table—every eye devoured it—the wheel turned—my blood stopt—it was done—Fate had spoken —all my hopes were blasted—the horrible *black* struck my eyes and my brain like thunder and seemed like annihilation!

ROD. Receive the lesson as a voice from Heaven and renounce the accursed practice for ever!

GEO. Who asks your advice, sir? What! Shall I give up the hopes of victory because I have received one blow? No! I will conquer Fortune! If I had staked on the black I should now have been master of a million!

WARN. Aye! Think of that! If you had—

GEO. Silence! If I had not followed your advice I should not have been ruined.

WARN. Did I advise you to play like a madman? Have you not lost my money?

GEO. Your money! You have my note, sir.

WARN. Fie, fie! Tomorrow you will be rich. I am still your friend.

DER. Tomorrow. [*The gamblers retire by different ways*]

GEO. Tomorrow my marriage will be broken off.

WARN. What? For want of a set of diamonds? If that is all—I can procure them for you.

GEO. You?

WARN. I.

GEO. When?

WARN. Now.

GEO. Where?

WARN. Here.

GEO. You, Warner? My friend! I will give ten—twenty times their value for them. But where will you find this treasure?

WARN. On the floor above, a discreet dame carries on a traffic very convenient for unfortunate gamesters. Many a precious article finds its way into her hands. I am in credit with her; and by chance I saw today a most magnificent set of diamonds in her possession.

DER. The scoundrels!

GEO. Let us fly, my dear Warner! You are indeed my friend.

ROD. M^r. St. Germain! [*Following him*]

GEO. I don't know you, sir—Come, my dear Warner! All will be well. [*Exeunt L.H.*]

DER. I am thunderstruck! This is the man who was today to receive the hand of my dear Amelia. Thank Heaven I have come in time. [*Going L.H.*]

Rod. [*Returning L.H.*]   M^r. Dermont—you do not know me or you cannot believe that the son of your friend could be found here. I would have avoided your sight but that accidentally I have overheard that which is of moment for you to know.

Der. I thank you for your good intentions—I have heard and seen enough. Let us fly this infamous place before you communicate anything with an honorable purpose. This way—What is this? [*Going L.H. Drum L.H. Enter officer and guards of the Maréchausseé meeting them and stopping them. Soldiers guard the doors. Other soldiers bring in gamesters*]

Off. Let no one out who is not known.

Der. You will not prevent—

Off. I must execute my orders. Show your papers.

Der. Shall I be forced to dishonor myself by declaring my name in such a place?

Off. You should not have come to such a place. Diamonds of great value have been stolen from a neighboring house. It is suspected that they have been brought hither.

Der. And you dare to suppose—

Rod. Hold. My name is Rodolph Dericourt and I will answer for this gentleman.

Der. Thank you, generous youth.

Off. I must know the gentleman's name.

Rod. I answer for him.

Off. His name?

Der. Dermont. I am a merchant of Marseilles and arrived in Paris this evening. Is that sufficient?

Off. Yes, sir, when it is so proved. In the mean time I must conduct you before a magistrate.

Der. Just Heaven!

Off. [*Receiving a paper from a soldier*]   Four persons arrested. Sir, you also must follow me.

Der. Poor Amelia! Who shall inform you in time to prevent your misery?

Rod. What, sir? You are—?

Der. Her only relative! I seek to save her!

Rod. Entrust me with your orders—I will hasten—

Der. Fly to my hotel—take this. [*Gives a paper*] I shall owe you more than life. [*Exeunt L.H.*]

SCENE 2: *A saloon open to a garden. Chairs, particularly a chair for M*ʳ. *St. Germain. Ten o'clock in the morning. Two female attendants bring in a veil, gloves, flowers, etc. Enter Louisa discovered.*

Lou. Very well! Place them there. Ah, Valentine, how does Mʳ. St. Germain? [*Enter Valentine from door R.H.*]

VAL. No better. The doctor has just left him and appears very uneasy. He wishes to speak to his son, and this is the third time I have been sent to seek him. His father is very impatient.

Lou. Ah, Valentine, Mʳ. George makes more than one uneasy in this house. But it is too late now to examine into his conduct—in a few hours they will be married.

VAL. Madam Louisa—have you discovered—?

Lou. I know that he was out all last night.

VAL. Oh! if my old master knew it—Does Miss Amelia know how often he passes the night from home?

Lou. No. Yet I have found her repeatedly in tears. She begins to partake of my suspicions especially of that Warner who rules Mʳ. George in all things. But I dare not speak the word gamester to her.

VAL. It is a word would kill my old master if applied to his son.

Lou. Hush! It is Miss Amelia. Here she comes. [*Exit Valentine by the garden center. Enter Amelia L.H. Music*]

AME. Ah, Louisa! I have escaped from the noise, heat and compliments of the company.

Lou. Dear madam, I can sympathize in your anxieties—your fears.

AME. Fears, Louisa! Does it not appear to you, my friend, my instructress, that my wedding-day is fraught with omens of ill? My uncle, Mʳ. Dermont, the only relative I have, has not arrived at the time he appointed. He abandons me! And I hear whispers—though no one tells me that the life of Mʳ. St. Germain is almost despaired of. What a moment for festivity and joy! And *that* Warner is to be present at the ceremony. I cannot express the feelings which the bold looks of that man cause in me—and yet my dear George seems to love him more than all the world.

Lou. Where is Mʳ. George?

AME. I have scarcely seen him this morning.

Lou. It is time you attended to your toilette.

AME. Sure—yes—it is Mʳ. St. Germain! He is better. Heaven be praised. [*Enter Mr. St. Germain from his chamber. Music. Amelia and Louisa run and aid him, instead of the servants, to his chair*]

Sт. Ger. Where is my son? I have enquired for him several times this morning and now—

Ame. He is coming, sir. Run, Louisa. [*Enter George from garden, center down on R.H.*]

Lou. Here he is.

Geo. [*Approaching*] Warner not yet here! I fear he has not obtained the diamonds! I wait upon you, sir. Amelia, your presence is required in the saloon.

Sт. Ger. Stop, Amelia. Let me enjoy the presence of my beloved daughter. I cannot conduct her to the altar—that is a subject of regret to me. But how is this? My son—Amelia is not yet decorated to my mind. Have you forgotten?

Geo. The multiplicity of preparation—Warner not yet come—nothing is ready yet—we want time—. Ha, there he is—[*Enter Warner center*] The diamonds—

Warn. I have them. [*Advancing*] Lovely Amelia—and you, venerable sir, excuse my arriving so late. [*Takes the casket from his pocket*] I thus perform my promise to my friend. [*Gives it to George*]

Geo. Dear Amelia, deign to accept these poor tokens of my love.

Ame. What! These are indeed magnificent.

Warn. [*Aside*] They have cost us dear.

Ame. See, my father!

Warn. [*To George*] I have promised twenty thousand francs to be paid this evening on account.

Geo. The money shall be ready.

Ame. Dear George, I go to adorn myself with these diamonds, only valued by me as the gift of love.

Warn. [*Offers his hand*] Permit me, madam. [*Going over to center*]

Ame. [*Refusing it*] Sir! [*Crosses to L.H. to Louisa*]

Sт. Ger. George—remain with me.

Geo. Willingly, sir. [*To Amelia*] Don't be long away. [*To Warner*] It is the last sermon. [*Exeunt Warner R.U.E., Amelia and Louisa L.H.*]

Sт. Ger. My son, in becoming a husband, you, by the custom of our country, are liberated from paternal authority. You become independent and take possession of your fortune. But, my son, this is a moment fraught with peril to you. The most fatal of all passions has shown itself in you from infancy— the passion for gaming—the basest of all propensities. But you have promised—you have sworn that this odious vice should never more debase you. George—you have kept this promise to your father?

Geo. Why this doubt, sir? If you wish renewed oaths, I swear—

Sᴛ. Gᴇʀ. No—Heaven reads your heart; it is to Heaven that you shall answer for the fate of Amelia. But if you have deceived me—or if you suffer yourself anew to be drawn from the path of honor by this detestable passion —if you should ever merit the infamous name of a gamester—may Heaven pardon me for having sacrificed the most lovely of women by entwining her destiny with yours. But you, my son, you will be punished by all the complicated misery which this infamous vice must bring upon you. Contempt, dishonor, poverty, guilt. Yes, the blackest of crimes and the most ignominious of punishments follow in the train of a gamester!

Gᴇᴏ. My father—sir—is this a moment—?

Sᴛ. Gᴇʀ. Yes, my son—for it is the moment that decides your fate.

Gᴇᴏ. Heaven be praised, they are coming.

Sᴛ. Gᴇʀ. Your hand, George. Let our friends find us as a father and son should be—united. [*Warner and the company enter from the garden. Music. Amelia and Louisa attended by women from L.H., Amelia dressed and ornamented with the diamonds. Amelia kneels to the old man, who rises and kisses her. All go off in procession but St. Germain and Valentine*]

Sᴛ. Gᴇʀ. Go, my children; my heart and my prayers go with you. [*Music. All the ladies and gentlemen go out through the center*]

Vᴀʟ. Will you return to your chamber, sir?

Sᴛ. Gᴇʀ. No. I will remain in this hall; I will here await their return. Valentine! I am much affected—much moved! Oh, that I may realize the hope I have founded on this union! He has sworn to abandon gaming—he has abjured play! His friend Warner has sworn the same! By this time they are about to be united by the indissoluble bond—Valentine.

Vᴀʟ. Sir.

Sᴛ. Gᴇʀ. Run to the church—even here I would assist at the union of these beloved beings. You can hasten back and announce the moment when the priest shall give them his blessing.

Vᴀʟ. I understand, sir—[*Exit by garden*]

Sᴛ. Gᴇʀ. I ought to feel happy—but I am not so. I experience fears— almost do I repent the—[*Enter Rodolph from the garden*]

Rᴏᴅ. [*Advancing timidly*] I see no servant—

Sᴛ. Gᴇʀ. A stranger—

Rᴏᴅ. Have I the honor of speaking to Mʳ. St. Germain?

Sᴛ. Gᴇʀ. Yes, sir.

Rᴏᴅ. My name is Rodolph Dericourt. Your friend, Mʳ. Dermont—

Sᴛ. Gᴇʀ. Dermont! Has he arrived? Why is he not here?

Rᴏᴅ. This letter will explain.

St. Ger. [*Reads*] "I have discovered a secret of the utmost importance. I pray you, do not conclude the union of my niece with your son until I have seen you and explained these hasty lines." Merciful Heaven! Sir—do you know—my fears? Sir—my son is now at the altar! If there is yet time it shall be broken off—[*Attempts to rise*] Call my servants.

Rod. [*Assisting him*] Be calm, sir. [*Valentine rushes in from garden*]

Val. Sir! Sir! It is done! They are married!

St. Ger. O Heaven! [*Enter Dermont L.H. Rodolph meets him. Valentine replaces his master in his chair*]

Rod. It is too late. They are married. Hide the dreadful truth from the poor old man.

St. Ger. [*Stretching his feeble hand towards his friend*] Dermont!

Der. My friend!

St. Ger. That letter?

Der. Forget it.

St. Ger. Never! Explain—immediately explain!

Der. It must be so. Last night—in a gaming house—

St. Ger. O my fears! Finish—

Rod. Hold! They come. Spare the innocent bride—Spare the honor of your son—Let the secret remain with us forever.

St. Ger. No! I will know all! declare all!—[*Music. Procession from the garden. Enter George, Amelia, Louisa, Warner and others*]

Ame. My uncle! My friend! My father! [*Rushes into his arms*]

Geo. [*To Warner*] Is not that the stranger—?

Warn. Hush! It is he.

Geo. And Rodolph? We are betrayed!

Ame. You turn from me—you do not speak to me. My uncle! My father! My dear George, it is my uncle Dermont.

Geo. I am very sorry that he arrived too late to be present at the ceremony.

St. Ger. Perhaps you ought to thank Heaven. My daughter, retire to your apartment.

Ame. Me, sir!

St. Ger. Retire. I must speak to my son.

Geo. Remain, Amelia. I prohibit your departure. You have now no other master than your husband. I see the blow that is prepared for me, and whence it comes. [*Looks at Rodolph*] The cowardly assassin is before me. You, sir, shall account to me for this treachery.

Rod. Me!

Ame. O Heaven!

DER. Insult no one here, young man. I, alone—

GEO. You dared not, you were one of the company and would be silent for your own sake. [*Enter Valentine L.H.*]

VAL. A police magistrate would speak with you, sir.

ST. GER. With me?

WARN. [*To George*] We are lost.—The diamonds!

DER. [*To St. Germain*] Save the honor of your family. Let all strangers be requested to depart. [*Dermont gives directions to servants. Music. The company disperse through the garden. Enter magistrate and two officers of justice L.H.*]

MAG. I am sorry to trouble you, sir.

ST. GER. Speak, sir!—Explain, I pray you.

MAG. I must, sir. [*To George*] Is your name, sir, George St. Germain?

ST. GER. My son!

GEO. It is.

MAG. Diamonds of great value have been stolen in the neighborhood of a house which you, M^r. George St. Germain, are known to frequent. We know from the depositions of persons arrested, that you received, in that house, from a suspected woman, a casket of diamonds which could not belong to a person of that class.

AME. George—you—

GEO. Silence!

ST. GER. Is this true? Deny it or I renounce you for ever.

MAG. He cannot deny it.

GEO. Why should I deny it? Am I not the master of my own actions? Who shall prohibit my purchasing any thing I may desire? And if the thing purchased was not the property of the vender, how should I know it?

WARN. That's right; be firm.

MAG. Your deposition in court is necessary and I must invite you to follow me.

GEO. Me!

AME. O Heavens!

ST. GER. My name—my family dishonored! For pity, sir!

AME. O sir, in the name of Heaven I intreat you to spare my husband! Pity his aged father, who is sinking into the grave! Do not give the mortal blow to the venerable man.

MAG. Your prayers, madam, the tears of an aged father all plead—but—what—what do I see? Those diamonds—

AME. Horror! Horror!

GEO. Come hither, Amelia!

MAG. Stop, madam, I recognize on you, by the description given, the diamonds which were stolen—they decorate your person.

AME. Horrible! [*Tears off the jewels*]

WARN. [*To George*] Do not name me.

AME. There—there—there they are! Oh save me from infamy. [*Flies to Dermont*]

DER. [*Receiving her in his arms*] My child!

ST. GER. Accursed day!—I feel that my end is nigh—I—[*Faints. Amelia, Louisa, Rodolph, etc., support him*]

DER. You see, sir, the danger which threatens the life of this venerable man, and doubtless there is no thought of accusing this impudent young man of robbery. I therefore beg that you will not insist upon his following you at this moment. I will be answerable for his appearance.

MAG. Your word shall be sufficient, sir, for the present. [*To the officer*] You may withdraw. [*The magistrate and followers go off L.H. Mᴿ. St. Germain is borne off to his chamber accompanied by Amelia, Louisa, Rodolph and servants. Warner goes off by the garden*]

DER. Thus far, sir, I have been silent through respect to a father overwhelmed by the shame and ignominy of an unworthy son.

GEO. How, sir—

DER. Hear me, sir. Unfortunately I have a right to be heard. You cannot expect that after this exposure of your infamous conduct I will suffer you to be the arbiter of my niece's fate. The daughter of my brother shall not be a victim to your vices. It is for me to protect her—to save her from the abyss into which a gambler would drag her. I could not prevent, but I will dissolve your marriage.

GEO. You dissolve my marriage! But for the respect I bear that wife you would wrest from me, that word had been your last. So, then, it is to be my accuser that you pursued me? And by what right do you pretend to regulate my actions and set bounds to my will? I am now free, in possession of fortune, master of myself and of my wife! I am in my own house, and remember, sir, that I have a right to drive from my doors the man who insults me.

DER. Ungrateful wretch—who saved you but now, from the shame of being carried to a court of justice?

GEO. Dare you, sir, to brave me?

DER. I am in the house of my friend. My niece shall never belong to a gambler.

GEO. Out of the house—Away! or I will not answer for your life. [*Amelia rushes from Mᴿ. St. Germain's apartment*]

AME. Hold! Hold!

DER. [*Going to her*] Amelia.

AME. George! For Heaven's sake calm this fury. Your father is recovering his senses. You know the danger of again agitating him. You will kill him, George, if he hears these sounds of fury—

DER. Wretched man, you are murdering your father!

GEO. Away, sir!—hence or—

AME. [*Clinging to Dermont*] My uncle! [*Enter Louisa from the chamber*]

LOU. Madam! Madam! Sir! Your father is coming. He threatens you—he—

AME. O my husband! fall at his feet and implore his forgiveness.

GEO. Away—let me drive this man from my house! [*The company return from the garden. M*^{r}*. St. Germain enters struggling with Rodolph, from whom he disengages himself*]

ST. GER. Hold!

GEO. O Heaven!

AME. Mercy! Mercy!

ST. GER. No! The voice of Heaven shall be heard in the last words of a dying man! Listen! The fate of a gambler is written upon the gates of Hell. Ungrateful son! Already a parricide, you will be a guilty husband and unnatural father. Gaming will overwhelm you with every evil! Your days will be numbered by your crimes; and your life will end in misery, tears and remorse.

GEO. My father!

ST. GER. I curse the parricide! [*Falls*]

GEO. My father! [*Amelia and Louisa kneel by M*^{r}*. St. Germain. The company stand horrorstruck*]

CURTAIN

SECOND DAY

SCENE I: *An apartment adjoining the bedchamber of Amelia. A door on each side and one at the bottom. Amelia is discovered writing and occasionally wiping the tears from her eyes. Two candles and extinguisher, burnt to the sockets, indicate that she has passed the night thus. It is daylight. Enter Louisa L.H.*

LOU. So!—Another sleepless night, passed in writing. She weeps!—Yes, always when alone she weeps. Fifteen years of wedlock and not a day of happiness. My poor mistress! Yours indeed is a life of sorrow. [*Arranges the furniture*]

AME.   Yes! This last effort must be made. Not for myself—I am the wife of a gamester! I am resigned to my fate! But my boy! If I can save him—[*Writes*]

LOU.   Madam!—Did you speak of your son? Shall I bring him?

AME.   My dear Albert! Thank you, Louisa—I cannot see him now.

LOU.   You have not been in bed, madam. You have been weeping—I must chide you, madam.

AME.   Louisa, you see me during the absence of my husband, occupied in writing. It is to my uncle.

LOU.   What, madam! To Mr. Dermont, whom your husband drove from his door with reproaches and insults?

AME.   Do not call to my recollection that terrible scene. But he knows that I am innocent—my boy is innocent. For years I have implored his pardon! He, alone, can save my boy! For this purpose at night whilst my husband is—

LOU.   At the gaming table! Always at the gaming table and always with that infamous Warner. How can my master be so blind as not see that the hypocrite is ruining him, while he dares to prefer his infamous suit—?

AME.   Louisa!

LOU.   I must speak, madam. You are too good—too patient. If I were in your place I would unmask the villain to my husband and to the world.

AME.   I dare not. You know the violence of my husband's temper. I shudder at the thought of exciting his resentment—What is that?—My husband has returned. Louisa!—If he has lost at play—do not leave me. [*Enter Valentine by door in flat down L.H.*]

VAL.   Mr. Warner.

LOU.   Warner!

AME.   You know that I will not see him in the absence of my husband.

VAL.   This is the third time, madam, that he has been here—even before it was day. Not finding my master, he says he must speak to you instantly, to prevent a great misfortune.

AME.   What misery awaits me now! My husband has lost—and despair perhaps—admit him.

LOU.   Madam!

AME.   No—no!—He deceives me!—He has not seen my husband—it is a plot—I will not see him. Stop, Valentine—Before your master returns take this letter to the post office. [*Folds and seals it*]

VAL.   I have not dared to tell her—the furniture will be seized today if—[*Noise*]

AME. [*Coming forward with the letter*] What noise?

LOU. Your husband, madam. [*Goes to the door*]

AME. My husband! [*Hides the letter in her bosom*]

LOU. [*Returning from the door*] He has sent Warner away and is coming alone—he is in a paroxysm of rage.

AME. I tremble!—Louisa!—Do not let my boy come. Do not let him witness these scenes of horror. [*Enter George from door in flat. The others stand immovable. He advances to the center*]

GEO. How is it, madam, that you arrogate to yourself the right to shut my doors against my best friend Warner?

AME. So—early.—In your absence—

GEO. Frivolous excuse! You hate Warner, because he is my friend.

AME. Warner your friend!

GEO. As to you, sir, I'll turn you out of doors if you treat him with disrespect.

VAL. Me! Turn me out of doors! The old servant of your father—Me! in whose arms he died!

GEO. Silence!!

AME. [*Entreats Valentine by signs to silence*] Valentine!

GEO. He is always bringing to my recollection—[*To Louisa*] What do *you* here?

LOU. I am waiting on my lady.

GEO. You are not wanted. Away! Both!

VAL. [*Giving papers*] Today, sir, these—were left—

GEO. [*Crushing the papers in his hand*] I defy them! Leave us! [*Valentine goes L.H., Louisa R.H.*] Fate has this night done her worst. I have drank the very dregs of the bitter draught. No sermonizing, madam. To all you can say, I answer, Chance can enrich me as easily as it has ruined me. You have more than once seen and felt the effects of Fortune's smiles. These remains of splendor—these wrecks of opulence which surround us, are the proofs. I take my turn to rise and fall—but tonight! All is lost—I must have money today or all is over with me.

AME. George—my husband—you have already had my jewels. I possess nothing—the furniture of our house only remains.

GEO. That is levied upon.

AME. Have we then nothing?

GEO. No. I repeat—I must have money or it is all over with me. [*Sits gloomily*]

AME. You make me shudder, my husband. Have we not always been miserable even in the midst of occasional splendor? Incessant alarms—quarrels—insults and disgraces! for fifteen years—

GEO. No more, madam!

AME. I do not reproach you—I only beg of you to pity me—to save your child! A portion of my dowry yet belongs to me. The interest it produces, though nothing in the mode of life we have been accustomed to, will be sufficient to support us in peace and independence, in some humble but happy retreat. Oh, my husband, if you will from this day quit this splendid house—this fatal city—your false friends—you will find *that* peace, so long lost; and my life shall be dedicated to your happiness! Our little Albert will grow under our eyes far from the seductions of vice! [*Kneels to him*] George! My husband! Let us fly from this Hell in which we have been plunged.—Renounce gaming! On my knees I beg for *my* life and *your* happiness!

GEO. [*Raising her and himself standing up*] You have repeated this discourse to me a thousand times at least. A scanty revenue—a village habitation—an existence miserable! Unsupportable!—Riches and splendor are the objects of my ambition! I have already possessed them.—Besides it is too late. Amelia, you offer me the remains of your dowry—it is *that* I ask—confide in me—only until tomorrow and I will return it doubled.

AME. Can you ask me to give away all that remains to me—to your child?

GEO. Only till tomorrow, I tell you.

AME. That morrow will never come. Today you will go to the gaming table and tomorrow my child will be a beggar.

GEO. Amelia, am I not your husband? If I *command* you to—

AME. George, I am in your power. I have no protector. You may take my life, but you shall never make me disinherit my child.

GEO. You would prefer seeing me dragged to the scaffold?

AME. O Heaven! My husband!

GEO. Yes—learn—since you will know it—that driven by want, rage and despair—I obtained money by forging—

AME. Mercy! Mercy, Heaven!—The prophecy of your father is fulfilled, and you will die a criminal!

GEO. [*Seizing her arm*] Wretched woman, would you drive me to despair?

AME. George! pity me! [*Valentine L.H. and Louisa R.H. run in*]

LOU. My lady!—

GEO. Who called you?

LOU. I thought, sir—

GEO. Away!—Both!—Away—leave us.

AME. Leave us, Louisa—Valentine—we wish to be alone. [*They go out R.H. and L.H.*]

GEO. You now know the whole truth. Forged notes made by me, will, tomorrow—be in the hands of the police if the money—

AME. What's the sum? Does it require all?

GEO. All. I have prepared this paper—it will empower Warner—

AME. Warner!

GEO. To draw your dowry from the hands of your banker.

AME. Oh! My son!

GEO. I must not appear in the business. You see that my situation is desperate.—You see me resolved.—Sign this paper or witness my self-immolation!

AME. Hold—give me—

GEO. You consent?

AME. In saving my husband from infamy, I save my Albert. [*Goes to the secretary and signs*]

GEO. She signs it!

AME. Take it, my husband, and hasten to annihilate the proofs of your guilt—George, I give you all. I ask in return that you will renounce—

GEO. For ever, dear Amelia. Valentine!—Valentine, I say! [*He enters L.H.*] Prepare the great saloon for company. [*Exit Valentine L.H.*]

AME. At such a moment?

GEO. The world must be blinded. Fear nothing. Adieu, Amelia.

AME. In the name of Heaven redeem the forged notes without loss of time.

GEO. I have time enough. [*Aside*] Now to double this sum. Fortune must be kind today to make up for the ill-treatment of last night. Adieu, Amelia! Now to my friend Warner. Adieu, Amelia. [*Exit L.H. Enter Louisa R.H.*]

LOU. What has happened—dear madam!

AME. My misery is too great for my strength! My child is doomed to want!—My husband—[*Enter Valentine center*]

VAL. Madam, a moment after my master went out, a person whose features did not appear unknown to me, gave me this billet and desired me earnestly to deliver it immediately.

AME. Some further misfortune. It is—it is my uncle's hand! He is here! I thank thee, Heaven! Thou has sent me a protector! [*Kisses the letter. Enter Dermont center*]

DER. Amelia!

AMELIA. My uncle!—My more than father! [*She rushes into his arms. Pause. Valentine and Louisa go out center*] You have not yet called me your niece.

DER. Have I not pressed you to my heart?

AME. My letters unanswered—

DER. I have been abroad. All your letters were waiting my return—instead of writing I have flown to assist you.

AME. Indeed I have need of a friend.

DER. I already know that George has lost the inheritance of his father.

AME. All is lost.

DER. And—debts?

AME. Oh yes!

DER. But your dowry?

AME. I gave him all.

DER. What? Did you forget that you are a mother?

AME. Oh—if you knew—

DER. His violence, his tyranny! An ungrateful son, an unkind husband, an unnatural father—all is comprised in the name of gamester!

AME. He is the father of my son—he is my husband!—Oh, spare him!

DER. Generous victim! But his vices shall not destroy you. I am your protector! Your fate shall be separated from his—I must break this union—I must—

AME. Hold, sir! I never will desert my husband. He had my vows at the altar. If he had made me happy I should have thanked Heaven; he has filled my days with anguish and bitterness, but I will *follow* him through every woe, and strive to soothe him in misery and death.

DER. What, then, do you expect from *me*?

AME. I am a mother. *My* life is devoted to sorrow—but my boy—

DER. Shall be mine! Bring him to me.

AME. Louisa! [*She appears*] Seek my son—bring him hither—Hark!— What is that?

LOU. It is my master's voice. He has returned and is coming up stairs.

DER. I must avoid him. I am with Rodolph Dericourt.

LOU. If you go *now,* sir, you must meet him.

AME. Remain, sir.

DER. No, I cannot.

LOU. If you will consent— [*Points to L.H. door*]

DER. That chamber.

AME. It is mine.

Der. I must avoid the presence of a man at whom my soul sickens. [*Exit L.H.2E. Enter George, Valentine and servants. Exit Louisa L.H.*]

Geo. [*Giving a purse to Valentine*] Let the saloons dazzle every eye with their splendor! Spare no cost—[*Exeunt Valentine and servants*] Amelia—you have paid no attention to your dress.

Ame. Have you secured the notes?

Geo. This evening—tomorrow morning—will be time enough. Now let us think only of our ball. It shall be the most splendid thing Paris ever beheld. We will have masks—opera—dancing.

Ame. Speak lower.

Geo. I have ordered a new set of jewels for you—Warner chose them. Superb!—All the world shall envy your splendor.

Ame. Why so loud?

Geo. Why not? We will have a concert. You must show your skill on the harp—Warner reminded me that you had no harp and an elegant one is ordered.

Ame. I cannot play tonight—

Geo. Madam, you can do whatever I desire.

Ame. Do not speak thus—

Geo. What are you afraid of? Why are your eyes incessantly turned to that chamber? Some one is there—you tremble. By Heaven I will know—

Ame. [*Holding him*] George!—My husband!—Stop—

Geo. Ha!—By Heaven I will—[*Is going to door. Enter Dermont L.H.2E.*]

Der. Hold!

Geo. Dermont here!

Der. I *expose* myself, to save innocence from outrage.

Geo. What brought you here, sir?

Der. To see once more the daughter of my brother. To judge if my predictions are verified. You have fulfilled your promises—she knows what it is to be the wife of a gamester! Nay, sir—I fear you not—I have nothing to say to you. [*Going*]

Ame. Will you not ask him to remain?

Geo. No!

Der. Innocent and noble victim! Do not sink under the weight of your chain. Remember that you have a father who watches over you. [*Exit Dermont; Amelia in tears*]

Geo. This is too much!—Madam, I prohibit your ever seeing him again.

Ame. [*Advancing*] And this is my return for having sacrificed all. I have but one friend in the world and you drive him from me! Your disinherited child has but this one protector—and you deprive him of that sole support!

GEO. I hate him because he despises me and teaches you to hate me.

AME. O George, how little do you know my heart.

GEO. Silence. Some one comes. Dry your tears—[*Enter Valentine followed by a jeweller with a casket and two porters with a harp in its case. Warner enters a moment after*]

WARN. Here I am, my friend! Madam, permit me. [*He attempts to take Amelia's hand. She withdraws it*] So! So!—She has been weeping. So much the better. You see, my friend, that I have executed all your commissions. Carry those jewels into Madam St. Germain's chamber. The harp must go into the saloon, but the case may go into the chamber also. [*Pointing to R.H. door*] So; that's right. [*They obey him*]

GEO. Amelia, I expect you to do the honors of my house. [*Takes her hand and leads her into the chamber L.H.2 door. The jeweller and porters return with Valentine, who dismisses them and goes off with them*]

WARN. So far, well! My project succeeds admirably. My agents are intelligent and will be tonight at their appointed stations. Haughty woman—tomorrow you are mine! [*Exit*]

SCENE 2: *A street. Time night. Enter Warner L.H.*

WARN. Now to get George out of the way and employ him while I carry my plot into execution and secure Amelia. He will be too late to take up the forged notes. I have put the bloodhounds of the police upon the scent.—He will soon be in the hands of justice and I will bear off the proud Amelia in triumph. [*Enter George R.H.*]

GEO. My dear Warner, I have been in luck—I profited by my run of good fortune!

WARN. I lost ten thousand francs.

GEO. A bagatelle! But, Warner—we must not neglect those damned notes—

WARN. You will use the money you got from your wife for that purpose.

GEO. Certainly—I have it all—except a few thousands expended in the entertainment of tonight—but a few hours will double the funds I have in hand!

WARN. Doubtless! Remember, that at midnight, all our friends meet at the Russian prince's. The sport will be high—I have pledged my word that you will be there.

GEO. Depend upon me. What! give up this money before Fortune shall have doubled or trebled it? No! We will divide our funds and by assisting each other—

WARN. I cannot be with you—I must be at the Persian ambassador's playing an equally sure game. Tomorrow we meet and divide the spoil. I will take what money you can spare.

GEO. [*Gives notes*] There—half my funds. Tomorrow at six we meet—

WARN. And divide!

GEO. And annihilate those evidences—

WARN. Hush—adieu!

GEO. Success attend you! [*Exit L.H.*]

WARN. So! I have the night to myself! Success must attend me! [*Exit R.H.*]

SCENE 3: *Amelia's bedchamber. A rich bed and curtains. A window in flat (practicable). A door on each side of the stage. The harp-case is seen and a toilette table with a hand-bell. Music is heard without. The harp-case is opened and Warner's boy comes forth. He examines the chamber—listens—retires and shuts himself up. Enter Louisa with a light R.H. She proceeds to light the candles on the toilette.*

LOU. What can have happened?—A midnight visit from Mr. Dermont! I do not know that I do right to introduce him secretly to my lady's bedchamber—[*Two taps are heard on R.H. door*] Here he is. [*She opens door. Enter Dermont and Valentine; the last retires after introducing him*]

DER. Please to say to Mr. George St. Germain that I must speak to him instantly.

LOU. That is impossible, sir.

DER. Why?

LOU. Do you not know, sir, that he never passes the night at home? He is at the gaming table.

DER. Wretch! But tonight—this ball?

LOU. My lady does the honors of the house.

DER. At such a moment! Run, madam, and call my niece.

LOU. My lady!—You terrify me, sir!

DER. Haste—lose not a moment!

LOU. More misery! More misfortune! [*Exit R.H.*]

DER. How can I hide from my poor Amelia the horrors that await her? And this infatuated wretch is engaged at play while chains and perhaps the gallows is preparing for him. [*Enter Amelia R.H. door*]

AME. O my uncle! What can have brought you at this unseasonable hour?

DER. Summon your courage, my child. You must know the worst. Your husband is lost if he does not instantly fly—he has committed a forgery.

AME. All then is discovered!

DER. You knew—

AME. Only today.

DER. It is but within a few hours that the police have had notice of the forgery. The officers of justice are now in pursuit of him.

AME. Oh save him! Save him!

DER. For your sake—for the sake of your child—but—where is he? He must be found instantly—

AME. Alas! I know not. [*Enter Louisa hastily R.H.2E.*]

LOU. Madam, a stranger who says he has something of importance to communicate to Mr. Dermont.

DER. It is Rodolph Dericourt. Admit him. He will serve you with zeal. [*Enter Rodolph R.H.2E.*]

ROD. Madam, pardon—

DER. My niece knows your motive.

ROD. There is but a moment for your husband to escape—

AME. What! What is to be done!

DER. You must take refuge in my arms—Albert is already my child. You must put an end to your sufferings and abandon—

AME. Never! [*Enter Louisa R.H.2E.*]

LOU. Madam! Madam!—It is rumored among the company that officers of justice are in pursuit of my master.

DER. Let the company be dismissed—shut the doors—I must attend to it— [*Crosses R.H. Enter Valentine L.H.*]

VAL. All are flying from the house, sir.

DER. So much the better. Put out the lights! Shut the doors! We will prepare for the flight of George. Do you, Amelia, shut yourself in this apartment. If George returns, let him come instantly to the house of Rodolph— when we have put his person in safety, we will endeavor to save his honor.

AME. Oh, save my husband!

DER. We will, if Heaven has not abandoned him. [*Exeunt Dermont and Rodolph and Valentine L.H.*]

AME. Ruined! Dishonored! And while I await him in agony, he is surrounded by the accomplices of his guilt.

LOU. O madam—promise me, that whatever new misfortune falls on you —I may share it.

AME. Dear Louisa! But where is my son?

LOU. He sleeps in my apartment.

AME. Let him sleep—poor boy—[*She approaches her toilette and sees herself in her glass. Starts*] What a dress for misery. Help me, Louisa—assist me to take off these jewels—I should have worn a mourning dress from the moment of my marriage. [*Louisa takes a light and follows Amelia into door R.H. As soon as they are off, the harp-case is opened softly and the boy comes out. He listens, examines the door of cabinet, goes to the window, opens it softly and waves a white handkerchief. He returns to the case and takes a silk ladder of cord, fastens it to the window sash and throws one end out. Warner enters the window by this means, with his sword in his hand. The boy points to the door of the cabinet, then runs to the toilette, takes the bell and wrenches out the tongue or clapper. This done he goes out at the window. Warner throws the silk ladder after him and comes forward*]

WARN. So all is safe! She is mine! George cannot return—I have secured him. Friend Warner, this is thy master-stroke! She must be alone by this time. No—if she does but send away Louisa—my victory is secure! [*Retires into the harp-case. Enter Amelia dressed plainly in white and Louisa with light. Music*]

AME. Now, Louisa, leave me.

LOU. Let me pass the night *here*.

AME. No—do *you*, at least, sleep—and be near my dear boy. See that the house is safe—the doors all fastened. Take the key of that door which leads to the private stair-case. If my uncle or Mr. Rodolph return, bring them by that way. If my husband comes home I will admit him by the way of the cabinet. [*Pointing to R.H. door*]

LOU. I obey you, madam. [*Exit Louisa L.H. Amelia seats herself. Warner comes from the harp-case and gliding to the R.H. door turns the key. Amelia starts. He has put his sword on a chair*]

AME. Louisa!—Is that you? [*Warner retires from door*] Louisa! Some one is here—Who is there?

WARN. It is I. [*She shrieks*] Hear me.

AME. Leave me! I will summon—[*She runs to the toilette, takes the hand-bell and finds that it has been broken*]

WARN. You see all has been provided for—you are in my power. [*Shows his pistols*]

AME. I am lost.

WARN. No. I come to save you. In spite of your cold disdain, my love—

AME. Away! Or by my shrieks I'll call my servants to my succor—to drive with infamy from these doors the most vile of men! Away, sir, instantly—by that door [*R.H.*]—openly—in presence of my servants—without concealment or mystery!

WARN. No, madam, it has cost me too much trouble to obtain this interview. I have no fears of interruption. Your husband is otherwise employed—*your* servants are taken care of—*mine* wait my orders under that window. Nay, fear nothing—I love you and spite of your disdain will save and make you happy. George St. Germain is ruined, lost, dishonored. Tomorrow sees him a detected criminal at the bottom of a dungeon. I offer you riches and happiness—love, opulence, pleasure—

AME. Base, cruel, cowardly hypocrite. You alone are the cause of all my husband's follies and—guilt. You alone have led him to ruin and dishonor—and *now* would deprive him of his last—his only remaining consolation—the support of a wife! Villain! I will unmask you to him.

WARN. Do you brave me! Then let vengeance and love be united. You do not know me yet!

AME. Ruffian! Heaven! [*Seeing the sword*] I am saved! [*Seizes it*] Stand off! Death rather than infamy!

WARN. Rash woman! Hold! [*He seizes and wrests the sword from her*]

AME. Help! I—die. [*She sinks fainting—her hair is dishevelled and floats around her; he supports her. Knocking at the door R.H.*]

GEO. Open the door, Amelia.

WARN. Curses! It is George's voice.

GEO. I say, open the door!

AME. It was my husband's voice!

GEO. Open the door, I say!

AME. Fly, wretched man! Fly!

WARN. I cannot—but—hush! [*He runs and puts out the lights*] You will be dishonored if you betray me. [*Hides in the harp-case*]

GEO. Open the door, or I will burst it open!

AME. This is worse than death! [*She attempts to go to the door but sinks, faints and falls near the toilette. George breaks open the door and enters. He throws off his cloak*]

GEO. Nobody! Darkness! Silence! I thought I heard voices—my imagination must have deceived me. Amelia no doubt is asleep. She is yet ignorant of the ruin and dangers that surround me. Warner abandons me too at this moment of utter desolation! I must fly instantly. Fly?—Alone?—No, Amelia must go with me—my only friend—my only consolation. Ah! I now feel her worth! She loves me; she will follow me through every ill—I must awaken her—[*He goes towards the bed and stumbles on the sword of Warner*] What is this? [*Lifts it*] A sword!—It it not mine. Some one then has been here—Ah, I recollect—the door was fastened on the inside—I *did* hear voices—which were hushed when I knocked! Hell! Hell! I am betrayed! Betrayed by my wife at the moment that destiny overwhelms me! Oh, for vengeance! Vengeance on the traitress! Blood! Blood! [*He opens the curtains—searches the chamber—at length sees her*] What?—Cold!—Dead! [*Raises her tenderly*] Amelia! Amelia!

Ame. My husband's voice! Oh, mercy! Mercy! [*Kneels*]

Geo. Mercy! That word condemns you. You are then guilty!

Ame. No! No! Fly! Oh, fly! Who do you look for? He is gone—

Geo. Ha! He is gone! Wretch! Who is your paramour?

Ame. George! I am innocent!

Geo. Where is he?

Ame. You will murder him!

Geo. Yes, by Heaven, I will have his blood! Wretch! And *you* have dared to condemn me! You! Adulteress!—But your infamous accomplice shall die before your eyes! He cannot escape me—[*He searches the chamber and, trying the door L.H., finds it locked*]

Ame. [*Holding him*] My husband!

Geo. Where is the key of this passage?

Ame. I have not got it—fly this way!

Geo. Do you fly—if you would save your life. [*Forces the door and rushes out*]

Ame. May Heaven in mercy prevent further guilt! [*Enter Louisa R.H. door with a light and Rodolph following her*]

Lou. Madam, Mr. Rodolph—at his desire.

Ame. [*Running to him*] Heaven has sent me succor!

Rod. Madam, I seek your husband. He was seen to enter his house—he is followed—he must fly instantly—

Ame. Do not leave me, sir. Save me—My husband—There will be bloodshed! [*During this Warner escapes from the harp-case and unseen follows George*]

Rod. Your distress, madam—! Gracious Heaven! What does this mean? [*Re-enter Warner leading George, to whom he has given his pistols; points to Rodolph*]

Warn. Behold your wife's seducer! [*George advances. Amelia, shrinking, throws herself between him and Rodolph. Louisa pushes Rodolph into R.H. door. George puts aside Amelia and follows them. Two reports of pistols are heard. Louisa shrieks and re-enters. Warner exit*]

Lou. He has murdered him! [*Amelia faints. Re-enter George, and Dermont rushes in L.H. door with Valentine*]

Der. Fly! A carriage and horses await you—all is ready—

GEO. [*Showing the R.H. door to Dermont*] Yes—I go—but I am revenged. You—traitress—shall share my fate! [*Lifts Amelia and bears her off L.H. door. Re-enter Dermont*]

DER. Horror! Horror! [*Valentine places himself before L.H. door and prevents Louisa from following her mistress. Soldiers enter with officers of justice at R.H. door*]

LOU. [*Running to window*] They are safe! They are safe! [*The officers and soldiers put aside Valentine and go off L.H. door. Louisa rushing down*] They have escaped!

DER. For the boy's sake, I thank Heaven!

CURTAIN

THIRD DAY

The stage represents the courtyard of an inn, giving on the highway. At the actor's left, the house decorated with the sign of the Golden Lion. At the other side, the entrance to a cellar. In front of the house and the cellar, and in other parts of the courtyard, rustic tables, surrounded with benches, stools, and many species of games usual in village taverns.

MRS. B. [*Coming from the house*] Babet! come, quick! be brisk! hasten! set the great table in the large dining room. Guerll! come, Guerll! [*Guerll appears, carrying pots of stoneware or tin*] Go to the cellar to draw the new beer into pots. [*While Guerll goes into the cellar, enter from one side four brewer's men carrying, two by two, vats of beer on their shoulders in the Flemish manner; and from the other side a servant girl with her hands and arms loaded with fish-baskets.—To the brewer's men*] You arrive in good time; there will be drinking today, it is the holiday of the country. Take that into the cellar. [*To the servant girl*] Come here, Goth. [*Looking into the baskets*] Let's see what you have. Game, poultry—that's good. Have the chickens plucked and put a couple on the spit; serve one of them at once to the traveller in No. 4. [*Birman enters at the bottom of the stage; Guerll and Babet run to meet him*]

BIR. [*From behind the scenes*] Take my portmanteau; lead Grisette to the stable and give her a peck.

MRS. B. Ah! there is my husband!

BIR. Good day, my dear wife. [*He gives his cloak, his whip and a package to Guerll and Babet, who carry them away*] A peck, do you understand? [*To his wife*] Let me embrace you once more—Excellent little beast! two leagues in three-quarters of an hour!

Mrs. B. Did you see the bailiff? Do you bring the permit to place on our sign-board "The Bavarian Arms"?

Bir. Pardie—a coat of arms six feet high and with golden letters as big as that.—Within six weeks, you shall see, no one will talk of anything except the "Golden Lion" inn; and there will not be a better frequented one on the highway to Munich; look here, you see that it is all regular. [*He takes from his pocket the permit, which he gives to his wife. At the same time he takes out two sealed letters*]

Mrs. B. [*Noticing the two letters*] What do you have there?

Bir. These? These are two letters that the messenger of Weissbruck brought; I met him on the way. [*Giving one of the two letters to his wife*] This is for your cousin Ghurt; you will send it on soon.

Mrs. B. Very well!—and the other?

Bir. The other? Ah! the other is for someone whom I do not know, and who is not from around here.

Mrs. B. Is that so?

Bir. Yes, it for a French captain who is travelling, who is to pass over this road and stop at our tavern.

Mrs. B. That's strange.

Bir. Faith, it's on the address; there, see.

Mrs. B. [*Reading*] Yes—"in care of M^r. Birman, at the Golden Lion inn, on the road to Munich." Well, take care of this letter and if the French captain comes, you shall give it to him.

Bir. Certainly. [*He puts it back in his pocket*] Say, did anyone come while I was away?

Mrs. B. Yes, a commercial traveller, he has slept here, he leaves this morning—and you, tell me of your journey.

Bir. I, just as you see me, I have breakfasted *tête à tête* with the bailiff.

Mrs. B. Indeed!

Bir. Ah! what wine, what rabbit pasty! and what a worthy man is the bailiff! Apropos of the pasty,—no, I mean of the bailiff, I have a proud piece of news to tell you; you will see, a piece of news that will make a holiday in the whole country.

Mrs. B. Is that so? What is it anyhow?

Bir. You know the wretched man who arrived one fine morning two years ago, who came, he said, from Hungary, from Bohemia, from all sorts of countries, with a wife and little daughter; the scamp who has so poverty-stricken an air; in short, George, the stranger of the Red Mountain.

Mrs. B. Very well, George—what then?

Bir. What then? He is going to pack off.

Mrs. B. Good! George will quit the country?

Bir. Yes, thank God; he is a whole year behind in his taxes and in the rent for his hut. This is a fine opportunity, you see, to turn him out of doors; and as nobody in the village would now consider giving him lodging, to-morrow morning he will be driven from the parish like a vagabond and without a place of refuge.

Mrs. B. That is well done—that is to say—Ah! my God! and his poor wife and little daughter?

Bir. Why yes! on the road along with him—Oh! it's already done, you know; I saw the order on official paper; and that is not a bad thing for our house, do you see; because, since this accursed man came to live on the mountain, it is worse than if it were inhabited by a pack of wolves.[2] No one dare travel in the evening by the Kleinfield road! As soon as the sun is down all our customers are off for fear of meeting the man of the mountain. And if by bad luck, on a holiday, he calls in for a half-pot of beer you will see every one sheering off from him as if he had the plague.

Mrs. B. Ah now, husband! You are too hard on the poor man. I hope you don't think that he killed the traveller whose body was found under the precipice.

Bir. There are more than one that suspect it.

Mrs. B. If I thought so, I should never dare go to his hut again.

Bir. What, *have* you dared to go there?

Mrs. B. I never saw him there—but his poor wife and his little daughter—. Such misery! So poor!—they had not bread to eat—

Bir. You should not encourage—[*Enter George slowly at the bottom of the stage. He comes forward. Pale, haggard, gloomy, he advances to a table in front, and sits down*]

Bir. Look!—Just as I told you!

Mrs. B. But see, husband, how pale he is. Poor creature, he is faint from hunger—

Bir. He must not stay here.

Mrs. B. Don't be hard with him.

Bir. He must go. Holla! Mister! I say—

Geo. [*Looks up*] Your wish, sir?

Bir. Your pardon, friend, I want to know what it is *you* wish here?

Geo. A little rest upon this bench.

Bir. This table is intended for other customers.

Geo. I found a vacant place and thought I had a right to sit down.

Bir. Right! A right!—

[2] After this point Dunlap's manuscript resumes.

MRS. B. Gently, husband—[*Pulling his sleeve*]

BIR. Do you think I am afraid of him? Those who call for something *have a right.*

GEO. [*Rising and looking gloomily at him*] You are too charitable.

BIR. That depends upon—

MRS. B. You will get into a quarrel—

GEO. [*In a humble manner*] I can call for nothing. I have no money, I have had a long walk—give me a drink of water and I can go my way.

MRS. B. Poor creature—[*Looking at her husband*] He only asks water.

BIR. I can't find it in my heart to drive him away.

MRS. B. Drive him away! No—when all comes to all, he is a man. Give him a mug of small beer and a piece of bread.

BIR. Well, well, I will go and get it. It will be the last time, you know, for tomorrow the mayor[3] will drive him off.

MRS. B. As it is the last time, put some butter on the bread and bring some cold meat. [*George prepares to go*]

BIR. Stop; I will bring you something. [*Exit into the house. Mrs. Birman goes to the different tables*]

GEO. How shall I enter my hut without carrying bread to my wife and child? How shall I witness their sufferings and listen to their stifled sobs? How shall I tell them that they are to be driven from the miserable hut that shelters them—that after this night they will only have the sky for a canopy—the rocks to pillow their heads? If I had met a solitary traveller—Horror! [*Shudders at the suggestion. Mrs. Birman comes forward*]

MRS. B. Poor man, you seem fatigued.

GEO. I have walked all night.

MRS. B. A long journey?

GEO. No.

MRS. B. No? Where do you come from then?

GEO. From the forest. [*Music. She recoils from him. Enter Birman with a mug of beer, a piece of bread and some cold meat. Enter a traveller from the house; he advances and looks with compassion on George*]

BIR. There. Never say again that the landlord of the Golden Lion is not charitable. Drink—eat—and if you deserve it—may Providence guide you—

GEO. Providence! [*He heaves a sigh—recovers himself. Cuts the bread and meat in two and hides the greatest portion*] For my wife and child. [*Eats eagerly*]

TRAV. Unfortunate man!

[3] Apparently in the lost pages Dunlap had converted the bailiff of the original text into the mayor.

Mrs. B. [*To her husband*]   Here is the traveller who is going to Munich. I hope you have been well served, sir.

Trav.   Excellently, my good hostess! I see, my host, you have poor in this country.

Bir.   No, sir—Oh, that man—he is a stranger—from—France who lives on the mountain near this.

Trav.   He has made a slender repast. When one is going a journey, it brings good luck to do a charitable act before starting. Bring me a bottle of wine—I will take a stirrup-cup; I think this poor man will not refuse to *hob-or-nob* with me.

Bir.   With him!

Mrs. B.   Run, Babet—John—a bottle of the best wine.

Trav.   Hostess, my bill! I must be on my way to Munich.

Mrs. B.   Bring me the slate, Babet. I have only to add it up, sir. [*Babet runs into the house and returns with a slate. John brings wine and glasses. Mrs. Birman sits down with the slate. The traveller directs the wine and glasses to be put down upon the table and fills the glasses. George looks up surprised*]

Trav.   Taste this wine, my friend. You will find it better than small beer. [*He holds his glass to George, who, astonished, holds out his to meet it. Music. They touch glasses*] May the mercy of Heaven succor the unfortunate! [*George turns from him and is going to put down his glass*] Drink, my friend. [*George looks at him and they drink at the same time*]

Geo.   This revives me.

Trav.   I am glad of it. Come, again! To a happy futurity.

Geo.   A happy futurity! [*Aside*] And tomorrow my wife and child will be without shelter or bread!

Bir.   [*To his wife*]   This bodes no good to the stranger.

Mrs. B.   Four and two are six—you put me out.

Trav.   Do you know the roads in this country?

Geo.   Perfectly, sir.

Trav.   Is there not a shorter way than the high road to go to Munich?

Geo.   There is, sir, by the Red Mountain. It saves half.

Trav.   That is a great difference indeed. Is the road sufficient for a horseman?

Geo.   For one who is acquainted with it. [*Looking at him*] You are not, then, of this country?

Trav.   No.

Mrs. B.   Your bill, sir.

Trav. Eight florins. Very reasonable. [*Takes out a purse and puts down gold on the table*]

Geo. Gold!

Trav. I shall remember the Golden Lion on my return. Order my horse.

Geo. No—he has been kind to me. No, never! [*Is retiring*]

Trav. But I must have a guide. My friend, do not go yet. I am in haste to reach Munich—I will go by the mountain way if you will be my guide.

Geo. Me!

Trav. I will compensate you.

Geo. Me! No! No!

Trav. Why not? You know the way. I will give you two florins. It will be a good day's work for you.

Geo. True—true! Be it so, sir—I will go.

Trav. Finish your bottle and be ready to go with me. [*Exit*]

Geo. [*At the table*] May Heaven preserve me from this horrible temptation.

Bir. [*To his wife*] I must warn him.

Mrs. B. Would you hinder the poor man from earning a little for his wife and child? Besides, it is broad daylight. [*Re-enter Traveller prepared to ride*]

Trav. Come! My horse is ready. Good-by, good host and hostess.

Bir. and Mrs. B. A good journey, sir.

Bir. Don't stop on the way, sir—

Trav. Come, friend! [*Exit, George following. Music*]

Bir. Heaven send him safe I say. Come, wife, come—it is a busy day. [*Exeunt with servants. Enter Albert R.H. in front. Music*]

Alb. This is the place. The Golden Lion. Here I am to receive further instructions. Hollo! House! [*Throws his cloak on the table*] Have I at last come to the end of my researches? My parents, my virtuous suffering mother! My father! Once faulty, but I hope chastened by misery! Oh, let me hasten to bestow those blessings on them which the decease of my uncle—my more than a father has put in my power! What! House, I say! [*Enter Birman by door in flat*]

Bir. Who calls?

Alb. Are you the master of this inn?

Bir. At your service, sir. This must be the officer. Are you from Munich, sir?

Alb. I am.

Bir. And do you not look to receive a letter at the sign of the Golden Lion?

Alb. I was going to ask for it.

Bir. Your pardon, sir, I must make no mistake—your name is—?

Alb. Albert St. Germain.

Bir. [*Looking at the letter*] Albert St. Germain, Captain—

Alb. Give it me. [*Takes it and reads in silence*]

Bir. A captain and so young!

Alb. Yes, this confirms all! My friend, you doubtless are acquainted with all inhabitants of this neighborhood.

Bir. All, sir.

Alb. Do you know—a stranger—about fifty-five years of age—poor and probably avoiding notice—who came hither about two years ago?

Bir. Two years?

Alb. My instructions say he is a woodcutter.

Bir. His name?

Alb. Probably he calls himself George.

Bir. I—yes, I know him—a tall, stout man—I know him, not that I boast of his acquaintance.

Alb. Do you know his wife?

Bir. She is a very different kind of person, poor creature.

Alb. My dear mother!—Where do they live?

Bir. About a league from the village, half way to the hermitage on the Red Mountain, in a miserable hut—near the great precipice.

Alb. So very poor—

Bir. Poor! Why it is not ten minutes since I gave George a morsel of bread for charity. He has just gone to guide a stranger over the mountain. [*Albert sinks on a seat*] What is the matter, sir? Why, wife! Babet! John!

Alb. [*Rising*] Fatigue—fatigue! [*Enter Mrs. Birman and servants from the house*]

Bir. Quick! Wife! Wine! Refreshments!

Alb. Nothing at present. I must depart instantly. This evening my servants and baggage will be here from Weissbruck. I engage the best rooms in your house. My family will be here tomorrow.

Mrs. B. Your family, sir!

Alb. Here is money in advance. [*Gives gold*] Direct me the way to the Red Mountain and the hut of George, the woodcutter.

Mrs. B. Why, sir! There is a thunderstorm coming on. See the lightning.

Alb. I must away—direct me. [*Music without*]

Bir. Here come the holiday lads and lasses. [*Enter villagers*] In, lads and lasses, take shelter and dance in the hall. In, in and take the tables and benches in with you. [*They carry the tables, etc., into the house*]

ALB. Why do you detain me! The way to the hut?

BIR. If you *will* go, sir—this way—I will show you the way through the village and give you such directions—[*Exeunt L.H.*]

SCENE 2: *The hut of George. On the R.H. is seen a fireplace without fire. Further on, a curtain of serge ragged or torn; almost hid by the curtain appears a poor bed. On L.H. is a kind of cabinet or second chamber, of which the door is open. There are two windows in flat without shutters or glass and a door between them roughly put together without hinges and openings between the boards. The mountain with practicable pathways is behind. There is a rough board table, on which are two cushions for making lace. An old buffet with a pitcher and some plates. Four old chairs and a joint-stool. In the corner an axe. The wind is heard and some flashes of lightning seen. Enter Amelia from behind the serge curtain.*

AME. The storm bursts upon the mountain, and my husband not returned! He has not found any one to employ him. What shall I do if he does not return tonight? Or if he comes without bread for my poor child? [*Thunder*] The thunder will wake her. [*Looks into the cabinet*] No! Sleep on, poor girl, and spare me the torture of hearing you ask for a morsel of bread! But it is not tears—*labor* must save my child from hunger. [*Takes the cushion and sits*] One child has escaped this misery. Oh, why did Heaven send another, and that a girl to share my sufferings! Albert is happy. Oh! shall I never see him? [*Music. The storm becomes furious and the door in flat falls into the hut. She rises and shrieks. A shriek is heard in the cabinet and Georgette runs to the arms of her mother*] Don't be frightened, my Georgette! It is only the storm and the falling of this door. Your father will fasten it when he comes back.

GEORG. Where is he, mama? Not back yet? But don't weep—I will take my cushion and we will work together. [*She takes the cushion, places the stool near her mother and sits*]

AME. We had need to make haste—

GEORG. I can't work, mama! I am cold—

AME. Cold and hunger. [*Throws by her work*] I can only warm you in my bosom. [*Embraces her*] Hark! some one comes—[*Georgette runs to the door in flat*]

GEORG. Mama! It is papa! He comes, he comes! [*Music. Enter George from flat with a basket. He enters rapidly and his manner indicates fear. His features are disturbed, his look gloomy. He puts down the basket which is covered with a napkin*]

AME. O my husband, how happy I am to see you!

GEORG. Oh, we have been so frightened, papa!

GEO. Frightened! At what?

AME. The storm. But what accident has—

GEO. Accident—why? What do you mean?

AME. What has kept you from home last night?

GEO. Ah—true—no accident. [*He gives his hat and stick to Georgette, who puts them in a corner*]

AME. But you have returned safe to us and brought—

GEO. There—there. [*Pointing to the basket*]

AME. [*Uncovering the basket*] Heavens! What generous hand has been so bountiful? Come, Georgette, let us return thanks to Heaven—but first kiss your father.

GEO. [*Putting away the child*] Thank no one. [*Amelia, astonished, takes the hand of Georgette, then covers the table with the napkin and places the food and the bottle and glasses on the table with knives, forks, etc.*] Be quick; I am exhausted by fatigue—I am burning with thirst. My blood boils in my veins—quick—quick! [*He sits*]

AME. All is ready. Yes, you are fatigued—you have suffered. [*She sits and helps Georgette*]

GEO. Suffered! No matter! We have enough for today. Give me a glass of wine; it will restore me. [*He puts a piece of meat on his plate. Amelia pours out a glass of wine; he lifts it to his mouth, then suddenly puts it away and rises*] No! keep it—it is for you—I want none—

AME. [*Rising*] Take nothing? And just now you said—

GEO. Yes! I burn with thirst—Georgette, give me a glass of water.

AME. [*Pours it out*] Take it to your father.

GEORG. Here, papa! [*He drinks and gives her the glass*] You are hurt, papa. There is blood on your hand.

GEO. Blood!

AME. My husband! Are you hurt?

GEO. No—no—in removing a rock I scratched—It is nothing. I am cold —make some fire.

AME. With what?

GEO. True, we have no fuel! [*With a forced laugh*] Ha! ha! Good news for you, wife! We shall quit this abode of misery. Yes—yes—we must be off by sunrise tomorrow! The mayor of Kleinfield gave me this order, though on my knees I begged for a month respite. [*Shows a paper*]

AME. Driven away! Without shelter. [*Weeps*]

Geo. Why weep? Do you regret to leave these wretched walls incapable of covering you from rain or wind? You shall no longer sleep on the straw you have drenched with your tears.—Tears! Always tears! I tell you our fortune has changed. Tomorrow we will set off for some city. Vienna! Hamburg! Berlin!

Ame. Still farther from France and from my son.

Geo. Your son! Has not your uncle taught him to curse us?

Ame. Oh, no! But where shall we get money?

Geo. I have it—see—gold!

Ame. O Heaven! Who has been so good to us?

Geo. [*After a long pause*] I found it.

Ame. [*Terrified*] George!—Found it!

Geo. Half this money will carry us to one of the great cities; and with the other half!—Fortune does not always frown! Only place me where money circulates, and wealth is still within my reach!

Ame. What! Would you again—?

Geo. Peace! Hark! Some one is coming! Hide the victuals. Not a word of the gold! [*Music. Amelia hastens to clear the table but has not time. Enter Warner. He is covered with rags and bears a wallet on his back. He stops at the door in flat and leans on his staff. He advances a little extending his hands*]

Warn. Good folks, pity a poor wanderer! Charity, for the love of Heaven!

Geo. Let no one come in! Drive him away.

Georg. Only let me give him some bread. I am sure it is very hard to be hungry, papa.

Geo. It is—you know from experience. Well—well—[*Looks at his hands; fear overcomes pity and he repulses the child*] No! I prohibit it! [*Georgette goes frightened to her mother*] Drive him hence!

Warn. [*Advancing between George and Amelia*] You are very hard, sir. But this good lady, happily for me, has more compassion. May Heaven reward her—What? Is it?—Amelia!—George!

Geo. Warner! Ha! Hell has sent him hither to give him to my vengeance. [*Seizes the axe and rushes to strike Warner. Amelia throws herself between them with the child. George stands brandishing the weapon. Warner coolly folds his arms*]

Ame. Hold! Would you shed more blood? [*George lowers the axe and supports himself by its aid*] Do you not see, in this man's face, how Heaven punishes murder?

GEO. Murder! [*Lets the axe fall. Georgette takes it and carries it to the corner*]

WARN. Still the same! Always rash and passionate! And what would you have gained by stretching me on the earth? [*George sinks on a chair; his wife stands by him. The child goes to him; he takes her on his knee and occasionally leans his head on her as if not wishing to hear Warner*] I confess I did not use you well. But you have long known the truth, and fifteen years of poverty have been your avengers on me. Come, come, forget and forgive—and let us think of some means of making Fortune propitious to us.

GEO. No! No! You are the cause of all my misfortunes! You caused me to shed blood!

WARN. To save myself! As to the rest, we have been companions in guilt and have shared the same punishment—exile and misery. Here you see me travelling towards Munich a beggar. Hunger, the storm and the approach of night drove me for shelter to your hut—little thinking to find old friends here. I am sinking from fatigue and the want of food. Relieve me and give me shelter tonight and tomorrow. If George says so—we part. At daybreak I will resume my staff and my wallet, and go my way to Munich.

AME. What say you, my husband?

GEO. As you think best. [*Rises and goes up the stage*]

AME. I cannot refuse shelter even to you. Come, Georgette. [*She goes with the child into the closet*]

WARN. [*Putting down his wallet with his staff*] You don't choose my company, madam. Very well. But as you gave me shelter I suppose I may feed on the remains of your supper. [*Sits*] The Devil! Judging by *this,* you are not so poor as you look for! Wine! [*Drinks*] And good wine! George! Why do you keep aloof? Let us drink together. What? You refuse. May be you still think of—[*Puts his hand on his staff*]

GEO. No. A *word* has disarmed me. I have no right to revenge my injuries on you. But my wife! She has reason to hate and despise you.

WARN. Too true! But it is a pity she should separate us for your sake. [*Eating and drinking*]

GEO. For my sake!

WARN. Why, you do not appear to be over rich. Now, I only want opportunity, and my fortune is made. I have discovered a secret!

GEO. Discovered! A secret!

WARN. I have thought again and again of you—and to find you so poor. In fact, George, the remembrance of former times and the regret at having been an instrument in ruining you, makes me desirous of repairing your shattered fortunes.

GEO. *You!*

WARN. I know that my appearance contradicts my words. I know that you will not believe me. But the day will come—you will see proofs.

GEO. Proofs? Of what?

WARN. This is no chimera! I have discovered a mode of always winning. I am sure of breaking every gambling bank in Italy. I am now on my way to Piedmont. [*George listens eagerly*] I would not impart my secret for a million.

GEO. [*With hope and distrust*] And you would be willing to share with me—

WARN. I want an assistant—but your wife's hate—

GEO. She will obey me.

WARN. Well, then—but no—there is another obstacle. We have no money. You are as poor as myself. We must have something to begin with.

GEO. Perhaps—

WARN. How! [*George shows gold*] Is that all you have?

GEO. It is.

WARN. That's a pity. But you could get more by the same means.

GEO. [*Hiding the gold*] By the same means! Hark! I thought I heard a traveller passing. No. Warner—I have been ordered away from hence, but by paying an arrears of taxes, I can gain permission to stay. You must remain with me and—

WARN. Not here—only till morning.

GEO. Why? To be sure the place is poor—

WARN. Not *that*—but—I am a stranger, without passport, a beggar,—one of those called vagabonds, on whom suspicion is ready to fix *any* crime—and —coming hither, having quitted the highroad to shorten my way—I fell in with a heap of stones, earth and grass that attracted my curiosity. I opened the heap with the end of my staff and discovered—

GEO. [*Seizing his arm*] Silence!

WARN. *You* know then—

GEO. Did you see him?

WARN. I saw—

GEO. You uncovered the body?

WARN. Yes.

GEO. Come! Quick! It is almost night; help me to hide it.

WARN. It was you that—

GEO. No! No! It was Misery and Despair!—Come! Come!—It must be buried. [*Warner takes his wallet and staff. Georgette comes from the closet with a lighted lamp*]

GEORG. Mama has lighted the lamp with the flint and steel, and—

GEO. Carry it back. We are going out. If your mother asks for us—say we are gone to the hermitage. [*They go out and are seen passing the window R.H. Georgette, who follows them almost to the door, returns. Thunder*] The storm begins again. I will call mama. [*Is going to the closet. Music. Albert is seen passing the window L.H. and then enters the door. Georgette, seeing him, returns and puts the lamp on the table*] A stranger!

ALB. Don't be frightened, my little dear—I only came to enquire if this is the road over the Red Mountain?

GEORG. Yes, sir.

ALB. And is this the hut of George the woodcutter?

GEORG. Yes, sir. There is no other on the mountain.

ALB. And in this wretched place! O Heavens! [*Sits*] Where is the master of the house? [*Takes her hand*]

GEORG. He just now went out.

ALB. And, my—his wife?

GEORG. Mama is there. [*Pointing*]

ALB. And you then, you are—is it possible!

GEORG. Yes, sir, I am Georgette. [*Albert takes her on his knee and kisses her. Amelia calls "Georgette"*] Mama calls me, sir. [*Exit running to the cabinet*]

ALB. The voice of my mother! Let me—. No—not yet. She has suffered so much that I must prepare her by degrees for the happiness that awaits her. Heavens, do I see—a mother! [*Enter Amelia and Georgette*]

AME. A stranger, my dear? And where is your father?

GEORG. He went to the hermitage with the beggar.

AME. To the hermitage! Take your work and go in. [*Georgette takes her cushion and goes*]

AME. A gentleman! An officer? Did you ask to speak to me, sir?

ALB. I did, madam. The motive must excuse me. Have you no recollection of having seen me before?

AME. Where, sir, could I have seen you?

ALB. When you were—happy.

AME. I never was—happy.

ALB. Never? [*He attempts to take her hand; she retires*] In France, madam.

AME. In France! Oh, yes! I had then a son! [*Looks at him earnestly, bewildered*] But how could it be? So long ago. You are agitated, sir. You seem to fear—Do you come from France? From my dear native country?

ALB. And bring you news of one—

AME. Of my son? Have you seen him? Does he live—? Can it be? Your age—your emotion—

ALB. My mother!

AME. It is he! My Albert! My son! [*Throws herself in his arms*]

ALB. My good, my tender mother! I come to bring you fortune and happiness.

AME. I *am* happy! I *am* rich! I have my son! You will not leave me?

ALB. Never! Since my uncle's death, whose fortune I inherit, I have unceasingly sought you. Heaven has guided me and my sister was the first to receive me.

AME. Your sister! Georgette, come hither. [*Re-enter Georgette; she puts her cushion on the table*]

ALB. Do not tell her yet. Let me first gain her love. In this pocketbook I have bills to the amount of a million. But I have what is worth more—a pardon for my father.

AME. Your father—yes—[*Albert leads Georgette to the table and gives her a purse of gold intimating that it is for her mother. She pours it out on the table*] What shall I do? Warner must not know of this change—he must not meet my son! I will find and give notice to my husband. I shall meet him on the road.

ALB. Are you going out? The storm threatens.

AME. Not far.

ALB. I will go with you.

AME. I have reasons for denying you. Georgette, take good care of your friend. I will soon be back. [*Exit and is seen passing window L.H.*]

ALB. Georgette! I wish for pen and ink. [*She runs into the cabinet*] I must write to the landlord of the Golden Lion for a carriage. And these papers must be arranged. [*Georgette returns*]

GEORG. Come this way! Here is pen and ink in my little cabinet, and I will take my work and sit by you. [*Albert takes the lamp and with his pocketbook in the other hand goes into the cabinet. Georgette takes her cushion and is going to follow but a clap of thunder frightens her and stops her. George and Warner pass the R.H. window and appear at the door. The child runs to her father. Enter George and Warner hastily*]

GEORG. Ah, papa! [*She takes his hand and draws him towards the cabinet. Warner comes forward to put his staff and wallet on the table. Sees the gold*]

WARN. What is this?

GEORG. Hush, papa—no noise.

GEO. No noise? Why?

WARN. Gold!

GEORG. Because you will disturb the gentleman. See! There he is! He is writing.

GEO. An officer! What? I am sorry—

WARN. A stranger. [*Takes George's hand and leads him forward, showing the gold. Georgette follows*] Look! Is this gold his?

GEORG. No. It is mine. He gave it to me. [*Thunder. Warner goes rapidly to look into the cabinet*]

GEO. Gave all this to you? He must be rich, then.

GEORG. Oh, yes! He said he had a million in his pocketbook—there—in that pocketbook by his side. Don't you see it?

WARN. Yes, I see it.

GEO. And where did this rich man come from?

GEORG. I don't know.

GEO. Where is your mother?

GEORG. She went to seek you.

GEO. Alone! I must follow—[*Going*]

WARN. [*Stops and seizes his arm*] By and by. [*George stands with his eyes fixed on the table. Georgette takes her cushion and is going to the cabinet*] Leave your cushion and go look for your mother. She must be returning as she did not find us. If you see her coming, run and tell us.

GEORG. Why do *you* not go?

WARN. Do as I bid you. Your father orders you. [*He takes her hand and leads her to the door, pointing the way she must go*] Stop there—on the top of the rock. [*She goes. He shuts the door of the cabinet softly and comes to George*] Now we have an opportunity of realizing our wishes! And when we have this money, away to Italy and put in practice the scheme I confided to you! The opportunity is here.

GEO. [*His eye fixed*] What opportunity? For what?

WARN. This is the moment.

GEO. I do not understand you.

WARN. Look at our tatters! Think of what I told you. We have a million in our hands.

GEO. Hold! Thou art the infernal enemy of man and com'st to tempt my misery and despair. Avaunt! Leave me!

WARN. George! Hear me!

GEO. Avaunt, I say! Thou art my evil genius and lead'st to my damnation! Do you not see the livid corpse we came from burying? Do you not hear the last groans of my father? Have I not filled the measure of iniquity?

Am I not yet fitted for eternal night? [*Sinks on the table. The wind and storm of rain increases. Warner tries to rouse him*]

WARN. Are you mad? George!

GEO. [*Looking up*] Where is my wife?

WARN. Afar off.

GEO. My daughter?

WARN. Following her mother.

GEO. My son?

WARN. It is fifteen years since you had a son—George, recall your senses!

GEO. [*Rising with an air of desperation*] Yes! You *will* that I should murder the stranger.

WARN. It is night. He is alone. A million! Who shall know that he stopped here?

GEO. My wife saw him—received him—

WARN. You can say that you sent him away.

GEO. The traces of the murder will be left. [*Loud thunder*]

WARN. Hark! The storm redoubles! If the lightning falls on the hut and burns it and all within, are we answerable? See, these planks are dry as tinder. The wind will in a moment wrap all in flames. Give me this knife. Do you set fire to the hut by aid of this lamp.

GEO. I cannot. I am frozen with horror. I *will not*.

WARN. Coward! Is he more to be feared than the traveller? Remain here then; do not let your wife come near or—the child. Only come if I call for help—I will do it. [*He goes into the cabinet and at the moment a thunderbolt falls on the mountain and hut; the wind and rain redouble their fury. The child runs in and flies to her father, who takes her in his arms*]

GEO. Hold! Warner!—Hold!—Hold! [*Re-enter Warner with the pocketbook, which he throws at George's feet. He closes the door after him. The flames begin to appear within. Amelia rushes in followed by villagers*]

AME. My husband! O my husband! A murder has been committed—the body is found! Soldiers are coming to arrest you! Call your son—

GEO. My son! [*Warner escapes by door in flat*]

AME. He is there! [*Pointing to the cabinet*]

GEO. My son! My son! [*The flames appear bursting from the cabinet. He rushes in. Amelia would follow; the villagers hold her. George returns through the flames bringing Albert, wounded, and places him in the arms of his mother. He has the bloody knife in his hand*] He is saved! I give you your son! My hour is come—I am—

ALB. Mother, my father has saved my life! [*Re-enter Warner pursued by soldiers*]

Geo. [*Seizing Warner*] Come, I will never again quit you! I swear by Hell! [*He drags him towards the burning cabinet. The flames appear to gain fury. The roof and walls of the hut fall and discover the mountains and rocks covered by soldiers and villagers. George and Warner appear surrounded by flames. George plunges the knife into the bosom of Warner, who falls, and then into his own. Rushes forward and sinks, surrounded by his wife and children*]

Geo. Forgive me, Amelia! My son! See the miserable end of a gamester! [*Dies*]

END

America's Lost Plays